DUE PROCESS

NOMOS
XVIII

N O M O S

NOMOS XVIII

Yearbook of the American Society for Political and Legal Philosophy

DUE PROCESS

Edited by

J. ROLAND PENNOCK   *Swarthmore College*

and

JOHN W. CHAPMAN   *University of Pittsburgh*

New York: New York University Press · 1977

Due Process: Nomos XVIII
edited by J. Roland Pennock and John W. Chapman

Copyright © 1977 by New York University

Library of Congress Cataloging in Publication Data
Main entry under title:

Due process.

(Nomos 18)
Includes bibliographical references and index.
1. Due process of law—United States—Addresses, essays, lectures. 2. Due process of law—Addresses, essays, lectures.   I.   Pennock, James Roland.
II.   Chapman, John William, 1923-   III.   Series.
KF4765.A75D8   347'.73   76-40511
ISBN 0-8147-6569-6

Printed in the United States of America

PREFACE

Due process of law is a concept—or at least an idea—that has played a most important role in American constitutional law for the past century. During that period its path has negotiated many turnings, as Charles Miller's essay in this volume details. But at this particular stage in our history, it has taken on special interest and significance. The concept of "substantive" due process, for a long time moribund, has received increasing attention, sometimes under the guise of "equal protections." As more and more of the Bill of Rights has been "incorporated" into the Due Process clause of the Fourteenth Amendment, increasingly the Court has turned its attention to the exploration, elucidation, and definition of "fundamental rights" not expressly set forth in those amendments, or elsewhere in the Constitution, but presumably included in the "liberty" term of the Due Process clause. Also, during this period of growing judicial sensitivity to "rights" and to "fairness," the concept has been broadened in at least two directions. Its application has been extended in old areas and it has been applied to new areas—e.g., to the procedure to be used for suspending a public school pupil for misconduct. Moreover, it has been increasingly used as a concept of fairness in areas not at present regulated by law. Doubtless, it was for such reasons as these that the membership of the Society selected the topic of Due Process for the subject of its meetings in 1973.

These meetings were held in December in New Orleans in connection with the meetings of the American Association of Law Schools. With one exception, the participants in the program of those meetings are contributors to this volume, although in several cases the content of their original papers has been considerably expanded or otherwise altered. In addition, three other scholars have made major contributions to the volume: Kearns, Miller, and Marshall.

The general plan of the book is as follows: after an introductory chapter by one of the editors, Part I is devoted to historical (Miller) and comparative (Marshall) dimensions that were missing in the necessarily compressed program of the meetings.

Part II comprises six papers exploring the nature and the rationale of due process from a variety of points of view. If testimony were needed as to the richness of the concept and of the modes of justification for it, here it is. Although three of these papers originated as comments on two of the others, only one retains that form or substance, that of Pincoffs on Michelman. If a logically best way of ordering these papers is to be found, it has eluded the editors. Pincoffs's comments on Michelman apart, two of the papers are perhaps less technical, more broadly philosophical than the others. One of these, that of Scanlon, seeks to show the extent to which due process claims are derived from moral principle, especially the principle that arbitrariness should be avoided; and how far, on the other hand, they depend upon the requirements for prudently designed institutions. The other, that of Kearns, argues that due process is a requirement of system, wholly removed from moral precepts. It has seemed best to allow these two papers to bracket the other contributions to this part, all of which, including those by Grey and Resnick, in one way or another, accept the conventional wisdom that due process is intimately related to morality.

Part III is devoted to some of the more extended applications of the idea of due process, to what may properly be called "political due process." Thus Gerald Kramer devotes his full attention to the "due" implementation of the majority-rule principle. It turns out that, among the various ways in which the majority principle can be formulated, some are more "reformist" or "activist," as compared with others that might properly be designated "conservative"—even as with due process of law. Arthur Kuflick, not so much taking off where Kramer ends as taking off in a retrospective direction from where Kramer begins, examines the philosophical bases for the majority principle itself. This investigation eventually leads him to the conclusion that there is no such thing as *the* majority principle, although (and because) rule by the majority may be construed and supported in many different ways, no one of which is appropriate in all contexts.

Richard Epstein also deals, in large part, with political due process in his discussion of voting procedures for the discovery of majority rule in the context of collective bargaining. He links political and legal due process by injecting the interesting idea that courts might consider invalidating voting procedures established by legislatures for trade unions, when they clearly violate the majority principle.

Professor Bruce Ackerman, of the Yale Law School, was chairman of the Program Committee for the meetings that gave rise to this volume. To him, and of course to the contributors, the editors owe a deep debt of thanks.

J. W. C.
J. R. P.

CONTENTS

PART II

PART III

CONTRIBUTORS

DAVID J. DANELSKI
Government, Cornell University

RICHARD A. EPSTEIN
Law, University of Chicago

THOMAS C. GREY
Law, Stanford University

THOMAS R. KEARNS
Philosophy, Amherst College

GERALD H. KRAMER
Political Science, Yale University

ARTHUR KUFLIK
Philosophy, University of North Carolina

GEOFFREY MARSHALL
Political Science, Queens College, Oxford

FRANK I. MICHELMAN
Law, Harvard University

CHARLES A. MILLER
Government, Lake Forest College

EDMUND L. PINCOFFS
Philosophy, University of Texas

DAVID RESNICK
Government, Cornell University

T. M. SCANLON
Philosophy, Princeton University

INTRODUCTION

J. ROLAND PENNOCK

I

The meaning of the phrase "due process of law" takes us deep into history, deep into philosophy, and, were it to be fully expounded—which is impossible—far into the future, for it is ever-growing. Its roots grow out of an intriguing blend of history and philosophy—a blend also, as Charles Miller remarks, "of political symbolism and legal efficacy, both aided by semantic open-ness"*(infra)*. As is well known, the phrase "due process of law" became the official English translation, enshrined in numerous reissues of Magna Carta, of the original *per legem terrae*, "by the law of the land." It was intended to guarantee—at least to the barons—the common-law rights of Englishmen. These rights were both procedural (the right to trial by one's peers) and substantive (various liberties and rights of property). The barons were demanding justice, and justice is not confined to matters of procedure. Even John Rawls's insistence that his theory is a procedural one does not really contradict this point, for what he is seeking is a system of rules that have the best chance of achieving results that accord with our intuitive ideas of substantive justice.[1] Moreover, even these rules must be subject, to be consistent with Rawls's own reasoning—to the continuing process of reflective equilibrium. The illusory nature of the procedural-substantive distinction is more fully discussed by Miller in Chapter 1.

The foreshortened term "due process" omits a significant phrase, "of law." We generally think of the complete phrase as emphasizing the words "due" and "process"; but it would appear that the words "of law" are equally significant. In short, it may not be enough that the process in question is historically sanctioned, or even that it also be fair; it must also be a *legal* process, one that conforms to the idea of law, government by rules, nonarbitrariness.[2]

In medieval times, when virtually all law was customary law, and when custom was thought by its very nature to embody human reason (having passed the test of time), the idea of law that was not "legal" normally did not arise. That had to await not only the rise of statutory law (which in the early days was, theoretically, at least, declaratory only), but the idea of law as the command of the sovereign, something that was made rather than discovered, a deliberately man-made creation rather than the product of accretion. Law of this kind, not sanctified by tradition, by the fact that its origins were enshrouded in the immemorial past, lacked the presumption of validity that attached to customary law. Whether its provisions were in accordance with "due process" was no longer self-evidently true. The fact that something bore the title of law and had gone through the standard process by which law was made was no longer sufficient to guarantee it the cachet of "due process."

In England, however, as Geoffrey Marshall recalls to us in Chapter 2, the idea that an act of Parliament might still be lacking in due process did not come to prevail. For too long, one may conjecture, Parliament had been seen as the great protector against the possible arbitrariness of the royal prerogative for *it* to be thought of as the author of arbitrary actions. Moreover, Parliament had in its favor the fact that it was itself traditionally a court; the High Court of Parliament. Also, the dominance of utilitarian philosophy was not hospitable to claims of natural law or natural right. Bentham had declared all talk of "natural rights" to be "nonsense on stilts." Utility looked to the good of the whole, with little regard for claims by individuals or minorities against the expression of the majority.

In America, on the other hand, the colonial assemblies and their successors, the state (and federal) legislatures, had a different immediate background. They had been subjected to legislatively imposed taxes that they considered illegal. This and other experiences of what they considered arbitrary government led them to make wide resort to the rhetoric of rights; first common-law rights or "the rights of Englishmen," and then "natural rights." It was the philosophy of Locke ("constitutionalized natural law," in Miller's apt phraseology) rather than that of Bentham that prevailed on this side of the water. Since "due process of law" first gained currency in connection with the assertion of rights and of checks on government, and indeed is phrased for that purpose, its use as a limitation on government in all its branches came naturally in this country. For these and perhaps still other reasons, then, the traditional assertion of the individual rights not to be deprived of life, liberty, or property without due process of law was made applicable in the United States to governments as a whole, and specifically to legislatures.

But I have digressed. To return to the theme I was pursuing: the roots of due process grow out of a blend of history and philosophy. The Supreme Court's first stab at definition, in the *Murray* case,[3] sought to tie the concept exclusively to the common law, as that body of law was accepted in this country. But hardly a generation had gone by when it was forced to retreat from that overrestrictive concept.[4] From that time forward, historical precedent was no longer a necessary condition of due process.[5] A variety of streams of thought, some new and some traditional, fed the stream of evolving due process interpretation. All sought "justice." But what is justice? A venerable historical tradition comes down to us under the name of natural law, with its more modern offshoot of natural rights. In England today, the term "natural justice" is perhaps to similar effect, but is less freighted with history. Justice Frankfurter, frequently attacked by Justice Black for importing into due process interpretation the "accordionlike" qualities of natural law, in fact attempted to combine history and discretion.[6] He sought the best of the "Anglo-Saxon tradition," but at the same time attempted to blend it with a sympathetic sensitivity to current trends of thought regarding justice. Or perhaps what his ethical antennae sensed was what Edmund Cahn called the "sense of injustice."[7] Justice Black's attempt to escape judicial discretion by way of history was doomed to failure. Although he eventually won the particular battle with Frankfurter out of which originally arose their difference regarding the test for due process, it was Frankfurter's insistence that the meaning of due process was not all to be found in the explicit words of the Constitution that won the day.[8]

Although the historical tradition was individualistic, providing a framework for legal defenses against all forms of arbitrary governmental action, it contained no formula for growth. Yet such a formula was what was needed for the very first test of the historical formula that confronted the Court, the substitution of indictment by "information" for the traditional grand jury. (This was the *Hurtado* case, already referred to.) Justice Matthews did not really articulate a means for getting from there to here; he simply denied the exclusivity of the historical test and then advanced the test of "fundamental fairness" as an alternative. Apart from our intuitive understanding of the concept, "fairness" provides us with no philosophical basis for its elucidation. The literature of justice, from Plato and Aristotle to date, is, of course, voluminous and apt. It will not be reviewed here. It may be useful, however, to refer to two relevant modern traditions. One of them is especially useful for relating a particular claim to a particular legal system and for providing for the gradual development of the concept of due process. Without going back to Montesquieu and his predecessors, this tradition is most conveniently and properly related to Hegel. He and his jurisprudential successors, Savigny, Puchta, and Kohler, saw law generally as reflecting the spirit of the people from which it sprung.[9] This spirit was infused with rationality, of course, but its rationality was related to the needs, customs, beliefs, and stage of development of a particular people. It was that of incrementally developed adjustments to need and evolving sense of right rather than that of the excogitated efforts of legislators to provide the solutions to problems and to lay down general rules not immediately growing out of the necessity to solve a particular "trouble-case."[10]

Edmund Cahn's "sense of injustice," to which reference has already been made, likewise stresses the importance, for the development of just law, of trained minds, sensitive to evolving ethical concepts, grappling with individual cases demanding decision. Frankfurter has already been mentioned as a Supreme Court Justice who appealed, for the proper interpretation of due process, both to Anglo-Saxon traditions and to current concepts of right. One may also cite Holmes as a believer that standards of justice evolve with the growth of civilization.

II

Curiously enough, it may yet be true that it is Kant rather than Hegel who has provided us not only with the most useful standard of justice but also with a standard that at the same time allows for, and naturally leads to further development of the concept. Kant's second form of his Categorical Imperative has been shown to lend itself well for this purpose. The idea of respect for persons—or, in the Kantian formulation, the proposition that no man should be treated as a means only—provides the foundation. From it follow the ideals of liberty and equality.[11] Whether or not one derives a complete theory of justice from these concepts, they do provide a basis for criticizing the justice of any particular set of institutions or rules for distribution, whether it be slavery or some far more sophisticated set of rules that allows some men power over others with no advantage accruing to the latter. By far the most complete elaboration of a theory of justice based upon these Kantian principles is that of John Rawls.[12]

Not only is a central concept of due process—that of fairness—identical with Rawls's basic definition of justice, but the parallels extend much further. The historical development of the concept in this country, as detailed by Miller, appears largely to be in accordance with Rawls's theory. The rule of law, itself essential to liberty, in Rawls's words "requires some form of due process: that is, a process reasonably designed to ascertain the truth, in ways consistent with the other ends of the legal system, as to whether a violation [of law] has taken place and under what circumstances." [13] Although Rawls himself uses the term "due process of law" only in connection with procedural matters, it is clear that most if not all of the developments of substantive due process could be explained and justified by reference to his theory. Rawls believes that justice requires equal opportunity to secure the primary social goods of liberty and opportunity and the bases of self-respect.[14]

Both the incorporation of the freedom of expression provisions of the Constitution under the due process clause and the reallocation of legislative seats in pursuit of the goal of "one person, one vote" exemplify the same process of seeking the Kantian-Rawlsian goals of liberty and equality by way of the due process clause.[15]

One final remark in this connection. It is interesting to note that the way the Court goes back and forth between rigid rules and the concept of fairness or the sense of justice, is reminiscent of Rawls's method of "reflective equilibrium." In fact, it might be said that the judicial method—especially in due process cases—*is* the method of reflective equilibrium. For Rawls this means staking out a position with regard to the "original position," deriving rules from it, comparing them and the results to which they lead to our intuitive judgments of justice and then, if a conflict is found, modifying either the original proposition or the intuitive judgment, as rational reflection seems to dictate.

For the Court, to take a dramatic instance, one may start with the rule that liberty of contract is part of the liberty protected by the due process clause and that any law that interferes with that liberty must be presumed to be in violation of due process unless a strong public interest to the contrary can be shown. After roughly half a century, this rule (or principle) gave way to a simple presumption of legislative validity. It may be worth reminding ourselves of how this change came about. The emphasis on freedom of contract had led the Court to outlaw legislation regulating hours of labor and minimum wages. As belief in laissez-faire gave way to faith in governmental regulation, this interpretation of the Due Process Clause came increasingly into conflict with current views of justice. The impact of the Great Depression finally forced the Court to reverse itself, replacing the rule (or principle) that gave priority to freedom of contract by a simple presumption of legislative validity. Here the Court's sense of the requirements of justice in particular cases caused it to change its rule and its hierarchy of values (equivalent to an alteration of the assumptions about the "original position" for Rawls).

More recently, in the light of further experience and the continuing development of ideas and ideals, the process has been reversed. Thus the Court's evolving concept of the right of privacy has led it to invalidate legislation prohibiting abortions. Here the principle (for Rawls, read "assumption regarding the 'original position' ") was used to correct (in this case invalidate) a particular piece of legislation that presumably expressed the intuitions of right that prevailed among many people. Here the Court appears to be attempting partly to reflect changes in ideas of right that have taken place and partly to bring about such changes.

Interaction between historical and analytical or philosophical conceptions of the Due Process Clause are illustrated by the case of Apodaca v. Oregon, holding that the Clause's requirement of a jury trial for all but petty offenses does not require a unanimous verdict, although that requirement had great historical sanction and had theretofore been thought to be part of the due process concept.[16]

Finally on this point, it is undoubtedly true that, in its deliberations on particular cases, the Court often goes through the process of reflective equilibrium. It may "try on" a particular way of deciding a case, not like what it sees, and then find a way of reaching a result that suits it better. J. Woodford Howard, Jr., reports such an instance in the case of Mr. Justice Black. In the case of Colegrove v. Green, Black originally sided with Frankfurter and was appointed to write the opinion of the Court. In the course of writing it, he became convinced that his original position was wrong. He joined the dissenters, writing an opinion that gave no hint of the process he had gone through.[17]

III

Leaving Rawls and the broader question of the relation between due process and theories of justice, it may be useful to go a bit further in suggesting some of the interesting questions suggested by the dialectic of the law's development with respect to the Due Process Clause. On the procedural side, especially, history has played an important but diminishing role; "diminishing" as sensitivities to the requirements of human dignity have developed. Ways by which careful analysis of concepts can further this growth are well illustrated by David Resnick's contribution to this volume, with its interesting proposal, growing out of his analysis, for the equalization of "counsel-power" as between rich and poor.

On the substantive side of due process, we hear very little today (from the Supreme Court) about the right to contract freely, but we hear a great deal about the right of privacy, the right to travel, and other "fundamental rights." Some members of the Court subsume these rights (at least in certain of their applications) under the Due Process Clause, harking back to the right (freedom) of parents to have their children educated in schools of their own choosing (subject to certain limitations).[18] Others find them in or about the Ninth Amendment.[19] Whatever constitutional provision is relied upon, the ultimate justification is generally found in a blend of history, ideas of natural right, and the closely related philosophical concept of respect for persons. By whatever test, the Court seeks a "sense of right" that can command a broad consensus.

Once these rights are "found" (or at any rate denominated as rights), what are the limits of regulation? To what extent, if any, and by what justifications may they be abridged? In general, the Court seldom if ever holds rights to be absolute, Justice Black to the contrary notwithstanding, except in the case of such second-order rights as the right not to be deprived of liberty "arbitrarily," which is virtually a synonym for "without due process of law." [20] Rather, rights are strong but rebuttable presumptions.[21] In this case, however, the presumptive right that could not be rebutted was that of the state (school board) to require a teacher to take leave of absence after six months of pregnancy, regardless of her ability to perform her job. The right that was denied, it will be noted, was that of government to exercise a certain power; not a right of individuals. However, this is but the obverse of the right of the individual not to be subjected to such a regulation. When a presumptive right must yield to a law that meets the standards of due process, this standard is variously formulated. The older phraseology is "if the means are rationally related to a legitimate end" or to a "valid public purpose." More recently, the Court tends to speak in terms of a "compelling state interest," [22] at least where what it holds to be a "fundamental right" is concerned.

All of these substantive due process cases involve the weighing of claims of right. Sometimes it is the weighing of an individual's claim against society's claim on his own behalf. Thus the validity of laws requiring cyclists to wear crash helmets pits the rider's right to freedom against his safety. But generally it is a question of the claims of a specified individual or individuals against the claims of society (that is to say, of *any* particular individual against an indeterminate number of unspecified individuals within the polity).[23] The Court may, as it frequently does, attempt to simplify the problems of weighing (or "balancing") by designating certain claims of right as "fundamental," with greater or less basis in the Constitution itself for this distinction, and by insisting that the public interest be especially "compelling" in such instances. But such devices, whether or not they are helpful, can not conceal the fact of balancing.

It may be a matter of weighing the value (both to himself and to society) of an older person's claim to retain his job past a specified age limit as against the cost (again both individual and social) of the likelihood of unfair determinations being made if each case is decided "on its merits." Here, to be sure, various procedural devices (productivity tests, medical examinations) may be utilized as protections against unfairness, thus bringing in procedural due process in support of substantive due process. But even this does not end the matter. It might be that for most individuals the psychic cost of a determination in his individual case that he is no longer fit to hold his job would be greater than the cost to him of an automatic, "arbitrary" rule that frees him from risking the stigma of a determination made on the facts of his particular case.

I know no judicial decisions in which courts have taken into account all of the types of considerations enumerated above. (And it would be easy to add other relevant considerations.) The point of these remarks is simply to suggest that any final determination of what is due process is *in a measure* arbitrary (in spite of the fact that, as Scanlon argues, it is the nature of due process to eliminate arbitrariness), that relevant considerations are distributed out from the center in widening circles, and that how far they should be pursued is a matter of judgment, one for which courts will sometimes follow a fairly clear consensus and sometimes seek to create one. In the words of Charles Curtis, they may find "immanent law" or they may legislate.[24]

IV

These remarks about the selection of levels of relevancy lead us well into the next topic for comment. Can a developmental theory of due process be "value-free"? Can it be "neutral"? Nonactivist?

Passivist? Consideration of the cases of Frankfurter, the relativist-passivist, and Black, the absolutist-activist, should serve as warnings against hasty answers to these questions. In the abstract it would appear that a judge who sought to play a modest role would seek anchorage in the firmest rules possible, while an activist would chafe at their restraint and strive for discretion. But Black, detesting the uses to which discretion had been put in the past, in due process cases particularly, sought security against what he considered to be this abuse of power by relying on the incorporation theory, which gave somewhat more specificity. This move enabled him to be an activist at least in importing into the Due Process Clause of the Fourteenth Amendment the more specific liberties of the First Amendment. Frankfurter, strong believer in judicial modesty though he was, was an inveterate balancer. The law for him, and especially the Constitution, was not a code, not a matter of cut-and-dried rules and formulas. Rather the judicial craft required reading a text or a precedent in the light of history, and in the light of his interpretation of the Anglo-Saxon sense of justice and decency.

A developmental theory of due process, and its practitioners, must make use of values, and they must select values and weight them against other values. (Black clearly did so despite all his attempts to fasten his positions to the words of the Constitution.) This selection can be "neutral," in the sense of being uninfluenced by the biases of the members of the Court, only if the latter have some objective standard. If, for instance, they can find a "sense of right" of the community or of the nation, they need not import their own personal values. Or if they adopt some Kantian formula or Kantian-derived formula, à la Rawls, they may possibly approach neutrality. In practice, however, they can do no more than strive in one or another of these directions, even if they consider neutrality as a desirable goal. Also, it would seem that a Court that is trying to "develop" the concept of due process, whether in the direction of the national spirit or consensus or of some theory of justice, must be in some measure activist. One does not pursue a goal without activity—and activism.

Clearly due process of law is a concept that defies both Blackstone and Austin. It calls for other tools than the reading of history and of statutes. It calls for the exercise of discretion. It is open-ended. The courts may, indeed must, seek an ethical consensus. Perhaps they may even appeal to what Chaim Perelman calls a "universal audience," [25] though generally they must be content with standards of right that are more culture-bound. Why, perhaps along with seeking the standards of a "universal audience" and with appeals to the ethical ideas of those who have thought most about such problems, they must also seek out consensus is amply illustrated by the recent history of the Supreme Court's constitutional exegesis. The push for equality that so largely characterized the work of the Warren Court [26] on the whole struck a responsive chord in the American public. Nowhere was this fact more clearly evident than in the first big decisions on legislative reapportionment. This was a subject about which a strong reaction might have been anticipated, considering the vested interests of the politicians in the status quo. But efforts to reverse the Court's action by constitutional amendment were singularly unsuccessful, even in Congress. Developments regarding the rights of the accused also found wide support when they were directed toward equalizing the rights of the rich and the poor. Finally, even the great move for desegregation and the strengthening of civil rights generally, bitterly opposed though it was in most parts of the South, showed general support throughout the country in numerous ways, especially by the succession of civil rights acts enacted by Congress subsequent to the first desegregation decision.

In part, no doubt, the Court was finding a latent consensus; in part, it was creating one. But also in due time, in the latter two areas mentioned above in particular, it got too far out in front of whatever consensus had been emerging. In *The Self-Inflicted Wound,* Fred P. Graham, Jr., has strikingly told the story of how the Court got too far removed from its power bases in public opinion and in Congress. And it is unnecessary to note the backlash produced by certain busing decisions. In both cases, the Court has not only checked its forward momentum; but has also retreated somewhat from the positions to which it had appeared to be headed.[27]

A lack of popular support, a lack of agreement about the relative weight to be attributed to certain valued circumstances (e.g., school integration versus "neighborhood" schools) may take various forms, reflect itself in a variety of ways. Popular sentiment may be expressed by way of bumper stickers, letters to Congressmen, the ballot box, school boycotts, or violence. Congressmen may move for impeachment or refuse to increase judicial salaries and perquisites. Some of these activities may be clearly seen as expressions of a sense of right, and others may appear rather to be expressions of self-interest, with little regard for theories or feelings of justice. Courts must be concerned with both. In considering what process is "due" at any given time and place, a pragmatic concern for how far the Court can go in making law and have it still workable also has its place.

V

Distinguishable—but barely—from the question of the meaning of due process, which has been the subject of the discussion up to this point, is that of where the concept—and the legal requirement—is applicable. Most generally, to be sure, it is applicable to the polity and to lesser associations within the state. It incorporates aspects of justice, fairness, and rationality. While it deals with relations among people, especially in the context of the exercise of authority, it does not cover the full range of human relations. It would appear that due process, especially with respect to its procedural aspect, is less appropriate or valued less highly as one approaches the extremities of associational relations. Thus, for a very close community, the requirements of due process are both unnecessary and so crude and mechanical as actually to harm the social (or communal) fabric. The greater the mutual trust, the less the need to depend upon fixed procedures and the more such procedures interfere with the nuances of fraternal relations. This point is made explicit by David Danelski in his discussion of the ombudsman's role in a university setting, where it is the breakdown of consensus and mutual trust that has led to the demand and need for legalistic (due process) procedures.

In this connection, too, the *Roth* case, discussed in this volume by Danelski, Grey, Michelman, and Pincoffs, is of interest. The question is whether a nontenured teacher in a state college, who is not rehired, is entitled to a statement of the reasons why his or her employment was not continued. While the Court did not uphold Roth's claim as a matter of due process, two of the authors mentioned lean in the direction of feeling that it would be proper to insist on such a requirement. (A third, Michelman, also appears to feel that the procedure ought to be followed but fears that for the courts to require it would probably defeat its purpose.) Yet none of these authors suggests that the demand for a full statement and discussion of reasons would be legitimate in the case of an unsuccessful applicant for the position in question; and it seems to be implied that they would distinguish hiring and not rehiring. Why? Perhaps the person who is not hired is harmed less than the one who is not rehired; but it is by no means clear that this is always the case.

Possibly more to the point is the fact that the person who is not rehired was already part of the relevant association. The association of which he was a part is not such a tight community as to render due process inappropriate, but one consisting of persons sufficiently committed to continued association to call for the application of due process standards. The mere applicant, on the other hand, has not yet entered into the association in question. Even with respect to him, of course, the law may, and often does, impose constraints on the hiring entity. Thus far, these constraints have been legislatively imposed and do not appear to be judicially required as part of due process in the absence of legislation (except for the case of nondiscrimination on grounds of race, religion, or sex by a public employer). Nor have they been extended to the requirement that reasons be stated. In Michelman's terms, there is not even a shadow of entitlement to get the job in the first place, although there may be (in the case of public institutions, at least) some embryonic moral entitlement to a direct confrontation for the discussion of reasons in the case of nonrenewal. Grey would distinguish between interest (which the applicant might have to a greater extent than the person not rehired) and constitutional right. The latter, which might derive from general recognition of a moral claim, does not exist in *Roth*, or at least has not been recognized by the Court. He notes that this may be considered as an instance, perhaps a reemergence, of the old privilege-right distinction.

Let me elaborate and sharpen the issue somewhat. Edmund Pincoffs would make the entitlement to an explanation for nonreappointment derive from Kant's Categorical Imperative, in the form that no man should treat anyone as a mere means. A difficulty with this derivation is that it does not provide for the distinction between hiring and rehiring. Michelman apparently would make such distinctions, in general, depend upon intuited moral entitlements based upon general understandings and moral feelings, although in the case of Roth, for the prudential reason mentioned above, he reluctantly accepts the conclusion arrived at in *Roth*.

My suggestion is that these understandings and feelings, in turn, derive from, or are conditioned by, the nature of the bond uniting the individuals in question, the intensity or extent of community feeling. This theory would account for our finding of a moral entitlement to some statement of reasons in *Roth*, while denying it to the nonhired applicant. It would also account for our erstwhile feeling that due process requires less in the way of procedural protection for aliens (at least where their right to remain in the country is concerned) than for citizens. Today perhaps we are more willing than once was the case to consider common residency (without regard to citizenship) as a sufficient bond to trigger full due process protection. At the same time we still distinguish between the resident alien and the would-be resident, the applicant for permission to immigrate. The latter, though we certainly recognize him as a person, is not (*pace* Pincoffs) entitled to hearing, reasons, or other accoutrements of due process, if he is denied a visa.

In cases open to dispute, then, the right to due process may be derived from respect for the personality of a fellow member of a polity or other association short of an intimate community. Cases where there is a clear deprivation of life, liberty, or property are not open to dispute; they need not rely upon this theory, although it would surely apply. And more directly, they may rely upon our intuitions of moral entitlement. Yet surely some more reliable, some more objective test would be desirable where it can be found.

Michelman himself, in discussing the case of public housing, advances one. He suggests that housing is provided for the needs of the housed, but that jobs are made available for the needs of the state. This is a useful distinction, especially for the purpose of determining the degree of formalized due process that is appropriate. But it does not help me with my desire to provide a minimum of explanation for *Roth* and yet not the fuller hearing to which an occupant of public housing or a person denied unemployment compensation would, in my view, be entitled. Here, it seems to me, another distinction is useful. (Perhaps it may be viewed as only an extension or elaboration of Michelman's distinction.) I refer to the kind of facts appropriate for the administrative authority to take into account.

One important—often crucial—type of fact that is relevant in the nonrehiring case is at the same time so indeterminate as to render a judicialized procedure out of place. The educational administrator, as to some extent with other employers, [28] is looking for the person best qualified for the job. He is ever seeking to improve his staff. He may, therefore, not rehire an employee simply because he has good reason to believe that he can replace him/her with a better one. This may seem a harsh standard, in its effects, but it is generally accepted as required by the needs of the institution, at least for a probationary period. At the same time, it is apparent that the mere acceptance of this standard places great limits on what can be accomplished by any requirement of a statement of reasons. It may be, as Grey argues, that the fundamental variable here is the extent to which public recognition of a moral right to the benefit has solidified; and that the legislature is merely reflecting that fact when it specifies more precisely the conditions for entitlement in the case of unemployment "insurance" than it does in the case of welfare "benefits." All of this is intended to be suggestive rather than complete, for Scanlon seems clearly to be right in arguing that many considerations influence the decision as to where due process is required.

It has already been intimated, however, that it is not just a question of where due process is required; it is also a question of what process is "due," or how much due process is required under given circumstances. Thus I have suggested earlier that nonhiring and nonrehiring are to be distinguished by the test of intimacy of association, implying that something in the way of due process—in this instance, some statement of reasons—is called for in the latter but not in the former case. On the other hand, I have suggested, in the preceding paragraph, at least in certain types of nonrehiring cases, including the *Roth* type, that the kinds of facts relevant to the determination do not submit themselves easily, if at all, to normal due process procedures. In fact, a statement of reasons might, rightly, turn out to be substantially vacuous. Nonetheless, I am inclined to believe that the person aggrieved is entitled to such a statement, and whatever discussion that may call forth, if he desires it. With this understanding, I believe there is no inconsistency between the two kinds of tests I have proposed.

VI

These remarks have been largely confined to due process as it operates in the American system of government. Several of the papers in this volume to which at least passing reference has been made above rightly consider the concept in a broader context. Scanlon, in particular, sketches a more inclusive theory. For him, one must look to the nature of the authority or the institution in question before he can tell just what is entailed by due process's limitations upon arbitrariness. This takes him into what he describes as a "gray area between consideration of rights and considerations of public policy." This area is perhaps hardly different from what I was discussing in the paragraph before this, just as his theory of the "nature of the institution test" bears at least some resemblance to my earlier discussion of degrees of association and types of due process.

This reference back to the earlier discussion of degrees of association not only suggests that we have come full circle; it also provides a link to Kearns's discussion of due process in terms of the requirements for the maintenance of system. Kearns's idea of "demoralizing" due process, of relating it to system rather than to persons, runs counter to much of what has been said in the preceding pages (although less so, as I have remarked, to the first part of this chapter) and, indeed, to much of what has been said elsewhere in the volume. But it is intriguing, and it is perhaps unfortunate that the other contributors to the volume have not had an opportunity to react to it. Perhaps that would call for another volume—one in which, it would be hoped, Kearns would extend his discussion to a consideration of how (and whether) his theory could apply to substantive due process.

NOTES

1. John Rawls, *A Theory of Justice* (Cambridge, Mass.: Harvard University Press, 1971), esp. Chapter II.
2. For an elaboration of this point, see J. Roland Pennock, "Law's

Natural Bent," *Ethics,* 79 (1969), pp. 222-28. And see Scanlon's discussion, *infra.*

3. Murray's Lessee v. Hoboken Land & Improvement Co. (1856), 18 How. 272.
4. Hurtado v. California (1884), 110 U. S. 516.
5. Since Powell v. Alabama (1932), 287, U.S. 45, it is no longer even a sufficient condition.
6. Rochin v. California (1952), 342 U.S. 165 (Frankfurter's majority opinion and Black's concurring opinion).
7. Edmund Cahn, *The Sense of Injustice* (Bloomington, Ind.: Indiana University Press, 1949).
8. Note, for instance, the return to substantive due process in Cleveland State Board of Education v. LaFleur (1974), 44 U.S. 632, not to mention Roe v. Wade (1973), 410 U.S. 113.
9. The same theme, with a decentralizing twist, is provided by Hugo Krabbe's "sense of right of the community." See his *The Modern Idea of the State,* tr. Sabine and Shepard (New York: Appleton-Century, 1930), pp. 83-98 and Chapters V and VI.
10. The phrase is Karl Llewellyn's. He uses it in a discussion of how customary law develops out of particular cases in primitive tribes; but it reflects also his philosophy of law more generally and also that of his judicial hero, Benjamin Cardozo. See K. N. Llewellyn and E. Adamson Hoebel, *The Cheyenne Way* (Norman, Okla.: University of Oklahoma Press, 1941), p. 286.
11. See R. S. Downie and Elizabeth Telfer, *Respect for Persons* (London: Allen & Unwin, 1969) and Edmund Pincoffs's essay in this volume.
12. Rawls, *A Theory of Justice.* See especially pp. 251-57 for Rawls's own discussion of how his theory of justice derives from Kant.
13. Ibid., p. 293. The whole of Sec. 38, on "The Rule of Law," is relevant in this connection.
14. Ibid., p. 62. Rawls also includes in this listing "income and wealth." Thus far, at least, this aspect of justice is not thought of as subject to judicial application except as it may bear upon the most fundamental rights, such as the right to have effective access to the courts (right to free counsel for indigents accused of crime—or seeking a divorce).
15. The fact that some of the decisions that exemplify this trend, including the legislative apportionment cases, have nominally been accomplished by way of the Equal Protections Clause is of no great significance in view of the fact that the Court has now included so much of the substance of the latter in the former. It would appear that almost anything that is constitutionally lacking in equality can as well be held to be "arbitrary" under the Due Process Clause. Cf.

Cleveland State Board of Education v. LaFleur (note 9), which was argued as an "equal protection" case and decided as a "due process" case.

16. Apodaca v. Oregon (1972), 406 U.S. 404.
17. "On the Fluidity of Judicial Choice," *Amer. Political Science Rev.*, 62 (1968), pp. 43-56, 48. (In this case [328 U.S. 549], the Court held the issue of congressional reapportionment to be nonjusticable.) Howard cites other instances of justices reaching their ultimate conclusions, sometimes despite their ideological orientations, only after "tortuous processes of reflection and interchange. . . ." P. 56.
18. Meyer v. Nebraska (1923), 262 U.S. 390.
19. See Goldberg's concurring opinion in Griswold v. Conn. (1965), 381 U.S. 497.
20. By way of contrast, one may call attention to the theory of Robert Nozick. For him, substantive rights to property, for instance, are based entirely upon entitlements. Anyone who has acquired property in accordance with the principle of justice in transfer is absolutely entitled to that property. No process for taking it away is "due." Robert Nozick, *Anarchy, State and Utopia* (New York: Basic Books, 1974), p. 151.
21. Justice Stewart and a majority of the Court—admittedly in a slightly different context—go so far as to hold that a statute that creates an "irrebuttable presumption" of right violates the Due Process Clause. See *Cleveland State Board of Education* v. *LaFleur*, note 10.
22. The latter formulation is primarily found in opinions cast in terms of "the equal protection of the laws," but it also may be found in due process cases, for instance in the case of the pregnant schoolteacher referred to above (note 10).
23. To clarify still further what may be involved in a claim of individual right against "society," note that it may be a question of my (or anyone's) interest in having a fair trial, should I be accused of crime, against my interest in deterring would-be criminals. For useful distinctions regarding various types of balancing, see Scanlon (Chapter IV, below) on aggregate balancing, individual probabalistic balancing, and personal balancing.
24. Charles Curtis, *Lions under the Throne* (Boston: Houghton Mifflin, 1947).
25. Chaim Perelman, *Justice* (New York: Random House, 1967), Chapter V, especially p. 82.
26. See Philip B. Kurland, *Politics, the Constitution, and the Warren Court* (Chicago: University of Chicago Press, 1970).

27. Of course, "the Court" is not the same Court; but for present purposes, the question of whether the constraints were anticipatory or produced by new appointments is of no importance.
28. One might think also of a law firm's deciding whether or not to continue the services of an associate, or of a judge's (if a one-year rule had not been established) deciding whether to continue a law clerk, or of a legislator and his legislative assistant.

PART I

1

THE FOREST OF DUE PROCESS OF LAW: THE AMERICAN CONSTITUTIONAL TRADITION [1]

CHARLES A. MILLER

The protean tradition of American due process of law confirms in the life of the law what seventeen volumes of NOMOS have demonstrated in scholarship: that fundamental political and legal ideas, like great works of art, resist final definition and perhaps final understanding. Whether one accepts the jaundiced remark of Thomas Reed Powell that "due process is as due process does," or the more respectful view of Felix Frankfurter to the same effect, that due process has a "blessed versatility," a study of the American tradition yields few verities but many varieties of due process.[2] The idea of due process that lasts is that of individual freedom from arbitrary government imposition. It is an idea that assumes the existence of conflicts between the government and citizens and the resolution of those conflicts through lawful proceedings. In practice, the varieties of due process have depended on the rise and decline of social interests and on society's changing perceptions of what is arbitrary, unfair, or unjust. These are the general and hardly remarkable lessons of a study of due process of law as a central concept in the American constitutional tradition.

3

Why due process has become such a concept is, in hindsight, also not difficult to say. As will become clear, due process in the American tradition is a blend of political symbolism and legal efficacy, both aided by semantic openness.[3] The chronological progression of this essay permits an appreciation of these abstract features of due process in association with the concrete elements that have entered the due process tradition. The historical perspective also affords the opportunity to distinguish what is current from what is recurrent in due process thinking. Further, a historical view shows due process as an example of the method of the common law, both because it has evolved slowly and because its development has been so thoroughly in the hands of the judiciary. Finally, the history of due process is a model of the parallel and interrelated evolution, through a single phrase, of legal ideas connected with social interests.[4]

I. FROM MAGNA CARTA THROUGH THE BILL OF RIGHTS

The source of the concept—though not the phrase—"due process of law" is the original Magna Carta.[5] The Charter of 1215, by which King John agreed to feudal rights insisted on by the barons of Runnymede, contained sixty-three chapters. In Chapter 39 the king promised that

No free man shall be taken or imprisoned or disseised or outlawed or exiled or in any way ruined, nor will we go or send against him, except by the lawful judgment of his peers or by the law of the land.[6]

The key phrase is "by the law of the land"—*per legem terrae*. Like other words and phrases in Chapter 39, its early thirteenth-century meaning is not definite.[7] Historians generally explain "law" as a contrast to the decrees of King John, and "of the land" as a contrast with restricted bodies of law such as of the king (*lex regnum* appears elsewhere in Magna Carta), or of East Anglia, or even maritime law. In view of what the phrase and concept became, it should be noted that "law of the land" included both substantive and procedural aspects.[8] Whatever it was in contrast to, the "law of the land" was the customary law of England. As Sir Matthew Hale explained in the late seventeenth century, "Sometimes 'tis called Lex Angliae. . . . Sometimes 'tis called Lex et Consuetudo Regni. . . ; but most commonly 'tis called, The Common Law, or the Common Law of England. . . ." [9] This broad understanding of *per legem terrae* is characteristic of its successor phrase, "due process of law," as well. The later identification of the first expression with the second not only enhanced the constitutional status of Magna Carta by tying the Charter to common law, but simultaneously gave to the common law the blessing of the politically unassailable charter.

Within a year and a half of the ceremony at Runnymede, King John was dead. Because of the personalized nature of feudal government and the still unsettled situation among the barons and the royal representatives, Magna Carta was reaffirmed under the boy king Henry III in 1216. This reaffirmation was the first of over thirty reissues of the charter during political crises or changes of reign by successive British monarchs in the next two centuries. These periodic confirmations have a regularized American legacy in the constitutionally prescribed presidential oath of office to "preserve, protect and defend the Constitution"—the "supreme law of the land."

In the reissue of the Charter in 1225 (also under Henry III), Magna Carta was reduced from sixty-three to thirty-seven chapters, and the future due process clause, still *per legem terrae,* migrated from Chapter 39 to Chapter 29. It is Chapter 29 which is most commonly referred to in later writing (e.g., by Sir Edward Coke in the seventeenth century). A dozen years later the name "Magna Carta" was first officially applied to the document. [10]

"Process of law" is first recognizable as a law French phrase, *process de ley,* in a British legal document of the early fourteenth century. [11] Not long afterward, in the 1354 reissue of the charter under Edward III, Magna Carta appears officially in English for the first time. In Chapter 29, in place of *per legem terrae,* are the words "by due process of the law." By the end of the fourteenth century, Magna Carta, through its repeated confirmations, had become the accepted basic symbol of British constitutionalism. The due process clause, new in English, was the charter's central admonition against arbitrary government.

During the fifteenth and sixteenth centuries, though mentioned

in statutes or compilations of statutes, Magna Carta and due
process lay fallow in British constitutional disputes. Fortescue used
it in his opinions, but not in his treatises.[12] In the seventeenth
century, however, the Charter and the clause suddenly blossomed
again.[13] Under the scholarly and political influence of Coke and
other lawyers, Magna Carta was revived and transformed into a
source of liberties for all Englishmen (not just the barons) against
the monarchy.[14] In the *Second Part of the Institutes of the Laws of
England,* Coke examines Magna Carta chapter by chapter. Chapter
29 receives the lengthiest treatment by far, for "upon this Chapter,
as out of a roote, many fruitfull branches of the Law of England
have sprung." [15] He translates *per legem terrae* as "by the Common
Law, Statute Law, or Custome of England," but notes that "the
true sense and exposition of these words" are "without due process
of law." [16]

Coke's illustrations of due process of law are predominantly
procedural: indictment, presentment, warrants, writs. But he speaks
also of "liberties" of Englishmen guaranteed by the chapter, among
which is the freedom from monopoly.[17] In 1628, the same year the
Second Institute was published, Coke prepared the Petition of Right,
which quoted due process *and* law-of-the-land language from "the
great charter of the liberties of England." The petition charged that
recent executions and imprisonments had violated these clauses of
Magna Carta.

Just when the ideas of the Petition of Right exerted their most
dramatic effect and the Stuarts were deposed from the monarchy,
the ideas and language of Magna Carta Chapter 29 entered
American constitutional documents.[18] In 1641, the Massachusetts
Body of Liberties, prepared by men fleeing the turmoil of the
English Civil War, stated that life, honor, arrest and punishment,
family, and goods were to be protected "by some express law of the
country." A few decades later, the fundamental laws of New Jersey
and Pennsylvania provided for the protection of life and liberty in
the phrases of Magna Carta.[19]

In the 1760s, after the Stamp Act, and as if in anticipation of an
American need for an authoritative contemporary statement of
citizens' rights, Blackstone summed up and at the same time
expanded the ideas of Chapter 29 and due process of law. In
arranging his "three absolute rights of individuals," he followed the

order of Locke in justifying the existence of the state—for the protection of life, liberty, and property:

(1) "the right of personal security [which] consists in a person's legal and uninterrupted enjoyment of his life, his limbs, his body, his health, and his reputation." (2) "the personal liberty [which] consists in the power of locomotion, of changing situation, or moving one's person to whatsoever place one's own inclination may direct, without imprisonment or restraint, unless by due course of law;" (3) "the third absolute right, inherent in every Englishman, . . . of property: which consists in the free use, enjoyment, and disposal of all his acquisitions, without any control or diminution, save only by the laws of the land." [20]

The blend of due process ideas and phrases in Blackstone is in keeping with both the centrality and the ineffability of the concept. Personal security includes life as well as other protections. Personal liberty includes travel, but also the protection of the criminally accused by due course of law. Property rights are also absolute, though they may be both regulated and diminished by law. The plural "laws of the land," used in some early American state constitutions as well, indicates particularity, as in the case of statutes, and stands in contrast to the general, undifferentiated body of judge-made common law. Among the laws of the land, as is clear elsewhere in Blackstone and in American constitutional practice, are laws on taxation, eminent domain, and the police power. While Blackstone's list thus corresponds to life, liberty, and property, on inspection his discussion also yields a division between natural rights and criminal rights; and this manner of considering due process finds its way into the American tradition, too.

In their constitutional argument against king and parliament between the Stamp Act and the Revolution, American colonists referred to the common law, Magna Carta, and Coke, but not as often as one might expect on the basis of the substance of that heritage.[21] The more conservative hoped in the early years to retain the concrete heritage. John Adams, for instance, argued that the Stamp Act was "directly repugnant to the Great Charter itself." [22] The more liberal argument, reflected in James Wilson and John Dickinson, argued by analogy and became more significant in the 1770s: America needed its own Magna Carta in the form of a written constitution for the colonies.[23] The Declaration of Resolves

of the First Continental Congress, adopted in the fall of 1774, stated
that the representatives acted the way "Englishmen, their ancestors
in like cases have usually done," deducing their rights "by the
immutable laws of nature, the principles of the English constitution,
and the several charters or compacts" of the colonies. Among the
rights deduced were "that they are entitled to life, liberty and
property," and "that the respective colonies are entitled . . . to the
great and inestimable privilege of being tried by their peers of the
civinage, according to the course of the [common] law." [24]

The first constitution of an independent American state, that of
Virginia in June 1776, rearranged the due process ideas once more.
The first half of that constitution was its Bill of Rights, drafted by
Thomas Jefferson. It contains the two elements of due process
thought—natural rights and criminal rights—but cleanly separated
from each other. Section 1 of the Virginia Bill of Rights declares as
an "inherent right" of man "the enjoyment of life and liberty, with
the means of acquiring and possessing property, and pursuing and
obtaining happiness and safety." Section 8 contains the rights of the
accused in a criminal prosecution: notice, specificity, confrontation,
witnesses, speedy trial, no compulsory self-incrimination, impartial
jury of twelve men, and "that no man be deprived of his liberty,
except by the law of the land or the judgment of his peers." [25] What
Magna Carta had implicitly joined in Chapter 29, life, liberty and
property with due process of law, the Virginia Bill of Rights
distinguished, promulgating Lockean political theory at the outset
and standards for criminal procedure later.

Jefferson refined the language of Section 1 of the Virginia Bill of
Rights within a few weeks and produced the phrasing of the
Declaration of Independence: unalienable rights to life, liberty, and
the pursuit of happiness.[26] Although trial by jury is mentioned, the
Declaration does not speak of "law of the land" or "due process of
law." The omission of "law of the land" is understandable, since the
point of the Declaration was to declare a new land which could not
yet have agreed on any law. Due process of law, however, is the
implicit subject of the bulk of the Declaration, the grievances
against king and parliament.

State constitutions adopted in the months following the Declaration contain both the language and ideas of due process. Articles 8

and 9 of the constitution of Pennsylvania of August 1776, for
example, elaborate both sides of the social compact while declaring
rights of the inhabitants:

> . . . every member of society hath a right to be protected in
> the enjoyment of life, liberty and property, and therefore is
> bound to contribute his proportion towards the expense of that
> protection. . . . But no part of a man's property can be justly
> taken from him, or applied to public uses, without his own
> consent . . . nor can any man be justly deprived of his liberty
> except by the laws of the land, or the judgment of his peers.

The constitutions of Maryland and North Carolina (November
and December 1776) contain Chapter 29 of Magna Carta verbatim,
using "law of the land" rather than "due process of law" wording.
The Vermont constitution, adopted in July 1777, is a model
compilation from the previous constitutional handiwork. Its rights
are both "inherent and unalienable"; they include "enjoying and
defending life and liberty; acquiring, possessing and protecting
property, and pursuing and obtaining happiness and safety."
Vermont follows the criminal procedure article of Virginia (the
proto-Fifth Amendment) as well as the social compact and incipient
just compensation clauses of the Pennsylvania constitution. Later
New England constitutions, particularly those of Massachusetts
(1780) and New Hampshire (1784) are in the same mold. All use
"law of the land" language, as does the Northwest Ordinance: "No
man shall be deprived of his liberty or property, but by the
judgment of his peers, or the law of the land." [27]

The Federal Constitution of 1787, though securing several
personal rights that can be associated with due process—the habeas
corpus, contract, ex post facto, and bill of attainder clauses—did not
establish a bill of rights comparable to those in the state constitutions. The principal reason for this omission is that the Philadelphia
Convention was framing a government to be limited both in theory
to enumerated powers and in practice to relatively little citizen
contact with the national establishment. In addition, the delegates
were exhausted after a summer's work on the frame of government
itself. And even if, as some members proposed near the end of the

debates, time had been set aside to develop a bill of rights, the diversity of state views on the subject would almost surely have led to problems in drafting and in ratification.[28]

In the spring of 1789 James Madison introduced in the First Congress the amendment to the Constitution which became the Fifth. It brought together in a concise phrase elements of due process that had been scattered in recent constitutional documents: "No person shall be . . . deprived of life, liberty, or property, without due process of law." Madison also introduced, but the House of Representatives did not approve, new language to be interpolated in the Preamble: "That Government is instituted and ought to be exercised for the benefit of the people; which consists in the enjoyment of life and liberty, with the right of acquiring and using property, and generally pursuing and obtaining happiness and safety." [29] This statement, which if in the Preamble would not have been "law," is adapted from the natural rights side of due process ideas, while the Fifth Amendment due process clause appears in the context of rights for persons accused of crime.

This distinction aids in understanding the first of several points worth noting about the Fifth Amendment; namely, that the Declaration's "pursuit of happiness" has been replaced by "property." The substitution may be explained by the fact that the "happiness" phraseology had just been proposed by Madison for the Preamble. But it is also a recognition that the Constitution is a legal, rather than a purely political document. Judicial interpretation of "pursuit of happiness" would be no easy task, especially as the tradition of British law from Magna Carta through Blackstone used due process wording while pursuit of happiness came from Lockean philosophy. Further, compared to 1776, the framers of the Constitution had a nonrevolutionary temper: property, not happiness, deserved special attention.

A second change in the Fifth Amendment from the most common previous wording is that "law of the land" has been replaced by "due process of law." As the principal constitutional models at the time used the former phrase, due process wording seems to deserve some explanation. The historical records are not helpful in this regard, but the Constitution itself contains the phrase "law of the land," and this may offer a clue. It is a reasonable, though by no means certain inference that as "law of the land" had already been employed with one meaning in the Supremacy Clause, it would be misleading to endow it with another meaning in the Fifth Amendment. The law-of-the-land clause in Article VI places federal written law (Constitution, laws, and treaties) above state constitutions and laws. The term "law" in the phrase "law of the land" (and elsewhere in the Constitution) therefore refers to positive enactments (except where explicitly qualified, as in the reference to common law in the Seventh Amendment). Yet "law" in Magna Carta's law of the land was not restricted to—in fact probably did not even refer to—positive law, but rather meant common law. This, too, had to be treated circumspectly in the Constitution, since the framers neither desired nor anticipated a federal common law "of the land." Still, federal criminal trials had to be conducted according to law. "Due process of law" was the most appropriate language to use in the circumstances.

A final observation on due process in the Fifth Amendment concerns its location in the Bill of Rights. The due process clause seems to be a general clause, certainly more general than the clauses on self-incrimination and just compensation, which immediately precede and follow it. But it is just because due process is surrounded both within the Bill of Rights and within the Fifth Amendment by other, more specific clauses, that it is difficult to construe its general terms with the generality many people (and the American constitutional tradition) have accorded it. To judge by its location—and this becomes more important when considering the meaning of due process in the Fourteenth Amendment—the federal due process clause is neither an introduction to nor a concluding summary of specific guarantees for persons accused of crimes.[30]

One thing about the Bill of Rights was certain, though not always explicit. The guarantees applied to the federal government, not to the states. The First Amendment alone is clear on this: "Congress shall make no law . . . ." The remaining provisions are written in the passive voice, or nearly so.[31] But the history of their adoption leaves no doubt that the first Congress intended them to apply to federal, and not state officials. By virtue of his longevity, if nothing else, John Marshall was the apt person to state this officially in Barron v. Baltimore (1833), a case in which the owner of land taken by the city to improve its harbor facilities was denied relief under the just compensation clause of the Fifth Amendment.[32]

II. THE NINETEENTH CENTURY THROUGH THE FOUR-TEENTH AMENDMENT

During the first half of the nineteenth century the traditional understanding of due process/law-of-the-land terminology was advanced through argument, commentary, and decision in the developing American constitutional law. Daniel Webster, defending the "old" Board of Trustees of Dartmouth College in 1819, stated, "By the law of the land is most clearly intended the general law; a law, which hears before it condemns; which proceeds upon inquiry, and renders judgment only after trial." [33] Justice Story, in his *Commentaries on the Constitution* (1833) cites Lord Coke and, in one of the briefest discussions of any constitutional matter in his two volumes, concludes that the due process clause "in effect affirms the right of trial according to the process and proceedings of the common law." [34]

The two major federal constitutional cases which addressed directly the meaning of the due process clause are Corfield v. Coryell, decided by Justice Bushrod Washington as circuit judge in 1823, and Murray's Lessee v. Hoboken Land and Improvement Company, decided by a unanimous Supreme Court in 1856, the opinion written by Justice Benjamin Curtis.[35] Corfield, an out-of-stater attempting to take oysters in New Jersey waters, claimed the privileges of a state citizen under the privileges and immunities clause of Article IV, Section 2. Justice Washington, denying the claim, defined privileges and immunities in terms of "fundamental principles." These principles, though not explicitly associated with the due process clause, are a remarkable compendium of due process/law-of-the-land ideas. They include "the enjoyment of life and liberty, with the right to acquire and possess property of every kind, and to pursue and obtain happiness and safety"; the right of habeas corpus and access to civil proceedings, and the right of suffrage—all subject to limits under law and for the good of the whole.[36]

The breadth of this view, presented by a member of the natural-law generation of the late eighteenth century, must be contrasted to the more narrow scholarly, legalistic, and historical view of Justice Curtis in *Murray's Lessee,* three decades later. The difference in the legal claim presented explains much of the specific distinctions between the opinions. But the contrast reflects as well contending styles of constitutional interpretation, with the more constricted style of Curtis the product of an era of greater legal formalism. In this case, the federal Treasury proceeded administratively against its former collector of customs in New York for retaining for personal use nearly $1.5 million in federal revenue. The specific issue was whether title to the Hackensack Meadows, once owned by the customs collector, had passed to the person to whom the collector had sold the property or to the company which had purchased the land from the government, which had in effect seized it to help recoup its tax losses. Justice Curtis first stated a principle of due process interpretation: History, particularly the British common law practice beginning with Magna Carta, rather than the courts or Congress, defines due process. Examining the history of British summary proceedings for the collection of crown debts, Curtis concluded that judicial power was, in this instance, not a requirement of due process of law, and that the government had therefore proceeded legitimately in the case.[37]

Although *Corfield* and *Murray's Lessee* establish an enduring contrast with respect to the method of interpreting due process, they are alike in arising from circumstances involved with property rights rather than criminal procedure. *Murray's Lessee* in particular is only ostensibly about legal procedure, and it is this side of due process/ law-of-the-land, the side of property rights and, to a considerable degree, natural rights, which is the genuine American "contribution" to the due process tradition.

The protection to property afforded by the due process clause must be understood primarily in terms of social and economic history rather than in terms of legal form. Such protection does run through the standard historical signposts of Magna Carta to Blackstone and the pre-1800 American constitutional documents. But it does not enter the mainstream of American law until the litigation of large economic interests becomes important; and even then, owing to the background of the clause, it enters under the auspices of constitutional provisions other than due process. Indeed, so long as due process language applied only to the federal government and, at least initially, only to judicial proceedings (as is suggested by its location in the Fifth Amendment), this is quite understandable. Prior to the Civil War, the federal government enacted little legislation that directly affected, or at least directly injured property. States, on the other hand, in particular through the promotion of transportation enterprises—bridges, turnpikes, canals, harbors, railroads—took, or allowed others to take, property, issued bonds, granted franchises and privileges, and in general vested legal rights in corporations.[38] Legislatures, especially of the Jacksonian persuasion, sometimes revoked these grants, and state courts attempted to protect property through just compensation and sometimes law-of-the-land clauses.[39] The U.S. Supreme Court developed the contract clause for the same purpose.[40]

Although the background in property rights is undoubtedly present, it is the social reform movements, beginning in the 1830s and cresting in the 1850s, that led to late nineteenth century due process usage. Due process ideas evolved both in and out of court and were fused into a new ideology of higher law. The due process phrase, which had sprung from and had usually been considered in the context of specific legal rights, now acquired philosophical force. Just as seventeenth century British and eighteenth-century Americans had transformed Magna Carta from a baronial agreement into a declaration of rights for all men, so the reform movements encouraged the modern metamorphosis of due process from common law procedure to higher law substance.

In particular, the temperance and abolitionist movements, in court cases in the mid-1850s, forwarded the development of the new due process. Wynehamer v. New York, decided in 1856, struck down an extreme state temperance law, a statute which forbade, virtually forthwith and with only trifling exceptions, the sale or possession of intoxicating liquor.[41] The vote was five to three, and the seriatim opinions of the majority by no means argue from the same grounds. But two points stand out. First, the law is invalid under the state constitution's due process clause for its destruction of previously acquired and uncompensated property. Due process of law in this sense was interpreted as a blend of ex post facto and just compensation provisions. Second, the state court held it was a judicial—not a legislative—function to determine what legal process is due process, or when a person may constitutionally be deprived of property.

The abolitionists' arguments about due process are more sustained and complex, and were for a long time historically submerged.[42] What rises above the surface is a statement by Chief Justice Tancy in the *Dred Scott* decision.[43] Taney invoked the Fifth Amendment due process clause in support of the Supreme Court's invalidation of the Missouri Compromise, which forbade the introduction of slaves into states, with the exception of Missouri, north of the parallel forming that state's southern boundary. In that respect, wrote Taney, the act denied slaveholders traveling away from the South their property without due process of law.[44] In a fifty-four-page opinion, the due process argument occupies less than a paragraph and is employed for illustrative purposes only. In constitutional history the reference has usually been regarded as a sport, an almost accidental precursor of later nineteenth century substantive due process. But although fleetingly dealt with in *Dred Scott,* due process is firmly rooted in the controversy over slavery.[45]

As in the Wynehamer case, and indeed in virtually all early "substantive" due process cases, the due process argument need not be understood in the rigid perspective of later theory. The Missouri Compromise, in this view and in judicial eyes, deprived a person of his property without due process precisely because legislative rather than judicial process had decided the matter. It was, therefore, a violation of separation of powers theory to deprive slave owners without a judicial determination. It was also, in this sense, a truly procedural issue, though certainly with substantive results. Further, Justice Curtis's dissenting rebuttal to Taney's due process argument paralleled his opinion for the Court in Murray's Lessee v. Hoboken Land and Improvement Co. of the previous year. His interpretation of due process is exclusively historical—he refers four times to Magna Carta in his one page treatment—and exclusively procedural as well.[46]

Neither Taney nor Curtis, however, hint at the contemporary and complex political usage being made of due process language and ideology. But Howard Jay Graham shows how "zealots, reformers, and politicians—not jurists—blazed the paths of substantive due process," and how Lockean phraseology and ideas rather than a specific Magna Carta-Fifth Amendment tradition led to identifying substantive due process with constitutionalized natural law.[47] From the abolitionist point of view, the due process clause granted slaves their physical liberty, or at least protected the children of slaves in their natural-born liberty.[48] Lockean theory and due process likewise protected slaves from being deprived of the property produced by their labor.[49] This natural law interpretation of due process on the part of the abolitionists was met by a positive law interpretation from the slaveholders. The two sides were engaged in the traditional American practice of turning a dispute over social policy into a contest for the sanction and public acceptance of a particular constitutional meaning.[50] The slaveholders' interpretation of due process was that by positive law slaves were property, and by positive law (and Blackstonian theory) the right of locomotion of slaveholders with their property was part of liberty.[51]

The irreconcilability of these interpretations of due process gives further meaning to the fact that *Dred Scott* was not successful in settling a moral issue by legal or constitutional means. When the Civil War was constitutionalized by the Thirteenth, Fourteenth, and Fifteenth Amendments, however, due process was reintroduced into constitutional language, but in a way and with results that bypassed the antebellum dispute.

The origins, language, and consequences of Section 1 of the Fourteenth Amendment are the most tangled in American constitutional history. The reasons for the complicated origins and language are, in brief, these. At least three distinguishable kinds of history are important in studying Section 1: the understanding and expectations of members of Congress and others involved in drafting and ratification; the general social, moral, and political aims of the abolitionist movement which Section 1 reduced to constitutional terminology; and the evolving legal significance of the key terms of the section.[52] These different histories, separately or together, point to no unambiguous meaning of the section. Nor does the language of the amendment, whether taken as isolated words and phrases or viewed as a web of related concepts. The relations, in particular, are intricate. They include the distinctions, if any, between United States and state citizenship (since the first sentence of Section 1 refers to both kinds of citizenship and the second sentence only to United States citizenship); the meaning of "No State" and its connection with the power of Congress under the fifth section of the amendment to enact appropriate enforcement legislation—that is, the problems of "state action" and congressional authority versus judicial interpretation; and, most important here, the relation of Fourteenth Amendment language and its meaning to identical phrases used earlier in the Constitution: the privileges or immunities and due process clauses.[53]

III. SUBSTANCE AND PROCEDURE UNDER THE OLD COURT

The constitutional consequences of Section 1 of the Fourteenth Amendment are even more unruly than its origin and language.[54] The first Supreme Court interpretation of the Fourteenth Amendment—the Slaughterhouse Cases—raises many of the issues that collect around due process of law for the following sixty years.[55] The case has several strands, one of which was a sentiment against monopolies that Lord Coke had associated with the "law of the land" in the seventeenth century and which the age of Jackson had made standard in American politics. But the monopolists won in the case, for the Reconstruction government of Louisiana had established a slaughterhouse monopoly for its friends, and the Supreme Court would not restore a livelihood to its enemies, a group of southern white rebel butchers. To reach this conclusion, the Court took up two issues apart from its interpretation of Section 1 of the Fourteenth Amendment. The first was whether the nature of the federal union had changed as a result of the Civil War and the Fourteenth Amendment; the answer to the inquiry was that it had not. The second was, who was to be the beneficiary of the Fourteenth Amendment; the answer was freedmen, primarily—certainly not New Orleans butchers. As to Section 1, both majority opinion and the chief dissent, Justice Field's, devoted most attention to the privileges or immunities clause, the Court virtually throttling the provision at infancy through the concept of "dual citizenship," under which there were few benefits of national citizenship.[56] The two opinions effectually ignored due process by treating it as similar to privileges or immunities.

It is the dissent of Justice Bradley in the case which eventually triumphed, for it concentrates on the new due process clause. Bradley's premise contradicted the Court's. "It is futile to argue," he wrote, "that none but persons of the African race are intended to be benefited by this amendment. They may have been the primary cause of its adoption but its language is general." [57] Quoting from

Magna Carta Chapter 29 and referring to Blackstone's "absolute right" of property, Bradley had developed a due process argument on behalf of the New Orleans butchers. He regarded "liberty" as the right to choose an occupation and "property" as the occupation itself, thus altering the more accepted meanings of liberty as the absence of physical restraint and property as real estate or goods. Bradley's opinion, though not directed at the situations which arose in the following decades, is expansive enough to embrace them. In the words of the least of the dissenting justices in the case, Noah Swayne, the Civil War amendments should be raised "to the dignity of a new Magna Carta." [58]

As the ideas and interest in substantive-economic due process developed in the late nineteenth century, the traditional use of due process was not set aside. That use did, however, change direction from the path marked out in 1856 in *Murray's Lessee.* The new procedural due process did not rely on British history. In Hurtado v. California the appellant, convicted of murder, claimed the Fourteenth Amendment due process clause was violated by the provision of the state constitution permitting trial after "information" filed by a prosecutor rather than after indictment by the time-honored grand jury.[59] Upholding the state, the Supreme Court abandoned the principle of interpretation in *Murray's Lessee,* the principle that due process be both explicated and confined by history. In an opinion characterized by seeming sensitivity to historical change, by sweepingly humanistic views on jurisprudence and society, and by confidence in the destiny of the United States, Justice Stanley Matthews presented one of the Court's most noted statements on due process, nevertheless denying the claim of the criminal defendant. Arguing that though Magna Carta might require grand jury proceedings, the Fourteenth Amendment need not, Matthew wrote:

> . . . owing to the progressive development of legal ideas and institutions in England, the words of Magna Charta stood for very different things at the time of the separation of the American colonies, from what they represented originally. . . . The Constitution of the United States was ordained, it is true, by descendants of Englishmen, who inherited the traditions of English law and history; but it was made for an undefined and expanding future. . . .[60]

Rejecting for due process "the unchangeableness attributed to the laws of the Medes and the Persians," and noting, therefore, the "difficulty if not impossibility of framing a definition" for the concept, Matthews held due process must be determined by a "gradual process of judicial inclusion and exclusion," drawing on "the best ideas of all systems and of every age." Due process, he said, was like the common law, its inspiration coming "from every fountain of justice." [61]

The single dissenter in *Hurtado* was Justice Harlan. With accustomed vigor, he met the majority on two grounds; history and the constitutional text. While the majority had abandoned the specific requirements of British legal tradition because times had changed, Justice Harlan clung to those requirements because they were "settled usages and modes" of English law "not unsuited" to American condition. For this position, Harlan adduced clear support from American authorities such as James Wilson, Kent, Story, Shaw, and Justice Field (who did not participate in the case) as well as the Court's approach in *Murray's Lessee*. Textually, the majority had claimed that it was "forbidden to assume" any part of the Fifth Amendment "superfluous," and hence, so long as both Fifth and Fourteenth amendments contained due process clauses, so long as the two clauses meant the same thing, and so long as the Fifth Amendment but not the Fourteenth Amendment explicitly required grand jury indictment in capital cases, then the Fourteenth Amendment due process clause left open the possibility of prosecution on information alone. To this argument Justice Harlan could reply only that the framers of the Fifth Amendment knew that due process encompassed the grand jury provision, but wanted to "avoid the possibility" that Congress would tamper with it.[62]

The significance of *Hurtado,* emphasized by the dissent and confirmed by the subsequent history of procedural due process litigation, is its focus on certainty within the law.[63] The majority was willing to resolve the case on the side of uncertainty, whether with regard to the tension between stability and change in a legal system; the adequate notice to affected persons—citizens, lawyers, judges—of what the law means and requires; or the degree of latitude possessed by the justices in interpreting the Constitution. These issues arise persistently in later cases of procedural due process as part of the search for standards under due process of law, and although Justice Harlan and his successors such as Justice Black have never made the law stand still, they have pressed for certainty in the law in such a fashion as to force their opponents, such as Justice Frankfurter and the second Justice Harlan, to develop increasingly careful statements of due process as an evolutionary concept.[64]

In the middle of his *Hurtado* opinion, Justice Matthews wrote that due process of law was "not alien" to the code "which has given us that fundamental maxim of distributive justice—*suum cuique tribuere.*"[65] With this rhetorical reach back to the Code of Justinian, a natural law definition of justice, and perhaps the legal thought of Aristotle, Matthews felicitously, though probably not purposely, considered as a whole what was soon to be separated in due process thought, procedure and substance. The *Hurtado* case was at least a matter of process, but *suum cuique tribuere* and distributive justice are at least a matter of substance. That a conceptual division between procedure and substance in due process was not an assumption of the era is evident in two cases related to *Hurtado*. In Davidson v. New Orleans, from which Matthews took the method as well as the phrase "gradual process of judicial inclusion and exclusion," the Court held that so long as an official assessment on land could be challenged in court, and was not made final by legislative or executive action alone, due process standards had been met.[66] Due process, therefore, meant essentially that the courts were to have the final word, whether over property claims or procedural ones.[67]

Although asserting in *Davidson* that it had the last word in due process cases, the Court professed reluctance to speak it. Contrasting nearly a century of desuetude of the Fifth Amendment due process clause with the current docket "crowded with cases in which we are asked to hold that State court and State legislatures have deprived their own citizens of life, liberty or property without due process of law," the Court noted that "there exists some strange misconception of the scope" of the Fourteenth Amendment provision.[68] As it turned out, however, there was not. Justice Bradley, who thought and probably cared more about the meaning of due process than any other nineteenth-century justice, added a concurring note in *Davidson* objecting to the Court's parsimonious view of its work and emphasizing the property rights involved. As in the Slaughterhouse Cases, it was Bradley who saw, if he did not significantly determine, the future of due process litigation. He proposed that Fourteenth

Amendment due process be interpreted to include a just compensation requirement for the states.[69] And he explained what was involved in just compensation adjudication: "Respect must be had to the cause and object of the taking, whether under the taxing power, the power of eminent domain, or the power of assessment for local improvements [the *Davidson* situation] or none of these: and . . . if found to be arbitrary, oppressive and unjust, it may be declared to be not 'due process of law.' " [70]

With one important exception, Justice Bradley's statement is a virtual table of contents of the relation of due process to property for the next sixty years, and that exception—police power legislation—may be covered by his phrase "or none of these." [71] What united the taking cases with the police power cases is that both required the justification of "public purpose" for their constitutionality. When the Supreme Court upheld state price regulation in Munn v. Illinois (1877), it did so on the ground that grain warehousing was a "business affected with a public interest," therefore subject to police power legislation and immune from a challenge under due process.[72] To assure the immunity, the Court felt required to say that it was not the business of the judiciary to supervise such regulation, rather this was a matter to be taken up at the polls.[73] But this was 1877 and in the context of Granger reforms. Two years later, in *Davidson,* in the context of municipal real estate assessment, the Court insisted that process was not due unless accompanied by judicial oversight.

The case that best unites protection for corporate property with power for the courts under due process of law is the Minnesota Rate Case of 1890, in which the justices rejected a state commission's determination of railroad rates.[74] In a sentence of conjunctive equipoise between substance and procedure, the Court held:

> If the company is deprived of the power of charging reasonable rates for the use of its property, and such deprivation takes place in the absence of an investigation by judicial machinery, it is deprived of the lawful use of its property, and thus, in substance and effect of the property itself, without due process of law. . . .[75]

For good measure, and to secure more firmly in a developing jurisprudence corporate rights against popular legislatures, Justice

Blatchford completed the sentence by holding the Minnesota law also in violation of the equal protection clause.

The Court's initial unease about how to fasten its constitutional faith to the constitutional text is reflected in Thomas M. Cooley's *Constitutional Limitations,* the most influential treatise on constitutional law of the era. As several state courts prior to the Civil War had done, Cooley adduced principles of government and society to forbid certain restrictions on property regardless of due process:

> The bill of rights in the American constitutions forbid that parties shall be deprived of property except by the law of the land; but if the prohibition had been omitted, a legislative enactment to pass one man's property over to another would nevertheless be void. If the act proceeded upon the assumption that such other person was justly entitled to the estate, and therefore it was transferred, it would be void, because judicial in its nature, and if it proceeded without reasons, it would be equally void, as neither legislative nor judicial, but a mere arbitrary fiat.[76]

Property needed more than nontextual legal guides for its protection. It also needed, and received, the justices' faith in burgeoning capitalism. This faith the jurists had, buttressed by the distorted absorption of Locke, Adam Smith, and Darwin. The reformation of due process in late-nineteenth-century America to serve new social and economic interests is comparable, perhaps, to the transformation of Magna Carta in the mid-seventeenth century from a feudal agreement to an instrument of the middle class for political change. Both generations found a usable—indeed, nearly the same—political-legal banner from the past and raised it against a different wind to wage their own campaigns. Just as natural rights were united with the positive Magna Carta rights of Englishmen, the natural law was allied with the positive rights of due process to defend American private enterprise against public encroachment.[77]

In light of the already generous scope of due process of law, late-nineteenth-century substantive or economic due process was no illogical development. But to succeed it needed two legal refinements that earlier thought and litigation did not sufficiently provide, the "corporate person" and "freedom of contract." The problem of the corporate person has been fully explicated by Howard Jay Graham and can be briefly stated here.[78] The first section of the Fourteenth Amendment protects "citizens" in their privileges and immunities, but "persons" against due process and equal protection violations. Textually, therefore, "persons" and "citizens" are not the same, and "persons" is without doubt the broader term. The question is: how broad? "Citizen" itself, had already been held to include corporations under Article III of the Constitution concerning federal court jurisdiction, though not under the federal comity (privileges and immunities) clause of Article IV.[79] Although "person" could easily be restricted to natural persons, and therefore add to citizens only aliens in defining the scope of its coverage, it was not forbidden by history or precedent to include artificial persons as well.[80] On the other hand, while the Joint Committee of the Thirty-eighth Congress had purposely used "persons" rather than "citizens" for the due process and equal protection clauses, the citizenship and privileges and immunities clauses were inserted on the floor of the Senate; consequently in the drafting history of Section 1 there is no direct relation of "citizen" to "person" at all. As to why and how the "constitutional corporate person" developed, Graham fully refutes the implications and "recollections" of Roscoe Conkling arguing before the Supreme Court in the 1880s, that twenty years earlier, the drafters of the amendment, whatever they wrote, intended corporations to be included under "person." Although this argument is most simply labeled a lie, Graham concedes it was nearly inevitable that corporations would benefit from due process protection.[81]

One of the due process benefits developed by the Court for corporations was "liberty of contract." [82] This liberty was based on a presumed parity of bargaining power between employer and employee, or between buyer and seller, guaranteeing both parties substantive due process "liberty" against police power legislation. The concept was inaugurated in a New York case of 1885, In re Jacobs, which held legislation prohibiting the manufacture of cigars in tenement houses unconstitutional.[83] The law was held to infringe, substantively and unconstitutionally, on the freedom of workers to practice their trade where they wished. Several years later liberty of contract was shepherded into federal constitutional law by Justice Peckham of New York. In 1897 he wrote for the

Court that a Louisiana insurance law violated the Fourteenth
Amendment due process clause by depriving a local firm of its
liberty to purchase insurance as it wished out of state.[84] Peckham
defined the new right:

> The liberty mentioned in [the Fourteenth] amendment means
> not only the right of the citizen to be free from the mere
> physical restraint of his person, as by incarceration, but the
> term is deemed to embrace the right of the citizen to be free in
> the enjoyment of all his faculties; . . . to pursue any livelihood
> or avocation, and for that purpose to enter into all contracts
> which may be proper, necessary and essential. . . ." [85]

With a unanimous Court behind him, Justice Peckham neatly
collapsed the liberty and property elements of due process terminology into one principle. Liberty originally related to imprisonment;
contract related to property. Bound together in a short phrase it was
difficult to recognize what had happened to the operative term; for
in the Court's argument, the phrase as well as the significance of
"without due process of law" had vanished. Notwithstanding the
Court's bow to the police power and its distinction between in-state
and out-of-state contracts, *Allgeyer* stands for the proposition that
almost no process of law could constitutionalize this or comparable
restrictions on the liberty of contract.

In Lochner v. New York, decided eight years after the Louisiana
insurance case, the Court was pressed by four dissenters to justify
the new liberty, and modified the idea considerably.[86] The New
York law restricting the hours which bakers could work would have
been valid, the Court admitted, if only it had demonstrated "a more
direct relation, as a means to an end" in its provisions.[87] The
majority agreed that the ends of wholesome bread and healthy
bakers were legitimate ones. Indeed, the Court had already upheld
an hours law as a valid exercise of the police power; but that was in
mining, a more dangerous occupation, and that, the Court implied,
made a constitutional difference.[88] A dissent by Justice Harlan met
the Court on its own means-ends ground. Justice Holmes directly
attacked the propriety of the Court's inquiry once the end of the
legislation was deemed constitutional. His test for the deprivation of
liberty without due process of law was whether "a rational and fair

man necessarily would admit that the statute proposed would infringe fundamental principles as they have been understood by the traditions of our people and our law." [89] It was a very difficult test to meet.[90]

The demise of liberty of contract in the Constitutional Revolution of 1937 was not justified on the basis of Holmes's latitudinarian view of due process. Nor did it come about simply through the marshaling of data in Brandeis briefs. Further, the Court continued to hold that liberty in due process of law meant more than the absence of physical restraint, so it did not return to the traditional meaning of the term. But in acquiescing to liberty as an economic right Chief Justice Hughes deliberately shifted the Court's emphasis from liberty for the individual to protection for the community. "Liberty in each of its phases," he noted, "has its history and its connotation." [91] While liberty is at heart individual, it is nevertheless safeguarded "in a social organization which requires the protection of law against the evils which menace the health, safety, morals and welfare of the people." [92] Adopting the ostensible standard of *Lochner,* but basing it on the wider premise occasioned by the Depression, Hughes concluded that "regulation [of liberty] which is reasonable in relation to its subject and is adapted in the interest of the community *is* due process of the law." [93] In a few sentences, Hughes had recognized the nature and realities of constitutional change and had transformed constitutional liberty— at least with regard to social welfare legislation—from an individual right to a community responsibility.

IV. CIVIL LIBERTIES, DOUBLE STANDARDS, AND INCORPORATION

During the decades that due process liberty expanded from a safeguard against arbitrary incarceration to a prohibition against "unreasonable" economic and social legislation, the Supreme Court began to apply the Fourteenth Amendment liberty to the freedoms protected by the First Amendment as well. This expansion of liberty on a second front was accepted—indeed, unintentionally encouraged—by the justices intent on utilizing freedom of contract. At the same time it was consciously, if sometimes reluctantly, forwarded by those justices, in particular Justice Brandeis, who found distasteful the means by which the "new liberty" was achieved.[94] Several cases of the 1920s mark the Court's path to the protection of substantive civil liberties under the Fourteenth Amendment due process clause.

In a case of 1920, when the Court upheld the power of a state to punish a person for speaking against American participation in the World War, Brandeis dissented: "I cannot believe that the liberty guaranteed by the Fourteenth Amendment includes only liberty to acquire and enjoy property." [95] The following year, when the Court denied power to a state to restrict the injunctive power of Courts in labor disputes, Chief Justice Taft had recourse to natural law language against four dissenters: "[T] legislative power of a State can only be exerted in subordination to the fundamental principles of right and justice which the guaranty of due process in the Fourteenth Amendment is intended to preserve." [96] Throughout his dissent in the case, Justice Brandeis deliberately and repeatedly characterized the right to carry on business as "liberty or property," thus accustoming his colleagues to think as favorably toward other kinds of "liberty rights" as they did toward property rights.

Not long afterward, Justice McReynolds, who could not abide Brandeis, brought to fruit the seed his brother had planted. Holding invalid a state ban against the teaching of modern foreign languages to schoolchildren, McReynolds wrote:

> Without doubt, [Fourteenth Amendment liberty] denotes not merely freedom from bodily restraint but also the right of the individual to contract, to engage in any of the common occupations of life, to acquire useful knowledge, to marry, establish a home and bring up children, to worship God according to the dictates of his own conscience, and generally to enjoy those privileges long recognized at common law as essential to the orderly pursuit of happiness by free men.[97]

This breathtaking proposition not only brought together traditional property (contract) and liberty (spread of knowledge and religion), it also included natural law (the family), the common law, privileges and immunities beyond due process, and a general blessing for "the pursuit of happiness by free men."

Although adopted in this informal manner by very divergent justices, an expanded notion of due process liberty under the

Fourteenth Amendment had not yet been officially authorized by the Court. This happened in 1925 when the Court explicitly recognized that the First Amendment was valid against the states under the Fourteenth Amendment due process clause.[98] The development in Gitlow v. New York immediately drew a sharp attack from the constitutional scholar Charles Warren. Warren argued not only that it was historically unjustified to use the due process clause, or its "liberty," to decide cases on freedom of expression, but that it was textually illogical and worse, fraught with danger. "It is hardly conceivable," he wrote, "that the framers of [the Fifth] Amendment, having already provided in the First Amendment an *absolute prohibition* on Congress to take away certain rights, would in the [same] Amendment declare or imply that Congress *might* take away the same rights by due process of law." [99] The crucial assumption in Warren's argument, of course, is the identity of meaning of the Fifth and Fourteenth Amendment due process clauses. While this is sensible as an assumption, it turns out not to predict what happened. So long as the Fifth Amendment clause did not permit any diminution of the First Amendment applied to the federal government, the meaning of the Fourteenth Amendment clause might be enlarged to include, to any degree, First Amendment rights applied to the States. Civil libertarians, if they were interested only in results, need not have worried.[100]

Justice Brandeis, more sensitive to the current of constitutional reasoning than Warren, made the doctrinal leap the next year:

> Despite arguments to the contrary which had seemed to me persuasive, it is settled that the due process clause of the Fourteenth Amendment applies to matters of substantive law as well as to matters of procedure. Thus all fundamental rights comprised within the term liberty are protected by the Federal Constitution from invasion by the States. The right of free speech, the right to teach and the right of assembly are, of course, fundamental rights.[101]

By the end of the 1920s, therefore, political liberals had joined economic conservatives in expanding the due process clause so that the Supreme Court could protect First Amendment freedoms under the same language that it protected corporate property.

If the chief due process issue in the early 1930s was how to contain substantive due process, the issues in the two decades following the constitutional revolution of 1937 were the degree to which economic due process had been laid to rest and the way in which the new liberty, the application of the Bill of Rights to the states, came to take its place.[102] Personal liberties not only crept up to economic liberties as the objects of Supreme Court favor, but quickly overtook them. This raised—and still raises—a theoretical problem in due process adjudication. What, if anything, justifies the distinction between property and personal rights; and, assuming the distinction, what justifies different standards of judicial review for them? This is the problem of the double standard.[103] The case which best symbolizes the turn from the old to the new era and establishes the double standard is United States v. Carolene Products Co. (1938).[104] In this case Justice Stone for the Court accepted the extreme and essentially impossible to meet standard of Justice Holmes in judging economic legislation: a law was constitutional unless its provisions precluded the assumption of resting on a rational basis. At the same time, in his well-known footnote 4, the Justice outlined areas of litigation in which there would be no presumption of constitutionality. The footnote forecast the general direction of the Court for the next thirty years in civil rights and civil liberties.[105]

The New Deal Court had little trouble suddenly rejecting economic due process arguments that had held force for half a century.[106] Freedom of contract, business affected with a public interest, "reasonable" regulation, judicial determination of a "fair return on a fair value of property" in rate making—all of these constitutional concepts vanished. As Hugo Black, the New Deal legislator put it after a quarter century as Justice:

> There was a time when the Due Process Clause was used by this Court to strike down laws which were thought unreasonable, that is, unwise or incompatible with some particular economic or social philosophy. . . . The doctrine that prevailed in Lochner, Coppage, Adkins, Burns, and like cases . . . has long since been discarded. . . . Whether the legislature takes for its textbook Adam Smith, Herbert Spencer, Lord Keynes or some other is no concern of ours.[107]

Where economic activities were concerned, the constitutional law of due process essentially gave way to administrative law.[108] But the remaining areas—procedural due process for persons accused of crimes, and the new civil liberties substance—flourished as never before.

At about the time that the *Carolene Products* case distinguished so sharply between economic and civil liberties, Palko v. Connecticut, through Justice Cardozo, proposed a distinction within civil liberties: between those liberties which were, and those which were not "of the very essence of a scheme of ordered liberty." [109] This elusive doctrine—and to a large extent the classification which accompanied it—became the Court's "standard," slowly abandoned over the next three decades. The core of the essence lay with freedom of expression. Outside the essence lay most federal protections for criminal defendants, including the jury trial and the right against being compelled to testify in one's own case.[110]

The analytical approach to the "incorporation" or absorption of the provisions of the first eight amendments under the due process clause of the Fourteenth was dramatically supplemented in 1947 by Justice Black's essay on the intent of the framers in Adamson v. California.[111] *Adamson* revived the dispute begun in Hurtado v. California, where Justice Harlan's dissent, like Justice Black's, argued that whatever, indeed precisely whatever, the Bill of Rights requires of the federal government the Fourteenth Amendment requires of the states, because members of the Thirty-ninth Congress intended it that way. The biting reply of Justice Frankfurter to this argument is summed up in a sentence:

> Those reading the English language with the meaning which it ordinarily conveys, those conversant with the political and legal history of the concept of due process, those sensitive to the relations of the States to the central government as well as the relation of some of the provisions of the Bill of Rights to the process of justice, would hardly recognize the Fourteenth Amendment as a cover for the various explicit provisions of the first eight Amendments.[112]

As in *Hurtado,* the jurisprudential nub of the *Adamson* dispute is the issue of certainty in the law. With its flawed details, Justice

Black's approach is, in theory, the most "certain." Due process in the Fourteenth Amendment means exactly what the first eight amendments mean. The possibilities for being less certain are numerous. Justices Murphy and Rutledge advocated "incorporation plus," by which Justice Black's definition would be a minimum that might be exceeded.[113] Justice Frankfurter, basically following Cardozo, and succeeded by the second Justice Harlan, held that Fourteenth Amendment due process should neither "comprehend" the specific provisions of the Bill of Rights nor be confined by them.[114] Finally, Justice Brennan has proposed a "nearly certain" method through "selective incorporation," according to which not everything is taken over from the Bill of Rights, but what is absorbed is absorbed intact.[115]

Only Justice Frankfurter's approach, as he insisted, corresponds with the history of due process. So long as constitutional litigation exists, there will be no static and "true" meaning of any provision or of all of the Bill of Rights to carry over into the Fourteenth Amendment. In addition, since most of the recent due process cases originate in state courts, the direction of incorporation—from the Bill of Rights to the Fourteenth Amendment—has lost its meaning. Instead of federal cases supplying a standard for cases that come from the states, the situation is now one of interaction of the state cases building upon each other or even contributing to national standards.

Finally, in historical perspective, the incorporation controversy is now moot, for two reasons. On the one hand, the outlook of Justice Frankfurter has been vindicated. To paraphrase Holmes, the history of due process has been that of experience, not logic. Due process in regard to the relation between the Bill of Rights and the Fourteenth Amendment has developed its own requirements independent of formulas of incorporation. It has not become fixed. On the other hand, Justice Black seems vindicated as well, for with almost no exception the first eight amendments are now the principal standard for Fourteenth Amendment adjudication.[116]

This does not mean that due process theory is of no use. Nor have we reached the situation in which Justice Black's goals have been achieved by Justice Frankfurter's methods. Black's aim was not merely the extension of rights for those accused of crime; nor was Frankfurter's method a kind of judicial uncertainty principle. Black

firmly believed that his literal approach to constitutional exegesis—
and in this the incorporation controversy was only one aspect—was
best for American constitutional government because, in theory, it
left sovereignty with the people, diminished the political power of
the judges, and kept the Constitution predictable for litigants and
plain for citizens. And Frankfurter, always arguing that flexible due
process was far from being without standards, firmly believed, in his
words, that the "history of liberty has largely been the history of the
observance of procedural safeguards." [117] The contrasting theories
and interests of the two justices, then, are important as contemporary evidence of the dialectic of due process. So long as men attach
fundamental juridical values to "due process of law," the phrase
with its evolving legal implications remains vital to the resolution of
constitutional problems.[118]

V. THE DUE PROCESS TRADITION AND RIGHTS FOR NEW INTERESTS

The Supreme Court's effacement of substantive due process after
1937 was in many ways complete.[119] But ultimately a reaction
began, emerging from and reaffirming principles and practices of
the American constitutional tradition which were independent of a
specific due process history as well as of the constitutional revolution
of the 1930s. What the tradition provided was the right of the
judiciary, with the tacit approval of the people, to check elected
legislatures and executives. Thus, although the Court's due process
destruction of social welfare legislation had strained the legitimacy
of its exercise of judicial review generally, that exercise has
remained, in fact flourished, in two forms related to the old due
process. One form has been the transfer of due process discussion to
other constitutional language. This has avoided unpalatable phraseology but has accomplished what jurists unrestrained by historical
consciousness could certainly have explained and evolved under due
process of law. The second form retains due process language but
refines it to take account, as due process always has, of contemporary social interests and needs.

The use of alternative language for due process purposes illustrates a common phenomenon in the development of legal institutions. Assuming that "due process purposes" exist, for example to

protect vested rights of property, then other constitutional provisions—ex post facto, obligation of contracts, and the just compensation clauses—have already been shown to be at least partial
substitutes for the due process clause. At the same time, different
social interests—sometimes even incompatible ones such as slavery
and abolitionism or employer versus employee interests—have
gravitated to, if not clutched at, due process language for their
constitutional justification. The relationship between constitutional
language and the interests claiming constitutional protection is a
complex one. Language, as language, may be more or less specific
and therefore seem more or less suited to covering certain kinds of
claims.

But should claims always be decided under the provision, or by
the concept, that, in terms, seems most apt? Yes, if we wish to
confine the case to the clause; no, if we hope to expand the case to
other claims. More important than the unglossed words of the text
is current constitutional practice, which in turn is affected by
historical usage. When a social claim seeks constitutional protection,
lawyers and judges are inevitably affected by the contemporary
juristic *Weltanschauung*. It seems likely, for instance, that only at the
time of its ratification and again since the mid-1960s would the
Ninth Amendment have appeared a feasible constitutional clause
under which to claim any rights at all, and that now—but not
then—could it be related to concepts akin to due process. Whether
language or historical contingency plays the principal role in
associating social interest with constitutional phraseology, the due
process clauses and the principles developed under them provide the
best example of this association in the American experience.

For one thing, the asymmetry of the Constitution regarding
prohibitions against state and federal action has led to some
linguistically peculiar practices with the due process clauses. The
strain of judicially enforcing formal federalism has had the effect of
using these clauses as shields behind which other provisions of the
Constitution can be relocated, so that standards are the same
against both states and nation. This has been discussed above with
respect to moving the Bill of Rights "forward" into the Fourteenth
Amendment. Of equal interest is the fact that the contract clause
and the equal protection clause, both explicitly applicable only

against the states, have rather openly been applied against the federal government as if they were included in Fifth Amendment due process.[120]

Prior to 1937, substantive due process purposes were sometimes advanced by other, more direct, means. In the first child labor case, the Court held that Congress had overrun the limits of its authority under the commerce clause and invaded states rights.[121] In the second child labor case, the Court held that Congress had unconstitutionally used the federal taxing power in pursuit of the same goal.[122] These grounds no longer suffice. Yet in maintaining a national economy through interpretation of the commerce clause against the states, the Court has sometimes seemed to permit the continuation of substantive due process judgments.[123] Similar substantive due process situations have arisen under the equal protection clause.[124]

Twenty-five years after the constitutional victory of the New Deal, a justice—apparently approvingly—referred to "the present Court's allergy to substantive due process." [125] In the ensuing decade, however, the allergy has been treated, albeit in part allopathically through other constitutional clauses. As Joseph Tussman and Jacobus tenBroek suggested in 1949: "Due Process is, after all, a weapon blunted and scarred in the defense of property. The present Court, conscious of its destiny as the special guardian of human or civil rights may well wish to develop some alternative to due process as a sanctuary for these rights. The equal protection clause has much to recommend it for this purpose." [126] Yet despite the extensive use of the equal protection clause since the 1950s to accomplish aims which earlier might have been achieved through due process reasoning, due process adjudication continues to thrive well beyond the sphere of criminal procedure. The covering reason for this is that since Magna Carta due process has afforded protection to individuals against arbitrary and "unjust" government action in a way that equal protection, with its origins in the abolitionist movement, has not. But two significant contemporary trends explain more.

First, as the activities of government have expanded in the areas of welfare, housing, medicine, and employment, the potential for arbitrary official action has also increased. There is much more to be protected against. And this protection, in the form of fair administrative procedure or just legislative classification, is typically a legal means to securing more substance—that is, money or its equivalent—or for achieving the opportunity to secure more substance. Judges may value procedure for its own sake and for the sake of a legal system, but litigants have the substance of cases in mind. As it is the government rather than private enterprise which legally controls this new substance, an important distinction exists between the new property and the old, one which allows the Court to believe it is not returning to its former stance but is instead reemphasizing the traditional meaning of due process, protection of citizens from arbitrary governmental action.[127] Due process adjudication or its equivalent, then, has reentered the field of substance. With regard to the new property, due process has usually followed the traditional path of fair procedure while equal protection, concerned with rational (sometimes "reasonable") classification has been refined with concepts such as "suspect criteria," and "compelling" state or "fundamental" personal interests.[128]

The second reason for the continued expansion of due process adjudication is an increasing sensitivity to individual human claims against society, not only with regard to the new property, but also in criminal procedure, the "new substance" of privacy, refinements of first amendment rights, and areas not formerly governed by constitutional law. The thought and language of substantive due process has been applied to government intrusions into genuinely private activities, sex and marriage. Procedural rights have been extended to realms identifiable by traditional state control over the parties (juvenile offenders, aliens, prisoners, mental patients, military personnel), by new claims based on the interest at stake (right to travel, professional licensing, and job retention), or by a groping attempt to hold back the tide of McCarthyism in the 1950s and 1960s.[129] Due process decisions have forced the revision of administrative procedures and have been the main legal impetus to the development of public defender offices throughout the country. The expansion of due process within the legal system has also encouraged—in part because of potential legal consequences—the conscious development of due process standards in many nongovernmental organizations such as educational institutions.

In the course of the cases dealing with the new property and other recently fashioned rights, the Court has often reworked distinctions traditionally thought important in constitutional law. The most important sets of distinctions are between procedure and substance and between liberty and property.

All cases have substantive outcomes no matter how judges and lawyers see the issue under discussion.[130] The effect that procedures have on outcome is obvious when one considers what is meant by "parliamentary strategy," an activity dominated by lawyers. Although one could argue for the outcome-neutrality of procedure on the ground that some recognized standards are necessary to reach any substantive outcome that will be accepted as legitimate, particular procedures do help determine particular outcomes. And not only does procedure significantly determine substance, but the reverse may be true, as well. As the old economic due process cases demonstrate, the more highly valued a substantive end, the more rigorous the procedures in its protection are likely to be.[131] Contemporary constitutional law has also had to cope with the liberty-property distinction. The "new property" has led the Court explicitly to bind the two concepts together. Justice Stewart, citing Locke and Blackstone for support, wrote for the Court in a due process case of 1972:

> . . . the dichotomy between personal liberties and property rights is a false one. Property does not have rights. People have rights. The right to enjoy property without unlawful deprivation, no less than the right to speak or the right to travel, is in truth a "personal" right, whether the "property" in question be a welfare check, a home, or a savings account. In fact a fundamental interdependence exists between the personal right to liberty and the personal right in property. Neither could have meaning without the other.[132]

The realms, classifications, and doctrines of contemporary due process may arise from contemporary social needs, but only living jurists can articulate them in constitutional law. During his service on the Supreme Court, Justice Frankfurter was the most thoughtful, if adulative, due process justice.[133] But it is the second Justice

Harlan, Frankfurter's less passionate successor to the guardian of the tradition, who developed the most comprehensive modern view of due process on the Court.

Harlan's due process thought is distinguished by three characteristics. First, it takes meticulous account of the role the concept has played in constitutional history, with regard both to the jurisprudential disputes that have surrounded it and its persistent function of protecting important social interests in different eras. Second, while insisting that due process is a broad idea, Harlan sharply distinguishes it from related clauses, such as equal protection and—along with Frankfurter—prefers not to innovate with other constitutional clauses or concepts when the due process tradition provides a solution.[134] Tied to no tradition, other constitutional clauses would be at the mercy of ephemeral Court majorities and might suddenly add or subtract large areas of law from constitutional protection. Finally, and most striking, Harlan is the first justice since 1937 clearly to hold that due process should not be restricted to procedure but should also protect "fundamental" substantive rights, such as privacy, in particular with respect to marriage and sex. Other justices have now accepted this approach, as the abortion cases of 1973 make plain.[135]

With the abortion cases, due process has not gone full circle—or even in a seventy-five-year epicycle. The crucial constitutional language is the same, but the equally crucial social context has changed. The tradition of due process, precisely because it is a tradition of social thought and practice as well as a meandering stream of judicial precedents, continues to provide the materials for determining what claims and interests deserve protection from governmental action. If the future is like the past, due process language and ideas will accompany the development of legal concepts and litigation in new areas of social concern as well as in recurring ones such as economic crises and criminal justice. Women's rights and environmental protection are two areas in which the due process tradition may contribute to rapidly developing bodies of law.

It was against a due process claim, the right to an occupation—the pursuit of happiness—that the Supreme Court once agreed that states could prohibit women from practicing law.[136] It was in spite of the due process claim, by corporations, that the Court upheld welfare legislation designed to protect women.[137] In the 1970s the principal argument for the Equal Rights Amendment has also involved the due process tradition and it has squarely opposed it. In the first place, due process and equal protection do not contain the specific content desired—equality between sexes. Second, due process is usually, and has been regarding the claims of the women's rights movement, a slow-moving instrument of social and legal change. These, of course, are normally considered the virtues of due process: nothing specific, nothing fast, rather society's evolving sense of fairness. Opponents of the amendment, therefore, apart from views they may hold on the "role" of women, look to due process of law as the model for constitutional development and are at heart afraid of the years of judicially created confusion likely to result from a new and unqualified principle of fundamental law.

The contemporary law of the environment, propelled by social, political, and economic forces, and developed from other, established areas of law ranging from nuisance to admiralty, is also likely to confront the due process tradition.[138] Judges are understandably reluctant to prescribe policy in an area which is technical, normally the province of legislatures or agencies, and almost surely not best dealt with piecemeal. But as they recognize that environmental litigation is often based on an attrition strategy of procedural battles in a substantive war, judges have not been reluctant to enforce the standards of due process, usually through administrative law.[139] The mixing of procedure with substance is well illustrated in the Mineral King case, in which the Sierra Club was denied standing to sue the Secretary of the Interior in order to prevent commercial development in a national wilderness area.[140] The dissent of Justice Blackmun relied on the Administrative Procedure Act in an attempt to secure the club a hearing. Justice Douglas proposed that the environment itself—rivers, forest, animals—be given substantive rights in court.[141] Both are due process arguments. The old-fashioned substantive due process approach was suggested in 1970 by a United States District Court judge who, while dismissing a case for lack of jurisdiction, found that under the Fourteenth Amendment due process clause "each of us is constitutionally protected in our natural and personal state of life and health" from environmental pollution.[142]

The most significant discussions of constitutional due process in recent years, while refining the subject with new perspectives and distinctions, all proceed from the view that under "due process of law" fall the basic issues of American constitutional government and the function of the judiciary. In view of the history of due process and the social interests and legal doctrines that have transiently or permanently become associated with it, this is not remarkable. From its inception in Magna Carta, due process of law has attempted to provide a standard, both as norm and as emblem, for resolving instances of the persisting confrontation between man and his government. The recent discussions, like earlier ones from Coke through Frankfurter, make due process central to the rule of law and to society's sense of justice and fundamental values. Whether viewed in terms of fair procedures, claims to property and to various liberties, or the assignment of roles and limits to the courts, the language and ideas of due process have offered guidance.[143] To courts, commentators, and commoners, the hold of due process of law is a blend of history and reason, as Justice Frankfurter said, though on another plane it might be described as a compound of habit and imprecise language. Either way, due process of law consists in the political and legal doctrines that have developed, and in some cases undergone demise, in its name; of ordinances and rulings that protect individuals and groups from arbitrary impositions; and of arguments for political reform, social and economic justice, and the proper place of courts in a constitutional system. With its historical and ethical connotations, due process of law brings together *per legem terrae* with *suum cuique tribuere.* The durability of due process over seven and a half centuries, as phrase and idea, is a tribute to a law-minded people whose traditions have enjoyed continuity and whose aspirations for a just life are consciously and finely attuned to the relation between individual fulfillment and social welfare.

NOTES

1. I owe the "forest" image to Walton Hamilton's study of substantive due process, "The Path of Due Process of Law" and Thomas More's insight on procedural due process: "This country's planted thick with laws from coast to coast . . . and if you cut them down . . . d'you really think you could stand upright in the winds that would blow then?" Hamilton's article is in Conyers Read (ed.), *The Constitution Recon-*

sidered (New York: Columbia University Press, 1938), pp. 167-90. More's lines come from Robert Bolt, *A Man for All Seasons* (London: Heinemann, 1960), p. 39. For its source, see William Roper, *Life of More* (Early English Text Society Edition, London: Oxford Univ. Press, 1935), pp. 41-42. This reference was kindly supplied by R. S. Sylvester, executive editor of the *Yale Edition of the Works of St. Thomas More.*

2. T. R. Powell is quoted in Howard Jay Graham, *Everyman's Constitution: Historical Essays on the Fourteenth Amendment, the "Conspiracy Theory" and American Constitutionalism* (Madison: State Historical Society of Wisconsin, 1968), p. 590; Felix Frankfurter, "Social Issues before the Supreme Court," 22 Yale Rev. 476, 490 (1933).

3. The combination is reflected in a news story. In the spring of 1974, when the House Judiciary Committee's impeachment inquiry was temporarily thwarted by the White House, the committee extended a subpoena deadline. Representative Barbara C. Jordan, a member of the committee who had visited the National Archives to commune with the constitutional parchment in preparation for her task, defended the extension: "It has been our practice since the beginning to give the President not due process but due process quadrupled." *New York Times,* April 26, 1974, p. 1.

4. Charles H. McIlwain discusses general reasons for retaining constitutional terminology to cover changes in constitutional function and purpose in "Some Illustrations of the Influence of Unchanged Names for Changing Institutions," in Paul Sayre (ed.), *Interpretations of Modern Legal Philosophies* (New York: Oxford Univ. Press, 1947), pp. 484-97. Arthur O. Lovejoy might term the inquiry here one of

> philosophical semantics—a study of the sacred words and phrases of a period or a movement, with a view to a clearing up of their ambiguities, a listing of their various shades of meaning, and an examination of the way in which confused associations of ideas arising from these ambiguities have influenced the development of doctrines, or accelerated the insensible transformation of one fashion of thought into another, perhaps its very opposite. It is largely because of their ambiguities that mere words are capable of this independent action as forces in history. A term, a phrase, a formula, which gains currency or acceptance because of one of its meanings, or of the thoughts which it suggests, is congenial to the prevalent beliefs, the standard of value, the tastes of a certain age,

may help to alter beliefs, standards of value, and tastes, because other meanings or suggested implications, not clearly distinguished by those who employ it, gradually distinguished by those who employ it, gradually become the dominant elements of its signification.

The Great Chain of Being: A Study of the History of an Idea (New York: Harper and Row, 1960), p. 14.

5. The standard works, all entitled *Magna Carta*, are by William Sharp McKechnie (Glasgow, 1905), Henry Elliott Malden (ed.) (London, 1917), Faith Thompson (Minneapolis: Univ. of Minnesota Press, 1948), and J. C. Holt (Cambridge: Cambridge Univ. Press, 1965). See also Charles H. McIlwain, "Due Process of Law in Magna Carta," 14 Colum. L. Rev. 27-51 (1914).

6. The Latin reads: *"Nullus liber homo capitur, vel imprisonetur, aut dissaisiatur, aut utlagetur, aut exultetur, aut aliquo modo destruatur, nec super um ibimus, nec super eum mittemus, nisi per legale judicium parium suorum vel per legem terrae."* The computation and possible significance of the fact that the words of Chapter 39 lie precisely in the middle of the Magna Carta are presented in Gottfried Dietze, *Magna Carta and Property* (Charlottesville: Univ. Press of Virginia, 1965), p. 30, n. Rodney L. Mott noted that the expression "by the laws of the Empire and the judgment of his peers" can be found in an eleventh-century edict of the Holy Roman Emperor, but it has no known connection with Chapter 39. *Due Process of Law* (Indianapolis: Bobbs-Merrill, 1926), p. 1.

7. Richard L. Perry succinctly lays out alternative meanings in *Sources of Our Liberties* (New York: McGraw-Hill, 1964), p. 6, n. 13.

8. McIlwain, "Due Process of Law" (note 5), pp. 46-47.

9. *The History of the Common Law of England* (published posthumously, 1713), ed. Charles M. Gray (Chicago: Univ. of Chicago Press, 1971), p. 36.

10. Albert B. White, "The Name Magna Carta," 30 Eng. Hist. Rev. 472-75 (1915) and 32 Eng. Hist. Rev. 554-55 (1917). Also Ivor Jennings, "Magna Carta and Constitutionalism in the Commonwealth," in William H. Dunham, Jr., et al., *The Great Charter* (New York: Pantheon Books, 1965), p. 75.

11. Ibid., p. 26. Dunham judges this "perhaps" the first use of due process of law in a constitutional context.

12. See generally Max Radin, "The Myth of Magna Carta," 60 Harv. L. Rev. 1060-91 (1947).

13. See generally Maurice Ashley, *Magna Carta in the Seventeenth Century* (Charlottesville: Univ. Press of Virginia, 1965).

14. A baronial invocation appears in Elizabethan literature. Shakespeare's Duke of Clarence speaks to one of the murderers sent against him by his nephew, the would-be Richard: "Before I be convict by course of law / To threaten me with death is most unlawful." Richard III, I.iv.192. The play was written in the 1590s, but its setting is somewhat over a century earlier.

15. Edward Coke, *Second Part of the Institutes of the Laws of England* (4th ed., London, 1671), p. 46.

16. Ibid., pp. 46, 50.

17. Ibid., p. 47. "No man shall be . . . dispossessed of his Freehold (that is) lands, or livelihood, or of his liberties, or free customes, that is, of such franchises and freedomes, and free customes, as belong to him by his free birthright, unlesse it be by the lawfull judgment, that is, verdict of his equals (that is, of men of his own condition) or by the Law of the Land (that is, to speak it once for all) by the due course, and processe of the Law. . . . Generally all monopolies are against this great Charter, because they are against the liberty and freedom of the subject."

18. The best collection of materials is Perry, *Sources of Our Liberties*. All quotations in the text from documents antedating the Constitution, unless otherwise noted, come from Perry. See also H. D. Hazeltine, "The Influence of Magna Carta on American Constitutional Development," 17 Colum. L. Rev. 1-33. (1917); and A. E. Dick Howard, *The Road from Runnymede: Magna Carta and Constitutionalism in America* (Charlottesville: Univ. Press of Virginia, 1968).

19. The New Jersey document, but not the Pennsylvania one, contains a "due course of law" clause. William Penn, who drafted the Pennsylvania Frame of Government, probably prepared the Concessions of West New Jersey as well. In 1687 Penn was responsible for the first publication of Magna Carta in the colonies. Perry, *Sources*, pp. 180-88, 204-21.

20. * 129, 134, 138.

21. See, generally, Bernard Bailyn, *The Ideological Origins of the American Revolution* (Cambridge, Mass.: Harvard University Press, 1967). For the American Bicentennial the British Parliament offered an original Magna Carta to be displayed in the Capitol. Congress accepted the offer in a joint resolution: "In drafting the Constitution and the Bill of Rights of the United States, our founding fathers sought to guarantee to the people the freedom of the church, an independent judiciary, the right to a speedy trial, and the concept of due process of law, which principles were clearly derived from Magna Carta." *New York Times*, October 26, 1975, p. 22.

22. Henry Steele Commager (ed.), *Documents of American History*

(5th ed.) (New York: Appleton-Century-Crofts, 1949), vol. I, p. 57.

23. Bailyn, *Ideological Origins,* p. 173, n.

24. *Documents Illustrative of the Formation of the Union of the American States* (Washington, D.C.: Government Printing Office, 1927), pp. 1-5.

25. In Magna Carta, the order is "judgment of his peers or law of the land." The reversal may be an accident. The original order reappears in the Northwest Ordinance. The significance of the order is difficult to perceive.

26. On the formation of the Declaration generally, from its ideas to its composition, see Carl Becker, *The Declaration of Independence: A Study in the History of Political Ideas* (New York: Knopf, 1966 [orig. 1922]). Just as the protection of property—a function of the state—can be traced to Locke's political theory, the pursuit of happiness, a fundamental human right, can be found in his moral theory *(Essay on Human Understanding).* The close relationship between the two is evident later in due process cases on the right to pursue a lawful calling. See generally Howard Mumford Jones, *The Pursuit of Happiness* (Ithaca: Cornell Univ. Press, 1966 [orig. 1953]).

27. Due process provisions in state constitutions (until 1968) are collected in Howard, *The Road from Runnymede,* pp. 479-82.

28. Hamilton's defense of the omission of a Bill of Rights at the end of *The Federalist* is only in part disingenuous. He argued that any list of rights would imply that the new federal government, instead of being restricted, retained the authority to delimit and define rights; that is, it would be able to control those areas of activity not explicitly stated as rights. No. 84. The Ninth and Tenth Amendments are an attempt to meet Hamilton's argument. For the complications associated with one right that might have been elaborated in a Bill of Rights, the right to a jury trial in civil cases guaranteed in Article III, see Federalist No. 83, and compare the Seventh Amendment.

29. Perry, *Sources,* p. 422, from Gales, *Debates,* I. 433-34.

30. It is quite probable that the order of clauses in the Bill of Rights was not as carefully conceived as later legalistic minds tend to expect, or as was the original constitutional text, which benefited from a Committee on Style. Within the Bill of Rights as a whole, the provisions relating to criminal law are not gathered together. Within the Fifth Amendment, the clauses seem almost randomly collected, although one could argue that they deliberately begin with guarantees for criminal trials alone, go through a guarantee which is applicable in both criminal and civil situations (the due process clause) and conclude with a noncriminal provision (just compensation). As ratified, the due process clause is located almost precisely in

the middle of the Bill of Rights, by a word count from either end. This middle position is surely an accident, however, since originally the clause was in the seventh of twelve amendments, not at the end of the fifth of ten amendments. Nevertheless, a middle position may have a kind of architectonic significance, regardless of its origin. This, at least, is the subject of the speculation of Gottfried Dietze on the location of *per legem terrae* in Magna Carta. See Dietze, *Magna Carta and Property.*

31. Only the Sixth and Tenth Amendments use the active voice grammatically, and even they are unclear as to the source of the guarantees. But we ought not charge a generation of men accustomed to natural rights declarations with deliberate ambiguity born of our own positivistic mode of reading legal documents.

    32. 7 Pet. 243.

33. Dartmouth College v. Woodward, 4 Wheat. 518, 581 (1819).

34. Sec. 1789.

35. The citations are 6 Fed. Cas. 546, No. 3230, E. D. Pa., and 18 How. 272.

36. 6 Fed. Cas. at 552-53. " [T]he reach of Fourteenth Amendment due process ... was suggested," wrote the second Justice Harlan, " ... long before the adoption of that Amendment [namely to] those concepts which are considered to embrace those rights 'which are fundamental; which belong ... to the citizens of all free governments.' Corfield v. Coryell. ...." Dissenting in Poe v. Ullman, 367 U.S. 497, 541 (1961).

37. Hannis Taylor, a constitutional authority of the early twentieth century, strongly condemned both Curtis's method of constitutional interpretation and his historical scholarship in the case. "Due Process of Law: Persistent and Harmful Influence of Murray v. Hoboken Land and Improvement Co.," 24 Yale L. J. 353-69 (1915).

38. In an early Supreme Court case, a justice defined a vested right as one which entitled a citizen "to do certain actions or to possess certain things, *according to the law of the land.*" Justice Chase in Calder v. Bull, 3 Dall. 386, 394 (1798) (emphasis supplied).

39. An early example is North Carolina v. Foy, 2 Hayw. (N.C.) 310 (1804), in which a state court held void under a law of the land clause the repeal of a land grant. Several ideas come together in the case: the vested rights of property, retrospective legislation, and law designed not for general purposes but to reach (or punish) a named party (hence usurping the function of the judiciary). See, generally, Edward S. Corwin, *Liberty against Government: The Rise, Flowering and Decline of a Famous Juridical Concept* (Baton Rouge: Louisiana State Univ. Press,

1948), Chapter 3, "Liberty into Property, Before the Civil War"; and Wallace Mendelson, "A Missing Link in the Evolution of Due Process," 10 Vand. L. Rev. 125-37 (1956).

40. The close connection of these constitutional ideas was manifest as early as the Northwest Ordinance. In Article II of the Ordinance, the law of the land clause (due process) and the just (there "full") compensation clause appear in the same sentence, as they do in the Fifth Amendment, and are followed immediately by the prohibition of all laws that "in any manner whatever interfere with or affect private contracts."

41. 13 N.Y. 378.

42. The arguments are the subject of decades of research by Howard Jay Graham, whose studies are relied upon here. See Graham, *Everyman's Constitution* (Madison: State Historical Society of Wisconsin, 1968), in particular Chapter 5, pp. 242-65, which appeared originally as "Procedure to Substance—Extrajudicial Rise of Due Process, 1830-1860," 40 Calif. L. Rev. 483-500 (1952-53).

43. Scott v. Sandford, 19 How. 393 (1857).

44. 19 How., at 450.

45. Taney's argument was not unprecedented even in Supreme Court opinions. Justice Henry Baldwin, a learned and acerbic Jacksonian, had written in dissent in a slavery case of 1841: "Being property by the law of any state, the owners are protected from any violations of the rights of property by Congress under the Fifth Amendment of the Constitution," Groves v. Slaughter, 15 Pet. 449, 515. As Baldwin did not specify what in the Fifth Amendment he had in mind, one could support his statement by the just compensation clause as well as by the due process clause, though slaves would not have been "taken" for a public purpose, in the standard sense of the term. Substantive due process is also implicitly recognized in the wartime proposal of Lincoln that owners be compensated for the emancipation of slaves.

46. 18 How. at 626-27.

47. *Everyman's Constitution,* pp. 250, 258, 249.

48. In 1783 Chief Justice Cushing of Massachusetts had interpreted the declaration of his state's constitution that "all men are born free and equal" to prohibit being born into slavery. See Walker v. Jennison, in Commager (ed.), *Documents of American History* (5th ed.), p. 110.

49. E.g., James G. Birney, in 1837; see Graham, *Everyman's Constitution,* p. 232. See also Theodore Weld, "The Power of Congress over the District of Columbia," 1837, printed as an Appendix in Jacobus tenBroek, *Equal Under Law* (New York: Collier Books, 1965), pp. 243-80, esp. pp. 271-72.

50. *Cf.* Arthur Bestor, "The American Civil War as a Constitutional Crisis," 69 Am. Hist. Rev. 327-52 (1964).

51. That the South had no doubts about its views is manifest from the constitution of the Confederacy, in which Art. 1, Sec. 9, Cl. 16 is identical to the Fifth Amendment. The fourth clause of the same section prohibits "impairing the right of property in negro slaves."

52. Section 1: "All persons born or naturalized in the United States, and subject to the jurisdiction thereof, are citizens of the United States and of the State wherein they reside. No State shall make or enforce any law which shall abridge the privileges or immunities of citizens of the United States; nor shall any State deprive any person of life, liberty, or property, without due process of law; nor deny to any person within its jurisdiction the equal protection of the laws."

53. The language is not actually identical. The due process clause shifts from the passive voice of the Fifth Amendment (with "federal government" presumed to be the subject) to the active voice in the Fourteenth ("Nor shall any state deprive. . . ."). In the Fourteenth Amendment privileges or immunities clause, the "or" replaces the "and" of Article IV. The distinction between privileges *and* immunities and "privileges *or* immunities" has had no legal significance, whether or not it has more than an accidental historical explanation.

54. Howard Jay Graham asserts that federal and state due process clauses "have been the sources and bases of at least one-third, and during certain critical periods, possibly more than one-half of our aggregate constitutional litigation." *Everyman's Constitution,* p. ix; see also p. 587. An indication of the significance of the due process clauses can be seen in the five editions, spanning half a century, of the Library of Congress publication *Constitution of the United States of America (Annotated),* in which the due process clauses have had competition from only the commerce clause (which was accorded more space only in the first edition). The number of pages devoted to the due process clauses, and the percentage this number is of the total pages in the various editions, are as follows:

Edition	Pages	Percent of Volume
1923	68	8
1938	212	17
1953	189	14
1964	224	13
1973	190	9

The percentage figures appear to be correlated with the "truth" concerning the relative importance of due process issues in then current constitutional law; the historical accumulation of substantive due process cases and rules in the late 1930s; the impress of the due process scholarship of the volume's editor, Edward S. Corwin, beginning in 1938; the rise of the equal protection clause as the swiftest current in the stream of constitutional litigation from the 1950s on; and the dispersion in later volumes, to other portions of the Bill of Rights, of the discussion of specific issues that may formally be litigated under the Fourteenth Amendment due process clause.

Another, perhaps less telling, indication of the decline of due process as a category of thought is its disappearance as a main entry in the *International Encyclopedia of the Social Sciences* (1968) in comparison to the article, by Robert E. Cushman, in the *Encyclopedia of the Social Sciences* (1931) (vol. 5, pp. 264-68). In the *I.E.S.S.*, Robert G. McCloskey discusses due process under "Constitutional Law: Civil Liberties" (vol. 3, pp. 307-12).

55. 16 Wall. 36 (1873). The Slaughter-House Cases are the starting point of Walton Hamilton's scholarly journey on "The Path of Due Process of Law," cited above, note 1.

56. The Court utilized Justice Bushrod Washington's broad definition of privileges and immunities in Corfield v. Coryell, though not to define the phrase generally, as might be expected, but, unhistorically, to distinguish broad Article IV state privileges and immunities from narrow, Fourteenth Amendment federal privileges or immunities.

On the fortunes of the privileges or immunities clause see Arnold J. Lien, *Concurring Opinion* (St. Louis: Washington Univ. Studies, 1957).

57. 16 Wall., at 123.

58. 16 Wall., at 125. Concerned more with the Court's discrimination against southern rebels than with closely reasoned analysis of the new constitutional clauses, Swayne probably unconsciously reflected the dominant thought of his time by holding to traditional due process reasoning while subsuming Bradley's thought under the innovative equal protection language.

" 'Due process of law,' " Swayne said, "is the application of the law as it exists in the fair and regular course of administrative procedure. 'The equal protection of the laws' places all upon a footing of legal equality and gives the same protection to all for the preservation of life, liberty, and property, and the pursuit of happiness." 16 Wall., at 127. When white southerners regained control of the Louisiana government and abolished the slaughterhouse monopoly, the Supreme Court held unanimously that the later act did not deprive the formerly privileged butchers of their liberty or property without due process of law. Butchers' Union Slaughterhouse v. Crescent City Live-Stock Landing Co. 111 U.S. 746 (1884).

59. 110 U.S. 516 (1884).

60. 110 U.S., at 529, 530-31.

61. 110 U.S., at 531. Justice Matthews quoted the rule of "gradual process of judicial inclusion and exclusion" from Justice Miller for the Court in Davidson v. New Orleans, 96 U.S. 97, 104 (1878); 110 U.S., at 534.

62. Harlan pointed out, however, that when the Fourteenth Amendment was adopted all states required grand jury indictments in capital cases. Thus, aside from British history indictment seemed part of the understanding of the framers of the Fourteenth Amendment.

63. Early confirmations of the *Hurtado* approach, accompanied by Harlan's continued dissents alone, are Maxwell v. Dow, 176 U.S. 581 (1900), and Twining v. New Jersey, 211 U.S. 78 (1908).

64. If due process were considered not under the aspect of predictability but under that of veracity, that is, not according to the character of the determining process but according to the quality of what is determined, then the dispute between the Court and the dissent in *Hurtado* is whether grand jury indictment in fact leads to factually more justified prosecutions than does an information proceeding; or perhaps whether this was true in the case at hand. If the dispute is seen in this fashion, however, and the modern terminology of Herbert Packer is applied to it, Hurtado's and Harlan's side seems to represent the "due process model" of criminal procedure, while the Court's side is the "crime control model." See Packer, *The Limits of the Criminal Sanction* (Stanford: Stanford Univ. Press, 1968), pp. 149-73. This is so because the due process model, in Packer's explication, is disposed to distrust the efficacy of official fact-finding as well as to be skeptical "about the morality and utility of the criminal sanction," p. 170. It is therefore disposed to find or create ever more "rights" for criminal defendants.

65. 110 U.S., at 531.

66. 96 U.S. 97 (1878).

67. The significance of a judicial determination of due process of law is not merely that courts assert power for themselves, but that an historical problem is laid to rest. The problem, in the Court's words, was this: The due process clause "which the great barons of England wrung from King John at the point of the sword . . . meant . . . the ancient customary laws of the English people, or laws enacted by the Parliament of which those barons were a controlling element. It was not in their minds . . . to protect themselves against the enactment of

laws by the Parliament of England." 96 U.S. at 101-02. That no
"parliament" existed in 1215 did not disturb, or was not known to the
Court. The Court's conclusory answer to the problem that a
legislative body determined what was or was not due process of law,
was that American due process clauses would be "ineffectual" if not
applied to state legislatures and upheld by courts. The chief step to
this conclusion, which the Court perhaps felt uneasy elaborating, was
that judicial review, separation of powers theory, and checks and
balances, already authorized courts to examine legislative and
executive action. There was no reason why due process, including the
"law" according to which due process was to be granted, should be an
exception to such judicial examination. J. A. C. Grant writes that
"random decisions" prior to the Civil War held that due process was
no limit on the legislature, "a statute, whatever its content, necessarily
being part of the 'law of the land,' and hence due process of law."
"The Natural Law Background of Due Process," 31 Colum. L. Rev.
56, 66 (1931). But mentioning "the great principles of Magna Carta,"
Justice Story wrote the dominant view for the Court in 1829: "That
government can scarcely be deemed free, where the rights of property
are left solely dependent upon the will of a legislative body, without
any restraint." Wilkinson v. Leland, 2 Pet. 627, 657. Two years after
Hurtado, in a leading equal protection clause case, the Court, speaking
again through Justice Matthews, combined process and property.
Yick Wo v. Hopkins held that a law "fair on its face and impartial in
appearance" violated the Constitution if it was administered "with an
evil eye and an unequal hand." 118 U.S. 356, 373 (1886). The Court's
citations in support of this holding about procedure deal exclusively
with property rights.

68. 96 U.S., at 103-4.
69. He thus raised, although not explicitly, the relation of the Fifth to the
Fourteenth Amendment. Representative Bingham of Ohio, a leading
member of the Joint Committee of Fifteen on Reconstruction, had
tried and failed to insert a just compensation clause into the
Fourteenth Amendment. Graham, *Everyman's Constitution,* p. 33. This
deliberate omission might have been invoked to exclude a just
compensation interpretation of the new due process clause. But as it
involved a property rather than a personal right, the argument would
have been futile at the time. Recall, on the other hand, the successful
use of this kind of textual exegesis by the majority in the case of the
grand jury indictment.
70. 96 U.S. at 107-8.
71. Bradley's particular branches of government "taking" were the

subject of scores of due process cases in the Supreme Court under the due process clause. For a leading case relating just compensation and due process to the taxing power, see Henderson Bridge Co. v. Henderson, 173 U.S. 592 (1899). Just compensation requirements for eminent domain were first applied to the states under the equal protection rather than the due process clause. Reagan v. Farmers' Loan & Trust Co., 154 U.S. 362, 388 (1894). But shortly afterward Justice Bradley's due process view on the matter was adopted. Chicago, B.&Q. R.R. Co. v. Chicago, 166 U.S. 226 (1897). In general, see the exhaustive study by Rodney G. Mott, *Due Process of Law: A Historical and Analytical Treatise on the Principles and Methods Followed by the Courts in the Application of the "Law of the Land"* (Indianapolis: Bobbs-Merrill, 1926).

Howard Jay Graham, in "The Economic and Constitutional Significance of Frontier Tax Titles, 1800-1890," explores the role of the land tax bar in the development of substantive due process. According to Graham, this bar, "like the antislavery and the railroad and Chinese habeas corpus bars, pioneered substantive due process and equal protection." *Everyman's Constitution*, p. 500. The original setting was the Illinois Military Tract in the decades prior to the Civil War, where tax rates were often specific and regressive; penalties, dates, and payment procedures, capricious; and records in confusion. Out of litigation over the taxes came the influential *Tax Titles* (1855) by Robert S. Blackwell, an Illinois lawyer. It was Blackwell who molded the cases of several states into a theory protecting land ownership from arbitrary legislation, and thus contributed to the new due process.

72. 94 U.S. 113. For background, see Harry N. Scheiber, "The Road to *Munn:* Eminent Domain and the Concept of Public Purpose in the State Courts," 5 *Perspectives in American History*, 329-404 (1971); also J. A. C. Grant, "The 'Higher Law' Background of the Law of Eminent Domain," 6 Wis. L. Rev. 67-85 (1931).

73. Justice Field (with whom Justice Strong agreed) dissented against this doctrine, as well as against the outcome of *Munn*—"subversive of the rights of private property." 94 U.S. at 136. Since the Slaughterhouse Cases four years earlier, however, Field had learned that due process, rather than privileges or immunities, was the appropriate constitutional clause to take a stand on. His goal was unchanged. The liberty and property which due process protected, like the earlier privilege or immunity, was the pursuit of happiness, a person's right "to pursue such callings and avocations as may be suitable to develop [one's] capacities, and give to them their highest enjoyment." 94 U.S. at 142.

Although Field is the archetypical judicial protector of property rights through due process, he was also, particularly as circuit justice in California, a guardian of human rights through due process. See, generally, Graham, "Justice Field and the Fourteenth Amendment," in *Everyman's Constitution,* pp. 98-151. Field was also not a principled opponent of the exercise of the police power against corporations. See his opinion for a unanimous Court in Missouri Pacific Ry. Co. v. Humes, 115 U.S. 512 (1885), in which he quotes and affirms the Court's *Davidson* language about litigants' "strange misconception of the scope" of due process; and, contrary to the implication of Bradley's concurrence in *Davidson,* which would use due process to protect against "arbitrary, oppressive, and unjust" laws, Field held, in *Humes,* that if laws were "within the legitimate sphere of legislative power" and enforced with "security of private rights" in mind, then "the harshness, injustice, and oppressive character of such laws will not invalidate them as affecting life, liberty, or property without due process of law." 115 U.S. at 520.

74. Chicago, M. & St. P. Ry. Co. v. Minnesota, 134 U.S. 418.

75. 134 U.S. at 458. Justice Bradley dissented, protesting that the Court in effect had overturned Munn v. Illinois. "The important question always is," he wrote, "what is the lawful tribunal for the particular case?" 134 U.S. at 465. His answer in this case was, as the Court had asserted in *Munn,* the legislature. See also Smyth v. Ames, 169 U.S. 446 (1898), the case in which the Court stipulated a particular accounting method for determining "unreasonableness" of rates and thereby deprivation of property without due process of law.

76. Cooley, *Constitutional Limitations* (6th ed.) (Boston, 1890), p. 208. Cooley was by no means opposed in principle to restrictions on private property in behalf of the public welfare. See, generally, pp. 429-509, "Of the Protection to Property by 'The Law of the Land.' " For the government to take property from A and give it to B had violated natural law or the Constitution from the beginning. Calder v. Bull, 3 Dall. 386, 388 (1798); Davidson v. New Orleans, 96 U.S. 97, 102 (1878); Thompson v. Consolidated Gas Utilities Corp., 300 U.S. 55, 79-80 (1937). As a justice said in dissent against upholding a federal law in 1917: "Such legislation, it seems to me, amounts to the taking of the property of one and giving it to another in violation of the spirit of fair play and the due process clause." Wilson v. New, 243 U.S. 332, 370 (Justice Day).

77. See generally Sidney Fine, *Laissez Faire and the Welfare State: a Study of Conflict in American Thought, 1865-1901* (Ann Arbor: Univ. of Michigan Press, 1956); Loren P. Beth, *The Development of the American Constitution, 1877-1917* (New York: Harper & Row, 1971); and Charles Grove

Haines, *The Revival of Natural Law Concepts* (Cambridge: Harvard Univ. Press, 1930), esp. Chapters V-VII, on due process and natural law.

78. Graham, *Everyman's Constitution,* pp. 23-95, 367-437.

79. Louisville R.R. v. Letson, 2 How. 497 (1844) held that a firm may be sued in federal courts where it is incorporated regardless of where the stockholders live. Graham reports on the unsuccessful attempts of out-of-state insurance companies to utilize the comity clause against discriminatory state legislation in the 1850s. *Everyman's Constitution,* p. 75.

80. For the use of "person" to include corporation under the equal protection clause, see Santa Clara County v. Southern Pacific Ry. Co., 118 U.S. 394, 396 (1886); for the "corporate person" under the due process clause see Minneapolis & St. L. Ry. Co. v. Beckwith, 129 U.S. 26, 28 (1889). The Court held in the abortion cases of 1973 that Fourteenth Amendment due process "person" does not include the unborn. Roe v. Wade, 410 U.S. 113, 156-59.

81. That history was on the side of the corporations is evident both from the fact that corporations had functionally replaced persons as the dominant controllers of property, and that corporate interests had become so powerful in American society. After fifty years of the constitutional corporate person when Justice Black (later joined by Justice Douglas) unsuccessfully tried to halt the tide of history, the Court paid him little attention. Connecticut General Co. v. Johnson, 303 U.S. 77, 83 (1937) (Black, dissenting); Wheeling Steel Corp. v. Glander, 337 U.S. 562 (1949) (separate opinion by Justice Jackson and dissent of Justices Douglas and Black).

82. The Court was aided by constitutional commentators. See Clyde E. Jacobs, *Law Writers and the Courts: The Influence of Thomas M. Cooley, Christopher G. Tiedeman, and John F. Dillon upon American Constitutional Law* (Berkeley: Univ. of California Press, 1954). In general, see Margaret Spahr, "Natural Law, Due Process, and Economic Pressure," 24 Am. Pol. Sci. Rev. 332-54 (1930).

83. 98 N.Y. 98.

84. Allgeyer v. Louisiana, 165 U.S. 578. The interstate commerce aspect of the case was not crucial in the holding. The Court had held three decades earlier that the interstate insurance business could be regulated by states in disregard of apparent commerce clause problems. Paul v. Virginia, 8 Wall. 168 (1868).

85. Allgeyer v. Louisiana, 165 U.S. at 589.

86. 198 U.S. 45 (1905).

87. 198 U.S. at 57.

88. Holden v. Hardy, 169 U.S. 366 (1898).

89. 198 U.S. at 76.
90. The leading contemporary examination and critique against the Court's doctrine was Roscoe Pound, "Liberty of Contract," 18 Yale L. J. 454-87 (1909), reacting against the transfer of liberty of contract from the Fourteenth to the Fifth Amendment due process clause in the federal "yellow-dog" contract case, Adair v. United States, 208 U.S. 161 (1908). But a powerful warning against uncontained constitutional uses of "liberty" had been issued in 1891 by Charles E. Shattuck, "The True Meaning of the Term 'Liberty' in those Clauses in the Federal and State Constitutions which Protect 'Life, Liberty, and Property,' " 4 Harv. L. Rev. 365-92. Shattuck argued for a restrictive, that is traditional, use of liberty on the grounds that it had always referred to physical restraint in a criminal process; that it would, if broadened to include religious liberty, necessarily imply that such a liberty could be limited so long as it complied with due process requirements; and that society should not be hindered from meeting the evils of modern working conditions by reworked constitutional language.

The *Lochner* majority's implied invitation to prove the validity of the means-end relationship led to the Brandeis brief and the upholding of an Oregon hours law for women. Muller v. Oregon, 208 U.S. 412 (1908). A law of the same state applicable to all workers was upheld in Bunting v. Oregon, 243 U.S. 426 (1917) by the same means. But the Brandeis brief, though acknowledged by the Court for its aid, was no guarantee of constitutional vindication. In Adkins v. Children's Hospital, a five-man Court returned to *Lochner,* stressing that "freedom of contract is the general rule and restraint the exception." 261 U.S. 525, 546 (1923). The dissents in *Adkins* paralleled those in *Lochner.* Chief Justice Taft, as Harlan earlier, was concerned with the "evils of the sweating system." Justice Holmes noted that "liberty of contract" was not Fourteenth Amendment language but had been developed "within our memory." "It is," he continued, "merely an example of doing what you want to do, embodied in the word 'liberty.' " 261 U.S., at 562, 568.
91. West Coast Hotel Co. v. Parrish, 300 U.S. 379, 391 (1937). Nebbia v. New York, 291 U.S. 502 (1934), in ending the constitutional usefulness of the doctrine of a business "affected with a public interest," foreshadowed *West Coast Hotel* on due process; but Roberts's opinion in *Nebbia* does not match the sweep of Hughes's in the later case.
92. 300 U.S. at 391.
93. Ibid. (Emphasis added.) Such language was not invented by Hughes for the occasion. As associate justice in 1911 he had written for a

unanimous Court, in a railroad injury case: "Liberty implies the absence of arbitrary restraint, not immunity from reasonable regulations and prohibitions imposed in the interests of the community." Chicago, B. & Q. R. Co. v. McGuire, 319 U.S. 549, 567. A year prior to *West Coast Hotel*, Justice Stone, dissenting, had depicted the consequences of the freedom of contract theory and stated the solution: "There is a grim irony in speaking of the freedom of contract of those who, because of their economic necessities, give their services for less than is needful to keep body and soul together. But if this is freedom of contract no one has ever denied that it is freedom which may be restrained, notwithstanding the Fourteenth Amendment, by a statute passed in the public interest." Morehead v. Tipaldo, 298 U.S. 587, 632 (1936).

94. Brandeis was evidently torn between wanting to excise the due process clause from the Constitution entirely because of the harm it had worked on social legislation at the hands of the judiciary, and recognizing that the clause might yet be canalized in that area through the technique of the Brandeis brief while being developed to promote first amendment liberties. For the Justice's view in 1924, see Louis L. Jaffe, "Was Brandeis an Activist? The Search for Intermediate Premises," 80 Harv. L. Rev. 986, 989 (1967). This was at the height of the controversy over a constitutional amendment proposed by Senator LaFollette which would have permitted a two-thirds congressional vote to overturn a Supreme Court decision. The purpose was to restrain the Court's use of substantive due process. Felix Frankfurter, in an anonymous *New Republic* editorial at the time, supported the amendment: "We have had fifty years experiment with the Fourteenth Amendment. . . . The due process clause ought to go." Frankfurter, *Law and Politics* (New York: Harcourt, Brace, 1939), p. 16. An example of Brandeis's "brief" at the time is his unsuccessful attempt to persuade the Court that a state could prescribe standard weights for bread without depriving companies of property without due process. Burns Baking Co. v. Bryan, 264 U.S. 504 (1924) (dissent).

95. Gilbert v. Minnesota, 254 U.S. 325, 343.

96. Truax v. Corrigan, 257 U.S. 312, 329 (1921).

97. Meyer v. Nebraska, 262 U.S. 390, 399 (1923).

98. Gitlow v. New York, 268 U.S. 652. *Gitlow* overturned a passing remark to the opposite effect which the Court had issued three years earlier. Prudential Life Insurance Co. v. Cheek, 259 U.S. 530, 543 (1922).

99. "The New 'Liberty' Under the Fourteenth Amendment," 30 Harv. L. Rev. 431, 441 (1926). (Emphasis in original.)

100. Warren recognized, though he did not advocate, two other avenues

that would more cleanly secure the First Amendment freedoms against state infringement: a reversal of Barron v. Baltimore, and a new understanding of the privileges or immunities clause of the Fourteenth Amendment. Justice Brandeis had proposed a variant of this second course of reasoning in Gilbert v. Minnesota, 254 U.S. 325, 337 (1920) (dissent) by way of the privileges and immunities clause of Article IV.

101. Concurring in Whitney v. California, 274 U.S. 357, 373 (1927).
102. See, generally, Henry J. Abraham, *Freedom and the Court: Civil Rights and Liberties in the United States* (2d ed.) (New York: Oxford Univ. Press, 1972), pp. 29-88, "The Bill of Rights and Its Applicability to the States." A book of enormous industry that covers the transition period is Virginia Wood, *Due Process of Law 1932-1949; The Supreme Court's Use of a Constitutional Tool* (Baton Rouge: Louisiana State Univ. Press, 1951). The principal chapters of the book discuss due process and the First Amendment, socioeconomic legislation, criminal proceedings, administrative actions, and the taxing power.
103. Robert G. McCloskey, in "Economic Due Process and the Supreme Court: An Exhumation and Reburial," 1962 Sup. Ct. Rev. 34-62, concludes that the Court's complete abandonment of economic due process was largely a reaction to the earlier extremism of the conservatives. The body of McCloskey's essay is a discussion of attempted distinctions between economic and civil rights. Among the points raised are these: that perhaps the Court should decide in neither area; that limits on expression may "impinge on the human personality more grievously than do laws curbing economic liberty" (p. 45); that most men, however, would find a right to work at least as vital as the right to speak; that social progress or self-government depends on freedom of expression; that the Supreme Court may be peculiarly ill-equipped to decide economic cases; that a number of cases (e.g., on picketing and occupational licensing) mix the two areas; and that the Court may have sufficient constitutional and political burdens without reentering the province of economic due process.
104. 304 U.S. 144.
105. The three paragraphs of the footnote indicated that the Court might not presume the constitutionality of government acts in the following areas, which were essentially noneconomic: specific prohibitions of the Constitution; restrictions on the political process (e.g., voting, expression, and political organization); and acts directed at religions or minorities.
106. State courts, however, did not at the time and have not since followed

the national Court's capitulation. See the review articles [note] "State Views on Economic Due Process: 1937-1953," 53 Colum. L. Rev. 827-45 (1953); and Monrad G. Paulsen, "The Persistence of Substantive Due Process in the States," 34 Minn. L. Rev. 91-118 (1950). A wide-ranging and thorough discussion that focuses on one state is Hans Linde, "Without 'Due Process': Unconstitutional Law in Oregon," 49 Ore. L. Rev. 125-87 (1970).

107. Ferguson v. Skrupa, 372 U.S. 726, 729, 730, 732 (1963). See also Justice Frankfurter, concurring in American Federation of Labor v. American Sash Co., 335 U.S. 538, 542-57 (1949), in which the former New Deal adviser distinguished economic legislation, which the courts should not meddle with, from "matters like censorship of the press or separation of Church and State, in which history, through the Constitution, speaks so decisively as to forbid legislative experimentation." 335 U.S. at 550.

108. "The only relevant function of law in dealing with this intersection of government and enterprise," wrote Justice Frankfurter in 1939, "is to secure the observance of those procedural safeguards in the exercise of legislative powers which are the historic foundation of due process." Driscoll v. Edison Light and Power Co., 307 U.S. 104, 122 (concurring). Justice Cardozo, far less charitably, wrote that a regulatory commission must set revenue "something higher than the line of confiscation. If this level is attained . . . there is not denial of due process though the proceeding is shot through with irregularity or error." West Ohio Gas Co. v. Public Utilities Commission, 294 U.S. 63, 70 (1935).

109. 302 U.S. 319, 325 (1937). Although Justice Cardozo's discussion is elaborate and renowned, it pays little attention to two issues which would seem to be of importance, the relation between the Fifth and Fourteenth Amendment due process clauses, and the significance of federal privileges and immunities in the determination of constitutional requirements on the states.

110. Another scheme for classifying rights had been proposed at the turn of the century in the *Insular Cases*. There, the Court noted a distinction between "natural" and "artificial" rights, both in the Constitution, but the latter peculiar to American jurisprudence. Among the natural rights listed were First Amendment freedoms, Fourth and Eighth Amendment immunities, access to the courts, and the right to due process of law. Artificial rights included the franchise and unidentified "particular methods of procedure." Downes v. Bidwell, 182 U.S. 244, 282-83 (1901). However distinguished, the two grades of rights set the scene for a double standard within the

province of civil liberties, the contemporary idea of "preferred freedoms." See Robert B. McKay, "The Preference for Freedom," 34 N.Y.U.L. Rev. 1182-1227 (1959).

A few months before the *Palko* doctrine was announced, Chief Justice Hughes had achieved substantially the same result without relying on the Bill of Rights. He wrote simply, "Freedom of speech and of the press are fundamental rights which are safeguarded by the due process clause of the Fourteenth Amendment. . . ." DeJonge v. Oregon, 299 U.S. 353, 364 (1937). This left open the possibility that criminal procedure rights were also fundamental. The Fourteenth Amendment end of the funnel can also be opened, as Justice Douglas has noted: "The Court has frequently rested state free speech and free press decisions on the Fourteenth Amendment generally rather than on the Due Process Clause alone." Lehman v. Shaker Heights, 418 U.S. 298, 305 n. 1 (1974) (concurring).

111. 332 U.S. 46. See the rebuttal of Charles Fairman, "Does the Fourteenth Amendment Incorporate the Bill of Rights? The Original Understanding," 2 Stan. L. Rev. 5-139 (1949), and generally, the introduction by Leonard Levy to *The Fourteenth Amendment and the Bill of Rights: the Incorporation Theory* (New York: Da Capo Press, 1970). Justice Black was never convinced. See his concurring opinion in Duncan v. Louisiana, 391 U.S. 145, 162-71 (1968) and the chapter "Due Process of Law" in his *A Constitutional Faith* (New York: Knopf, 1969), esp. pp. 33-34.

112. 332 U.S. at 63. Whether intended as a condensation of the Bill of Rights or not, the migration of the due process clause from a complex context to a simpler one in the Constitution is reminiscent of Magna Carta's combining Chapter 39 and 40 of the document of 1215 into Chapter 29 of the 1225 and later versions of the Charter.

In his position on the right of the states to develop criminal procedures different from each other, that is, on the positive value of federalism, Justice Frankfurter was influenced by the old Court's due process tendencies. He had agreed with an opinion of Justice Jackson a few year earlier: "The use of the due process clause to disable the States in the protection of society from crime is quite as dangerous and delicate a use of federal judicial power as to use it to disable them from social or economic experimentation." Ashcraft v. Tennessee 322 U.S. 143, 174 (1944) (dissent).

113. Dissenting in *Adamson* at 123-25. Justice Douglas, who concurred with Justice Black in *Adamson,* later said of Justices Murphy and Rutledge: "Perhaps they were right." Doe v. Bolton, 410 U.S. 179, 212, n. (1973) (concurring).

114. 332 U.S. at 66. See also Frankfurter, "Memorandum on 'Incorporation' of the Bill of Rights into the Due Process Clause of the Fourteenth Amendment," 78 Harv. L. Rev. 746-83 (1965). The "Memorandum" is for the most part a compilation of cases.

115. See Louis Henkin, "'Selective Incorporation' in the Fourteenth Amendment," 73 Yale L.J. 74-89 (1963). In a comprehensive article that appeared shortly after the *Adamson* case was decided, John Raeburn Green anticipated much of Brennan's position and Henkin's critique. "The Bill of Rights, the Fourteenth Amendment and the Supreme Court," 46 Mich. L. Rev. 869-910 (1948). See also Justice Frankfurter in *Adamson,* 332 U.S. at 65.

116. One exception, traditionally held up as proof that the total incorporation theory was not really sensible, is the right preserved by the Seventh Amendment for a jury trial in federal civil suits in which the value in controversy exceeds twenty dollars.

    Two of the significant overrulings, nationalizing the Bill of Rights by absorbing into the Fourteenth Amendment formerly unabsorbed provisions, or, more accurately, formerly unabsorbed interpretations, concern the right to counsel in felony cases (Gideon v. Wainwright, 372 U.S. 335 [1963] overruling Betts v. Brady, 316 U.S. 455 [1942]), and the right to introduce into trial evidence unconstitutionally seized (Mapp v. Ohio, 376 U.S. 643 [1961] overruling Wolf v. Colorado, 338 U.S. 25 [1949]). In the right to counsel case, the flexibility of Justice Frankfurter's due process theory permitted it to "catch up" to Justice Black's goals; at least Frankfurter is reported, from retirement, to have agreed with the new outcome. Anthony Lewis, *Gideon's Trumpet* (New York: Random House, 1964), p. 222.

    The Court provides a summary of incorporated provisions and cases in Duncan v. Louisiana, 391 U.S. 145, 147-49 (1968), probably the final case to take up, full scale, through four opinions, the various incorporation arguments. As Justice Black states in his dissent, although absorption or incorporation has been fought almost exclusively in terms of due process, it is as historical—not to say logical—to invoke the privileges or immunities clause for the purpose; only the burden of the Slaughterhouse Cases has kept it from rising to this end. Justice Harlan's dissent in *Duncan* is the most balanced and comprehensive discussion of the incorporation problem and Fourteenth Amendment due process to be issued from the Court. Explaining, but opposing, both the selective and total incorporation approaches, Justice Harlan accepted the "gradual view" as the mainstream of Court precedent and constitutional history, the view of Davidson v. New Orleans, Maxwell v. Dow, Palko v. Connecticut, and Justice

Frankfurter in Adamson v. California. The important point about the relation between the Bill of Rights and the Fourteenth Amendment due process clauses, wrote Harlan, "is the fact that the Bill of Rights is evidence, at various points, of the content Americans find in the term 'liberty' and of American standards of fundamental fairness." 391 U.S. 145, 177 (1968).

An important recent dispute over incorporation continues the particular issue of *Duncan*—whether state jury trial requirements must be identical to federal requirements, in this instance whether the jury must be unanimous to convict in a criminal case. With respect to federal juries, the Sixth Amendment is silent. Four members of the Court held that neither the Sixth nor the Fourteenth Amendment requires unanimity. Four members held that the Sixth Amendment does and therefore the Fourteenth Amendment must. Justice Powell, in the tradition of Justice Frankfurter and the second Justice Harlan, argued that Fourteenth Amendment due process is not identical to the meaning of the Bill of Rights. He therefore provided the crucial vote, holding that due process did not require unanimity in state criminal trials, but that the Sixth Amendment required it in federal courts. Johnson v. Louisiana, 406 U.S. 356 (1972).

117. McNabb v. United States, 318 U.S. 332, 347 (1943).

118. Wallace Mendelson, *Conflict in the Court* (Chicago: Univ. of Chicago Press, 1961) presents, in sharp terms, the jurisprudential contrast between Justices Black and Frankfurter.

119. Not only did the American judiciary finally react against substantive due process, but other countries, in the course of drafting their constitutions, also reacted against it. On the one hand they feared the development of a comparable judicial power, and on the other they had an interest in socialism or social welfare legislation which the American framers—and American judges—definitely did not share. No matter how benign the phrase looked, or how confined to criminal proceedings its ancestry, due process of law has not had the allure for others that it has had in the United States.

In England, where one might have thought due process would thrive, the phrase "has received practically no judicial construction in litigated cases." Hugh Evander Willis, "Due Process of Law under the United States Constitution," 74 U. Pa. L. Rev. 331, 334 (1926). When other countries have framed constitutional documents, the American experience with due process has led to carefully circumscribing or avoiding the phrase altogether. Wallace Mendelson, in "Foreign Reactions to American Experience with 'Due Process of Law,'" 44 Va. L. Rev. 493-503 (1955) systematically presents many of these instances. He quotes Lord Bryce defending a due process clause for the Government of Ireland Bill in 1893 in language that makes one wonder about Bryce's understanding of America: "We are dealing with words which have received in the Courts of the United States a perfectly clear, perfectly uniform, perfectly definite, and perfectly unambiguous construction." Ibid., p. 495. The bill, with its due process clause, was not enacted. Prime Minister Asquith, on the other hand, opposed a due process clause with far more insight about American practices (and after twenty years more history). Due process language, he argued in the debate over the Government of Ireland Bill of 1914, is "full of ambiguity abounding with pitfalls and certainly provocative of every kind of frivolous litigation. . . . If you introduce into your Bill a limitation of this kind . . . you are really enthroning the judiciary as the ultimate tribunal of appeal. There is no question whatever about that. Look at what is going on now in the United States." Ibid., p. 496.

The clause in the draft constitution for India was modified from "life or liberty without due process of law" to "life or personal liberty except according to procedure established by law." Ibid., p. 497. For Felix Frankfurter's role in dropping the due process clause from the draft of the Indian constitution see B. Shiva Rae (ed.), *India's Constitution in the Making* (Madras: Orient Longmans, 1960), p. 303, cited in Theodore L. Becker (ed.), *Political Trials* (Indianapolis: Bobbs-Merrill, 1971), p. 39 n. Property had already been deleted from the clause in the socialist-leaning constitution, and now the ghost of liberty of contract was exorcised. One delegate to the constitutional convention said of the first wording: "This clause may serve as a great handicap for all social legislation, for the ultimate relationship between employer and labour, for the protection of children and for the protection of women." Quoted in William O. Douglas, *We the Judges* (Garden City, N.Y.: Doubleday, 1956), p. 273 n. The Indian Supreme Court has held that the "deliberate omission of the word 'due' lent strength to the contention that the reasonableness of a law was not a justiciable question under the Indian Constitution." Nobushige Ukai and Nathaniel L. Nathanson, "Protection of Property Rights and Due Process of Law in the Japanese Constitution," 43 Wash. L. Rev. 1129, 1133 (1968). For commentary on due process of law in British colonies which became independent nations in the mid-twentieth century, see Thomas M. Franck, "Due Process in Developing Nations," in Bernard Schwartz (ed.), *The Fourteenth Amendment: A Century in American Law and Life* (New York: New York Univ. Press, 1970), pp. 192-203.

The Israeli draft constitution states: "No one shall be tried save by due process of law," restricting the phrase to its traditional use. The West German Basic Law, drafted under American, if not New Deal eyes, separates and clarifies the concepts of property and liberty. Article 14 states: "Property and the right of inheritance are safeguarded. Their scope and limitations are determined by legislation." (Although the second sentence seems intended to qualify and explain the first, the use of "legislation" would seem at the same time to restrict the judiciary.) Traditional due process, on the other hand, reads this way (Article 104): "The freedom of the individual may be restricted only on the basis of a formal law and only with due regard to the forms prescribed therein. . . ."

The Japanese Constitution of 1946, drafted under the supervision of General MacArthur's lawyers, is even more influenced by the American experience. For instance, the "right to own or to hold property is inviolable" (Article 29), but the "right to life, liberty and the pursuit of happiness shall be the supreme consideration in legislation and in other governmental affairs, to the extent that it does not interfere with the public welfare." (Article 13). The traditional due process concern reads (Article 31); "No person shall be deprived of life or liberty, nor shall any other criminal penalty be imposed, except according to procedure established by law." See Ukai and Nathanson, "Protection of Property Rights," esp. p. 1131.

In 1974, when Australia debated the desirability of adopting a national bill of rights, one of its most prominent jurists (and friend of Felix Frankfurter), former Prime Minister Sir Robert Menzies, "questioned whether Australians would like to have their rights guaranteed by 'somewhat vague phrases,' interpreted by judges in accordance largely with their own political convictions. Modern experience in the United States has shown the broadly expressed guarantees of individual rights have recently been interpreted by their Supreme Court in the light of the political and social concepts of the judges, whose judgments will, in very truth, be legislative." *New York Times,* March 24, 1974, p. 10.

120. In the Legal Tender Cases, the Court held invalid on contract grounds (as well as on independent Fifth Amendment due process grounds) the issuance of greenbacks during the Civil War. Hepburn v. Griswold, 8 Wall. 603, 622-23 (1870) (overturned in Knox v. Lee, 12 Wall. 457 (1871)). When the Court, through Justice Brandeis, unanimously overturned New Deal legislation granting mortgage relief to farmers in the guise of a bankruptcy act, it also in effect read the contract clause into the Fifth Amendment. Louisville Joint Stock

Land Bank v. Radford, 295 U.S. 555 (1935). On the other hand, the Court held the New Deal gold clause legislation constitutional in part on the opposite reasoning—the absence of a federal contract clause. Norman v. Baltimore and Ohio Rr. Co. 294 U.S. 240, 306-11 (1935). In Choate v. Trapp, 224 U.S. 665 (1912), the Court held that a privilege of tax exemption once granted by the federal government could not be rescinded because of the due process clause: the exemption amounted to a contract, which was property and had to be treated as such under substantive due process

As to equal protection, the Court in the Japanese Evacuation cases was faced with determining whether race was a constitutionally valid means of classification by the federal government. Chief Justice Stone noted: "The Fifth Amendment contains no equal protection clause and it restrains only such discriminatory legislation by Congress as amounts to a denial of due process." Hirabayashi v. United States, 320 U.S. 81, 100 (1943). But his following sentences show how weak a reed this argument was, and Justice Murphy, whose attention to detail did not always match his vision of a democratic society, spoke in dissent of the "equal protection of the laws, as guaranteed by the Fifth Amendment." Korematsu v. United States, 323 U.S. 214, 235 (1944).

In the school desegregation case from Washington, D.C., the Court wrote: "The concepts of equal protection and due process, both stemming from our American ideal of fairness, are not mutually exclusive." Discrimination might "be so unjustifiable as to be violative of due process." In the circumstances, since the Constitution prohibited the states from maintaining racially segregated schools, "it would be unthinkable that the same Constitution would impose a lesser duty on the Federal Government." Bolling v. Sharpe, 347 U.S. 497, 499 (1954). See also Schneider v. Rusk, 377 U.S. 163, 168 (1964), Shapiro v. Thompson, 394 U.S. 618, 641-42 (1972), Frontiero v. Richardson, 411 U.S. 677, 680 n. 5 (1973), and Johnson v. Robinson, 415 U.S. 361, 364 n. 4 (1974).

121. Hammer v. Dagenhart, 247 U.S. 251 (1918).
122. Bailey v. Drexel Furniture Co. 259 U.S. 20 (1922).
123. Justice Black, dissenting in such a case in 1949, wrote: "The judicially directed march of the due process philosophy as an emancipator of business from regulation appeared arrested a few years ago. The appearance was illusory. That philosophy continues its march." Hood v. DuMond, 336 U.S. 525, 562.
124. In Kotch v. Board of River Port Pilots, 330 U.S. 552 (1947), the Court agreed that New Orleans port pilots could continue to choose their

associates essentially by nepotism, keeping others from such employment. See also Railway Express Agency v. New York, 336 U.S. 106
(1949), in which the Court, and Justice Jackson, concurring, discuss
the differences between due process and equal protection. The "new
substantive equal protection" is discussed in the text below.
125. Justice White dissenting in Robinson v. California, 370 U.S. 660, 689
(1962).
126. "The Equal Protection of the Laws," 37 Calif. L. Rev. 341, 364
(1949). For discussion in historical perspective, see Wallace Mendelson, "From Warren to Burger: The Rise and Decline of Substantive
Equal Protection," 66 Am. Pol. Sci. Rev. 1226-33 (1972). Also
Kenneth L. Karst and Harold W. Horowitz, "Reitman v. Mulkey: A
Telophase of Substantive Equal Protection," 1967 Sup. Ct. Rev. 39-
80. For discussions of other substitutes for due process see [Note] "The
'New' Thirteenth Amendment: A Preliminary Analysis," 82 Harv. L.
Rev. 1294-1321 (1969); William O. Bertelsman, "The Ninth Amendment and Due Process of Law—Toward a Viable Theory of Un-
enumerated Rights," 37 U. Cin. L. Rev. 777-96 (1968); and Philip B.
Kurland, "Privileges or Immunities Clause: 'Its Hour Come Round
at Last'?" 1972 Wash. U.L.Q. 405-20. "[O]nly the privileges or
immunities clause speaks to matters of substance," Kurland notes,
"certainly the language of due process and equal protection does
not." p. 406.
127. Charles A. Reich, "The New Property," 73 Yale L.J. 733-87 (1964), is
the most influential statement. Reich organizes modern instances of
government control of wealth and argues for the development of legal
and constitutional theory to protect personal liberty in the face of this
control. Two years earlier, Arthur S. Miller proposed a similar
development in "An Affirmative Thrust to Due Process of Law?" 30
Geo. Wash. L. Rev. 399-428 (1962). His argument, too, was based on
the expansion of governmental authority. See also Archibald Cox,
"Constitutional Adjudication and the Promotion of Human Rights,"
80 Harv. L. Rev. 91-122 (1966); William Van Alstyne, "The Demise
of the Right-Privilege Distinction in Constitutional Law," 81 Harv.
L. Rev. 1438-64 (1968), on a "demise" necessary before the new
property could be protected; James J. Graham, "Poverty and
Substantive Due Process," 12 Ariz. L. Rev. 1-34 (1970) which
discusses both the old substantive due process and the contemporary
reactions to it by Justices Black, Douglas, and Harlan; and the
exhaustive note, "The Growth of Procedural Due Process into a New
Substance: An Expanding Protection for Personal Liberty and a
'Specialized Type of Property . . . in our Economic System,'" 66 Nw.

L. Rev. 502-53 (1971). A critical examination of the arguments in these articles, suggesting among other things that equality and the material well-being of society are not philosophically or practically compatible goals, is Ralph K. Winter, Jr., "Poverty, Economic Equality, and the Equal Protection Clause," 1972 Sup. Ct. Rev. 41-102.

128. Leading cases include Shapiro v. Thompson, 394 U.S. 618 (1969) (one-year residency requirement for welfare eligibility is invalid); Sniadach v. Family Finance Corp., 395 U.S. 337 (1969) (hearing required before wages can be frozen under a garnishment law); Goldberg v. Kelly, 397 U.S. 254 (1970); (hearing required before welfare benefits can be terminated); Boddie v. Connecticut, 401 U.S. 371 (1971) (court fees must be waived for indigents seeking a divorce); U.S. Dept. of Agriculture v. Moreno, 413 U.S. 528 (1973) (food stamps cannot be denied individuals on the ground that they live with persons not legally related to each other). Justice Marshall, concurring in a case decided with *Moreno,* noted that his analysis combined "elements traditionally invoked in what are usually treated as distinct classes of cases, involving due process and equal protection. But the elements of fairness should not be so rigidly cabined." U.S. Dept. of Agriculture v. Murry, 413 U.S. 508, 519 (1973).

The *Sniadach* case differs from the others listed here in that the suit is between private parties. No state largess is involved. But one of the parties, the creditor, relied on a state law to enforce a contract, and the Court, having regard for the new property, modern equalitarianism, and the claims of the poor, decided that the law could not be invoked without adhering to due process requirements. In general see Allison Dunham, "Due Process and Commercial Law," 1972 Sup. Ct. Rev. 135-55.

129. Among the recent arguments in due process adjudication is that of the "irrebuttable presumption." This presumption, by creating a class of persons from which no individual can escape through a demonstration of the presumption's inapplicability in a particular case, violated current due process standards that a governmental rule must have an individualized rational relationship to a valid state interest and that there be no "reasonable alternative means" for achieving the same end. See Vlandis v. Kline, 412 U.S. 441, 452 (1973) and Cleveland Board of Education v. LaFleur, 414 U.S. 632 (1974). Because an irrebuttable presumption establishes a class of persons, equal protection reasoning might also have been developed to meet the argument. The irrebuttable presumption discussion may fade from constitutional law, however. See Weinberger v. Salfi, 422 U.S. 749 (1975).

Among the most dismal due process decisions are those made during the McCarthy era affecting aliens. See, e.g., Justice Jackson's discussion of procedural due process in Shaughnessy v. Mezei, 345 U.S. 206, 218-24 (1953) (dissent), and the several opinions in Fleming v. Nestor, 363 U.S. 603 (1960), a case which held, against essentially substantive due process arguments, that social security rights are not vested. Walter Gellhorn analyzes an extensive catalog of due process problems associated with "The Right to Make a Living" in his *Individual Freedom and Government Restraints* (Baton Rouge: Louisiana State Univ. Press, 1956), pp. 105–51. Erwin N. Griswold, *The Fifth Amendment Today* (Cambridge: Harvard Univ. Press, 1955) is an eloquent statement of the due process tradition focused on the protection of persons called before legislative investigating committees.

130. A good example of the rules-outcome problem in constitutional law is the determination of which jurisdiction, and therefore which rules, control a case. See, e.g., Alfred Hill, "The Erie Doctrine and the Constitution," 53 Nw. L. Rev. 427, 449-56 (1958). For another area of law, see Edmund M. Morgan, "Rules of Evidence—Substantive or Procedural?" 10 Vand. L. Rev. 467-84 (1957), which proposes that judges mold "outcome determinative rules" to peer through the haze of the procedure-substance relationship. In spite of intimate connection with each other, procedure and substance are still distinguished in legal and moral philosophy. See, e.g., John Rawls, *A Theory of Justice* (Cambridge: Harvard Univ. Press, 1971), p. 59.

131. The death penalty cases of 1972 are an instructive example of the procedure-substance problem in civil liberties. Furman v. Georgia, 308 U.S. 238. Five justices held capital punishment unconstitutional, but three of them found the defect in procedure (capricious imposition of the death penalty) and two of them in the substance (no procedure could save the death penalty). First Amendment provisions are also perplexing, for both as rights and in lawsuits they seem to have the attributes of procedure as well as substance. Is free speech a valuable right for substantive or procedural reasons? If the Court hears a case on the regulation of loudspeakers in public parks, is it deciding substance or procedure? The traditional distinction is not very useful here, and jurists have devised other categories of analysis in such cases. See, generally Henry P. Monaghan, "First Amendment 'Due Process,' " 83 Harv. L. Rev. 518-51 (1970).

132. Lynch v. Household Finance Corp. 405 U.S. 538, 552. It would be easy to see the distinction between human and property rights in such a case vanish in the face of an analysis based on "whose rights?"—

formerly the rights of the wealthy, now the rights of the poor. This is not the language the Court normally speaks, however, even though cases from Griffin v. Illinois, 351 U.S. 12 (1956) to San Antonio School District v. Rodriguez, 411 U.S. 1 (1973) focused on poverty as a defining characteristic under either the due process or equal protection clause. Liberty and property are treated as separate, though related, concepts in contemporary moral theory. See, e.g., Rawls, *A Theory of Justice,* p. 60.

133. Frankfurter wrote on due process—procedural due process—often, particularly during the middle years of his Court tenure. The flavor of what he believed, and how he wrote, apart from the application to particular circumstances such as right to counsel or the introduction into trial of unconstitutionally-seized evidence, may be appreciated from these passages:

> The history of American freedom is, in no small measure, the history of procedure. . . . Judicial review of [the due process] guaranty of the Fourteenth Amendment inescapably imposes upon this Court an exercise of judgment upon the whole course of the proceedings in order to ascertain whether they offend those canons of decency and fairness which express the notions of justice of English-speaking peoples even toward those charged with the most heinous offenses. Malinski v. New York, 324 U.S. 401, 414, 416-17 (1945) (concurring).

> Due process of law . . . conveys neither formal nor fixed nor narrow requirements. It is the compendious expression for all those rights which the courts must enforce because they are basic to our free society. But basic rights do not become petrified as of any one time, even though, as a matter of human experience, some may not too rhetorically be called eternal verities. It is of the very nature of a free society to advance in its standards of what is deemed reasonable and right. Representing as it does a living principle, due process is not confined within a permanent catalogue of what may at a given time be deemed the limits or the essentials of fundamental rights. Wolf v. Colorado, 338 U.S. 25, 27 (1949).

> Representing a profound attitude of fairness between man and man, and more particularly between individual and government, "due process" is compounded of history,

reason, the past course of decisions, and stout confidence in
the strength of the democratic faith which we possess, . . .
Joint Anti-Fascist Refugee Committee v. McGrath, 341
U.S. 123, 162 (1951) (concurring).

Due process is that which comports with the deepest
notions of what is fair and right and just. Selesbee v.
Balcom, 339 U.S. 9, 16 (1950) (dissent).

On Frankfurter, see Louis H. Pollak, "Mr. Justice Frankfurter:
Judgment and the Fourteenth Amendment," 67 Yale L.J. 304-43
(1957); and Richard G. Stevens, "Reason and History in Judicial
Judgment: Mr. Justice Frankfurter's Treatment of Due Process,"
unpub. diss., Univ. of Chicago, 1963.

134. As to the equal protection clause, Harlan evidently feared the
consequences of fastening decisions on a particular social value which
the Court was embracing, namely equality. See Williams v. Illinois,
399 U.S. 235 (1970). Harlan's concurring opinion in the birth control
case, Griswold v. Connecticut, 381 U.S. 479 (1965), relied on the
suttantive due process grounds of privacy and rejected the pen-
umbral right-emanation theory of the majority, the Ninth Amendment emphasis of Justice Goldberg concurring, and the restrictive due
process views of the dissenters. Justice Frankfurter had warned
against the "mischievous uses" to which a revived privileges or
immunities clause might be put in cases which he felt amenable to
due process adjudication. Adamson v. California, 332 U.S. 46, 61
(1947) (concurring). See also his concurring opinion in United States
v. Lovett, 328 U.S. 303 (1946), arguing for a due process solution to a
case which the Court, through Justice Black, decided under the bill of
attainder clause. For a discussion of procedural due process by Justice
Harlan, see his separate opinion in Re Gault, 387 U.S. 1, 68-72
(1967).

135. Roe v. Wade, 410 U.S. 113. See, generally, Richard A. Epstein,
"Substantive Due Process by any Other Name: The Abortion Cases,"
1973 Sup. Ct. Rev. 159-85. Justice Harlan's most extensive discussion
of due process, including his new substantive due process, appears in
Poe v. Ullman, 367 U.S. 497, 539-55 (1961) (dissent). This antedates
the rise of the "new property" rights. Justice Stewart, concurring in
the abortion cases, recognized the force of Harlan's views when he
wrote that although the Court had "purported to sound the death
knell for the doctrine of substantive due process" a decade earlier, and
although he himself had tried to keep the knell ringing, he had
become convinced that a new right—the right of a woman to control

her body—needed recognition under due process. Roe v. Wade, 410 U.S. 113, 167 (1973) (concurring). Laurence Tribe believes that the dissents in the abortion cases can be read in such a way that "the Court is evidently unanimous in accepting a fairly sweeping concept of substantive due process, although various Justices continue to resist that characterization." Tribe, "Toward a Model of Roles in the Due Process of Life and Law," 87 Harv. L. Rev. 1, 5 n. 27 (1973).

Chief Justice Burger and Justice Rehnquist, the dissenters, surely are among the resisters. See Chief Justice Burger's dissent in Einsenstadt v. Baird, 405 U.S. 438, 467 (1972) and the dissents of both justices in Vlandis v. Kline, 412 U.S. 441 (1973). Justice Douglas, in the abortion cases, mentioned three kinds of rights that he thought were covered by the Ninth Amendment, the "Blessings of Liberty" in the Preamble, and "liberty" in the Fourteenth Amendment. They are a compendium of contemporary rights outside of the new property: "the autonomous control over the development and expression of one's intellect, interests, tastes, and personality"; "freedom of choice in the basic decision of one's life respecting marriage, divorce, procreation, contraception, and the education and upbringing of children"; and "freedom to care for one's health and person, freedom from bodily restraint or compulsion, freedom to walk, stroll, or loaf." Doe v. Bolton, 410 U.S. 179, 211-13 (1973) (concurring).

136. Bradwell v. Illinois, 16 Wall. 130 (1873). The Court treated the claim under the privileges or immunities clause rather than the due process clause, but referred to the Slaughter-House Cases, just decided, for a discussion of the scope of the Fourteenth Amendment generally.

137. Muller v. Oregon, 208 U.S. 412 (1908), deviated from in Adkins v. Children's Hospital, 261 U.S. 525 (1923) and returned to in West Coast Hotel Co. v. Parrish, 300 U.S. 379 (1937). The protective legislation, considered a victory for women at the time, has been called into question by the women's rights movement because it discriminates between sexes.

138. See, generally, Ronald E. Klipsch, "Aspects of a Constitutional Right to a Habitable Environment: Towards an Environmental Due Process," 49 Ind. L. J. 203-37 (1974).

139. An example is Citizens to Preserve Overton Park v. Volpe, 401 U.S. 402 (1971).

140. Sierra Club v. Morton, 405 U.S. 727 (1972).

141. For his argument, Justice Douglas relied on Christopher D. Stone, "Should Trees Have Standing?—Toward Legal Rights for Natural Objects," 45 S. Cal. L. Rev. 450-501 (1972).

142. Judge William D. Murray in Environmental Defense Fund, Inc. v.
      Hoerner Waldorf Corp., No. 1694, D. Mont., Aug. 27, 1970 (3 Env. L.
      Reptr. 20794). An important aspect of property and the environment,
      traditionally related to due process, is discussed from Magna Carta to
      the present in Fred Bosselman, et al., *The Taking Issue: An Analysis of
      the Constitutional Limits of Land Use Control* (Washington, D.C.: Council
      on Environmental Quality, 1973).

      When private property and American foreign policy clash and
      result in court cases, "the taking issue" may arise in another context.
      For the history, see Willard Bunce Cowles, *Treaties and Constitutional
      Law: Property Interferences and Due Process of Law* (Washington, D.C.:
      Public Affairs Press, 1941). A brief discussion which does not
      anticipate the expansion of due process of law in foreign affairs is
      Louis Henkin, *Foreign Affairs and the Constitution* (Mineola, N.Y.:
      Foundation Press, 1972), pp. 255-57. This is confirmed with respect to
      the expropriation of American-owned property by foreign govern-
      ments in violation of international law in Banco Nacional de Cuba v.
      Sabbatino, 376 U.S. 398 (1964) in which the Court decided, eight to
      one, not to examine the validity of the taking.

143. Four of these commentaries deserve mention for their range of
      considerations. Although they are not explicitly built on one another,
      they demonstrate an evolution from Judge William Hastie's use of
      traditional categories to propose new human-rights distinctions in
      1956; through Leonard G. Ratner's new categories which make order
      out of due process goals and adjudication, and Harry H. Wellington's
      perception of the bearing of due process on the constitutional
      "allocation of competences" among agencies of government; to
      Laurence H. Tribe's full-scale proposal that due process be seen as the
      guide to a "role-allocation model" in society as a whole. The
      references are Hastie, "Judicial Method in Due Process Inquiry," in
      Arthur E. Sutherland (ed.), *Government Under Law* (Cambridge:
      Harvard Univ. Press, 1956), pp. 326-44; Ratner, "The Function of the
      Due Process Clause," 116 U. Pa. L. Rev. 1048-1117 (1968); Well-
      ington, "Common Law Rules and Constitutional Double Standards:
      Some Notes on Adjudication," 83 Yale L. J. 221-311 (1973); and
      Tribe, "Toward a Model of Roles in the Due Process of Life and
      Law," 87 Harv. L. Rev. 1-53 (1973), and "Structural Due Process,"
      10 Harv. Civ. Rights-Civ. Lib. L. Rev. 269-321 (1975).

2

DUE PROCESS IN ENGLAND

GEOFFREY MARSHALL

An American constitutional lawyer might well be surprised at the elusiveness of references to the term "due process of law" in the general body of English legal writing. We all recall (dimly) its occurrence in the Petition of Right in 1628 where it is linked to "the law of the land," as it was by Sir Edward Coke, who spoke of "the process of the law"—that which is carried out "in due manner or by writ originall of the common law." [1] Today one finds no space devoted to due process in Halsbury's *Laws of England*, in Stephen's *Commentaries*, or Anson's *Law and Custom of the Constitution*. The phrase rates no entry in such works as Stroud's *Judicial Dictionary* or Wharton's *Law Lexicon*. So it becomes a nice question what items in the legal and constitutional arrangements of the United Kingdom might best be discussed under the due process rubric.

Natural justice is perhaps too narrow for the purpose, and the rule of law too broad. Nevertheless, the rule of law probably comes nearest to the mark. When Dicey popularized the phrase in the 1880s, its implications were primarily the absence of arbitrary power or wide discretionary authority. It also entailed the rejection of any exemption for particular classes of persons from the duty of obedience to the law which governs citizens in general. In the 1970s these questions have taken on a new twist. The king's prerogative and special commands no longer threaten the equal rule of law, but other agencies and groups have laid claims to prerogatives and powers that may be equally difficult to reconcile with the universality of legal obligations and the regular and certain application of legal principles.

Whether we think of the rule of law or of due process, we could probably agree that its elements consist at least of the following: fairness, impartiality, independence, equality, openness, rationality, certainty, and universality. Parceling out the territory thus, we can at least set off on a lightning tour of the juridical landscape, picking out new additions to the skyline and marking the oddity of some of the existing configurations.

I. FAIRNESS

The imposition of fairness by legal rules is a form of restraint, and since constitutionalism is always a compromise between restraint and liberty, we might expect fairness to involve conflict with other social values that involve freedom from restraint. One aspect of the contest is the fair trial versus free speech dilemma. In some ways, at least, the balance in the United Kingdom has obviously been pushed further in the direction of protection for the trial process than it has in the United States. The point was underlined in 1973 by the decision of the House of Lords in *Attorney-General* v. *Times Newspapers*.[2] The *Times* set out to publish a series of articles on the manufacture and marketing of the drug thalidomide. One of the articles was objected to by the manufacturers, the Distillers Company. What precisely was its subject matter is not known since it was held that its publication would have constituted a contempt by prejudicing the trial of pending actions against the manufacturers. The *Times* argued in its defense that though there was a public interest in the fair administration of justice, there was also a competing public interest in free discussion which, even in the law of contempt, ought to be weighed by the court.

The argument seems to have surprised Lord Widgery in the High Court since he suggested that the balancing of interests might be a suitable form of activity for an administrative body but was not appropriate for a court exercising a judicial function. This straight-batting jurisprudence failed to carry the day on appeal, and when the case reached the House of Lords, Lord Reid and his colleagues were prepared to accept that a balance had to be struck between the two forms of public interest. But Lord Simon added—oddly—that the balance could not be struck anew in each individual case. (Where else could it be struck?) When proceedings were pending the paramount interest lay in protecting the due administration of justice; this being necessary in the words of Lord Cross to prevent a gradual slide towards trial by newspaper or television. So no balance came down in favor of the *Times,* and the article remained unpublished.

On another part of the contempt front, however, things have gone better for the rights of the individual. Direct contempts in the face of the court [3] seem no longer to be viewed with the traditional severity. In 1970 a group of Welsh Nationalist protesters who sang and scattered leaflets in court were merely bound over and released after an appeal.[4] In earlier times, missile throwing in court had more serious consequences as in the case recorded by Samuel Pepys: "A prisoner being condemned at Salisbury for a matter . . . while they were considering to transport him to save his life, the fellow flung a great stone at the judge, that missed him but broke through the wainscote. Upon this he had his hand cut off and was hanged presently." [5]

The threat of libel actions as well as the contempt danger remains, however, an obstacle to the freedom of press investigation and publication. It seems; for example, quite probable that if British newspapers had been faced with the situation as it appeared to the *Washington Post* in June 1972 after the Watergate break-in, they would have found it impossible to publish an analogous series of articles. The impending trial of the burglars would have placed severe restraints on any inquiry into the background of the affair and no doubt (since distributors are equally in peril with journalists and publishers) a great many dangerous pages would have had to be torn from imported copies [6] of *Time, Newsweek,* and other incautious alien publications. Secretaries of State, attorneys-general, and public officials would also have been at least as free as ordinary citizens to sue for defamation.

It is perhaps just conceivable that the American doctrine laid down in *New York Times* v. Sullivan and its successors operates a little hardly when spread over every possible category of public servant, both elected and nonelected (not all of whom have the elected politician's capacity and a public platform for counter-speech that is sometimes advanced as a partial rationale for the freedom to denounce public officers). After all, the doctrine of personal liability of public officials for their wrongful acts might suggest the reciprocal entitlement to the ordinary remedies available to fellow subjects. Nevertheless, the balance struck in Britain between free comment and the protection of reputation is certainly over-tender of both public and private susceptibilities.

Even a local government authority has been held entitled to defend its reputation. In 1972 the Council of the seaside resort of Bognor Regis successfully sued an outspoken critic of its policies. The defendant had accused the Council of undemocratic behavior and "Toy Town Hitlerism." Damages of 2000 pounds were awarded against him, and his costs were in the region of 30,000 pounds.[7]

Almost every day, moreover, newspapers carry small inside-page items recounting the payment of what are usually called "undisclosed sums" in settlement of actions for defamatory reports whose offense is generally some minor factual misstatement or incautious inference. The *Times* of July 31, 1974, for example, records two such episodes. In one, the publishers of the *New Statesman* offer damages and the costs of the action for publishing a suggestion that Beaverbrook Newspapers are intending to cease publication of the *Daily Express* (a particularly incestuous example of watchdog not biting watchdog). In the other case, the *Guardian* expresses regret and makes amends for criticizing a television program which was attributed to the wrong television company. In the same issue, a (mercifully unsuccessful) attempt is reported to commit a journalist and newspaper editor to prison for contempt allegedly committed in reporting the trial of seven women charged with causing a disturbance in a public house. One offending headline had referred to a "Women's Lib bar-room battle," but the Lord Chief Justice, after due consideration of an application by the defendants, ruled that the imputation was unlikely to influence the course of justice.

II. IMPARTIALITY AND INDEPENDENCE

One topic given added interest by recent American constitutional history is the independence of the processes of justice and their divorce from political influence or control. It is surprising that so fundamental an issue should remain one of the gray areas of our constitutional law, though there are a number of firm conventions in existence. In both Britain and America, the actual and potential involvement of senior members of the executive government in activities that may bring them into conflict with the law makes it necessary to have as much clarity as possible about the extent to which those who are in charge of the machinery of prosecution and investigation may pursue their activities under a guarantee of immunity from interference. The practical issues on which questions arise are the institution or cessation of criminal investigations, the institution and withdrawal of prosecutions, the granting of immunity from prosecution, and the general policies and methods adopted in the enforcement of the law. In terms of the traditional categories of political science, these are in principle executive functions. But the discomfort of that description is that it suggests that executive policy is ultimately a matter for decision by executive politicians and that there should be some form of accountability to elected persons for decisions that may have important political consequences. What has happened is that a curious and uncertain compromise has been struck between these conclusions and a not fully worked out view that law enforcement ought to share some of the characteristics of the judicial function—that it should not be subject to either legislative accountability or executive control. The implication is that either the law enforcement function should be a *sui generis* function standing outside the legislative-executive-judicial trinity, or that it should benefit from some form of internal separation of functions within the executive branch.

In England the attorney general is one of the Queen's ministers who shares the collective political responsibility of the administration and is responsible to Parliament for the advice given to the cabinet and for the actions taken in his name. He may be questioned in the House of Commons on the reasons for his decisions to authorize or to withdraw prosecutions. But can the cabinet and Prime Minister direct him to exercise his powers in a particular way? One answer is that it would not be illegal to do so or to dismiss the attorney general for failure to comply with a collective decision of the cabinet. The sanction would, as for any other minister, be removal from office, formally by the Crown, on the advice of the prime minister. In 1919 Attorney General Sir Gordon Hewart said that in relation to prosecutions for such offenses as sedition the question of prosecution was one of policy and one for the consideration of ministers. In 1924 the Labour cabinet of Ramsey MacDonald issued an instruction that no prosecution of a political character was to take place without cabinet sanction.

Since 1924, however, when MacDonald's government fell over the issue of suspected political interference to secure the withdrawal of a prosecution, the received convention has been that it can never be the right of a cabinet to veto or to insist upon a prosecution though it is permissible and even a matter of duty for the attorney general to seek the views of ministers where matters of public policy are involved. Such a consultation occurred when Mr. Heath's Attorney General Sir Peter Rawlinson decided against proceeding with charges against the Palestinian Leila Khaled for offenses committed in the course of an attempted aircraft hijacking. It is not clear whether consultation on the public policy aspects with political colleagues implies that such colleagues' views should be sought on the desirability of prosecution or whether the consultation should be merely directed to assessing the political consequences of prosecution which the attorney general must then weigh in the balance. At any rate, it will be insisted that the decision must be his.

If one were to search for a possible legal basis for such independence, it might be that the case is stronger where statutes make the assent of the attorney general or the director of public prosecutions (who works under his direction) necessary to the institution of a prosecution than where the attorney general is exercising his prerogative power to stop proceedings on indictment by entering a *nolle prosequi*. In the latter case, the prerogative is that of the crown and the crown by convention is advised on the exercise of the prerogative by ministers.

Luckily England, unlike Scotland and the United States, has not embraced the notion that the prosecution function ought to be monopolized in the hands of state officials. In principle (though there are now many statutory exceptions), anyone may start a prosecution. A striking example occurred in 1974 at the time of the general election. Police Constable Joy, a policeman on traffic patrol, reported a well-known local politician for a number of traffic offenses. His superior officer decided not to prosecute, but P.C. Joy, though charged with a breach of police discipline, insisted on bringing the prosecution himself and obtained a conviction. Of course the principle of constabulary independence runs wider than the prosecution function, embracing law enforcement decisions generally. In 1968 in R. v. Metropolitan Police Commissioner *ex parte* Blackburn the Master of the Rolls said that "every constable in the land . . . is independent of the executive. . . . No minister of the crown can tell him he must or must not keep observation on this place or that, he must or must not prosecute this man or that—nor can any police authority tell him so. The responsibility is on him. He is answerable to the law and to the law alone." [8] The legal and historical foundations of this thesis are debatable, but it has been moderately successful in keeping politics out of law enforcement.

III. EQUALITY AND UNIFORMITY

Blackburn raised a number of points about the equal application of law and about discretion in enforcement. There is room for puzzlement here. Uniform enforcement cannot mean automatic prosecution of every offense, since no society has enough policemen, and because offenses vary from the murderous to the trivial. There must be discretion in disposing of scarce police resources to meet these inherent difficulties in the imposition of legal sanctions. Yet it seems intolerable if those whose duty it is to apply the law pick and choose the laws that they think it necessary to enforce. This seems to be another dilemma of due process.

In 1951 Sir Hartley Shawcross, attorney general in the Attlee government, said, "It has never been the rule in this country . . . that suspected criminal offenses must automatically be the subject of prosecution. The public interest is the dominant consideration." [9] It had been supposed until recently that prosecutory discretion could not be challenged. But in 1968 Mr. Raymond Blackburn upset that assumption by asking for an order to compel the Metropolitan police commissioner to withdraw a policy instruction which laid down that no action was to be taken to detect offenses in licensed clubs against the Betting, Gaming and Lotteries Act of 1963 unless there had been complaints of cheating or evidence that criminals were regularly using a particular club. As a result, police observation stopped, and an important section of the act was not in fact enforced in London gaming clubs. This was a policy decision that the exercise of enforcement was, in the uncertain state of the law, an inefficient use of police manpower.

Mr. Blackburn, however, took the view that the police had no such power to make a general decision not to enforce a particular part of the law. The police capitulated and withdrew the policy instruction so Mr. Blackburn did not get his mandamus. The Court of Appeal made it clear, however, that they would have been prepared in a suitable case to enforce the performance of a duty to enforce the law.

What would be a suitable case is unclear. Two separate issues are raised. One is whether the police owe a duty to the public to enforce the law and whether a decision not to prosecute in a particular case can be a breach of such duty. The other issue is whether a breach of duty can be inferred merely by reason of there being a general policy of nonprosecution in particular types of case. This latter view would bear a plausible resemblance to the general rule that a body on whom a discretion is conferred must exercise it and not disable itself from exercising judgment in each case by a self-fettering policy rule. Perhaps this amounts only to saying that there is nothing objectionable about formulating policies for the exercise of discretion provided that the body or person exercising the discretion is prepared in each case to consider whether grounds exist for making an exception to the policy.

The Court, however, did not commit itself to this view, and various examples were mentioned of proper general policies in prosecution and nonprosecution matters. Instances cited were the nonprosecution of attempted suicide (when suicide and attempted suicide were crimes) and the nonprosecution of certain classes of juvenile sexual offenses. On the other hand, said Lord Denning, a decision by a chief police officer not to prosecute any person for stealing goods worth less than 100 pounds would be improper, and it would appear that the court could countermand it. What it seems to amount to is that there is a clear discretion to formulate policies of nonprosecution but the discretion is not an absolute one. The police owe a duty to the public to enforce the law and in proper cases (which remain uncertain) citizens with zeal and money enough can compel the performance of this duty in the courts.[10]

In the absence of any constitutional guarantee of equal protection, substantive equality in English law is a fragmentary topic. Two essays in establishing equality in particular areas are the Race Relations Acts of 1965 and 1968 and the equal opportunities legislation designed to prevent certain kinds of discrimination against women. The 1965 Act deals, among other things, with racial incitement; while the 1968 legislation seeks to prevent discrimination in the supply of goods, services and facilities where such discrimination is based upon grounds of color, race, or ethnic or national origins, and where the services in question are supplied to the public or any section of the public. Many of these terms have posed difficult questions of statutory interpretation,[11] but a more fundamental difficulty has been the drafting of the acts so as not to conflict too dramatically with existing concepts of ownership, disposal, and rights to property and privacy. Consequently, the exceptions and proposed exceptions to the scope of the legislation are of some interest.

The race relations legislation does not extend to the employment of persons in a private household, residential occupation of premises shared with the owners, sleeping and sanitary facilities on ships or aircraft, the sale of houses by their owners, and jobs requiring special attributes. It is a curious feature of the legislation that though discriminatory acts in these areas are not unlawful, the intention to perform them cannot be advertised. So although it is lawful to employ Chinese waiters, Scottish cooks, and Balinese dancing girls, one cannot say in public print that that is what one intends to do by way of advertising the vacancy.

Still further and better entertainment has been furnished by the attempt to legislate for sexual equality. Proposals published by the Conservative government in 1973 related only to employment. They made provision for five probable and three possible exceptions from the scope of the act, namely: (1) where the nature of the job requires it to be performed by a man or a woman (e.g., modeling at

least some kinds of clothing); (2) where a man or a woman is
required for purposes of authenticity (e.g., casting a play about
heavyweight boxing); (3) where the employment involves maintaining a team including persons of each sex (staffing a dancing
academy?); (4) where single sex employment is legitimately related
to the nature of the institution (e.g., female domestic staff in a
convent—but a wide field for argument is indicated); (5) where
there is communal living accommodation (no mention of aircraft or
ships here); (6) where it would be offensive to public taste or
decency for a man (or a woman) to do the job (a grammatically
obscure proposal which seems to indicate that only hermaphrodites
need apply); (7) where strong customer or client preferences exist in
the provision of personal services (possibly this includes massage
parlors but excludes striptease establishments); and (8) where
twenty-five or fewer persons are employed.

In 1976 the Labour government enacted proposals broadly
following those suggested by its predecessors in office. The Sex
Discrimination Act is somewhat broader, however, in that it
prohibits discrimination on the grounds of marital status as well as
sex. Meanwhile, some institutions have not waited for the imposition of legal sanctions before liberalizing their establishments. It has
been reported in the press that one Scottish golf club has already
amended its rules to provide that "ladies may play without
restriction during the hours of darkness."

IV. RATIONALITY

One might perhaps have expected the giving of reasons for
decisions to figure more prominently than it does in the notions of
due process and natural justice. Equality, fairness, and justice imply
that like cases should be treated alike. And how can it be
determined that cases treated alike are in fact alike if no grounds are
suggested for equating them or distinguishing them from similar
but distinct cases? Some have indeed supposed that the right to a
reasoned decison was one of the principles of natural justice, along
with the right to a hearing and the absence of bias. The Report of
the British Committee on Ministers' Powers of 1932 (of which Sir
William Holdsworth and Harold Laski were part-authors) said that
it "may well be argued that there is a third principle of natural

justice, namely that a party is entitled to know the reason for the decision be it judicial or quasi-Judicial." [12] It may well be argued also, of course, that there is a right—natural justice apart—to have reasons given for an *administrative* decision. But none of these propositions seems to have been universally admitted. One possible reason is that the greater part of decisions in English courts would on such a view be given in disregard of natural justice, since they are given by magistrates, who generally do not give reasoned decisions but (unless stating a case for appellate purposes) simply find defendants guilty or not guilty. For that matter , so do juries. Many magistrates would think it impossible to give reasons which went beyond saying that one witness was believed and another not. Still, that is not always the reason, and if it is, it could possibly be stated in terms that did not obviously impute perjury to the losing party.

Similar issues arise where decisions are given by administrative tribunals, such as rent, national insurance, social security, or valuation tribunals. Here a statutory obligation was placed by the Tribunals and Inquiries Act of 1958 on tribunals, and in ministers making decisions after the holding of a public inquiry, subject to the specification of reasons being restricted on grounds of national security. If the government wishes to exempt any class of such decisions from the necessity to give reasons, it must consult a statutory body—the Council on Tribunals—which has set its face against giving such exemptions. Tribunals considering conscientious objectors' applications for exemption from military service were one such case. Of them the council said, "In very many cases the reasons given by the tribunal would not and indeed could not amount to more than a statement that the tribunal accepted or rejected the truth and sincerity of the applicant's or appellant's objection on grounds of conscience. But ... we could not regard the giving of even so limited a statement of reasons as unnecessary." [13] The same view was taken of various categories of arbitrators. So if quasi-judicial and administrative officers can articulate their reasons, why, we may wonder, should justices of the peace lag behind? Clearly, questions may arise about what constitutes a reason (distinguish between "not a satisfactory reason" and "not a reason at all"). But no insoluble difficulties have yet emerged.[14]

One area in which reasons for action have traditionally not been forthcoming is that in which prerogative powers have been exercised by ministers and civil servants. Examples are the granting of honours by the Crown, the exercise of the prerogative of mercy (before the abolition of capital punishment), the control of immigration and the issuing or refusal of passports. In all such cases one theoretical and convenient pretext for nonreasoned decision has been that in theory the decisions are those of the Queen whom it would be disrespectful to cross-examine. The reality is of course that ministers advise the Crown and are capable of explaining, if they wish, on what principles advice has been given. In immigration matters, statute has taken over from the prerogative. Instructions to Immigration officers are now published together with the relevant legislation and regulations and a system of appeals tribunals exists. Passports, however, like patronage, remain in the area of ineffability. No reasons are given for refusing them, and there is no appeal against refusal. Their status is perhaps odd. Though purchased for money, they bear the words "This passport remains the property of Her Majesty's Government in the United Kingdom and may be withdrawn at any time." That may simply be bluster by Her Majesty's Principal Secretary of State for Foreign Affairs (a capacity for bluster now being one of the requirements for the job), but at any rate he may certainly choose not to renew passports when they expire. Luckily, no such document as a passport is needed by a British subject to leave the country, though the police might delay him long enough to miss his flight by pretending to believe him to be an alien.

V. OPENNESS

Many things may be contrasted with and sometimes conflict with openness—for example security, secrecy, confidentiality, and privacy. All of these have entered in various ways in Britain and America into the argument about the limits of executive privilege. The result of recent adjudications in Britain has been to bring the law into a state not too different from that which has emerged from United States v. Richard M. Nixon. There may be come reason to assert indeed that no such thing as executive privilege exists to be claimed by the crown. In the first place, the crown is not the sovereign; second, no separation of powers argument for inherent executive authority can be adduced; and third, the courts seem now to have suggested that what was traditionally dubbed "crown privilege" is a misnomer.[15] The privilege of objecting to the production of evidence in court is not confined to the crown or to documentary evidence in the possession of the crown. It seems to be merely an aspect of public policy that a claim for the confidentiality of evidence should sometimes be upheld in the courts. However, where ministers do make such claims they are no longer regarded by the courts as conclusive. In Conway v. Rimmer [16] it was held that there was a residuary power to inspect documents privately in order to strike a judicial balance between the interests of the parties and the general interest in the administration of justice. In that case, confidential reports on police officers and on criminal investigation were in issue. Other recent cases [17] have involved confidential information given to government agencies such as the Gaming Board and the commissioners of customs and excise.

Information furnished in confidence to government by private bodies is one category of information likely to figure in an a priori catalog of material which can reasonably be excluded from general statutory provisions about public access to official information. A committee under the chairmanship of Lord Franks [18] has recently compiled such a list. The committee was set up as the result of almost universal disquiet about the provisions of the existing Official Secrets Acts. In general, these make it an offense for anyone holding a governmental office to communicate any information obtained in the course of his duty to anyone (for example to reveal the time at which tea is taken in the Home Office). It is also an offense for any person to receive such information having reasonable grounds to believe that it has been communicated in contravention of the Act.

In 1971 there occurred on a minor scale a British version of the Pentagon Papers affair. A secret diplomatic and military report on the Nigerian civil war prepared for the Foreign Office was leaked and published in the *Sunday Telegraph*. The author of the report, a journalist to whom he had given it, and the editor of the *Sunday Telegraph* were charged under the act. No one having been discovered breaking into their psychiatrists' offices, the case was allowed to go to the jury which after a strong direction from the judge acquitted all three defendants. In his summing up, Caulfield

J. strongly suggested, that the document in question did not endanger national security, that the government's case was "a barren waste," and that Section 2 of the Official Secrets Act might have reached retirement age and should be pensioned off.

Its successor may well be a new Official Information Act. The Franks Committee's suggestion is that criminal sanctions should be confined to a number of specified categories of information comprising: (1) defense, security, foreign relations, currency, and foreign reserves; (2) cabinet documents; (3) information facilitating criminal activity; (4) information supplied in confidence to the government by private individuals; and (5) official information used for private gain. Only material classified as "Top Secret" or "Secret" or "Defense Confidential" would be protected in the first category, and a minister's certificate that the information was correctly classified at the relevant time would be binding on the court.

There are signs that civil servants have found these proposals too much to swallow. They have been heard complaining—in the nicest possible way—that considerable—not to say insuperable—difficulties may arise, for example, in defining communicable and incommunicable forms of economic and diplomatic information. Overprecipitate—not to say reckless—action seems unlikely to commend itself, therefore, given the need to consider the matter with due deliberation, from all its aspects and in proper perspective.

VI. CERTAINTY

There is much to be said for the view that the rule of law is best protected by a clear enunciation of public rights. The question then arises why the English, who have not been backward in claiming to have rights, have nevertheless failed to get themselves a proper Bill of Rights and consistently display very little eagerness to have one? The traditional arguments have, after all, been muddled and unpersuasive. There was Dicey's contrast between rights and remedies (though remedies *are* rights). There was also the allegation that English law does not favor the positive statement of rights as distinct from the negative procedure of leaving wide areas of behavior legally unconstrained. That was never really true and is becoming less so. We have, for example, the right to strike, the right to picket, and the right to vote.

Other elements in the opposition to Bills of Rights have been a supposed distaste for European and American political machinery and the belief that to commit oneself to a formal statement of rights implicitly suggests the notion that such rights might be suspended (though it is not clear why the enactment of fundamental rights suggests it any more than the enactment of anything else). It is also the case that Bills of Rights imply judicial review and that, as every English schoolboy knows, leads to undemocratic obstruction of legislation desired by the people.

It may well be, however, that postwar developments in Europe, the Commonwealth, and the United States have weakened the psychological resistance of Englishmen to formal constitutional guarantees and to judicial review. The Commonwealth is full of Bills of Rights drafted in part by English draftsmen. The European Human Rights Convention is now, though circuitously, available for use by citizens of the United Kingdom. In addition, the image of judicial review in the United States has been transformed for many by the libertarian maneuvers of the Supreme Court during and even since the Warren era. A Court that cuts down executive privilege, undermines capital punishment, safeguards contraceptive supplies, guarantees abortion and protects, the careers of pregnant servicewomen seems far removed from, the Nine Old Male Chauvinists whose pedantic notions of due process endangered the New Deal. So perhaps the time is ripe for a serious attempt to protect our own rights and liberties whilst the opportunity offers and the sovereignty of Parliament, once such a lion in the path, is beginning to look unsteady on its feet.

At least three questions, however, need to be distinguished. First, are there serious or numerous invasions of civil, political and administrative rights in the United Kingdom? Second, should what is wrong be put right by more piecemeal legislation, by adoption of the European Human Rights Convention as a parliamentary enactment, or by a new, home-grown statement of fundamental rights? Third, how should any such legislation, if adopted, be enforced and entrenched against repeal, infringement, or evasion.

Then there is the question of measuring and expressing the degree of absoluteness of the protected rights. How far, for example, need the freedom of speech be explicitly qualified by the need for regulation of judicial proceedings, the need for impartiality in radio and television broadcasting and the protection of reputation, livelihood, and literary copyright, as well as by an inherently unspecifiable group of circumstances many of which have not yet arisen.

The problem occurs right across the spectrum of rights and liberties. Everyone (well, almost everyone) is against sin, discrimination, censorship, and the like, and in favor of openness, freedom, equality, and natural justice. But how far should the qualifications, modifications, limitations, and exceptions to these desirable generalities be set out in the legislation? Could any committee or assembly that one can envisage in the British Isles ever happily agree about what these elaborations and modifications should be? Since the answer is obviously no, we seem impelled towards the view that all must be left to judicial interpretation. This presents us with a dilemma, since such a course implies that we should abdicate to future judicial instincts the settlement of major questions of principle about the meaning and application of rights.

Equality or equal protection is one field where almost nothing is settled by the general enunciation of principle. The statement that there should not be discrimination conceals both the issue as to which criteria are legitimate bases for discrimination between groups of citizens and an important question about the extent to which the relevant enforcible obligations should be placed upon everybody or only upon state or government agencies. It seems pleasant to decree that no one shall be disadvantaged on irrelevant grounds; but the proposition that the law should not discriminate does not in itself conclusively establish either that nobody should, or that the law should be used to punish all discriminatory activities.

No one believes that there are no areas in which private choice should be tolerated in the interests of freedom. But which are they to be? Paradoxically, there is perhaps more chance of such issues being genuinely debated in a judicial forum than in a democratically elected legislature, which is where ideally they ought to be debated. Though most men are moved by fashion, ideology, self-interest, and self-importance there is probably more of each in the latter place than in the former. The best argument for a British Bill of Rights is that it is impossible to overestimate the collective partisanship and irrationality of Members of Parliament.

VII. UNIVERSALITY

In explaining the rule of law, Dicey's *Law of the Constitution* stressed the idea of universal application of the law. "Every man whatever his rank or condition is subject to the ordinary law of the realm.... With us," he added, "every official from the Prime Minister down to a constable or a collector of taxes is under the same responsibility for every act done without legitimate justification as any other citizen." [19] But by 1914 Dicey was complaining of the tendency to diminish the sphere of the rule of law by conferring special powers and exemptions on various administrative bodies and on the crown. At one point he remarks that the equal rule of law was exposed to a new peril, quoting Sir Frederick Pollock, who in 1908 had written that "The Legislature (had) thought fit by the Trade Disputes Act, 1906, to confer extraordinary immunities on combinations of both employers and workmen." [20]

The Trade Disputes Act of 1906 in fact effectively immunized trade unions from tort liability. Damage caused by withdrawal of labor or the effects of picketing was primarily in contemplation, but the act went very wide. In the second edition of his *Law and Opinion in England*, Dicey pointed out that "if a Trade Union possessed say of 20,000 pounds, causes a libel to be published of A, an employer of labor, or B, a workman who refuses to join the union, or excites some fanatical ruffians to assault A or B, neither A nor B can maintain an action against the union." As the result of the Trade Union Act of 1913, when unions were authorized to apply their funds to political objects, it might be, Dicey thought, that they could freely publish libels on parliamentary candidates of whose politics they disapproved.[21]

Since 1914 no political party has been very successful in regulating trade union activities. The Labour Party, of course, has an inherent constitutional disinclination for any such activity. Nevertheless, in the decade since 1965, both parties have felt the need and both have failed. In 1969 after the report of the Donovan Royal Commission on Trade Unions, the Labour Party had a plan for legislation. It was designed to avoid unofficial and wildcat strike action by providing for cooling-off periods and to give the government powers to require union ballots before strikes involving

serious threats to the economy. It was a moderate enough plan, but
the prime minister and his cabinet were told to abandon it and they
did so.

In 1971 the Conservative government enacted a more comprehensive measure into law as the Industrial Relations Act to
encourage the making of binding collective agreements, and to set
up an industrial relations court to enforce a code of fair practice for
employers and employees. The major trade unions declined to
accept the act or any such act. Some trade union leaders said that
though passed by Parliament it was not a law at all. When orders
were made by the National Industrial Relations Court against
"unfair industrial practices," the transport, engineering, and dockers' unions did not obey them. When the Amalgamated Engineering Union was fined a total of 130,000 pounds for contempt, it
refused to pay. So an anonymous and mysteriously philanthropic
group of employers paid the fines, thus vicariously (and mirac-
ulously) purging the engineers' contempt. When dockers were
imprisoned for contemptuous disobedience of court orders [22] and a
general strike was threatened urgent steps were taken to find
grounds for releasing the dockers from jail and for pretending that
their contempt (which was greater than ever) had vanished away.
When miners and power workers struck, armies of coal miners
invested power stations, defied the police and engaged in large-scale
illegal picketing [23] and intimidation.

Some, though not all, trade union leaders made it clear that they
were not prepared to tolerate conservative policies or a conservative
government and would stop the country to prove it. Under the
threat of an indefinite miners' strike, the electorate took the hint,
stood down the conservative government, and engaged Mr. Wilson
to pay the money, switch on the lights, and repeal the Industrial
Relations Act as being a wicked and arrogant attempt to meddle
with the prerogative power of the unions in industrial affairs.
Nobody in either party has managed to explain what else was
wrong with the Industrial Relations Act.

Nevertheless, the world is now not what it was, and we are aware
that there are a number of things that trade union leaders do not
like. They do not like collective agreements solemnly entered into to
be treated as if they were intended to be binding or enforceable.

They do not like to see pickets who act illegally subjected to legal penalties. They do not like workers or citizens who decline to listen to pickets, and they are inventing a new law to allow pickets to stop and detain nonlisteners. They do not like cartoons in newspapers that misrepresent the motives of trade unionists. They do not like regular contributions to newspapers by writers who are not members of the National Union of Journalists. They do not like incomes policies that limit wage bargaining though incomes policies that limit prices are acceptable. They do not in general like right-wing economic policies or right-wing governments and might not let the electorate have one even if the electorate wants one (though they do not go so far as to say—as do the militant members of the National Union of Students—that right-wing speakers should be physically prevented from making speeches that advocate provocative or reactionary policies).

In 1974 some novel dislikes were made known and supported by the threat of "blacking" or industrial action. There were attempts to remove private patients from hospitals operating under the National Health Service and threats to take action to prevent the building of private hospitals. In Australia there were—possibly double-edged—threats to prevent Mr. Frank Sinatra from returning to the United States. So far no action has been taken to force the abolition of private education, first class railway carriages, or trips to the seaside.

Any practical assessment of due process in England must take account of these developments. In Dicey's analysis of the nineteenth-century constitution, the privileges of the crown constituted an awkward exception to the universal application of the rule of law. Today the crown is no longer an over-mighty subject, but the trade unions collectively have inherited the royal prerogative. Social customs also have changed in a manner appropriate to this transformation of the political system. In all ranks of liberal and polite society criticism of the monarchy as a palpable social evil (comparable perhaps to sweat shops or tuberculosis) is acceptable and commonplace. On the other hand any such denunciation of, say, the Transport and General Workers' Union would be thought impolitic and vulgar. The implications do not make for light-heartedness about the future of due process in England.

NOTES

1. 2 Inst. 50. Coke was commenting on chapter 39 of the Magna Carta: "No free man shall be taken or imprisoned or disseised or outlawed or exiled or anywise destroyed; nor will we send upon him, unless by the lawful judgment of his peers, or by the *law of the land" (lex terrae).* Pollock and Maitland sum up the import of the charter as being "that the king is and shall be below the law." *History of English Law* Vol. 1, p. 173. As to what was intended by chapter 39, see W.S. McKechnie, *Magna Carta* (1905) pp. 441-43 and C.H. McIlwain, "Due Process of Law in Magna Carta," 14 Colum. L. Rev. 27-51 (1914).

2. Attorney General v. Times Newspapers Ltd. [1973] 3 all E.R. 54.

3. Some doubt exists as to the meaning of this expression. In June 1974 an attempt to introduce laughing gas into a courtroom through a ventilation shaft was held not to be a contempt committed in the face of the court. Balogh v. St. Albans Crown Court Times Law Rep. 4 July 1974.

4. Morris v. Crown Office [1970] 2 Q.B. 114.

5. *The Diary of Samuel Pepys* Vol. VIII (ed. R. Latham and W. Matthews) p. 429. The judge happened to be leaning on his elbow at the time and is reported to have said, "If I had been an upright judge, I had been slain."

6. Prudence now frequently dictates this practice as the result of a prosecution in 1957. The Queen v. Griffiths *ex-parte* Attorney General [1957] 2 Q.B. 194.

7. Bognor Regis U.D.C. v. Campion [1972] 2 Q.B. 169.

8. *R.* v. Metropolitan Police Commissioner *ex parte* Blackburn [1968] 2 Q.B. 118. Cf. Report of the Royal Commission on the Police 1962 (Cmnd 1728); G. Marshall *Police and Government* 1965 Chap. I; and J.L.J. Edwards *The Law Offices of the Crown* 1966 Chaps. 10 and 11.

9. 483 H. C. Deb. 5s. col. 679.

10. Mr. Blackburn returned to the charge in 1973 with a further (unsuccessful) attempt to compel the stricter enforcement of obscenity laws. *R.* v. Metropolitan Police Commissioner *ex parte* Blackburn (No. 3) 1973 2 W.L.R. 43.

11. E.g., on the meanings of "national origin" and "section of the public," see Ealing Borough Council v. Race Relations Board [1972] A.C. 342; Race Relations Board v. Charter [1973] 2 W.L.R. 299; Race Relations Board v. Applin [1973] Q.B. 815; Race Relations Board v. Dockers Labour Club and Institute [1974] 2 W.L.R. 166. At the time of writing an amended Race Relations Act has been introduced into Parliament, in part to reverse decisions in the courts on "national origin" and to cover discrimination by private clubs.

12. Cmd 4060 (1932) p. 80.
13. Report on the Council on Tribunals 1959, pp. 65-66.
14. In some cases it has been held that the giving of inadequate or unintelligible reasons does not comply with the statutory duty to give reasons. See Re Poyser and Mills' Arbitration [1964] 2 Q.B. 467 and Givaudan v. Minister of Housing and Local Government [1967] 1 W.L.R. 250. French Keir Developments Ltd. v. Secretary of State for the Environment (The *Times,* 15 October, 1976).
16. Conway v. Rimmer [1968] A.C. 910.
17. R. v. Gaming Board *ex parte* Benaim and Khaida [1970] 2 Q.B. 417 Norwich Pharmacal Co. v. Customs and Excise Commissioners [1972] 3 W.L.R. 870.
18. Departmental Committee on Section 2 of the Official Secrets Act, 1911 Cmnd. 5104 (1972).
19. *Introduction to the Study of the Law of the Constitution* (10th ed.) p. 193.
20. Ibid., p. 204. The citation from Pollock is from *Law of Torts* (8th ed. 1908) p. v.
21. *Law and Opinion in England* (2 ed. 1914) pp. xlv and xlviii.
22. Churchman v. J.S.S.C. *Times Law Rep.* 15 June 1973.
23. The right to picket does not imply a permission physically to obstruct persons or the highway. Piddington v. Bates [1961] 1 W.L.R. 162; Tynan v. Balmer [1967] 1 Q.B. 91; Hunt v. Broome [1973] 2 W.L.R. 773; Kavanagh v. Hiscock [1974] 2 W.L.R. 422.

PART II

3

DUE PROCESS

T. M. SCANLON [1]

In this paper I will offer a general account of how the absence of "due process" can give rise to legitimate claims against institutional actions. I will be concerned particularly to show in what ways claims to due process are grounded in moral principles of political right and how far they depend rather on strategic judgments about the prudent design of social institutions. My account will provide a demarcation of the area within which due process claims are appropriate—an area much broader than "state action"—and provide at least a rough framework for determining when given procedures are adequate responses to these claims. I will also offer an account of substantive due process and undertake to explain why it is that when a legal right to due process is recognized courts, in enforcing this right, will find themselves making substantive as well as merely procedural decisions.

The account I will offer sticks close to the truism that due process is concerned with protection against arbitrary decisions, and one can find a place in my account for many of the phrases that have been used in interpreting the Fifth and Fourteenth Amendments to the United States Constitution. But while I will have a certain

amount to say in the abstract about the role of courts in providing
and enforcing due process, my account is a philosophical and not a
legal one. It is grounded in a conception of the moral requirements
of legitimacy for social institutions and not on what the law of the
United States or any other country actually is. I hope that what I
have to say may be of some use in legal arguments about
constitutional rights to due process of law, but I have not
undertaken to defend my theory as an interpretation of the
constitution.

I

The requirement of due process is one of the conditions of the
moral acceptability of those institutions that give some people
power to control or intervene in the lives of others. Institutions
create such power in several ways. They do so directly by giving
some the authority to command others and providing the force to
compel obedience to these commands. Less directly, but no less
effectively, institutions give some people a measure of control over
others by securing their control over resources or opportunities that
are important ingredients in the kind of life that people in the
society want to live. I have referred to these forms of control in
terms that emphasize their negative and threatening aspects, but
they are an aspect of social life one could not reasonably seek to
avoid altogether. To begin with, some dependence of this kind is in
a trivial sense unavoidable. To the extent that any one person has
the right and ability to determine how some choice is to be made,
others are to that degree "subject to his will." In addition, nontrivial
forms of authority are important and valuable means to many
social goals.

But even if rights and powers giving some people a measure of
control over others must be a feature of any plausible system of
social institutions, the way in which these rights and powers are
distributed is one of the features of social institutions that is most
subject to moral criticism and most in need of justification.
Questions of due process become interesting only on the supposition
that such justifications can be given. The importance of due process
arises from the fact that these justifications are in general limited
and conditional. Even a person's rights to move his body and to

dispose of his possessions as he sees fit are limited by requirements that he not bring specified kinds of harm to others. More interestingly, the authority of public officials is, typically, not only limited (e.g., by their jurisdiction) but also conditional. Thus they are empowered not simply to disburse a certain benefit or impose a certain burden but rather to do so *provided* certain specified conditions are met. For example, the authority of a judge to order penalties or fines, and the authority to issue or revoke licenses are both of this form. Authority not tied to special justifying conditions is in fact quite rare. (Perhaps the presidential power to pardon is an example.)

This conditional character is typical not only of the authority of public officials but also of that of persons occupying positions of special power in nongovernmental institutions such as schools, colleges, and businesses. School administrators have the authority to suspend or expel students on academic or disciplinary grounds and to impose other disciplinary penalties. Employers have the right (absent specific contractual bars) to fire workers when this is required by considerations of economic efficiency, and perhaps also when it is necessary as a means of discipline within the firm. In each case, these limits and conditions on a given form of authority flow from the nature of the justification for that authority. The authority of school administrators and employers is presumably to be defended on the ground that it is crucial to the effective functioning of these enterprises.[2] But there would be no prospect of constructing on this basis a defense for unconditional authority to fire or suspend someone for any reason whatever; e.g., because you didn't like his looks, his politics, or his religion, or because he was unwilling to bribe you.

But once de facto power to suspend or fire is conferred, one may ask what reason there is to believe that it will not be exercised in these unjustifiable ways. Thus, beyond the requirement on institutions that the power they confer be morally justifiable, there is the further moral requirement that there be some effective guarantee that these powers will be exercised only within the limits and subject to the conditions implied by their justification. In some cases, nothing need be done to provide such a guarantee. It may happen that, given the motives and the scruples which those in a particular position of power can be expected to have, and given the structural features of their position (e.g., the competitive pressures active on them), there is little reason to expect that they will act outside their authority. Where this is not the case—when obvious temptations or even just clear opportunities for laxness or capriciousness exist—an effective counter may be provided by a system of retrospective justice, levying penalties for the improper use of power and requiring compensation for those injured.

Beyond (or in addition to) this, further guarantees may be provided by introducing special requirements on the way in which those who exercise power make their decisions. Due process is one version of this latter strategy. It aims to provide some assurance of nonarbitrariness by requiring those who exercise authority to justify their intended actions in a public proceeding by adducing reasons of the appropriate sort and defending these against critical attack. The idea of such proceedings presupposes, of course, publicly known and reasonably specific rules with respect to which official actions are to be justified.

The authority to decide whether the reasons advanced are adequate may be assigned to different persons or bodies by different procedures. If the grounds and limits of a given decision maker's authority are well known and taken seriously in a community, then even a hearing procedure that allows him to preside and pronounce the verdict may be a nonnegligible check on the arbitrary use of his power since he will presumably place some value on not being publicly seen to flout the accepted standards for the performance of his job. But in general the assurances provided by a system of due process will be credible only if there is the possibility of appeal to some independent authority which can invoke the coercive power of the state to support its decisions.

Appeal to the courts offers greater assurance against arbitrariness, in part, because of the expectation that the judge will be less a party to the original dispute than the decision maker himself, but also because a judge is presumed to have a greater commitment to an ideal of procedural justice and a greater long-term stake in his reputation as a maker of decisions that are well founded in the relevant rules and principles. At each stage in the appeals process other than the last, these factors of personal motivation will be supplemented by the more explicit threat of being overruled. When we reach the ultimate legal authority, of course, we will in practice be relying on personal commitment, pride, and aspiration alone and on the existence of a public conception of the ground and limits of this authority, which serves as a basis for public approbation or disapprobation of the way it is exercised.

II

Due process is only one of the strategies through which one may seek to avoid arbitrary power by altering the conditions under which decisions are made. It may be contrasted with strategies that seek to make power less arbitrary by making the motives with which it is exercised more benign; for example, by allowing decisions to be made by elected representatives of those principally affected. Rule by such elected representatives is an acceptably nonarbitrary form of authority in a given situation to the extent that it is reasonable to believe that the complex of motives under which representatives act—the desire to be reelected, the need for financial support, loyalty to and shared feelings with one's region or group, the desire to be a "good representative" in the generally accepted sense of this phrase, the desire to be esteemed in the society of representatives and politicians, etc.—will add up to produce decisions reasonably in accord with the rights and wishes of those governed.

As I have mentioned, the mechanisms of a system of due process also depends upon motives—e.g., on the professionalism of judges—but such a system need not in general attempt to influence the authority whose decisions it is supposed to control in favor of the interests of the affected parties. Indeed, the notion of due process is most often invoked in cases (such as the employment case discussed above, or cases of school or prison discipline) where it is assumed that the decision-making authority whose actions are to be checked will be moved (quite properly) by considerations largely separate from the interests of the persons most directly affected. The idea of a right to due process is thus much broader in application than that of a right to participation or representation; it involves the recognition of those subject to authority as entitled to demand justification for its uses and entitled to protection against its unjustified use but not necessarily as entitled to share in the making of decisions affecting them.[3]

The fact that imposition of due process requirements thus

involves minimal alteration in the established relations of power makes it a particularly easy remedy for courts to invoke. Its acceptability is also increased in a society like our own by the extraordinarily high public regard for legal institutions and the procedures that are typical of them. Given these facts one might expect that insofar as it falls to the judiciary to deal with important social conflicts the remedy of due process is likely to be over utilized.

I have not attempted to say what the *right* to due process is. The moral basis of my account of due process lies in something like a right, namely the idea that citizens have a legitimate claim against institutions which make them subject in important ways to the arbitrary power of others. But it is not easy to say in general when those who have such a claim are entitled specifically to what I have called a mechanism of due process. I described above a range of controls on the exercise of power extending from cases in which authority can be regarded as self-policing to systems of retrospective justice to systems of due process with increasing levels of judicial review.

Moral principles of political philosophy do not determine which of these mechanisms is required in any given case. This is a question of strategy that can be answered only on the basis of an analysis of the factors active in a particular setting. The situation is analogous to the case of representation. One might set forth as a principle of political philosophy that just institutions should provide means for people to participate effectively in decisions affecting them provided that power is distributed equally and that its exercise will not enable some to override the rights of others. But political philosophy can tell us little about what kinds of participatory and/or representative institutions will satisfy the requirement of effective and equal participation in a given case. The choice of suitable forms may depend on local tradition, the distribution of economic and social power in the society, the nature of other primary divisive conflicts, and other variables.

In deciding whether mechanisms of due process are required and in assessing the adequacy of particular mechanisms the main questions seem to be these:

(1)   How likely is it that a given form of power—if unchecked—will be used outside the limits of its justification?

(2) How serious are the harms inflicted by its misuse?

(3) Would due process be an effective check on the exercise of this power?

(4) Would the costs of a requirement of due process in cases of this kind be excessive? Is the additional effectiveness of due process over other forms of control worth the additional cost?

The costs at issue here will include, in addition to the delay of decisions and the costs of mounting the procedures themselves, the personal and social costs of depersonalizing decisions and reducing them to rules and procedures.

Due process, as I have characterized it, will be most effective where there exist reasonably clear, generally understood standards for exercise of the authority in question, standards which can serve as the background for public justification and defense of decisions. As the relevant standards—and even the starting points for arguments for and against the propriety of a given decision—become less and less clear, the constraints on the decision maker in a due process proceeding become progressively weaker, and the power of these decision makers itself comes to seem more and more arbitrary. The same thing may be true when the relevant standards—while quite precise—become less and less generally understood until finally they are the preserve of a small group including only the hearing examiners, their staff, and the main combatants.

The variation in the forms of due process mechanism that seem appropriate to different situations is not due solely to the different ways in which effective protection against arbitrary decisions can best be given. The procedures with which we are familiar in civil and criminal trials, disciplinary proceedings, and administrative hearings serve a variety of different functions in addition to the general one of providing protection against arbitrary power; and some of the features of these proceedings may be explained by these additional purposes. Thus, for example, many hearings are not merely fact-finding or rule-applying mechanisms; they also serve an important symbolic function as public expressions of the affected parties' right to demand that official acts be explained and justified. If the hearing is to serve this function, the procedures followed should be ones that take the complainants' objections seriously and place them on a par with the claims of authority. This provides an argument for adversary proceedings, for the right to counsel, and for the rights to call witnesses and cross-examine opposing witnesses which go beyond whatever advantages these procedures may have as mechanisms for ensuring a "correct outcome." [4] An argument of this kind is at its strongest in the case of a criminal trial or other proceedings in which a person is accused of wrongdoing. An accused person has an interest in having the opportunity to respond to the charges against him and to present what he takes to be the best defense of his action. This interest would not be met merely by ensuring that all the facts and the relevant legal arguments in the defendant's favor will somehow be brought before the court. There is a crucial difference between having these facts presented and having them presented as a defense by the accused or by someone speaking for him with his consent and participation. To the extent that this interest is a component in the rationale for the procedures of a criminal trial, it would be a mistake automatically to take these procedures as a model for what due process requires generally.

A different mix of purposes is represented in disciplinary proceedings in a school or university. Officials of an educational institution have, in addition to general duties to treat students coming before them fairly and not to use their power in an arbitrary manner, special fiduciary obligations to be concerned with its students' intellectual and personal needs.[5] It is therefore not sufficient merely that disciplinary proceedings follow clear and fair rules and that accused students be informed of their rights and given the opportunity to rebut charges against them. The institution may also be itself obligated (in a way that the state in a criminal trial is not) to investigate cases with the aim of uncovering evidence favorable to the defendant. It should also undertake to inform an accused student of the various alternatives open to him and counsel him in deciding what course to follow.[6] One would expect to see these special obligations reflected in differences between the procedures followed in cases of student discipline and in cases where faculty members or other employees face dismissal. But the requirements of *due process* in these cases are the same.[7]

III

I have described due process as one of the conditions for the moral legitimacy of power-conferring institutions. Suppose that a right to due process as I have described it were to be recognized as a legal right within a given legal system. What might a court be deciding in determining in a certain case that this right had been violated? There seem to be three possibilities:

(1) The court may decide that, given the nature of the authority in question, the nature of the harms likely to result from its improper use, and the likelihood of its being used improperly, procedural safeguards are required that were not followed in the given case. Here the court is appraising the decision-making process from the outside in its capacity as the guarantor of the legal right to (procedural) due process.

(2) On the other hand, the court may decide that while the procedures followed in the given case were formally adequate the reasoning accepted in these tribunals was faulty or in any case insufficient to justify the decision in question on the required grounds. Here the court is playing a role as one of the appeals stages in an established system of due process. Whether judicial authority to make decisions of this kind is required as a deterrent against tendentious verdicts at earlier stages is itself a question of procedural due process of type (1).

(3) Finally, the court may decide that, while the procedures followed in the given case were formally adequate and the reasoning offered in support of decisions unexceptionable, the rules that were applied in these proceedings must themselves be rejected because they exceed the assigned authority of the decision maker in question. Such rules (e.g., the disciplinary code of a school, prison, or labor union) might be struck down on the ground that their enforcement would infringe some specific constitutional guarantee (e.g., some First Amendment right), but this is just one way in which it might be shown that a given rule exceeded the authority of the agency in question. This same conclusion could also be reached by arguing that, given the nature of the institution in question, the given rule could not possibly be taken as part of its writ.

This third case is substantive due process as I understand it. Substantive due process decisions in their most characteristic and controversial form are those based not on any explicit constitutional limitation but rather on appeal to the nature of the authority whose power is in question. The notion of the nature of an institution is one likely to raise legal and philosophical eyebrows. It appears to be an attempt to resolve legal or moral issues by appeal to definitions, and it is apt to provoke questions as to where such definitions are supposed to come from. Surely, it will be urged, social institutions do not have "essences" which can be discovered and used as the basis for authoritative resolution of philosophical or legal controversies. But an important social institution enabling some to wield significant power over others is unlikely to exist without some public rationale—at the very least an account put forth for public consumption of why this institution is legitimate and rational. This will include some conception of the social goals the institution is taken to serve and of the way in which the authority exercised by participants in the institution is rationally related to those goals. If the institution is not merely rationalized by those wishing to maintain its power, but in fact generally accepted as legitimate then some conception of this sort will be fairly generally accepted in the society and rendered coherent with other aspects of the prevailing views. Such a conception may be more or less clearly articulated. It is almost certain to be vague and incomplete in some areas and may be gradually shifting and changing. But something of this kind will almost surely exist and can serve as a basis for argument.

In an argument of the kind I have in mind, an appeal to the current conception of an institution—even in its clearest and most explicit features—need not be final. One must also be prepared to defend the social goals appealed to as in fact valuable and to defend the forms of authority defined by the institution as rational means to those goals and as acceptable given the costs they involve. When a defense of this kind is given within the context of a due process proceeding, the social goals and judgments of relative value to which it appeals must themselves be defended by appeal to contemporary standards (or by an argument about what standards in the relevant area ought to be given other beliefs and values people in the society hold.) [8] But while the limits of debate are in this sense set by prevailing views, the fact that the dominant conception of an institution is not taken at face value but must be shown to be coherent and consistent with other social values provides a measure of independence and allows for criticism through which the prevailing conception of an institution can be extended, clarified and altered.

Appeals of this sort to the nature of social institutions lie behind many quite convincing commonsense political arguments, and even though our conception of an institution is often partly in doubt and in places controversial such appeals can yield quite definite conclusions. It seems to me clear, for example, that a labor union could not use its power of expulsion to collect dues to be used to support a particular religious group but that it could, at least in some cases, compel dues members to pay to support a political candidate or party. And this conclusion follows, I think, from our conception of the nature and purposes of a union rather than from any specific constitutional or statutory limitation.

Such arguments by appeal to the nature of an institution occupy a kind of gray area between considerations of rights and considerations of good policy. Take, for example, the question of academic freedom. It seems to me that the doctrine of academic freedom has its basis in the idea that the purposes of academic institutions are the pursuit and teaching of the truth about certain recognized academic subjects as defined by the prevailing canons of those subjects.[9] Relative to this conception of the purposes of academic institutions, it is rational that they be organized in such a way that the primary motivation of scholars and teachers will be to report and to teach whatever appears to them to be the truth about their subjects. In particular, if teachers and scholars are subject to power which is likely to be used to influence them to teach and report doctrines favored by certain people whether or not these doctrines appear to them to be the truth about their subjects, then it is rational (provided the costs are not too high) to shield them from this power.

The doctrine of academic freedom is generally defended as one such shield. The restraints it imposes on the authority of administrators and trustees over teachers are directly tied to a particular conception of the purposes of an academic institution. They would make no sense (or only a different and more limited kind of sense) as applied to a religious school whose main purpose was the dissemination of a particular faith or to a school founded for the purpose of offering an education which included a nonstandard version of some recognized subject, e.g., biology without evolution or some unorthodox version of history.

As I have described it, academic freedom appears more as a counsel for the rational design and wise administration of certain kinds of academic institutions than as a matter of right. But such a counsel of rationality may be transformed into a right through the application of a general moral or legal principle of due process, limiting the authority of academic officials to those powers and prerogatives that are consistent with and rationally related to the rationale for and purposes of their institutions. To defend the right of academic freedom so conceived, one must be prepared to defend the relevant kind of academic institutions as worth having and their activities as worth the costs of safeguarding them through this means.

Decisions of substantive due process and decisions of procedural due process both involve appeal to a conception of the institutions in question, their rationale and purposes. In making a procedural due process decision of the first type described above, a court must estimate the risk that the power exercised by an institution will be used in ways that go beyond its authority. The court must therefore employ, as a standard, some conception of what that authority is. In making a decision of substantive due process, however, a court goes further and appeals to such a conception in order itself to declare a particular exercise of power illegitimate.

The distinction between substantive due process decisions and procedural due process decisions may seem to coincide with that between judicial scrutiny of rule-making authority and judicial scrutiny of rule-applying authority, but the two distinctions are not the same. Rule-making authority may come under judicial scrutiny on grounds falling clearly within what I have called procedural due process. There may be serious doubts whether, in a particular situation, given rule-making power will be used only in a nonarbitrary fashion, and special procedures for the making of rules may be required to insure this. What is special about substantive due process scrutiny is not that it is directed to the limits of rule-making authority but rather that in exercising it courts directly apply a conception of what the rules of a particular institution may or may not be.

The potentially controversial grounds on which substantive due process decisions may be based—a conception of the nature and purposes of a particular institution—are thus already presupposed by decisions of procedural due process. Nonetheless, decisions of substantive due process deserve to be considered a more controversial form of judicial activity, for in making them courts exercise a further and more intrusive form of authority over the institutions concerned. Whether it is proper for courts to exercise this kind of authority, is itself a question of procedural due process [type (1)] in the broad sense I have described. In its favor, one might maintain that judicial oversight of rule-making and rule applying procedures, however careful, is empty as a protection against arbitrary authority if the authorities in question are free to make and apply whatever rules they wish. This would be an overstatement. Strong traditions, the opinion of a public informed by a clear conception of the limits of the authority in question, and the likely resistance of those affected by arbitrary rules all may provide some check on rule-making authority, a check whose effectiveness may be enhanced by an enforced requirement of appropriate rule-making procedures. But these same factors also provide a check on the manner in which rules are applied, and this check is not always sufficient, even when the relevant procedural safeguards are observed. This is shown by the fact that in at least some cases we think that courts should have the power not only to require due process at the level of original decisions but also to reverse the results of such procedures when they are clearly misapplications of the relevant rules. Thus the argument that substantive due process is sometimes called for is parallel to the argument that procedural due process of type (2) described above is sometimes called for.

It is very implausible to suggest that, while the threat of arbitrariness for which the second form of procedural due process is a possible remedy often occurs, the corresponding threat of misuse of rule-making authority never exists. But even where this threat exists, it is a further question whether substantive judicial review is called for, or even effective, as a protection against it.

One reason for doubting its effectiveness rests on skepticism about arguments by appeal to the nature of an institution. If such arguments are thought to be insubstantial rhetoric—not arguments at all but a mode of discourse in which there are virtually no useful standards and in which almost anything can be defended with equal plausibility—then a process of review based on such arguments would itself constitute a highly arbitrary form of authority, perhaps as arbitrary as that which is sought to be checked. I have expressed above, and tried to defend by example, the view that for most significant social institutions "the nature of the institution" is something one can argue about in a rational way. But even if this is conceded, there may be objections to empowering judges to strike down rules or other enactments of, e.g., private associations on the basis of the court's judgment that these fall outside of and cannot be defended by appeal to the current conception of the nature of the organizations in question. It may be thought preferable to allow organizations (through means meeting procedural due process standards) to define and alter their own purposes and rationale. Crudely described, what is at issue here seems to be a question of balancing—of finding the proper trade-off between the goal of protecting people from arbitrary regulations and requirements and that of allowing them to associate for common purposes and define the terms of their own association. I will have more to say about this problem and about the claims of institutional autonomy in the next section.

IV

I have argued that the basis of due process requirements lies in a condition on the legitimacy of power-conferring institutions. Since the state is only one such institution among many, it follows that the range of possible application of due process requirements is much broader than the extent of "state action." This conclusion seems to me to be in accord with our intuitions about particular cases. In considering rights to due process in cases of suspension or expulsion of students, for example, it seems arbitrary to distinguish between institutions on the basis of whether or not they receive state or federal funds. This seems arbitrary, first, because the very serious dislocation of a student's career which in our society can result from expulsion from college is not significantly different in the two cases. Nor is the likelihood of arbitrary action by administrators acting in the absence of procedural safeguards less in one case than the other. Given the importance attached to gaining admission to college, and the lack of real bargaining power on the part of applicants, student's freedom of choice in deciding what college to attend can scarcely be expected to serve as an effective check on administrator's authority, and the decision to attend a particular school can scarcely be taken as authorization of whatever powers the administrators of that school may wish to claim. At any rate, there seems to be little difference with respect to these matters between private and public institutions.

But while judicial enforcement of due process requirements does not seem to me to be limited to cases of state action, there does seem to me to be an area of activity, which might be called the sphere of purely voluntary organizations, within which due process requirements apply only with reduced force. In this section I will attempt to characterize this area more clearly and examine the ways in which the claims of due process seem to be reduced.[10] I will also indicate how the notion of state action retains some content and force even though it does not mark the outer limits of due process enforcement.

Even given the similarities noted above, the difference between state-supported institutions and private institutions might still be crucial for due process if the costs of imposing due process requirements on the two kinds of institutions were significantly different. But, at least as long as we confine our attention to procedural due process, and as long as we are concerned with colleges and universities in the traditional sense, this is not the case. One can imagine a religious school in which the tenets of the faith required relations of authority which would be entirely inconsistent with due process requirements of the usual kind. In such a case, the cost of imposing due process rights would be quite high, amounting to the serious alteration, if not the destruction, of valued aspects of institutional life. A school of this kind would be extremely special in offering not merely education of the kind required for the careers at which most members of the society aim but rather a special form of life chosen for its own sake by those few who happen to value it. Those who attend such an institution thus accept its requirements voluntarily in a stronger sense than those who accept the requirements of, say, Princeton or the University of Michigan or Harvard Law School, institutions which are principal means of access to some of the most highly desired positions in the society.

But as far as the weakening of procedural due process requirements is concerned, it is the former feature—the direct clash between the forms of due process and the goals of the institution—rather than its high degree of voluntariness that is crucial. For even where institutions are thoroughly voluntary, if the costs to individuals of the misuse of official authority are high and the chance of such misuse significant then there will be a prima facie case for procedural due process safeguards. In the present example, this prima facie case is overridden by the unusually disruptive consequences of due process forms.

In voluntary institutions of this kind, it is at least partly accurate to see the authority of institutional officers to order, discipline, and expel members as arising from a contract, and to see the limits and conditions of this authority as fixed by the terms on which members (voluntarily) enter. Since even full voluntariness at time of entry into membership does not preclude great inequality in the power unilaterally to interpret and act on the terms of the membership "agreement," the need to impose procedural due process is not eliminated by the voluntary nature of the institution.

But substantive due process is very different. It amounts to the power of a court to arrive at an independent judgment of the limits and conditions of the authority of the group and its officers, a judgment based on a conception of the nature of the institution that need not be determined by the understanding of its members. Where an institution is truly voluntary, this represents a serious inroad into the freedom of individuals to enter into such arrangements as they wish and to define the terms of their own association.

But few of the most significant institutions of society are voluntary in this strong sense. When institutions are not fully voluntary, there are limits on the degree to which it is permissible to allow present members or present officers freely to determine the conditions under which others may have access to the benefits their institution provides. These limits are in part determined by the nature of the institution in the sense described above.

Let me return to the case of traditional colleges and universities. Some limits on changes in university requirements and policies may arise from the requirement of fair warning and the obligation to comply with the legitimate exceptions of students already enrolled. In determining what expectations are (or were) legitimate, we may appeal to "the idea of a university" as it was understood at the time these students enrolled. Here appeal to the nature of an institution helps us to fill in a vague or incompletely articulated agreement. But the idea of a university may be invoked in a stronger sense in setting the limits on requirements for admission or requirements that are to apply only to students who enroll in the future.

It seems at the outset that almost any requirements of this kind would be immune from substantive due process review provided they were plausibly related to normal educational purposes or could be brought under the heading of educational experimentation. For requirements that are evidently idle or perverse, the matter is not so clear. I am thinking here of such things as a policy of restricting admission to persons over six feet tall or a university policy requiring freshmen to speak only when spoken to and to serve as lackeys to older students and faculty.

If we think that courts should not intervene to review and possibly strike down such policies, this is presumably because we feel that freedom to try out new and different educational forms is a good thing, that competitive pressures between institutions will curb excesses, and that the existence of many comparable alternative institutions prevents idiosyncratic policies adopted by one school from imposing a very high cost on would-be applicants. Such considerations are crucial to the case for nonintervention given the place universities occupy as means of access to the most desired positions in our society. If these conditions should fail to hold—if certain restrictions on admission unrelated to plausible academic purposes should cease to be merely the idiosyncrasy of a few particular institutions among many and should come to be quite general, thereby effectively excluding a group of people from university education and all those careers to which it is the main avenue of approach—then the case for judicial intervention on substantive due process grounds would be strong.

This is what has happened in cases of discrimination. What once was or might have been an idle preference which some institutions could be allowed to cater to—like a preference for people over six feet tall—comes to have unacceptable consequences once it becomes a general pattern. This preference then ceases to be an acceptable ground for admissions decisions. Antidiscrimination judgments of this kind can be seen as substantive due process decisions based on arguments about the nature of an institution in the sense discussed above. The judgment that university admissions officers cannot follow a white-only policy is based on the judgment that a

university cannot take being an all-white institution as one of its
defining purposes. It cannot do so because the cost of allowing
educational (and other) institutions so to define themselves is, in the
circumstances, unacceptable. What is the cost? It is, first, that a
whole group of people will be effectively blocked from important
areas of social life. Of course, any set of criteria—if uniformly
employed by all the institutions in a given category (e.g., all
universities)—will act as a bar to some "group," namely those who
fail to meet these particular criteria. Perhaps any such exclusion,
when it is sufficiently uniform, always represents a cost which must
be considered. But it is crucial to the costs typical of cases striking us
as discrimination that the criteria of exclusion express attitudes that
are demeaning to those towards whom they are directed. Once
circumstances arise in which such attitudes are widespread and
have been generally acted upon—once, that is, discrimination of a
certain kind has become a problem—the cost of allowing institutions
to define themselves as excluding the group discriminated against
become very high. This may provide grounds for refusing to allow
institutions so to define themselves even in areas of national life in
which such a definition would pose no threat of systematic
exclusion. For example, it would not be acceptable to form a lily-
white professional sports team in 1975 even though this would pose
no threat to black athletes.

The conclusion of a substantive due process argument of this kind
barring institutional discrimination against blacks is not that
institutional policies must be "color blind." A university admitting
blacks only would not be objectionable on the grounds I have
mentioned: there is at present no risk of whites being excluded from
higher education generally or from any important range of institutions within it. A policy of excluding whites need not be based on
antiwhite attitudes, and, even if it were, the threat posed to their
self-respect and standing in the society would be insignificant.
Finally, an institution with such a policy could conceivably be
thought to serve significant cultural value. (A similar asymmetry
exists in the United States of 1975 between institutions excluding
women and institutions for women only.)

I have suggested that the conclusion of a substantive due process
argument against discrimination is to be stated negatively as the
judgment that there are certain purposes which institutions may not

be allowed to adopt as part of their defining rationale or to appeal to in justifying their policies.[11] It might be suggested that such judgments could as well be stated positively as, for example, the judgment that universities must employ only admission criteria rationally related to their central academic purpose. I want to make two comments about this alternative formulation.

First, if this requirement is understood narrowly, as the claim that since the central purpose of universities is education, they must employ academic excellence, demonstrated or projected, as their sole criterion for admission, then the proposal is one that has never been imposed and should not be. Obviously, colleges and universities should be able to choose their own special character and be free in choosing students to supplement strictly academic criteria with other desiderata related to the kind of institution they wish to be. Substantive due process decisions which ruled out this kind of variation, even to the extent of requiring that nonacademic criteria be restricted to a tie-breaking role in admissions, would be mistaken. This shows, I think, that the correct arguments must be understood negatively—as ruling out certain purposes and standards rather than demanding others.

Second, it is a mistake to think that criteria of academic excellence are themselves sacrosanct. I have stressed the fact that universities are gateways to the most generally desired positions in our society. Criteria of academic success bear some relation to plausible efficiency-based criteria for selection to these positions. But this connection certainly can be, and for many positions no doubt commonly is, overrated. In any event, the general use of standard academic criteria for admission to colleges, universities and professional schools has costs, both in tending to preserve some forms of discrimination and in creating its own form of stratification, and these have to be weighed against its value as a means to increased efficiency. I am not here arguing that this balancing comes out against academic criteria. I am only pointing out that the standard of merit which they represent, while it may have great appeal both for its own sake and as a hard-won refuge from arbitrary and discriminating practices, still has to be defended as worth the costs it involves.[12]

Let me summarize the discussion of this section. There is an important distinction between those institutions of a society that are

truly voluntary and those that, because they are the means of access
to benefits desired by most in that society, are so important to life in
the society that their power cannot plausibly be justified merely by
saying that anyone who does not wish to deal with them on their
own terms may simply refrain from dealing with them. Obviously,
an institution that is truly voluntary at one time can cease to be so
at another as conditions and mores change. Perhaps colleges and
universities were once truly voluntary in our society; now they are
not. Procedural due process requirements apply to voluntary as well
as to nonvoluntary institutions, but for substantive due process the
distinction is crucial. The authority that truly voluntary institutions
have over their members can plausibly be seen as derived from
consent, and their more general justification lies simply in the value
of allowing individuals to associate for whatever purposes they may
choose.[13]

But as an institution ceases to be truly voluntary and comes to be
the mechanism for providing some important good, some further
justification for its power is required. This justification typically
rests on the institution's role in providing the good in question, and
the authority of individuals within the institution must then be
defended as part of a rational and acceptable mechanism for
providing that good. Thus, in the case of nonvoluntary institutions,
there arises both a case for and a basis for criticism on substantive
due process grounds. But this does not mean that a court would be
justified in imposing on any such institution its conception of what
is required by the central function of that institution. Institutional
autonomy and variety among institutions providing the same good
remain important values. Even where institutions of a certain kind
are not fully voluntary, the ability of individuals to choose among
various institutions of this kind may constitute an adequate
safeguard against capricious restrictions or unwarranted requirements. But when the exercise of institutional autonomy leads to
systematic exclusion or to the imposition of other unacceptable
social costs then judicial intervention may be called for to delimit
the purposes with respect to which institutional policies are to be
justified.

A remark on "state action." The state is a nonvoluntary
institution of the strongest kind. Everyone in the society is subject to
its requirements, and most are required to support its activities

whether they wish to or not. The activities of the state, however, are varied. Some of these, when considered with respect to their particular purposes, are in themselves what I have called nonvoluntary institutions (state-supported universities are an example); others are more akin to voluntary institutions (national parks and the support of scholarly research seem to me to fall into this category).[14]

But all of these activities, since they are supported by tax money, are the undertakings of a particular nonvoluntary institution. Accordingly, they are subject to conditions and limitations flowing from the nature of this institution, conditions and limitations that may not apply to other (voluntary or nonvoluntary) organizations pursuing the same purposes (e.g., nonpublic universities, private recreational areas, or foundations for the support of scholarly research). Thus, for example, tax-supported institutions may be barred from adopting religious or political activities as part of their function even though comparable private institutions may do so, and tax-supported institutions may be subject to especially stringent requirements of fairness in the distribution of their benefits. These conditions and limitations could be enforced under the heading of substantive due process as applied to the particular nonvoluntary institution of the state. But, since the state is only one nonvoluntary institution among many, this is a special case of substantive due process. To show that substantive due process applies to a given institution one need not show that it is an activity of the state but only that it, like the state, should be recognized as not truly voluntary.

V

Probably the most controversial substantive due process decisions are those in which a court overturns the action of a legislature. According to the general framework presented in Section III, such a decision could take either of two forms: the piece of legislation might conflict with a specific constitutional prohibition or it might be found to exceed the authority of the legislature in a more general sense as determined by an argument about the nature of legislative authority. Decisions of the first kind are, in themselves, relatively uncontroversial; although the way in which I have presented them may seem odd insofar as it suggests that any instance of judicial review is an example of substantive due process. I will return to this point. Decisions of the second kind are subject to the two objections to substantive due process discussed above—skepticism about arguments appealing to the "nature" of an institution and the belief that institutional autonomy is preferable to the imposition of judicial authority—which apply here in slightly modified form and with apparent added strength.

The first objection appears to be strengthened because the question at issue has become not merely whether there is some ground on which claims about the nature of an institution (in this case the nature of the legislature and its power) can rationally be established but rather whether such claims can be established by appeals to and interpretation of the Constitution. After all, it is the Constitution which is supposed to define the limits of governmental authority, and which therefore ought to be the only ground on which a court can delimit that authority. The second objection is also strengthened, since what is to be overridden by a substantive due process decision is now not merely the desire of some small group of people to be allowed to associate for their own purposes but a decision of the legislature which, after all, is supposed to be the political voice of all the people.

If we were to stipulate for the moment that the due process clauses of the Constitution can be taken to require due process in the sense I have outlined, then we might take a short way with the first objection. For on this assumption substantive due process arguments of the kind I have described would be, in a formal sense, arguments about what the Constitution requires just as much as, say, arguments about freedom of speech are: in each case there is a brief constitutional formula. In both cases, the subject at issue concerns the distribution of authority (in the case of the First Amendment, authority to regulate expression, in the other case, authority more generally). In neither case does the Constitution literally specify what constitutes an acceptable system of authority of the relevant kind. Thus, in applying either formula, a court must be working with some conception of authority not explicitly supplied by the Constitution, and it must defend these conceptions as tenable under prevailing conditions, arguing by appeal to the

Constitution and to generally accepted principles of political morality.[15]

There are, of course, a number of differences between the two cases I have just compared. One particularly relevant here is the difference in scope of the two principles. Freedom of expression is a fairly specific question, and only one of many with which the Constitution deals. But substantive due process, as I have described it, deals with the basis and bounds of authority in all branches of government (and even outside of it), i.e., with the subject matter of the Constitution as a whole. So it seems that either substantive due process arguments are just arguments about what the rest of the Constitution as a whole requires, in which case the due process clauses add nothing to the rest of the Constitution beyond procedural guarantees, or else the authority to make substantive due process decisions opens the door to general theoretical argument about what the powers of government ought to be, i.e., to judicial revision and extension of the Constitution.

Obviously the Constitution, which embodies fundamental political principles of our society, plays a central role in substantive due process arguments as I have described them. But in order to decide which of the alternatives just presented follows from my view one would have to know how far the forms of argument I have described are included within an adequate account of the methods of constitutional interpretation. For this one would require a general theory of constitutional adjudication, which I cannot provide.[16]

But arguments against substantive due process decisions and in favor of judicial modesty vis-à-vis legislative judgments have often been put forward not just as arguments about what our Constitution and legal traditions require but as arguments in political theory about what constitutes a proper distribution of authority in a democratic system.[17] So considered, these arguments fall within the framework I have been presenting: As I have already remarked, the question they are concerned with is a question of procedural due process of type (1) (as indeed are all questions about the propriety of various forms of judicial review). These arguments may be approached within my framework by considering the four questions presented above, these being (1) the likelihood of misuse [18] of the power in question; (2) the magnitude of the harms involved; (3) the degree to which substantive due process review would offer an improvement, and (4) the costs involved in invoking it.

Questions of types (1) and (2), about the likelihood of legislative excess and the degree to which legislative self-restraint can be relied upon, play some role in arguments against substantive due process, as do questions of type (4), concerned mainly with the loss of popular sovereignty to a dictatorial judiciary. But the most prominent role has been played by questions of type (3): is substantive due process review itself an acceptably nonarbitrary form of authority? This question divides into two: Are there acceptably clear standards for substantive due process arguments? And is there sufficient reason to think that courts will be held to these standards in making their decisions? Here the relation between "interpretation of the Constitution" and what I have called "argument about the nature of an institution" comes to be of putative importance as a matter of political theory as well as of law. For the idea behind some arguments against substantive due process in this more extended form seems to be that judicial review is an acceptably nonarbitrary form of authority only insofar as it consists in the application of reasonably specific constitutional formulas.

This idea may sometimes be motivated by the view that in reaching substantive due process decisions a court must either be (a) applying some relatively clear constitutional formula; or (b) registering what it takes to be prevailing public opinion; or (c) enacting into law its own personal philosophical views. It is then maintained that, since (c) is unacceptably arbitrary and (b) something better done by an elective representative body than by a court, (a) represents the only acceptable alternative. The strength of this conclusion depends, of course, on how the notion of "application" as used in (a) is understood. I cannot here go into the question of whether there is a plausible interpretation of (a) that would encompass what is generally accepted as legitimate constitutional adjudication in non-due process areas yet exclude the kind of reasoning I have described in discussing substantive due process. I have maintained above that if (a) is interpreted narrowly, then (a), (b), and (c) do not exhaust the relevant alternatives. It is possible to argue rationally about the acceptable distribution of authority in society, and the requirement that a court resolve issues by engaging in public debate of this kind may in some instances be a less arbitrary method of decision than the alternative of unrestrained legislative authority.

Of course, if courts have the authority to reach decisions on this ground, it is likely that they will sometimes do it wrongly. But one cannot infer from the fact that certain decisions are egregiously wrong that they would best be avoided by the adoption of a formal principle (e.g., a principle of judicial modesty) barring courts from undertaking such decisions at all. Such a principle is analogous to a formal principle of legislative behavior, say, one requiring representatives to vote the expressed wishes of their constituents or, alternatively, permitting them to vote their own consciences. Individual decisions can be outstandingly wrong on substantive grounds without violating any such formal principle.[19] Such a principle has to be argued for on general grounds of the kind just discussed by showing that, given the conditions under which decisions are made, the pressures on decision makers and the methods open to them, the adoption of the principle is a needed curb on arbitrariness or a valuable contribution to the efficiency or reliability of the process.

Rather than pursue this general controversy any further, let me close by considering one special case of the argument for judicial modesty. On my view, substantive due process decisions involve an element of balancing. In reaching such a decision a court may often have to decide, e.g., whether the instrumental value of allowing an institution to operate in a certain way or to pursue a particular purpose justifies allowing it to exercise a certain form of authority despite the costs of its doing so. It is often maintained that such questions are ones which a representative body is particularly designed to resolve, and that a court, in undertaking to reweigh a balancing decision previously arrived at by the legislature, is either inefficiently undertaking to act as a better barometer of public feeling than the legislature is or else placing its own preferences above those of the people as a whole in a way that is repugnant to democratic principles. I want to maintain, against this argument, that questions properly resolved by balancing come in different forms, and that for some balancing questions there is both an acceptable method of judicial determination and a reason why this method should be preferred to purely legislative resolution.

In the sense in which the term "balancing" is used in most legal (and some philosophical) theory, almost anything can be "balanced" against almost anything else. With no claim to exhaustiveness (or even to mutual exclusiveness), let me roughly distinguish three different forms of decision making in which competing considerations are balanced against one another. The first, which I will call "aggregative balancing," is the form typical of traditional utilitarian arguments. In this form, the sum of the advantages of those who may be expected to gain from a particular act or policy is compared to the sum of the disadvantages of those who will lose by it. It is an essential mark of aggregative balancing that the outcome can always be influenced by altering the *number* of people on each side, e.g., by sufficiently increasing the gainers or decreasing the losers.

One method of individual decision making that is parallel to aggregative balancing as a method of social choice might be called "individual probabilistic balancing." Here a single person, when faced with a choice between alternative actions leading to uncertain outcomes, considers, for each alternative, the sum of the values for him of the outcomes associated with that alternative, discounted in each case by the probabilities he assigns to these outcomes actually occurring. He then chooses the alternative with the greatest sum of values. Thus, for example, a person considering the desirability from his point of view of various policies concerning police searches may take into account, for each policy, the contribution that policy will make to his safety balanced against the negative value he attaches to being searched, this discounted by the likelihood under that policy of his being subjected to such a search. If, as may be the case in this example, a large number of people think it extremely unlikely that the disadvantageous consequences of a given policy will actually accrue to them, while this probability is much higher for a certain much smaller group, then, if each person reaches his decision on the basis of individual probabilistic balancing and the group decision is made by majority vote, the result is likely to be the same as if aggregative balancing were used.

I suggest that there are questions which, intuitively, strike us as questions of balancing but for which such aggregative arguments do not strike us as appropriate. They are not appropriate, for example, as a way of deciding where the line between reasonable and unreasonable searches and seizures is to be drawn. Surely this line *is* arrived at by a kind of balancing, and this is a balancing which involves the relative strengths of people's interests. This is shown by the fact that, as customs and patterns of life change, it may become proper to draw this line differently; the difference reflecting changes in the value people place on keeping various areas of their lives free from intervention.

But neither aggregative considerations nor estimates of probability are relevant to the kind of balancing that is involved here. To strike the relevant kind of balance, a person must ask himself not what his chances are of being searched, but what *he* would accept as adequate justification for having a certain intervention into his life *actually* take place.

Let me call this "personal balancing." Here we are typically balancing, on the one hand, the importance of the benefits to be gained by allowing officials to exercise a certain power, e.g., the power to carry out searches under specific conditions. Determination of this value may involve some aggregation, since we are concerned not with what will be gained by allowing a search to be carried out on a single particular occasion but the value of having such search power in general.[20] On the other hand, we have the value to *an* individual of being free from this kind of invasion. Here we are dealing not with the value to any particular individual but with a "normal" value– the value most people in the society would assign to being free from such searches.

If we were all perfect utilitarians, then perhaps the question posed in personal balancing is one we would settle by aggregative balancing. But utilitarianism is not an adequate account of our normal outlook. There is certainly an area of public policy choices within which aggregative considerations are generally thought, perhaps correctly, to have a dominant role. It seems appropriate, for example, that the goal of bringing the greatest benefit to the greatest number should guide decisions as to how funds available for medical research are to be allocated among the campaigns against various diseases. But a particularly high ratio of benefits to burdens would not, I think, generally be taken as in and of itself sufficient to justify a policy of compulsory organ donation (with monetary compensation) or a policy giving medical authorities the right to compel participation in (not at all dangerous but somewhat unpleasant) medical experiments.

Now there is no reason why legislatures could not reach judgments of the nonaggregative kind I have been calling personal balancing. But there is good evidence for thinking that they characteristically operate in a fashion more likely to yield aggregative judgments. Certainly this seems to be true of the behavior of many legislatures in civil liberties matters. But, even given well-founded suspicion of legislative judgments in areas where personal balancing is called for, a case for giving final judgment in these areas to the courts requires some account of how judges are equipped to do better.

What a court must ask in these cases is whether the benefits that are taken as grounds for a particular exercise of authority are really sufficient to justify it, given the value people generally set on being free from interventions of the kind in question. In determining what this value is, judges need not refer primarily to their own tastes and values. Ample evidence is available in the lengths to which people generally go in their private lives to protect themselves against such interventions, the ways in which they react when they suffer them, and the kinds of legal remedies (claims for damages, etc.) that they consider appropriate. When this evidence makes it clear that the value placed on being free from interventions of the given kind is indeed very high, then a court has an objective basis on which to claim that the authority to carry out such interventions cannot be justified by marginal considerations of social advantage (e.g., the expectation of a slight increase in convictions for certain crimes). An argument of this form would seem to me to support, for example, due process decisions of the kind sometimes based on the test of "conduct that shocks the conscience" while avoiding the subjective aura of that slogan. What is relevant is not that a given exercise of authority (e.g., certain searches) outrages a judge, but rather that it should outrage anyone because the grounds on which it purports to be justified manifestly fail to match the value we ourselves demonstrably place on being free from such interventions.

Arriving at a judgment by the method I have suggested is not the same thing as making an estimate of public opinion. Public opinion may clearly be that the law in question should be passed. In the kind of argument I am suggesting a court would offer evidence for a claim about the value most people demonstrably do set on the sanctity of the relevant aspects of their lives and argue that, given what this value is, the proffered justification for the law in question does not hold up. The conclusion to be drawn is that public opinion and the judgment of the legislature reflected an unacceptable willingness to set a lower value on the concerns of the assignable minority who would suffer from this law than they do on their own, i.e., to engage in aggregative balancing in a case in which this is not an appropriate method.

What is the area within which it is proper for a court to look behind expressed preferences and make judgments of this sort? One answer is that it consists of those cases in which the burden of a piece of legislation is being borne by a clearly identifiable minority that is unlikely to be able to defend itself effectively in legislative decision making (the classical "discrete and insular minority" [21]); but before this criterion becomes applicable one must, on the view I have sketched, already have determined that the question at issue is one of balancing and that it is one for which personal balancing is the required form. But which questions are these?

Here I have no clear-cut answer. One natural suggestion is that personal balancing is required where rights are at issue, but I am unsatisfied with this answer for several reasons. First, some issues of rights are not questions of balancing at all but rather arguments of principle which mark the limits of permissible balancing. Second, within these limits it is not clear that every question of balancing that concerns the subject matter of a recognized right is one for which purely aggregative methods are inappropriate. It may be, for example, that "the greatest happiness of the greatest number" is a proper ground for settling some policy questions about the regulation of expression but not the proper ground for others. Obviously this question of limits—as well as the definition of personal balancing itself—require further clarification before this distinction can be considered an adequate theoretical device. I offer it here in a tentative way as an example of how the judicial balancing that would form a part of substantive due process decisions as I have described them might be distinguished from the kinds of balancing properly reserved to legislatures.

I have tried here to give a general account of due process and to show how much of what seems to fall under this heading can be traced to a single intuitive idea—the unacceptability of arbitrary power—which constitutes its moral foundation. In giving an exposition and anatomy of the idea of due process as I understand it, I have probably given more emphasis to the appeal of this notion than to its problems and dangers. (This is particularly true of my discussion of substantive due process.) This emphasis is perhaps the natural tendency in a theoretical discussion, where intellectual coherence is an overriding goal and where relatively little can be said about questions of strategy and political judgment. The fact that the notion of due process is so situated as naturally to serve as a point of conflict between the pure demands of justificatory coherence and the real world of political institutions is no doubt one reason why this notion continues to be a subject of interest and an object of intense controversy.

NOTES

1. In revising this paper I have benefited from the responses of the commentators and discussants at the meeting at which the first version of the paper was delivered and from comments by members of the Society for Ethical and Legal Philosophy and members of Ronald Dworkin's seminar on the philosophy of law, all of whom heard later versions. I am grateful to the members of these audiences for their patience and help, and especially to Bruce Ackerman and Ronald Dworkin for many helpful discussions on the subject of this article.

2. Of course one also has to justify *having* such institutions given their costs.

3. Contrast Selznick, *Law, Society and Industrial Justice* p. 275: ". . . there is latent in the law of governance [as exemplified by due process] a norm of participation. . . . a legal order should be seen as transitional to a polity."

4. The inadequacies of a purely instrumental justification for trial procedures is pointed out by Laurence Tribe in "Trial by Mathematics," 84 Harv. L. Rev. 1329-93.

5. See W. A. Seavey, "Dismissal of Students: 'Due Process,' " 70 Harv. L. Rev. (1957) 1406-10; also, the unsigned note "Judicial Control of Actions of Private Associations" 76 Harv. L. Rev. (1963) 983-1100, esp. pp. 1002 ff.; and Z. Chafee, "The Internal Affairs of Associations Not for Profit," 43 Harv. L. Rev. (1930) 993-1029. I am grateful to Owen Fiss, who called my attention to the last two articles after the original version of this paper had been written.

6. This implies that what would normally be regarded as fair adversary

proceedings may not be enough. It is sometimes suggested that, for reasons like those considered here, adversary procedures are not appropriate at all for university discipline and that something more like traditional avuncular "dean's justice" better allows for the appropriate combination of concerned investigation, personal counseling, and rendering of justice. But the potential for arbitrariness here is apparent and familiar. One obvious alternative is a division of labor between (probably adversary) tribunals to apply the rules and separate officials to counsel and assist in uncovering the facts.

7. An alternative explanation of these differences would be that due process itself requires something different where the accused persons are young. But the special obligations of school officials seem to go beyond what general paternalistic arguments are usually taken to require.

8. A class of arguments of this form is discussed in Section V below.

9. Canons which may themselves be revised and altered of course. The following discussion draws on my essay, "Academic Freedom and the Control of Research" in E. Pincoffs (ed.), *The Concept of Academic Freedom* pp. 237-54.

10. For a discussion of the law relating to voluntary associations, in which many of the intuitive distinctions used here are clearly and perceptively drawn, see the sources referred to in note 5 above.

   By distinguishing, in the following discussion, between "purely voluntary" institutions and institutions that are "not fully voluntary" I do not mean to suggest that those who participate in institutions of the latter sort, e.g. as students in universities, do so *involuntarily*. All I am saying about such institutions is that, given the costs of refusal to participate in them, the authority they exercise over their members cannot be defended simply by appeal to the members' consent as expressed in their willingness to "join".

11. My analysis of discrimination is in this way similar to that offered by Ronald Dworkin in his "The Right to Go to Law School—The DeFunis Case," *New York Review of Books* 23 (Feb. 5, 1976) pp. 29-33. But I do not proceed, as he does, from a general theoretical distinction according to which all preferences to associate with or not to associate with others are suspect.

12. See Thomas Nagel, "Equal Treatment and Compensatory Discrimination," *Philosophy and Public Affairs* 2 (1973) 348-63.

13. In deciding how large a price nonmembers may be asked to bear in order that we can associate for our own private purposes one may, of course, have to take into account what those purposes are. The point

is only that with respect to the substance of its power over *members,* the particular purposes of a voluntary association do not have the same justificatory role as they do in the case of nonvoluntary institutions.

14. Some clarification of the nation of a voluntary institution is needed. Our concern is with forms of power some people are able to wield over others, and within a single institution several different forms of power may be involved. Thus, for example, a social club exercises one form of power over members, another over those who seek membership, and another over its employees. With respect to the first two, it is a purely voluntary institution; with respect to the last not so. Thus, the governmental agencies referred to are like voluntary organizations in the power they have over beneficiaries but like businesses or other employers in their authority over those they hire.

What about research-supporting agencies like NSF and NEH? Are the recipients of their grants like beneficiaries or like employees? The answer to this question depends on the role such support has in the economy of the relevant branch of academia. If grants provide temporary support for breaks within other long-term employment, they seem to belong to the voluntary sphere; but not so if they constitute continuing support without which a career of research in the field would be economically impossible.

15. Here I am close to the distinction between concepts and conceptions drawn by Ronald Dworkin. See his article, "Nixon's Jurisprudence," *New York Review of Books* (May 4, 1972), pp. 27-35.

16. Appeal to such a theory would also be required to decide whether the alternatives presented are fairly described. For a theory of adjudication that seems to encompass much of the kind of argument I have been describing, see Ronald Dworkin, "Hard Cases," 88 Harv. L. Rev. (1975) 1057-1109.

17. Insofar as these are distinct. Of course, arguments of the latter sort are apt to play an important role in arguments about what our constitution and political system requires. Here I am proposing only to pursue the questions of political theory without inquiring into how they figure in this larger argument.

18. There is here a slight problem of circularity in the interpretation of (1). Since what is at issue is the extent of legislative authority and the degree to which the word of legislatures is final, we cannot presuppose agreement on what constitutes misuse of legislative power. In order for the argument to proceed, therefore, we have to suppose that there is at least some agreement on the kinds of legislative action which are highly undesirable and which, if frequent, would at least raise questions about the acceptability of legislative authority. (Some such

agreement seems generally to be asserted by proponents of judicial modesty who, while arguing against judicial intervention, usually profess to deplore the legislation under attack.)

19. This is true, I would argue, of the famous substantive due process cases of the *Lochner* era. The view of liberty and of freedom of contract on which they are based could not be given a coherent defense of the kind required for a substantive due process decision on my account.

20. The question is one of allocation of competences; hence, in the terms of Charles Fried's distinction ("Two Concepts of Interests: Some Reflections on the Supreme Court's Balancing Test," 76 Harv. L. Rev. [1963] 755-78), we are concerned with a balancing of interests rather than of wants. My distinction is not the same as Fried's, since I am concerned with what is balanced against the benefits of allocating a competence in a given way. But another central distinction in Fried's article (p. 771), that between a court's assigning itself a certain role and its playing that role, appears to be the same as the distinction drawn above between due process decisions of type (1) and those of other types.

21. Cf. footnote 4 of Justice Stone's opinion in U.S. v. Carolene Products Co., 304 U.S. 144 (1938) at 152.

4

FORMAL AND ASSOCIATIONAL AIMS IN PROCEDURAL DUE PROCESS*

FRANK I. MICHELMAN

I. DUE PROCESS AS FORMAL AND NONFORMAL EXPLANATORY PROCEDURE

One familiar notion of due process is that of an obligation on the part of those who make decisions about the concerns of other individuals to engage in explanatory procedures—procedures in which agents state reasons for their decisions and affected individuals are allowed to examine and contest the proffered reasons. Perhaps also an impartial arbiter or judge may render judgment as to the adequacy of the reasons. A potentially adequate reason can typically be divided into two parts: (1) a general precept, rule, or maxim which is supposed to guide or govern the agent's decision and action, and (2) a specific ground—a fact in which the affected individual somehow figures—whose recognition supposedly determines the agent to act under his cited precept. The individual can challenge either the correctness of the precept or the existence of the ground.

Explanatory procedures may be either formal or nonformal. A procedure is formal insofar as it focuses on the question of legal justification—and lays the agent's decision open to reversal by an arbiter or judge in case the agent can point to no true ground which justifies the action under some legally valid precept.[1] A nonformal procedure does not aim at such third-party review of challenged action for legal adequacy. In a nonformal procedure, the individual questions the validity of the agent's precept (if at all) under some criterion other than legality—prudence, morality, fairness, or whatever; or he may do neither, merely hearing the agent out and accepting or concurring in the action. A nonformal procedure may—but need not—utilize an impartial third party and involve the parties in movements bearing some superficial resemblance to those occurring within a formal procedure. If a third party participates, his role will not be the arbitral one of imposing on the parties his considered view of their respective rights, though he may be asked to express a view. An important part of his role may be to help ensure that the agent discloses his real reasons for acting.[2] This sort of explanatory procedure might be called quasi-formal.

An obvious purpose of formal explanatory procedures is vindication of the private claims of individuals to have what belongs to them under the law.[3] What of nonformal, including quasi-formal, procedures? What compelling purposes might they serve? Such procedures seem responsive to demands for *revelation* and *participation*. They attach value to the individual's *being told why* the agent is treating him unfavorably and to his *having a part in the decision*. The individual may have various reasons for wanting to be told why, even if he makes no claim to legal protection, and even if no further participation is allowed him. Some of those reasons may pertain to external consequences: the individual may wish to make political use of the information, or use it to help ward off harm to his reputation. Yet the information may also be wanted for introspective reasons—because, for example, it fills a potentially destructive gap in the individual's conception of himself. Similarly, the individual may have various reasons for wanting an opportunity to discuss the decision with the agent. Some pertain to external consequences: the individual might succeed in persuading the agent away from the harmful action. But again a participatory opportunity may also be psychologically important to the individual: to have played a part in, to have made one's apt contribution to, decisions which are about oneself may be counted important even though the decision, as it turns out, is the most unfavorable one imaginable and one's efforts have not proved influential.[4]

A demand for nonformal procedures might issue from a certain kind of ideal conception of social relations and political arrangements, expressing revulsion against the thought of life in a society that accepts it as normal for agents representing the society to make and act upon decisions about other members without full and frank interchange with those other members, a kind of accountability to them even if not legal accountability. A nonformal view of an explanatory procedure would thus recognize a communal or fraternal aspect of social life of which a purely formal view, strictly concerned with ensuring that the private entitlements of individuals will be respected, may remain oblivious.[5]

The role of the mediator (or whoever) in a quasi-formal procedure, while it may be a very useful one, is plainly not essential to serving the nonformal aims of revelation and participation. The point of setting up a model of quasi-formal procedures involving an impartial third party, in a mediating role bearing some analogy to that of the judge or hearing officer in a formal procedure, is merely to call attention to the possibility that explanatory procedures of the sort we tend to associate with due process can and sometimes do simultaneously serve both the proprietary aims of formality and the relational aims implied by revelation and participation. In any explanatory procedure, formal or not, the affected individual obtains a more-or-less trenchant statement of the official's reasons for treating him unfavorably and has an opportunity to participate in a determination or the appropriateness of those reasons—at least under the criterion of legality, and perhaps also under criteria of prudence or fairness. (The latter sort of criteria will come into play even in a formal procedure, insofar as the legal standard purports to incorporate those others.)

If it is true that explanatory procedures of the type broadly connoted by "due process" can serve nonformal (communal, interpersonal) as well as formal (possessive, privatistic) aims, and we are not a priori disposed to say that formal aims are more important than nonformal ones, then what should we make of the view that the constitutional guaranty of due process does not extend to all cases of unwelcome official decisions about individuals, but operates only when such decisions arise in circumstances ripe for formal procedures—that is, where it seems prima facie that the only legally valid precepts to which the official could plausibly appeal would so limit his available justifications that it makes sense to think of asking an arbiter to decide whether justification actually exists?

II. SOME THEORETICAL NOTES

Before going on, I want to stipulate clearly the sense in which I mean to use the notion of "formality" in this essay. I am predicating formality of explanatory procedures, not of entire legal orders, using formality as a name either for an attribute of explanatory procedures or for a way of interpreting such procedures. In this usage, a procedure is formal insofar as its point of purpose is to vindicate legal entitlement, to secure to an individual that which is rightfully his; and we regard a procedure formally insofar as we thus construe its purpose.[6] I am not using formality as a name for some class of ideal conceptions or heuristic models of the whole legal order. Thus formality is not synonymous with legal positivism,[7] say, or with the libertarian vision of a *rechtsstaat*.[8]

Yet there *is* one of these global models or visions, recognizably positivistic and libertarian, with which the formal view of explanatory procedures seems to be linked.[9] The model embodies a goal of freedom measured in part according to whether and how thoroughly we may be imagined to have consented in advance to what appear as constraints or harms imposed on us by others. According to the model, all allowable impairments of our immediate freedom are clearly set out in general rules emanating from a legislative sovereign whose rule-enactments can be seen as somehow embodying our more fundamental and comprehensive consent. The rules thus have a double aspect. By their very effect of staking out the limits of each person's guaranteed freedom, they also stake out zones of autonomy wherein each is protected from exposure to unpredictable, arbitrary or discretionary interference by others.

In this model, the only, but necessary, job of judges is to make sure that the rules are applied as enacted. If the sovereign says—and we take it seriously to mean—that we are free to do or to have this or that unless such-and-such a fact is present, then the model demands that impartial officers have the last word about whether enjoyment of this or that has been denied despite the absence of such-and-such. The model requires confirmation from outside the arena of dispute that the rules being applied are the ones which the sovereign has legislated. It thus generates what we may call a modest judicial role.

This modest judicial role provides the link between the liberal-positivist model (if so we may call it) and the formal view of explanatory procedures.[10] Since (by definition) a formal procedure aims at the securing of entitlements, the decisions issuing from formal procedures must be open to criticism in terms of some set of objective criteria. Unless there are objective standards in terms of which decisions can be counted correct or incorrect, it is hard to see in what sense we can say that a decision serves to secure to an individual that which is *rightfully* his. Thus the role of rendering decisions in formal procedures—which we can call the judicial role—must consist of deciding in accordance with criteria external to, and capable of contradicting, the judge's own, Olympian or managerial view of what is best.[11] Rules supposed to emanate from a legitimate sovereign could apparently supply the necessary criteria for determining correct decisions, and the judge-as-rule-applier is an appealing—or at any rate an immediately accessible—interpretation of the judicial role.

In this essay I shall cite some data which seem to support the hypothesis of a link between the formal interpretation of explanatory procedures and adherence to the liberal-positivist model of a legal order.[12] But I do not want to suggest that such linkage as there may be is an analytical truth implicit in the concepts, as distinguished from an historically contingent matter of legal culture. At least, I want to leave open at this point the possibility of restraints on judicial decisions (or specifications of the judicial role) which are nonpositivistic yet sufficiently objective to allow one properly to speak of the proceedings in which those decisions are rendered as formal in the sense of being aimed at securing entitlements. For I shall also be citing data which I think suggest a connection between the formality of explanatory procedures and nonpositivistic conceptions of legal order.[13]

I find it hard to portray these nonpositivistic conceptions with any clarity.[14] Yet the opposition between formality and nonformality, as predicated of explanatory procedures rather than of whole legal orders, seems to me quite clear. The formal perspective is that of the isolated individual interested in getting what is his, while the nonformal perspective is that of a group member interested in his relationships with fellow members of the group. It might be said that formality is the standpoint of an individual momentarily regarding others solely as means to his ends, while nonformality is the standpoint of an individual steadfastly demanding to be treated as an end and not solely as means.[15]

On the surface, at least, the two perspectives do not appear mutually exclusive or competitive. Rather, they seem together to give a binocular view. Formality's aims and uses interpenetrate with those of nonformality. Formality—the articulation of disputes into claims and counterclaims of entitlement—may be put forward as a good way of coping with many problems of group life.[16] Yet systems largely characterized by formality will often—for good and understandable reasons—entitle certain classes of persons to settle certain classes of disputes by acts of discretion, and thus produce situations in which demands for nonformal procedures can be expected to arise.[17] In sum, the two perspectives are coexistent and apparently inseparable. Whether the two are at some level or in some sense also contradictory or incompatible is a question I shall be able neither to ignore nor finally to answer.[18]

III. THE POSITIVISM LATENT IN THE SUPREME COURT'S DOCTRINE OF ENTITLEMENT TRIGGERS

Consider Board of Regents v. Roth.[19] A state college official declines to renew the expiring one-year probationary contract of a novice professor and also refuses to state any reason, much less afford the professor any opportunity to probe or contest the reason. The professor is thus barred from all participation in the decision— which the Supreme Court aptly says is of "major concern" to him [20]—and can learn nothing about what (if any) supposed shortcomings on his part entered into it. The Court concludes that the professor has no constitutional due process right to any explanatory procedure. The due process guaranty pertains to deprivations of "life, liberty, or property"; and, says the Court, not every conceivably unwelcome impact on an individual, authored by a government official, necessarily amounts to an offense against any of that majestic trinity. Specifically, nonrenewal of a pretenure one-year teaching contract is not such a deprivation. It accordingly is an impact which state officials may engineer without ever staging any hearings or other explanatory procedures.

Due process rights are thus made to depend upon preexisting legal entitlements. These entitlements are not absolute claims which override all possible counterarguments, but rather are claims triggering requirements for some sort of justification—where justification means an objectively verifiable account of a person's conduct or the circumstances attending it, the truth of which will absolve conduct of legally wrongful quality despite its harmfulness to another. An entitlement is thus treatment which one person may not lawfully withhold from (impose upon) another, at the former's discretion. Entitlement's antithesis can be conceived as a legally valid rule saying that treatment is to be accorded or not, according to the actor's effectively irrefutable judgment or preference.[21]

Some entitlements are traced directly to the Constitution, perhaps as components of the "liberty" mentioned in the due process clause. (Examples recognized by the Supreme Court in the *Roth* decision include free speech, reputation, and permission to practice a profession.) [22] Other entitlements ("property") originate in statutes, in administrative promulgations authorized by statute, or in judge-made common law of equal dignity with statute; or they may originate in special transactions acquiring the force of law ("contract") under some master rule itself rooted in statute, common law, or the Constitution.

Obviously, a due process guaranty governed by an entitlement trigger is well fitted—in fact perfectly fitted—to a strictly formal interpretation of explanatory procedures. Just as obviously, that very perfection of fit means that the entitlement-tied guaranty is haphazardly suited to a nonformal interpretation. Whenever an entitlement beckons, an explanatory procedure will be required, and nonformal as well as formal aims may be incidentally served. But in other cases, where no plausible prima facie entitlement stands between an individual and the prospect of palpable harm—Professor Roth's case, for example—the entitlement-triggered due process guaranty ignores nonformal aims which might have been served by explanatory procedures.

Now it seems perfectly possible—and it has in fact happened—that courts might read the due process guaranty to require officials to offer explanatory procedures to individuals exposed to harm by official actions, despite concession on all sides that relevant entitlement is lacking and the procedure will thus be formally pointless.[23] We want to know why the Supreme Court should have rejected this possibility. It seems likely that the rejection would in some way reflect a commitment on the Court's part to a modest judicial role. No doubt the location "due process" is ample enough to encompass nonformal aims, and those aims have widespread recognition in our culture. Yet they are fuzzy notions nowhere explicitly recognized in the Constitution, so that to found a due process doctrine upon them would smack of judicial creativity or "activism."

On the other hand, a guaranty of explanatory procedures whenever—but only when—there are entitlements plausibly seeking vindication, though itself not quite explicit in the Constitution, seems to commit the judiciary to the recognition of no claims or values save those from time to time found explicit in the sovereign's laws. Procedure as the handmaiden of substantive rights thus seems a minimalist interpretation of due process.[24]

But this is so only if it be assumed that the method of determining rights in the future series of guaranteed formal proceedings will be of the relatively passive type associated with positivistic models of legal order. If the right-finding in those proceedings were to be attended by a degree of activism more characteristic of nonpositivist conceptions, then the decision to restrict the procedural due process guaranty to situations in which rights are claimed would be a confused way of honoring a commitment to judicial modesty. Thus the *Roth* decision, if we try to explain it in terms of such a commitment, exemplifies the connection I have suggested between the formal perspective on explanatory procedures and the positivist model of legal order. And what other explanation is there?

The recent decision in Arnett v. Kennedy [25] might appear to raise doubt about the thesis that the Court has a positivist model at least vaguely in mind when it asserts the dependency of procedural rights on the pursuit of plausible entitlements, but the appearance is misleading. *Arnett* involved a statute which (a) purported to protect tenured public employees against dismissal except on certain enumerated grounds, thus creating an entitlement; but (b) in the same breath curtailed access to explanatory procedures in support of the entitlement. Six justices agreed that the constitutional right to formal procedures would necessarily obtain once the statutory entitlement was established, despite explicit legislative intention to qualify the entitlement by restricting access to supportive explanatory procedures.[26] Now this conclusion of the six justices might seem inconsistent with the proposed interpretation of the *Roth* decision as deriving from a judicial disinclination to enforce rights or values not clearly enshrined in positive law. A procedural due process right so derived might seem to carry the seeds of its own destruction, since there is always the possibility of just what occurred in the *Arnett* case: the legislature, duly acting in accordance with the forms which mark its outputs as the consensual emanations of a legitimate sovereign, declares that no explanatory procedures need be afforded when violations of certain statutory protections are claimed. The answer is that under the implicit positivist model, the legislature's legitimate province extends only to issuance of those general, substantive rules which set the bounds on our zones of autonomy— more, that the legislature's legitimacy even in that restricted sphere presupposes the availability of formal explanatory procedures, of adjudication, to assure that the general rules are followed. The views of the six justices in *Arnett* thus accord with the model.[27]

IV. ADMINISTRATIVE DUE PROCESS UNDER THE DOCTRINE OF ENTITLEMENT TRIGGERS

Viewing Roth's case as a whole, one cannot say that he was denied all access to formal procedures to assure the legal validity of his treatment. It is not quite true, after all, that the official in *Roth* totally refused to name a ground for his nonrenewal decision. The ground he named was, in effect: "I *choose* (or I *judge it best*), for reasons I won't go into but which satisfy me, not to renew your contract." In tendering this ground, the official also implicitly cited as his maxim or rule: "Renew term teaching contracts or don't renew them, as you in your discretion choose (or judge best)." [28] The litigation culminating in the Supreme Court's decision provided Roth with ample opportunity to contest the validity of this rule, which the Court, in effect, held valid.[29] This conclusion made formally pointless a hearing on the reality or accuracy of the ground, since it will always be incontestably true that an official has some reason which satisfies him for doing as he does.

Roth's claim to a formal procedure was thus satisfied by the hearing given him *by judges* on his complaint against the conduct of *officials*. And it is generally the case that such direct judicial resolution, when available, will perfectly satisfy the formal aims of due process although the officials themselves have previously refused all direct interchange with affected individuals concerning the reasons for their actions. One therefore wonders what the *Roth* decision leaves of the notion of constitutionally required *administrative* due proces—the notion that officials *themselves* must provide affected individuals with explanatory procedures and that their failure to do this is itself a constitutional ground for judicial reversal of their actions.[30] Such a discrete requirement of administrative due process might seem to ascribe value directly to the explanatory transaction between the official and the concerned individual; the doctrine might seem, that is, to have in view the nonformal aims of revelation and participation.[31] But if so, the doctrine may not survive *Roth*. There is no evident reason why a doctrine having such aims should operate only when entitlements are at stake. As we have seen, the crucial place of entitlement in a due process doctrine restricted to formal aims is an analytical, a logical truth; but a crucial place for entitlement in a due process doctrine having nonformal aims is a mystery.

Other possibly persuasive accounts of administrative due process rights are likewise threatened by the theory of entitlement triggers propounded in the *Roth* decision. Some have thought that administrative due process should be understood as serving the goal of enlightened decision, by minimizing the chances of official action which—had the true facts and all the relevant considerations been brought out—would have been rejected as on the whole mistaken or imprudent, irrespective of whether a reviewing court could say that any entitlements were violated.[32] Someone might, for example, suggest this as a reason for judicial imposition of a due process requirement in regard to decisions by public school administrators about assigning students to various study programs or "tracks," where it is exceedingly hard to find a legal entitlement to be assigned to any particular program.[33] Such a suggestion seems gravely threatened by the *Roth* decision.

Now in contexts such as school assignment, a present lack of trenchant, objective standards for appraising particular decisions may make one question whether explanatory interchanges between officials and passionately interested individuals will in fact lead immediately to more prudent and enlightened decisions than would result without them. Even so, one might expect that such interchanges over a series of cases would contribute to the eventual emergence of standards sharp enough to make proceedings thereafter genuinely and worthily formal.[34] This might occur through case-by-case evolution, as decisions in the series seek principled explanation in terms of coherence with one another; or one might anticipate the intervention of legislative authority after knowledge and insight developed through the interchanges had ripened to the point of adumbrating standards both prudent and objectively compelling. Thus one might argue for a constitutional right to explanatory procedures at the adminstrative stage, regarding the procedures not as a device for securing extant entitlements but rather as a protected mode of access to a political, quasi-legislative process that might create entitlements.[35]

Nor need such an argument imply a right on the part of citizens that administration should *always* be driven as fast and as far as possible towards the formulation of entitlements; or that realms of official discretion are *always* disfavored; or that, in short, the Constitution enshrines the *rechtsstaat* ideal. The argument has force if only we believe that there are *some* situations in which an intuition can arise of newly developing, though still inchoate, "norms affecting interests widely agreed to be fundamental," and that due protection for *those* interests, in *those* situations, calls for placing decision makers "under an obligation to resolve [each relevant dispute] on its own terms, acting as appears just in the circumstances, but responsible for ultimately articulating some coherent explanation for the decision reached. . . . [T]he person responsible for decision would thereby enter into a dialogue about what rules," reflecting what "new moral consensus," should eventually prevail.[36]

Such a political-rights interpretation of administrative due process shares two important attributes with the otherwise radically different nonformal interpretation. *First,* the political-rights theory, like the nonformal aims theory, is at odds with the doctrine of entitlement triggers. There is no reason why political rights respecting administrative rule making should operate only in particular contexts of administrative action directly affecting individuals whom one could plausibly think of as *already* the bearers of relevant entitlements.[37] *Second,* reading the political rights theory into the Constitution's due process clauses requires no less a strain on judicial modesty than does finding there an ascription of transcending value to nonformal aims.[38]

Within the *Roth* framework an entitlement-triggered administrative due process right might perhaps be understood as a handmaiden to the main, formal due process right of judicial resolution—designed to conserve societal resources by filtering out petty cases and shaping up more substantial ones, before their entry into the expensive and heavily proceduralized judicial forum.[39] But it is hard to see the doctrine in this economic version as a constitutional *right,* which courts are to secure to an insistent individual despite the legislature's contrary economic judgment, or which federal courts are to secure to individuals despite contrary judgments of state legislatures and state courts.

An entitlement-triggered constitutional right to formal explanatory procedures at the administrative level can perhaps best be rationalized as either a supplement or a surrogate for a right to direct judicial resolution. On this view, administrative due process requirements arise out of an understanding that judicial resolution by itself (even assuming that the legislature may not withhold it altogether) [40] often cannot adequately serve the formal aims of due process. By legislative fiat or by institutional nature, courts find themselves with limited abilities to reexamine official fact-findings, as well as official judgments under complex legal precepts. To this extent entitlements are crucially at risk at the point of administrative decision: the net of judicial review is often too coarse to catch all administrative legal error. A possible response is to extend the requirement of formal procedure to the administrative level where the potentially conclusive determinations are being made.[41] It is believed, moreover, that a court may be better able to detect the taint of biased fact-finding or incorrect standards when it sits in review of a formal record made at a formal agency hearing than when it attempts direct resolution of the controversy between agency and affected individual.[42] These would be reasons why courts would require legislatures to provide for formal administrative procedures whenever they choose not to provide for judicial review tight enough to satisfy formal aims.

V. THE "RIGHT-PRIVILEGE DISTINCTION"
RESUSCITATED

So far, the thesis guiding our discussion of procedural due process law has been that the *Roth* doctrine, conditioning procedural rights upon the pursuit of entitlement, reflects an exclusively formal (rights-centered) view of the aims of explanatory procedures; that the doctrine also reflects a commitment to a modest judicial role; and that this view and this commitment suggest the Court's adherence to a positivist model of legal order, to which they together bear a coherent relationship. From here on, I shall be questioning one part or another of this thesis which up to now has stood up pretty well.

Earlier I suggested that the coherence of the Court's position would be undermined if it turned out that the method of determining when entitlements exist, so as to trigger procedural rights in particular cases, was to be noticeably activist.[43] My position in this section and the next two is that it does turn out that way.

Not so long ago, it was thought by many that the Fifth and Fourteenth Amendments conferred a general entitlement, good against public officials, not to be visited with significant harm of any kind for no ascertainable or plausible reason.[44] The due process clauses were thought to protect persons against harm from "irrational" official acts, while the equal-protection guaranty was thought to protect against "arbitrary and capricious" imposition of harm on selected individuals or groups. The general entitlement resulting from such doctrines I shall henceforth call the rationality entitlement.

It is at least a possible inference from the *Roth* decision that the rationality entitlement does not attach to all significant harms which state officials may impose on individuals.[45] If a professor's interest in renewal of his teaching contract were protected by even such a thin entitlement, the decision's apparent logic would further entitle him to explanatory procedures in which the officials of his college would be required to state a reason or reasons for any nonrenewal decision, he would have an opportunity to challenge both the genuineness and the rationality of those reasons, and an impartial hearing officer or judge would decide whether there were real reasons which were rational.[46]

Of course, a naked rationality entitlement might in reality provide no measurable security for state college professors. A requirement of rationality does seem to set *some* objective bounds on official action, insofar as we take the requirement to focus on the plausibility of belief in an asserted causal relationship between the challenged official action and the ends or purposes posited for officials by legislation. But these bounds are unlikely to be noticeably constraining. Even if (contrary to experience) we imagine a legislature providing a clear statement of a unique educational purpose, the range of plausible implementing judgments which officials might make, according to the situation, would probably be very broad.[47] Thus, if the aim of formal procedures is to vindicate entitlements for the sake of realizing such personal security as the positive law means or is able to bestow, we can see why the rationality entitlement standing by itself might fail to trigger procedural due process rights.

But courts have not always been content to leave the rationality entitlement thus naked of protection. When intent on protecting persons against highly discretionary official interference, courts have found ways of doing so. Occasionally they may invalidate legislative programs in which they can find no clear and unique statement of a purpose, capable of grounding worthwhile curbs on official discretion;[48] more often, they will read such statements into legislation which does not, at least to the naked eye, seem to contain them.[49] In addition, they may refuse to support official interference with individual activities or enjoyment of benefits unless officials have set about to define with precision their conception of appropriate means and to embody those definitions in general rules which effectively stake out zones of individual autonomy.[50]

Such a strategy is potentially adaptable to protect the jobs of state-college professors having no contractual tenure. The undoubted and central legislative purpose of getting and keeping able teachers and scholars could be judicially erected into the only purpose which may count in contract renewal decisions. College officials could be judicially required to enunciate generally applicable criteria for evaluation of teaching and scholarly performance and promise, with sufficient precision to make a formal procedure really worthwhile when nonrenewal impends.[51] The *Roth* decision indicates that the courts will not deploy any such antidiscretion strategy in order to protect the jobs of college teachers.

But does the decision mean to do away entirely with that part of due process doctrine that protects against uncontrollably discretionary incursions upon a broad array of interests, including some not within the select category of civil rights and liberties accorded special status by the Constitution (the category containing freedom of speech and association, freedom from governmental searches, the privilege against self-incrimination, freedom of interstate travel, access to the franchise on an equal footing, and so forth)? Consider governmentally subsidized housing for persons with restricted incomes. At one time it was common for leases in such housing to stipulate that they were good for a limited term such as thirty days; that they would be automatically renewed for an additional term unless officials gave notice of intention not to renew; and that the decision whether or not to renew was within official discretion. In offering such nonentitling leases, officials were thought to have been acting quite within the authority granted them by legislation. Yet it has been the prevailing view of lower federal courts that the due process clause overrides the antientitlement stipulations, establishing an entitlement to indefinite continuation of occupancy in the form of a requirement that terminations be justifiable on grounds of the occupant's (or applicant's) lack of need for the housing, propensity to abuse it, or perhaps, inability to pay enough to keep the project solvent.[52] And of course along with this constitutionally rooted entitlement came a procedural due process right to formal procedures whenever nonrenewal impended.[53]

Entitlement has even been imported into the admissions stage of public housing. Though there be a clear excess of applicants over available accommodations, and a dearth of substantively rational selection criteria capable of eliminating the excess, room still remains for the thinnest entitlement of all: the right not to be disadvantageously treated by some official's personally arbitrary, whimsical, or vindictive choice; and so at least one court has demanded that officials devise and promulgate a set of impersonal criteria and procedures (such as queues and lotteries), adherence to which is susceptible to objective determination in formal procedures.[54]

I want to insist that these housing entitlements are rooted in judicial applications (so to speak) of the due process clause and not in legislation, although some courts have modestly purported to find their sources in the obvious purpose of the housing statutes to provide subsidized housing for those who need it.[55] The trouble with appealing to statutory purpose as the source of entitlement is simply that there is no necessary or even compelling inference of entitlement from purpose. A legislature may well entertain the purpose of providing shelter—and even secure tenure of shelter—for the needy, and yet consider that a regime leaving lease terms to local official discretion is best adapted to achievement of its whole constellation of purposes (which perhaps include the creation and maintenance of a sociable, mutually supportive community of tenants; or the maintenance of a non-stressful environment for management).[56] A comparison with the *Roth* case is instructive. No doubt all would admit that in authorizing the employment of teaching personnel for a state college, the legislature probably has among its purposes the reward of meritorious service by extension of employment, and maintenance of institutional stability by continuing the employment of staff members who do good work. But from these purposes no inference of entitlement is drawn, one supposes because there are other purposes, too, and the legislature could well conclude that a regime of discretion is on the whole preferable.

Taken together, the housing and the public employment cases suggest this possibility: when legislation places various benefits within reach of individuals without meaning or purporting to create even the thinnest of entitlements, the courts will read the due process clauses to make entitlements out of some of these benefits though not all of them. If so, it seems that, *pace* Professor Van Alstyne, the "right-privilege distinction," like Frodo, lives;[57] only the line is no longer drawn, as once it seemed to be, between the private and public sectors—between "the limited power of the state 'reasonably' to regulate activities conducted by private means without substantial assistance by government" and "the unlimited power of the state to regulate advantages supplied by government without obligation." [58] Public housing and public employment are both on the public-sector side of the old line—but public housing (once the program has been established) is a right protected by substantive and procedural due process, including void-for-vagueness doctrine, while public employment remains a bare privilege.[59]

VI. ENTITLEMENT AND BENIGN DISCRETION

We have observed that courts have been prone to bring the full apparatus of formal due process to bear when governments and their officials set about to assign subsidized housing billets, but not when they assign job billets. Are the courts, then, engaged in some antipositivistic comparative evaluation of the moral weights of people's claims to housing and to jobs? Or can this judicial behavior perhaps be explained on technical and prudential grounds that would obviate resort to such a thesis?

It may strike us as obviously impractical and undesirable to devise a set of formalistically useful legal precepts to protect the teacher's interest in his job, though quite easy to do this on behalf of the housing occupant. Certainly a general inclination to the formal outlook would not rule out such differentiations. To accept them is simply to recognize that, whatever the values of private security and the rule of law, these values do not completely obliterate those of discretion and prudence. It seems manifestly desirable to confer upon many officials a breadth of discretion and flexibility of response that would evidently be defeated by any attempt to define their authorities in a finite list of maxims, jointly capable of determining correct decisions.

The case of teacher employment seems illustrative. One can say that it is desirable to allow administrators great flexibility in, say, allocating existing and anticipated resources among teaching and other needs, among teaching in one or another field and of one or another styles, among scholarship and other needs, and among scholarly efforts in various fields and of various styles; and in adjusting these allocations from time to time in light of changes in the overall resource picture, student-body composition, educational ideals, and so forth. Consideration of regional and social-group representation may also be thought relevant and important, as may concerns about compatibility and mutually supportive relations among fellow members of the institution. A rule allowing the administrator sometimes to reserve the question of contract renewal to his legally unfettered discretion is a device for conferring and protecting the requisite flexibility and prudential sensitivity. Such a rule will be needed for this purpose insofar as the allocational and other judgments having to be made cannot be reduced to a formula lending itself to useful statement in the form of objective grounds. At the same time, one might believe, strain on even a sternly rule-oriented model is not unbearable because, while the official is not the sovereign whose general enactments embody our consent, he is not rendered unaccountable—he cannot over the long run act quite arbitrarily—because his overall mission is well enough understood that his success or failure at it over time will be subject to effective, if inarticulate, legislative and political judgment.[60]

The interesting question is not whether a good case can thus be made for benign discretion in teacher hiring and retention, but whether the case would appear markedly less good as applied to tenant selection and retention in subsidized housing, were there not at work some moral intuitions about entitlements. The housing context invites consideration of factors such as sociability, compatibility, and mutual support; mixture, homogeneity and variety; deservingness; special consideration for those specially or unfairly burdened by other societal acts or practices; representation and equitable distribution across commonly identified social groups; and fiscal soundness. All these factors, and perhaps others, might well seem to enter into and constitute a prudential problem not satisfactorily reducible to a structured set of maxims and grounds. Of course maxims could always be stated, but their appropriate combinational properties—weights, priority relations, and so forth—would likely seem opaque to anything approaching formulary expression. That is the way it would seem, I suggest, were it not for our intuition that *the* driving aim of the housing program is to satisfy the just claims of those left in need of adequate housing. Perhaps it is this intuition which makes us feel that all precepts for assigning housing billets are inapposite except precepts of relative need so simple and straightforward that they can frame a formal entitlement.[61] And by the same token, what leaves us so open to conviction of the benignity of official discretion in the assignment of teaching jobs may be the absence of any comparable intuition regarding them.

VII. MORAL ENTITLEMENTS

Judicial responses to due proccss claims in the housing and other welfare contexts thus do suggest the workings of a legally inchoate entitlement to be adequately housed or whatever—an entitlement rooted in moral consciousness or in systematic moral theory which may serve as an ideal backdrop against which the legal order is viewed and comprehended but which is imperfectly represented in the actual legal order. Though courts as such are incapable of full and direct recognition and enforcement of the right (they cannot bring about the provision of ideally required housing which the political order fails to provide), they are quite able to recognize and act on the entitlement once embodied even imperfectly in legislative action.[62]

It is because we experience housing claims as appeals to moral entitlements that due process in the housing context has a clear, conventional, formal significance of vindicating private, possessive claims regarded as rights. Not only does due process promise to avoid a certain number of erroneous determinations that no entitlement existed under the political order's actual, if inadequate, translation of the conditions of the ideal entitlement into statutory rules of admission and exclusion. Due process also to some extent controls the content of the rules and the method of their administration. Beyond these effects there do, of course, remain numbers of cases in which the judicially modified statutory entitlement is admittedly withheld because of the political order's failure to provide necessary wherewithal which the judiciary is incapable of exacting.

But even as to these cases, there seems to be some expectation that due process probing of financial standards, priority groupings, and so forth will tend to minimize the number of such cases and even feed helpfully back into the political side of the problem.[63] The emergence of due process in the public-housing context thus seems consistent with a general conception of due process as a device for helping to secure to individuals their private rights. Yet the ultimate perception of the right seems to be rooted in moral consciousness—in supposedly shared values—and not in positive law.

But if there exists within judicial consciousness some inchoate, conception of a social ideal, capable of provoking judges to inject the regime of due process into the administration of public housing programs, why does it not similarly provoke judges to insistence upon the legalization of state personnel administration? The deceptively simple-looking answer has already been suggested: that the prevailing moral consciousness does not sense in a job, as it does in a housing accommodation, an arrangement which exists for the sake of its holder, in order to satisfy one of his basic needs.[64] It is by no means impossible to think of jobs that way—perhaps as niches in the ecology of social function and service providing an indispensable ingredient of self-respect.[65] But it seems we do not think of jobs that way now, at least not usually or primarily.

I say this answer is deceptively simple because additional explanation is required as to why a nonrenewed employee's needs for *revelation* and *participation*—as distinguished from his need for a job—are not themselves adequate to propel a morally responsible judiciary to the exaction of explanatory procedures under the due process clause. I want to postpone further discussion of that question.[66]

VIII. FAKE ENTITLEMENTS

In the three preceding sections I have contended that courts sometimes grant enforcement of formal procedural rights in support of entitlements whose ultimate sources lie beyond the positive law. If that is so, then the doctrine of *Roth*, tying procedural rights to the assertion of entitlements, cannot be explained simply as an implication of some general positivistic bias in our legal culture. I now want to continue questioning the thesis that purely formalistic and positivistic outlooks lie behind the judicial response to procedural due process claims, by suggesting that judicial decisions honoring such claims may sometimes be prompted by nonformal sympathizing with demands for revelation and participation, even when ostensibly responding to demands for formal protection of entitlements.

In the housing cases, for example, it may well be that there has sometimes occurred a process something like the following: (1) nonformal sensitivities propel a demand for explanatory procedures for persons facing denial of housing, and so—through the doctrinal linkage of due process with entitlement—suggest an entitlement to housing;[67] (2) once the notion of a housing entitlement is stirred in this way by nonformal sympathies, procedures in the housing context attract a formal significance—as well as a nonformal one— because the entitlement is really felt to exist although its existence cannot be demonstrated under the positive law. The total effect is that nonformal sensitivities work through formalistic habits of mind to help produce judicial intervention on behalf of moral en- titlements.[68]

If the formal outlook held exclusive sway over the legal mentality, the Supreme Court's *Roth* formula coupling explanatory procedural rights with entitlement could have only one meaning—could argue, so to speak, in only one direction. Entitlement would be the ground, procedural rights the consequent; entitlement the premise, pro- cedural rights the conclusion; entitlement the independent variable, procedural rights the dependent. If you would demand explanatory procedures, you must first find entitlement.

But if the formal outlook reigns only over our manner of speaking and arguing, if it cannot prevent inarticulate subversion by fuzzy, nonformal aims which we also entertain, then the argument binding entitlement to explanatory procedure may run as well in the opposite direction. To say that if you would insist on explanatory procedure you must first find entitlement would now be to speak with a forked tongue; for nonformal aims might prompt insistence on explanatory procedures in various settings irrespective of entitle- ment's prior presence there, and though a need to find (that is, to invent) entitlement would still exist, that need would be imposed (rather than expressed) by the verbal formulas of formalist logic which is really beside the point. Just because our ways of thinking about procedural rights are so habituated to the formal view (as our ways of thinking about legal order are habituated to the positivist model), judicial imposition of explanatory procedures in any context will make us feel, make us suppose, that an entitlement is present. If the entitlement has no fairly detectable source in positive law, the force of the inarticulate nonformal impulse will have opened a chink in the positivist armor of judicial modesty. The result may be judicial recognition of a moral entitlement. Or it may be the hatching of a fake entitlement—an entitlement which no one really credits as such and which serves no office except to provide the necessary ground for demanded procedural rights—and the fake entitlement, once born, may emerge from its shadowy origins to exert still further pressure on judicial modesty.

What about those school "tracking" cases I mentioned earlier? The argument is made, with fair hope of judicial acceptance, that the due process clause forbids assignment of public school students to special programs, including lower tracks, without revelation by officials of their reasons and provision to parents of ample opportunity to discuss and challenge the grounds and underlying maxims.[69] Perhaps such a development in the law will eventually founder on the *Roth* decision, but that is far from certain.[70] It seems at least equally likely that nonformal aims will prevail. Due process may be held applicable because the courts know that we simply do not want to live in a society that will permit its officials to make such decisions without full interchange with the interested parties.[71] But under the verbal logic of *Roth*, and the formalistic habit of mind it exemplifies, advocates and courts will also have to cite entitlements not to be assigned to lower tracks unless certain supposedly objective grounds (even if very vague ones like "need" or "suitability") exist.[72] The courts will have to say that these decisions are, at least in principle, subject to judicial review—and review not limited to policing against racial discrimination, punishment of free expression, and the like.

Such review will be of dubious propriety under prevailing conceptions of judicial role, and the courts will know it.[73] Some courts may nevertheless genuinely attempt it. Others may make a pro forma pretense of it. Neither solution comports with positivistic strictures or with judicial modesty. One wonders whether the true course of judicial responsibility would not be to recognize explicitly what everyone knows: that there are values in consultation and interchange with affected individuals quite discrete from the aim of protecting their substantive legal rights—values whose potential in a given situation need not depend on whether any entitlement is at stake; and that these values will irresistibly express themselves, through judicial decision if the legislatures and officials will not heed them. That would leave the courts in the uneasy position of deciding, case by case, with no simple rule to appeal to, whether the situation is such as to require judicial exaction of explanatory procedures; but it would relieve courts of an insupportable assumption of substantive review powers.[74]

The problem posed by the school-classification cases is that, except for the right not to be assigned for illicit reasons,[75] there is no readily detectable entitlement attached to assignment into or out of various public-school programs.[76] A reason there is no such entitlement seems to be that no one is yet capable of stating acceptable restrictions on official discretion in this area which are also objectively trenchant enough to support genuinely judicial oversight. As long as this incapacity persists, it is mere speculation that judges are likelier than school officials to achieve good results—to make beneficial, or prudent, or fair assignments.[77] For that matter, it is mere speculation to think that officials will do a fairer or more prudent job if required to reveal and defend their decisions in detailed face-to-face, embarrassing and potentially insulting confrontations with emotionally involved parents.[78]

Nevertheless, the conviction remains that to allow officials to proceed in such a matter without such interchange with those directly and vitally affected would be unacceptable. Is not at least a part of the reason for this conviction that such official behavior would have a meaning that clashes unbearably with a preferred conception of social and political life, in which self-respect is recognized as the fundamental human good that social life affects? Such a conviction can well ground a commitment to transactions akin to administrative due process, without at all implying a commitment to legal justification and judicial review. Yet the strictly formal view of procedures, legally codified by the *Roth* decision, requires that some entitlement be posited in order to ground a commitment to intrinsically valued interchange. The requirement of interchange is then explained by reference to the otherwise meaningless entitlement, and its own meaning thereby falsified.

IX. THE PROBLEM OF NONFORMAL RIGHTS

Why fall into these circumstances? Why not just admit that nonformal aims may sometimes dictate judicial enforcement of a constitutional guaranty of explanatory procedure although no substantive entitlement is involved? We are back to the question left hanging earlier.[79] We have to deal with a major paradox. Many have viewed with alarm what strikes them as a due process "explosion" in contemporary law. The "legalization," "formaliza-tion," or "proceduralization" of relations and transactions that had in the past been treated with supposedly benign informality is felt to bear deleterious consequences for the institutions containing those relations and transactions.[80] This experience of rampant legaliza-tion seems to reflect an increasingly anomic world in which private entitlement backed by formal procedure apparently arises to fill a vacuum left by the withering of that certain spirit we may call community. We may sense that there are other and better ways than entitlement-*cum*-formal procedure to "manage" such problems as pupil placement and teacher contract renewal; and at the same time we may sense and regret that our social life progressively loses touch with those other ways.

The "other ways" are typified by the sort of human or moral concern that, I have suggested, may often be seen as the true aim of administrative due process. But how could the formal legal order act on this premise? Every judge seems to be King Midas, converting whatever transaction he touches into an entitlement which may be coin of the positivist-formalist realm but is also, perhaps, poison to the communitarian spirit.

Within the formal vision, what is a *right* to due process, if not itself a privatistic, possessive entitlement? A due process entitlement is a concession to its holder of control over—one might as well say ownership of—bits of the behavior of the relevant officials. His assertion of control over those bits of behavior connotes his objectification of that behavior, his making of it a means, its becoming an instrument of his to be deployed in the pursuit of his own ends. On such grounds it can be argued that a due process entitlement can *only* have formal aims; that it cannot convey the nonformal, the interpersonal meanings of revelation and participa-tion, however much revelation and participation may be acciden-tally drawn into the formal procedural model, because an official whose explanations and interchanges have been *requisitioned* by someone who assertedly *owns* those elements of his behavior just will not be engaging in the kinds of acts which carry the interpersonal meanings that (possibly) we yearn for. If such a thing as a *right* to nonformalistic due process is conceivable, it must be a right of a sort of which we (or I) do not now have an adequate idea, a right existing outside the formalist-positivist framework, a claim or drive or value having a mandatory quality, yes, but not ultimately dependent upon judicial coercion because grounded in shared values.[81]

Insofar as we find ourselves trapped by insuperable skepticism about such possibilities, I think we must admit that judicial recognition of procedural duties in cases like Roth's can lead only to aimless and perhaps destructive exactions of arid procedural performances.[82] And, thus trapped, we would conclude that the Court judges correctly when it declines to exact procedural performances except in support of recognized entitlements.

This will surely strike some readers as conceding too much. They will say that to a worthwhile degree the aims of revelation, certainly, and even (as the case of collective bargaining suggests) those of participation, can be achieved through procedural engagements that are forthcoming only in response to threats of legal force, in a world quite empty of community or shared values. Perhaps so, but the matter is far from clear. The collective bargaining case may show no more than that where parties share a predisposition toward mutuality in decision making, born of a common experience of past cooperative relations and a common interest in future ones, government can assist the parties in carrying out their true purposes vis-à-vis one another by providing a code for bargaining.[83] As for legally compelled disclosure of the reasons for harmful decision, that can doubtless succeed in prying loose reasons in a form somewhat serviceable for the protection of entitlements. But whether reasons supplied under threat of legal retribution can at all satisfy the internal need for revelation must be seriously doubted. If what the affected individual wants is authentic, honest communication of the truth concerning the image others hold of him, then the pinched, clipped, strained, and anxious statements to be expected in response to judicial orders to speak are likely to distort that truth in ways important but undetectible, and are most unlikely to carry the ring of authenticity.

If I am correct in suspecting that the nonformal aims of explanatory procedures resist effective enforcement in the guise of rights in a formal legal order, then how could the same not be true of judicial attempts to enforce what I have characterized as moral entitlements as in the case of housing? Why is the notion of a moral entitlement, enforceable as a legal right in a formal legal order, not thoroughly self-contradictory? The question is most acute if we take it that the moral entitlement to housing draws on a belief that protection of each person's self-respect is a preeminent aim of society.[84] The idea of nurturing self-respect through provision of material goods clearly entails a notion of entitlement, yet also seems ultimately incompatible with resort to external enforcement. It is an idea that leaves the housing program teetering on the knife edge between whimsical charity and begrudging concession to external force.[85] It seems, like the idea of the humanistic aims of explanatory procedures, to demand a nonpositivistic conception of judicial role, one rooted in a belief in shared values, in which the judge's part is that of catalyzing, evoking, and formulating the community's conscious recognition of values and rights which the community is forever, if inexplicitly, engaged in collectively evolving.[86]

Perhaps it is just because public housing—though not a public job—strikes us as having been provided for the private good of the occupant, that judicial force can be used to exact procedural performances when housing is at stake without seeming to contradict either the interpersonal aims of due process or the prevailing, positivistic conception of the judicial role. The individual most obviously and directly claims legal ownership of an interest in *housing*, not in an official's behavior; and he claims *legal ownership* of the interest, not an objective, moral right to it. The legally contingent claim of ownership masks the objective moral claim which may underlie it. And because the official's procedural duties appear to be incidental to the litigant's demand for housing, the judicial act of enforcing those duties need not totally void them of nonformal significance.

Let me try to draw together some themes of this essay by posing a rather obvious hypothetical case. Suppose a statutory scheme for public employment makes an explicit differentiation between "probationary" or "term" teachers, as to whom no limits are set on official discretion to decline rehiring from year to year, and "tenured" or "regular" teachers, as to whom the only expressed limit on official discretion to terminate at the end of a year is an unadorned requirement of "cause" for such termination (and it is clearly understood that cause includes institutional circumstances, such as budgetary exigency, casting no reflection on a terminated teacher's character or competency). Under the *Roth* decision, is one of these so-called tenured teachers entitled to formal explanatory procedures when the responsible official proposes to terminate at the end of the current year? Since there is a statutory entitlement, albeit the merest of rationality entitlements, the answer appears to be yes. But since (as *Roth* also appears to establish)[87] the interest in being employed by the state is not one of those interests (like that in being housed by the state) which once placed within reach by legislation is translated by the due process clause into a "right," or "property," there is no apparent basis for judicial deployment of anti-vagueness doctrine to force the entitlement into a formalistically cognizable set of narrow rules or criteria limiting official discretion to terminate.[88]

Now a judicially required explanatory procedure under the naked "cause" (rationality) entitlement could serve only nonformal aims, not formal ones.[89] But what of the contention that a judicially exacted explanatory procedure is antithetical to nonformal aims? If that contention is correct, then in this case, although the verbal logic of *Roth* would require the court to order officials to grant an explanatory session, that session would be both formally futile and nonformally destructive.

What, then, are we to make of this case? I can think of two ways out. *First,* we might soften the thesis that a judicially demanded explanatory procedure absolutely cannot serve nonformal aims. Instead, we could say that under the habitual intuitions of contemporary legal culture, there is potential contradiction between judicial demand and nonformal aims, sufficient to explain why a court will not, on its own, read the due process clause to authorize judicial exaction of explanatory procedure where there is no entitlement to be vindicated or formal aim to be served. This leaves it open for the court to order such procedure when the legislature, by explicitly creating even a translucently thin entitlement, has indicated its view that, in the specific type of context in question, a legally exacted quasi-formal procedure would provide worthwhile service to nonformal aims despite the potential contradiction.

Second, we might say that the legislature's explicit creation of the thin "cause" safeguard is enough to draw the public-job interest into the sphere of moral entitlements. By enacting the thin entitlement, the legislature might be thought to acknowledge the community's sense that the job is for the sake of the teacher as well as for the good of the state; and that acknowledgement might be just enough to stimulate a further intuition that persons have a moral right to respectable employment just as they have a moral right to adequate housing. The court might then go on and give full due process protection to the job right just as it has for the housing right, including the use of antivagueness doctrine to force the explanatory procedure into a formally trenchant shape. What seems to me extremely interesting is that either of these two ways out involves the frank acceptance of associational as well as possessive ends as partially determinative in due process adjudication.

NOTES

* This paper was first prepared for delivery at the December, 1973 meeting of the American Society for Political and Legal Philosophy. Revision during the spring and summer of 1974 brought the paper to substantially its present state, with a view to publication in late 1974. I have not attempted any major revision of the paper to take account of developments occurring during the intervening delays in publication. Among relevant articles published during that period, Leonard Rubenstein, "Procedural Due Process and the Limits of the Adversary System," 11 Harv. Civ. R. Civ. Lib. L. Rev. 48 (1976), and David Kirp, "Proceduralism and Bureaucracy: Due Process in the School Setting," 28 Stan. L. Rev. 841 (1976), are two that seem especially germane to matters treated herein. During the same period, the United States Supreme Court has handed down a number of decisions bearing significantly on these matters, among them Goss v. Lopez, 419 U.S. 565 (1975); Paul v. Davis, 96 S.Ct. 1155 (1976); Hampton v. Mow Sun Wong, 96 S.Ct. 1897 (1976); Bishop v. Wood, 96 S.Ct. 2074 (1976); Hortonville Joint School Dist. v. Hortonville Education Assoc., 96 S.Ct. 2308 (1976); Meachum v. Fano, 96 S.Ct. 2532 (1976); Massachusetts Board of Retirement v. Murgia, 96 S.Ct. 2562 (1976). I have tried to call attention to these authorities at the appropriate points wherever I could do so by brief additions to the footnotes.

1. The definition does not stipulate that the precept must be a simple rule susceptible of mechanical application, nor does it incorporate any particular theory, such as legal positivism in some one of its variants, of how to understand legal validity. The precept may be a complex of nonrule standards (policies and principles) whose resultant vector is somehow to be found; and the precept's source may be something other than the command of a positivistic sovereign. See, generally, Ronald Dworkin, "The Model of Rules," 33 U. Chi. L. Rev. 14 (1967).

2. See Lon Fuller, "Mediation—Its Forms and Functions," 44 So. Calif. L. Rev. 305, 309 (1971).

3. Two widely noted contemporary statements of the dependency of the

formal rule of law on procedural due process are Charles Reich, "The
New Property," 73 Yale L. J. 733 (1964), and J. Skelley Wright, Book
Review, 81 Yale L. J. 575 (1972). See also Anthony Amsterdam, "The
Void-for-Vagueness Doctrine in the Supreme Court, 109 U. Pa. L.
Rev. 67 (1960). A particularly eloquent elaboration of the theme is
the dissenting opinion of Justice Brennan in McGautha v. California,
402 U.S. 183, 270 (1971). Jerry Mashaw, "The Management Side of
Due Process: Some Theoretical and Litigation Notes on the
Assurance of Accuracy, Fairness, and Timeliness in the Adjudication
of Social Welfare Claims," 59 Cornell L. Rev. 722 (1974), proceeding
from the premise that the aim of procedural due process is accuracy
in the determination of claims, suggests that in some circumstances
courts should require not only provision of hearings in individual
cases but also use of management devices to monitor the general
quality of agency decisions; and also suggests that demonstrably
successful use of such devices might excuse the agency from providing
individual hearings. Id. at 807. This essay will suggest reasons for
caution in appraising the latter suggestion.

4. See Laurence Tribe, "Technology Assessment and the Fourth Discon-
tinuity: The Limits of Instrumental Rationality," 46 So. Cal. L. Rev.
617, 631 n. 47 (1973); Note, "The Supreme Court, 1973 Term," 88
Harv. L. Rev. 41, 89 (1974); Robert Summers, "Evaluating and
Improving Legal Processes—A Plea for 'Process Values,' " 60 Cornell
L. Rev. 1, 20-21 (1974). Stephen Subrin and A. Richard Dykstra,
"Notice and the Right to Be Heard: The Significance of Old
Friends," 9 Harv. Civ. Rts. Law Rev. 449, 454-74 (1974); compare
Goss v. Lopez, 419 U.S. 565, 595 & n. 18 (1975) (Powell, J.,
dissenting); Donald Griffis and John Wilson, "Constitutional Rights
and Remedies in the Non-Renewal of a Public School Teacher's
Employment Contract," 25 Baylor L. Rev. 549, 570 (1973): "The
hearing is designed to present an opportunity for reconciliation where
a mistake has been made, for explanation where reasons for non-
retention are demanded, and for an exchange of views where
differences of opinion exist." This notion of participation corresponds
to the values of civility, dignity, self-respect, and self-expression
which, according to Edward Dauer and Thomas Gilhool, "The
Economics of Constitutionalized Repossession: A Critique for Professor Johnson and a Partial Reply, 47 So. Cal. L. Rev. 116, 147-49
(1973), ought to be counted among the benefits of procedural due
process. The notion of participation should be sharply distinguished
from the idea, developed at id. 144-47, of hearing rights as themselves
a form of power deployable in the pursuit of one's private goals.

5. In speaking of a "society" and of "social life," I refer to any group

(including but not limited to state or nation) encompassing both a representative agent and an adversely affected other member, such that the agent (and those whom he represents) and the other member are connected by their prior joint engagement in a common, mutually beneficial activity or arrangement requiring for its success the support and participation of both. Under these circumstances, I suggest without offering any defense of the suggestion, refusal of revelation and participation to those adversely affected by official action will seem especially outrageous. The suggestion is consistent with the fact that constitutional duties to provide due process are imposed only on governmental agents, those representing legally organized civil society at large. Whoever is adversely affected by the acts and decisions of such an agent is almost certainly a fellow member of the represented group.

In other cases, the relation of fellow membership may or may not exist. Since it may not, a flat constitutional duty to provide explanatory procedures may be inappropriate. If it does, the group's own charter is available for imposing the duty; or perhaps the courts will extend the constitutional duty by analogy. For a somewhat different explanation of the restriction of constitutional due process obligations to government agents, see Stephen Subrin and A. Richard Dykstra, "Notice and the Right to be Heard," 9 Harv. Civ. Rts. Law Rev. 449, 458-59 (1974). (For the thoughts set forth in this footnote, I am indebted to comments by Professors Bruce Ackerman and Leon Lipson of the Yale Law School; but they cannot be held accountable for my reworking of their suggestions.)

6. This seems to me an apt usage of "formal." The procedure is treated as a form (or method) potentially containing (or leading to) the substance (or result) of a determination of entitlements. When procedures are nonformal, there is no discrete substance to which they bear a form:substance relationship.

7. See, e.g., Herbert Hart, *The Concept of Law* (Oxford: Oxford Univ. Press, 1961).

8. See, e.g., Friedrich Hayek, *The Constitution of Liberty*, esp. ch. 13 (Chicago: Univ. of Chicago Press, 1960).

9. This is the model portrayed in Duncan Kennedy, "Legal Formality," 2 J. Legal Studies 351 (1973).

10. Compare Board of Regents v. Roth, 408 U.S. 564, 577 (1972): "To have a property interest in a benefit [so as to be entitled to explanatory procedures when officials threaten to disturb or withhold the benefit] a person must have more than an abstract need or desire for it. . . . It is a purpose of the ancient institution of property to protect those claims upon which people rely in their daily lives,

reliance that must not be undermined. It is a purpose of the constitutional right to a hearing to provide an opportunity for a person to vindicate those claims."

11. See Charles Fried, "Two Concepts of Interest: Some Reflections on the Supreme Court's Balancing Test," 76 Harv. L. Rev. 755 (1963); Ronald Dworkin, "The Model of Rules," 33 U. Chi. L. Rev. 14 (1967).

12. See pp. 131-137.

13. See pp. 138-148.

14. One such conception might see the judicial role as essentially that of allocating and delimiting decisional roles and competencies—a role objectively constrained by a requirement that the resulting collection of roles and competencies, including those unambiguously defined by constitutional and valid statutory material, constitute a coherent system. See Charles Fried, *supra* note 11; Laurence Tribe, "Foreword: Toward a Model of Roles in the Due Process of Life and Law, 87 Harv. L. Rev. 1 (1973). See also Laurence Tribe, "Ways Not to Think About Plastic Trees: New Foundations for Environmental Law, 83 Yale L. J. 1315, 1338-41 (1974).

15. This formulation in Kantian terms was first suggested to me by a draft of Professor Edmund Pincoff's comments which appear in this volume in Chapter 5.

16. See Lon Fuller, "Mediation-Its Forms and Functions," 44 So. Calif. L. Rev. 305, 328 (1971). It is not my purpose to disparage the virtues of formality, entitlement, property, privacy, and security. Perhaps this is the place to note that the private entitlements which formal procedures help secure are not all of material quality or essentially economic value. For example, the right to worship freely is such an entitlement. So, for that matter, is the right under certain circumstances to a formal explanatory procedure. And so would be the right, if there were one, to nonformal explanatory procedures. See pp. 149-50, *infra.*

17. See pp. 142-43, *infra.* For the sense in which I use the word "discretion," see note 21, *infra.*

18. See pp. 150-53, *infra.*

19. 408 U.S. 564 (1972).

20. Id. at 570.

21. For fuller discussion of this concept of entitlement see Frank Michelman, "The Supreme Court and Litigation Access Fees: The Right to Protect One's Rights—Part II," 1974 Duke L. J. 527, 541-44. See also the discussion by Circuit Judge Hufstedtler, dissenting in Geneva Towers Tenants Org. v. Federated Mortgage Investors, 504 F. 2d 482, 493-96 (9th Cir. 1974). The legal precept limiting discretion

need not take the form of a *"per se"* rule allowing of mechanical application. It may be a precept calling on a person to exercise judgment, such as by "weighing" or otherwise combining a number of relevant considerations. As long as the required exercise of judgment is reasonably open to possible judicial contradiction, there is an entitlement.

It will be seen that I am using "discretion" here in a rather "strong" sense, though not quite in the strongest sense of decision utterly unbound by authority, compare Ronald Dworkin, "The Model of Rules," 33 U. Chi. L. Rev. 14, 32-36 (1967). Doubts have recently been expressed as to whether it is proper or illuminating, when speaking judicial discretion, to distinguish that strongest sense of the word from the slightly less strong sense I intend here: that of judgment restrained, if at all, only by complexes of standards which, even if in principle objective and determining, are so intricate and opaque that honest, persistent disagreements are inevitable concerning their correct application to particular cases. See Kent Greenawalt, "Discretion and Judicial Decision: The Elusive Quest for the Fetters that Bind Judges," 75 Colum. L. Rev. 359, 368-70 (1975); Noel Reynolds, "Dworkin as Quixote," 123 U. Pa. L. Rev. 574 (1975).

22. Some recent decisions of the Supreme Court have suggested that the only "liberties" accorded substantive protection by the Constitution are those specifically mentioned in, or directly inferrable from, constitutional texts apart from the due process clause, and those (such as equal voting rights) thought derivable from the whole constitutional plan. See, generally, San Antonio Indep. School Dist. v. Rodriguez, 411 U.S. 1 (1973). Yet the interests in reputation and practice of one's trade or profession, included by the *Roth* opinion among the "liberty" entitlements, do not fit this conception. There remains at work a broader, though not very well defined, concept of constitutionally protected liberty, well illustrated by language from Meyer v. Nebraska, 262 U.S. 390, (1923), quoted in the *Roth* opinion, 308 U.S. at 572: ". . . the right of the individual to contract, to engage in any of the common occupations of life, to acquire useful knowledge, to marry, to establish a home and bring up children, to worship God according to the dictate of his own conscience, and generally to enjoy those privileges long recognized . . . as essential to the orderly pursuit of happiness by free men." Compare Hampton v. Mow Sun Wong, 96 S. Ct. 1897 (1976). But compare Paul v. Davis, 96 S. Ct. 1155 (1976); Meachum v. Fano, 96 S. Ct. 2532 (1976).

23. A clear example is Drown v. Portsmouth School Dist., 435 F.2d 1182 (1st Cir. 1970), cert. denied. 402 U.S. 972 (1971). But compare Drown v. Portsmouth School Dist., 451 F. 2d 1106 (1st Cir. 1971).

24. A similar explanation is offered in Comment, "Entitlement, Enjoyment, and Due Process of Law," 1974 Duke L. J. 89, 103, 117—an essay generally worth consulting on the entitlement-trigger theory of the *Roth* decision. Compare the Court's statement that "our analysis of the respondent's constitutional rights in this case in no way indicates a view that an opportunity for a hearing . . . would not be . . . wise. For it is a written Constitution that we apply. Our role is confined to interpretation of that Constitution." 408 U.S. at 578-79.

25. 416 U.S. 134 (1974).

26. The statute in *Arnett* provided for a full, formal hearing but only *after* the dismissal had been consummated and had taken effect. Three justices thought that Congress was free to create procedurally qualified "entitlements" quite as it saw fit to do. Six justices concluded that Congress could not rule out access to formal procedures to protect whatever entitlements it might create, but two of the six thought that a postdismissal hearing would suffice; and so the Government won the case.

27. Compare Laurence Tribe, "Structural Due Process," 10 Harv. Civ. R. Civ. Lib. L. Rev 269, 277-80 (1975). It is true, as pointed out in Note, "The Supreme Court, 1973 Term," 88 Harv. L. Rev. 41, 87 (1974), at 87, that the legislature can always cast limitations on procedural rights in the form of restricted definitions of substantive rights, e.g.: "Employees may not be dismissed except when either (i) *there exists* such cause as will promote the efficiency of the service or (ii) *the agency head has declared in writing* that such cause exists."

   But it does not follow, as the cited Note argues, that the only interest served by ruling out the form of legislation involved in *Arnett*, which separately asserts first the substantive right and then the procedural limitation, "would be to require greater candor when a legislature sought to limit the extent of an entitlement," or that the doctrine of the six justices in *Arnett* is inconsistent with *Roth*, see id. at 87-88. Within the model of legal order portrayed in the text, clause (ii) in the hypothetical statute presented above is *invalid*, except insofar as the Court would, as in Bishop v. Wood, 96 S. Ct. 2074 (1976), construe it to signify that the statute as a whole really means to leave the question of dismissal to the agency head's unfettered choice and so (despite the appearances created by clause (i)) creates no entitlement at all. The doctrine of the six justices thus has the quite significant effect of forcing the legislature to choose between (a) a nonentitlement regime of unfettered official choice (as in *Roth* and *Bishop, supra*) and (b) substantive restrictions on official choice, accompanied by whatever procedural rights due process requires. For related criticism of the position of the three Justices in *Arnett*, see

Comment, "Fear of Firing: Arnett v. Kennedy and the Protection of Federal Career Employees," 10 Harv. Civ. R. Civ. Lib. L. Rev. 472, 478-87 (1975).

28. That is, as long as the reasons for not renewing do not fall within a select group of illicit reasons. See note 46, *infra.*

29. That is, the federal-court litigation over procedural due process rights incidentally provided the due process hearing to which Prof. Roth was constitutionally entitled if he wished to challenge the substantive validity of the regime of unfettered official discretion. Cf. "The Supreme Court, 1973 Term," 88 Harv. L. Rev. 41, 87 (1974).

30. Compare Note, "Specifying the Procedures Required by Due Process: Toward Limits on the Use of Interest Balancing," 88 Harv. L. Rev. 1510, 1517 n. 35 (1975).

31. See Sindermann v. Perry, 430 F. 2d 939, 944 (5th Cir. 1970), affirmed, 408 U.S. 593 (1972). The court there says that the point of a formal administrative hearing "is not ... just to accommodate court procedures. More importantly, it is the process best calculated to reach a fair accord and to settle the problems which have arisen between the parties. After all, the candid settlement of differences that arise between men is the essence of the civil justice for which we strive."

32. See Note, "Specifying the Procedures," 88 Harv. L. Rev. at 1517 n. 35, 1541 n. 135.

33. David Kirp, "Schools as Sorters: The Constitutional and Policy Implications of Student Classification," 121 U. Pa. L. Rev. 705, 779 (1973); Paul Dimond, "The Constitutional Right to Education: The Quiet Revolution, 24 Hastings L. J. 1087, 1114, 1119-20, 1127 (1973); Merle McClung, "Do Handicapped Children Have Legal Right to a Minimally Adequate Education," 3 J. Law & Educ. 153 (1974). The three cited articles represent strong efforts to construct legal arguments for procedural rights respecting school classification and assignment. None really makes a confident claim to have located substantive entitlements respecting assignment to one "track" rather than another. See, e.g., Kirp, at 747-48, 752-54. But see id. at 776-78, discussing the stigmatizing effect of "slow learner" assignments, and compare note 74, *infra.*

34. See David Kirp, William Buss and Peter Kuriloff, "Legal Reform of Special Education: Empirical Studies and Procedural Proposals, 62 Calif. L. Rev. 40 (1974).

35. Consistently with such a view of the office of explanatory procedures, Kirp et al. suggest liberal allowance of intervention in individual proceedings by private or governmentally sponsored advocacy groups. The individual's right to quasi-adjudicative procedures is thus

partially translated into what looks more like an interest group's political right to quasi-legislative procedures—or, to use the appropriate legal word of art—rule makings. See id. at 78-81, 95, 120-21, 126, 131, 137-38. Thompson v. Washington, 497 F.2d 626 (D.C. Cir. 1973), and Burr v. New Rochelle Municipal Housing Authority, 479 F. 2d 1165 (2d Cir. 1973), may reflect a similar view.

36. Laurence Tribe, "Childhood, Suspect Classifications, and Conclusive Presumptions: Three Linked Riddles," 39 L. & Contemp. Prob. 8 (1975). For further elaboration of this argument for "interchange between state and citizen" as instrumental in "a legal system that aspires not to be frozen in time," see Tribe, "Structural Due Process," 10 Harv. Civ. R. Civ. Lib. L. Rev. 269, 304-310, esp. at 307 (1975).

37. With respect to that version of the political-rights theory that would require interchanges only in situations found to be instinct with inchoate norms respecting "interests widely agreed to be fundamental," one might want to say that a court's very act of classifying the case as one of that sort is tantamount to detecting the case's involvement of an entitlement. But discerning a pressing need now to address the question whether it is time for some entitlement to be brought into being cannot be the same thing as discerning an entitlement's present existence. Moreover, the sort of "entitlement" we would have in mind here is hardly harmonious with the positivistic view of the judicial role which, I have suggested, best promises to explain the entitlement-trigger doctrine. See pp. TAN 19-25, *supra*.

38. See p. 133, *supra*. As the text indicates, the political-rights theory entails a number of empirical assumptions and value judgments that cannot claim any clear constitutional certification: e.g., interchange promotes prudence; rules protect some interests better than discretion does; certain interests (an open and evolving set) are "fundamental."

39. Cf. Note, "Procedural Due Process in the Context of Informal Administrative Action: The Requirements for Notice, Hearing and Prospective Standards Relating to Police Selective Enforcement Practice," 53 B.U. L. Rev. 1038, 1059 (1973). Another suggested explanation for a judicially imposed requirement of formal explanatory procedures at the administrative level is that such procedures are much cheaper for the affected individuals—and in that sense much more accessible to them—than court litigation usually is. See Lamb v. Hamblin, 57 F.R.D. 58, 63 (D. Minn. 1972); Note, 5 Conn. L. Rev. 685, 690 n. 26 (1973). But how can one square such a reading of the due process clauses, as displaying such sensitivity to the unfairness of financial barriers to litigation, with the Supreme Court's recent decisions allowing the exclusion by court fees of ordinary civil

litigants who cannot afford to pay the fees? See, generally, Frank Michelman, "The Supreme Court and Litigation Access Fees: The Right to Protect One's Rights" Part I, 1973 Duke L. J. 1153; Part II, 1974 Duke L. J. 527.

40. Whether the due process clause confers a right to *judicial review,* as distinguished from a broader claim to formal explanatory procedure, is a question that remains unresolved. See, e.g., Ortwein v. Schwab, 410 U.S. 656, 662-63 (1973) (Douglas J., dissenting).

41. See, e.g., Willner v. Committee on Character, 373 U.S. 96, 104-5 (1963); Escalera v. New York City Housing Authority, 425 F.2d 853, 866 (2d Cir. 1970), cert. denied, 400 U.S. 853 (1970); Townley v. Resor, 323 F. Supp. 567 (N.D. Cal. 1970). Lamb v. Hamblin, 57 F.R.D. 58 (D. Minn. 1972), indicates that one reason for reading due process to require an administrative-level formal procedure is that in some cases it will be *too late,* by the time the case can be litigated in court, to protect the claimed entitlement as fully as the Constitution requires.

42. See Wayne McCormack, "The Purpose of Due Process: Fair Hearing or Vehicle for Judicial Review," 52 Texas L. Rev. 1257, 1263 (1974); Note, "Specifying the Procedures Required by Due Process: Toward Limit on the Use of Interest Balancing," 88 Harv. L. Rev. 1510, 1540 (1975).

43. Pp. TAN 24-25, supra.

44. See, e.g., William Van Alstyne, "The Demise of the Right-Privilege Distinction in Constitutional Law," 81 Harv. Law Rev. 1439 (1968). Compare Greene v. McElroy, 360 U.S. 474, 496-97 (1959) (dictum); Dixon v. Alabama Bd. of Educ., 294 F.2d 150 (5th Cir. (1961)). See also Hampton v. Mow Sun Wong, 96 S. Ct. 2562 (1976).

45. But see Thompson v. Gallagher, 489 F.2d 443 (5th Cir. 1973); Note, "Substantive Due Process: The Extent of Public Employees' Protection from Arbitrary Dismissal," 122 U. Pa. L. Rev. 1647 (1974).

46. It might seem that in cases such as this the ever-lurking possibility of violation of specific constitutional guaranties would lead to results hard to distinguish in practice from recognition of a rationality entitlement. The professor is entitled not to have a nonrenewal decision based on "invidious" (*e.g.* racial) discrimination, or on his having exercised certain constitutionally protected rights such as that of free speech. A court would entertain a suit on his behalf complaining of such a reason for nonrenewal, and award him relief if he could show that such an illicit reason was in fact operative. See Perry v. Sindermann, 408 U.S. 593 (1972). But how is he to show this, when the official is legally free to terminate his services for no reason at all? (On this question see generally William Van Alstyne, "The

Constitutional Rights of Teachers and Professors," 1970 Duke L. J. 841, 858-79.)

Simply in order to avoid the emasculation of the right not to suffer nonrenewal for various illicit reasons, a court might require the official to state reasons for the nonrenewal decision, once the complainant had produced evidence fairly raising a suspicion of illicit motivation. And if the reasons offered by the official appeared to be either false in fact or aimlessly irrational, the court could then conclude that the real reason was the illicit one and grant relief. See Comment, "The Scope of Judicial Review of Probationary Teachers Dismissal in California: Critique and Proposal," 21 U.C.L.A. L. Rev. 1257 (1974). Since these are just the conditions on which relief would be granted if a rationality entitlement itself were recognized, what difference does recognition of a rationality entitlement make? The easiest answer is that it makes a difference whenever the picture lacks any plausible suggestion of an illicit motive, capable of shifting to the official the burden of producing rational reasons for his action. Insistence on a prima facie showing of illicit motive before the official is required to state reasons seems to be the most important practical consequence of the doctrine that the contract-renewal interest is not itself property protected by a rationality entitlement. See Board of Regents v. Roth, 408 U.S. at 575 n. 14.

47. Cf. Drown v. Portsmouth School Dist., 451 F.2d 1106 (1st Cir. 1971).

48. E.g., Smith v. Goguen, 94 S. Ct. 1242 (1974); Papachristou v. Jacksonville, 405 U.S. 156 (1972). But compare Parker v. Levy, 417 U.S. 733 (1973).

49. See Kent v. Dulles, 357 U.S. 116 (1958); cf. United States Civil Serv. Comm'n v. National Ass'n of Letter Carriers, 413 U.S. 548 (1973).

50. See Raper v. Lucey, 488 F.2d 748 (1st Cir. 1973). Compare Hampton v. Mow Sun Wong, 96, S. Ct. 1897 (1976). In *Raper,* the court indicated its view that the official's obligation to articulate his maxims was implicit in the state's statutory scheme of administrative review. But the federal court's competency to adjudicate the case rested on a claim that Fourteenth Amendment due process rights were being violated.

51. I do not suggest that the results would be necessarily happy ones. See pp. TAN 59-61, *infra.*

52. Lopez v. Henry Phipps Plaza South Inc., 498 F.2d 937 (2d Cir. 1974). See Thomas v. Housing Authority of Little Rock, 282 F. Supp. 575 (E.D. Ark. 1967); Thompson v. Washington, 497 F.2d 626 (D.C. Cir. 1973); Short v. Fulton Devel. Co., Inc., 390 F. Supp. 517 (S.D.N.Y. 1975); cf. Hammond v. Housing Authority of Lane County, 328 F. Supp. 586 (D. Ore. 1971). Compare Fletcher v. Housing Authority of

Lousiville, 491 F.2d 793 (6th Cir. 1974), vacated and remanded, 95 S. Ct. 27 (1974), basing a similar conclusion on activist statutory interpretation. But cf. Manning v. San Francisco Housing Authority (N.D. Cal. Civ. No. 74-0266 (1974)) (housing authority may enforce rule excluding minors on grounds of legal incapacity to enter binding rental agreement).

53. See, e.g., Caulder v. Durham Housing Authority, 433 F.2d 998 (4th Cir. 1970), cert. denied, 401 U.S. 1003 (1971); Davis v. Toledo Metrop. Housing Authority, 311 F. Supp. 795 (N.D. Ohio 1970); cf. Neddo v. Housing Authority of Milwaukee, 335 F. Supp. 1397 (E.D. Wis. 1971). See also Aguiar v. Hawaii Housing Authority, 522 P.2d 1255 (1974); Escalera v. New York City Housing Authority, 425 F.2d 853 (2d Cir. 1970), cert. denied, 400 U.S. 853 (1971).

54. See Holmes v. New York City Housing Authority, 398 F.2d 262 (2d Cir. 1968); cf. Hornsby v. Allen, 326 F.2d 605 (5th Cir. 1964). But see Spady v. Mt. Vernon Housing Authority, 34 N.Y. 2d 573, 354 N.Y.S. 2d 945, 310 N.E. 2d 542, cert. denied, 95 Sup. Ct. 243 (1974), holding that a public-housing applicant has no right to an evidentiary hearing to challenge revocation of eligibility on grounds of a prior arrest and addiction record.

55. See McQueen v. Druker, 317 F. Supp. 1122 (D. Mass. 1970); Joy v. Daniels, 479 F.2d 1236 (4th Cir. 1973); cf. Geneva Towers Tenants Org. v. Federated Mortgage Investors, 504 F.2d 483 (9th Cir. 1974); Thompson v. Washington, 497 F.2d 626, 632-38 (D.C. Cir. 1973); Marshall v. Lynn, 497 F.2d 643 (D.C. Cir. 1973). But cf. Paulsen v. Coachlight Apartments Co., 507 F.2d 401 (6th Cir. 1974).

56. See the dissenting opinion of Hustedtler, J., in Geneva Towers Tenants Org. v. Federated Mortgage Investors, 504 F.2d 483 (9th Cir. 1974), at 496-98; Note, "Legislative Purpose, Rationality, and Equal Protection," 82 Yale L. J. 123 (1972). David Kirp, "Schools as Sorters: The Constitutional and Policy Implications of Student Classifications," 121 U. Pa. L. Rev. 705, 783 (1973), says that "comfort [of officials] . . . does not deserve to be treated as a legitimate interest." Yet, why doesn't it?

57. *Pace,* too, the Supreme Court. See Board of Regents v. Roth, 408 U.S. at 571: ". . . [T]he Court has fully and finally rejected the wooden distinction between 'rights' and 'privileges' that once seemed to govern the application of procedural due process rights." Compare Comment, *supra* note 24, at 98.

58. William Van Alstyne, "The Demise of the Right-Privilege Distinction in Constitutional Law," 81 Harv. L. Rev. 1439, 1442 (1968). For an argument that recent Supreme Court decisions have deeply eroded the position, seemingly established by Goldberg v. Kelly, 397 U.S. 254

(1970), that benefits under statutory welfare programs are "rights" rather than "privileges," see Barbara Brudno, "Fairness and Bureaucracy: The Demise of Procedural Due Process for Welfare Claimants," 25 Hastings L. J. 813 (1974).

59. Some passages in J. Skelley Wright, Book Review, 81 Yale L. J. 575 (1972), suggest that the line might be drawn between those public-sector programs which do and those which don't have a "regulatory" aim or impact on affected individuals. Id. at 588-89. Where the program has "regulatory" elements—a purpose of "bring[ing] primary conduct into conformance with agreed upon societal norms"—both efficiency and freedom may suggest a strong need for general rules clearly stated in advance. Whatever the merit of this approach, it doesn't seem that it would exclude public employment from the due-process protected category. Who doubts that official discretion to terminate or continue the employment of a state college teacher contains regulatory elements? See, e.g., Hortonville Joint School Dist. v. Hortonville Education Assoc., 96 S. Ct. 2308 (1976).

60. Moreover, it may well be argued that discretion can compete strongly with ruledness as a way of pursuing consistency and nonarbitrariness. "While [per se] rules do prevent reliance on 'trivial' difference of fact and other irrelevant and improper factors, they also prevent consideration of material differences of fact and other relevant and proper factors. Consistency cannot be defined in terms of the [per se rules themselves], but in terms of the statute's purposes and how the results reached in cases to which the rule applies compare to the results reached in all other cases decided under the relevant discretionary power." Abraham Sofaer, "Judicial Control of Informal Adjudication and Enforcement," 72 Colum. L. Rev. 1293, 1326 (1972). Compare Laurence Tribe, "Structural Due Process," 10 Harv. Civ. R. Civ. L. Rev. 269, 284-85 n. 47 (1975). In Hortonville Joint School Dist. v. Hortonville Education Assoc., 96 S. Ct. 2308 (1976), the Court indicated its receptiveness to the creation of discretionary regimes by holding, on highly debatable facts, that the Wisconsin legislature had granted unfettered discretion to Wisconsin school boards to fire teachers who went out on strike.

61. See pp. 140-41 & n. 52, *supra*, Laurence Rothstein, "Business As Usual? The Judicial Expansion of Welfare Rights," 50 J. Urban Law 1, 11-12 (1972), cites and discusses welfare-law cases to support the proposition that "the right to life is so fundamental that it cannot be burdened by eligibility conditions unrelated to the need of the recipient." There is no explicit constitutional guaranty of support for life. See Dandridge v. Williams, 397 U.S. 471 (1970).

A remarkable example is provided by the food-stamp cases, U.S.

Dept. of Agriculture v. Moreno, 413 U.S. 528 (1973), and U.S. Dept. of Agriculture v. Murry, 413 U.S. 508 (1973). In these cases the very legislation authorizing distribution of the benefit also specifically denied eligibility to certain classes of applicants. The Court, invoking the due process and equal protection clauses, invalidated the statutory exclusions because they were not tightly enough related to an applicant's need for food. See also note 68, *infra.*

62. Compare Frank Michelman, "In Pursuit of Constitutional Welfare Rights: One View of Rawls' Theory of Justice," 121 U. Pa. L. Rev. 962, 997-1010 (1973). A "moral entitlement" corresponds to the second of the two senses of "right" distinguished by Barbara Brudno, "Fairness and Bureaucracy: The Demise of Procedural Due Process for Welfare Claimants," 25 Hastings L. J. 813, 821-22 & n. 28 (1974), while positivistic entitlements correspond to the first sense. A comparison of sections V-VII of this paper with section VII of Professor Grey's contribution to this volume will reveal important similarities in our views, while note 17 of his paper identifies a basic difference.

63. For an apparent instance of such feedback, involving equal protection rather than due process, see Justice v. Board of Educ., 351 Supp. 1252 (S.D.N.Y. 1972) (school lunch program). Compare Paul Dimond, "The Constitutional Right to Education: The Quiet Revolution," 24 Hastings L. J. 1087, 119-20, 1127.

64. But compare Hampton v Mow Sun Wong, 96 S. Ct. 1897 (1976). In his opinion for the court in Lopez v. Henry Phipps Plaza South, Inc., 498 F. 2d 937 (2d Cir. 1974), Judge Friendly surmised that "[t]he [governments] which have extended aid to low and middle income housing hardly expected that a tenant could be evicted at the end of his term simply at the landlord's whim, when substitute housing could be obtained, if at all, only with delay, disruption in living habits and expense." Sure enough. But Judge Friendly was engaged in distinguishing the case before him (involving subsidized-housing nonrenewal) and the *Roth* case; and what he doesn't explain is: Why not make the same surmise about governmental expectations respecting the grounds on which jobholders might be "evicted" from their jobs?

65. See the dissents of Justice Marshall in Board of Regents v. Roth, 408 U.S. 564 (1972), and Massachusetts Board of Retirement v. Murgia, 96 S. Ct. 2562, 2571-72 (1967). In Norlander v. Schleck, 345 F. Supp. 595, 599 (D. Minn. 1972), the court wondered "whether ... the opportunity to be fairly considered for public employment, so as to be able to subsist and make a living ... [does] not rise to the same heights as a conditionally bought stove ..." (referring to Fuentes v.

Shevin, 407 U.S. 67 (1972)). Compare the suggestion that there is a "common law" right, under "the law of private associations," not to be arbitrarily expelled from membership in an organization (including a university)—the suggestion emphasizing that the doctrine protects membership *as such* (a "personality" interest) and not merely some linked proprietary or economic interest (such as a claim to some share of the organization's assets). Note, "Judicial Review of the University-Student Relationship: Expulsion and Governance," 26 Stan. L. Rev. 95 (1973). What is it that a court would do in recognizing the existence of such a right as a matter of "common law," which is any different from what a court would do in recognizing a "moral entitlement" to a public job?

66. A possible answer which seems to me inadequate is that the nonrenewed employee will typically have relinquished his procedural claim in advance. It is easy enough to imagine Professor Roth "waiving" his future procedural claims, as part of the same transaction—acceptance of a term contract with no trace of commitment to renewal—which results in his having no legal entitlement to keep his job. The professor, for reasons of his own, chooses to accept a job clearly marked by its exposure to the risk of unilateral, unexplained nonrenewal. He so chooses even though (I cheerfully assume) he might have found instead another job explicitly safeguarded by a commitment to explanatory procedures. This case is then clearly distinguishable from the public-housing case. The occupant's claim to the housing, and its actual accessibility to him, arise out of and are framed by his immediate need for housing and inability to obtain it elsewhere. Under those circumstances of state monopolization, the occupant cannot be said to have voluntarily relinquished any claim to explanatory procedures by accepting a lease which purports to negate those claims. See Aguiar v. Hawaii Housing Authority, 522 P. 2d 1255, 1268 (Hawaii 1974).

There are several difficulties with this explanation of the *Roth* decision, as one which does not so much deny a due process right to nonformal explanatory procedures as avoids the question through a finding of waiver. First and least interestingly, there is no indication at all in the Court's statement of the facts of any conscious, deliberate, relinquishment by Roth of any future claim he thought he might have to explanatory procedures in case of nonrenewal. Simply as a matter of precedent, Roth cannot be held to have "waived" any nonformal due process claims, under the Court's demanding standards for waiver of future procedural rights, as reflected in Fuentes v. Shevin, 407 U.S. 67 (1972), and D.H. Overmyer Co. v. Frick Co., 405 U.S. 174 (1972).

Second, if persons in Roth's position did ordinarily have a consitutional right to nonformal explanatory procedures (which is just the question we have under consideration), for a governmental agency to condition its offer of employment on the applicant's agreeing to forgo that right in the future would pose a serious constitutional issue (concerning an "unconstitutional condition") never noticed or discussed in the *Roth* decision. See, e.g., "Entitlement, Enjoyment, and Due Process of Law," 1974 Duke L. J. 89, 99-101; cf. Arnett v. Kennedy, 416 U.S. 134 (1974), discussed at pp. TAN 25-27, *supra.*

Third, most fundamental, and deserving of much more thought and discussion than I can here give: there is a serious question whether a doctrine of waiver—of contractual relinquishment of claims which may become apposite on some future occasion—can apply at all to a "fraternal" claim such as that to nonformal explanatory procedures. How can a person make a legally binding advance relinquishment of his claim to be treated as an end rather than purely as a means? How can another person presume to take legal advantage of the purported waiver? The problem is not that the act of taking the waiver seriously would put one in the position of treating the person who made it as a mere means—for that could be said whenever we demanded performance of another's contractually binding promise, and it would apparently be wrong (or at least contradictory) on most such occasions insofar as our willingness to enter into the agreement in the first place was an act of respect for the other's autonomous personality and a refusal to contract would have been the opposite.

But in this case the contractual commitment is one whereby the one who makes it treats *himself* as a mere means—trading away not just a portion of his future freedom of action but his very claim to be treated as a fully valued person. In that respect the waiver seems distantly akin to voluntary, contractual enslavement. The problem it raises is also akin to that which the Supreme Court has confronted when persons have purported to waive procedural rights which are theirs as criminal suspects or accused. The Court displays extreme reluctance to find effective waiver when the right is seen as bearing on the fairness of the guilt-determining procedure, rather than as protecting some discrete, possessive interest of the right-holder's. See Schneckloth v. Bustamonte, 412 U.S. 218 (1973).

67. Interaction of formal with nonformal aims seems to occur in Judge Wyzanski's opinion in McQueen v. Druker, 317 F. Supp. 1122 (D. Mass. 1970). In the course of concluding that the housing subsidy statutes imply an entitlement to continued occupancy which supports a due process claim to formal explanatory procedures in case of

proposed eviction, the opinion ascribes to the legislature the following perceptions: "[I]n many cases the tenant and his neighbors have come to consider him as a citizen of the housing project's community, as he is a citizen of city, county, commonwealth, and country. If he is evicted capriciously both he and his neighbors will feel a sense of injustice. This will create an atmosphere of hostility to the managers of the projects, and may deter desirable persons with a feeling of independence from applying for or renewing leases. There will be less basis for treating a public housing project as a venture in participatory democracy, and as a counterweight to the anomie and alienation often characteristic of modern urban communities."

68. Compare Robert O'Neil, "Of Justice Delayed and Justice Denied: The Welfare Prior Fair Hearing Cases," 1970 Sup. Ct. Rev. 160, 163. Consider U.S. Dept. of Agriculture v. Murry, 413 U.S. 508 (1973). This decision invalidated a statutory provision denying eligibility for food stamps to households containing persons over eighteen claimed as tax dependents by other persons. The Court held that the statute set up a "conclusive presumption" of lack of need, and thus violated the due process rights of claimants to individualized determinations of their actual need. Now the Court had previously made plain its view that there is no constitutional entitlement to sustenance in any positivistic sense, see Dandridge v. Williams, 397 U.S. 471 (1970); and there was no statutory entitlement apart from the very statute containing the challenged "conclusive presumption." By its decision in *Murry,* the Court effectively recognized a moral entitlement not to be denied stamps (that is, food) except on the sole ground of lack of need. And the Court's reliance on a procedural due process theory (as distinguished from the more obvious theory that the challenged eligibility criterion was an arbitrary classification violative of the equal protection guaranty) suggests that what provoked the Court to detect the moral entitlement was a nonformal reaction against the viciousness of a regime which wouldn't even bother to *ask* claimants whether they were *really* "eligible" or not. Compare Laurence Tribe, Foreword: "Toward a Model of Roles in the Due Process of Life and Law," 87 Harv. L. Rev. 1, 49 n. 224 (1973); Laurence Tribe, "Structural Due Process," 10 Harv. Civ. R. Civ. Lib. L. Rev. 269, 288 n. 54 (1975).

Also relevant to the speculations in my text are decisions in which it seems that statutory entitlements *to explanatory procedures* (but not, so far as appears explicitly, to any substantive protections) were judicially translated into rationality entitlements. See Scheelhaase v. Woodbury Central Community School Dist., 349 F. Supp. 988 (N.D.

Iowa 1972); Mil-Ka-Ko Research & Devel. Corp. v. OEO, 352 F. Supp. 169 (D.D.C. 1972) *(semble)*.

69. See, e.g., David Kirp, "Schools As Sorters: The Constitutional and Policy Implications of Student Classification," 121 U. Pa. L. Rev. 705, 775-93 (1973).

70. The argument has already found judicial acceptance as applied to assignment to special programs, *e.g.*, for the "retarded" or those with "learning disabilities," more patently and pointedly stigmatizing than assignment to a middle or lower "track." See Mills v. Bd. of Educ., 348 F. Supp. 866 (D.D.C. 1972); Pennsylvania Assoc. for Retarded Children, 334 F. Supp. 1257 (E.D. Pa. 1971) (consent decree); Merle McClung, "Do Handicapped Children Have Legal Right to a Minimally Adequate Education," 3 J. Law & Educ. 153 (1974).

71. Compare David Kirp, William Buss and Peter Kuriloff, "Legal Reform of Special Education: Empirical Studies and Procedural Proposals," 62 Calif. L. Rev. 40, 128 (1974): "Parents have a strong interest in knowing facts that vitally affect their child's education and future," irrespective of any formal rights they may have.

72. Compare id. at 137: "Unless a decision is predicated on identifiable and reasonable criteria, the requirement of procedural protection becomes an elevation of meaningless formality."

73. Compare Norlander v. Schleck, 345 F. Supp. 595, 599-600 (D. Minn. 1972): "This holding is in no way intended to restrict the ability of the City of St. Paul to determine the fitness of applicants, nor does it impose any duty upon the city to hire any particular person. What is required is timely notice of the basis of decisions and a reasonable opportunity for refutation." A substantive requirement that officials made a good-faith effort to provide the most suitable or beneficial education, cf. Rouse v. Cameron 373 F.2d 451, 456 (D.C. Cir. 1966), doesn't seem to help much, although at least one knowledgeable observer is more optimistic. See Merle McClung, *supra* at 163-66.

74. Paul Dimond seems to agree that any judicially enforceable substantive right would be "chimerical" except in rare and extreme cases. See Paul Dimond, "The Constitutional Right to Education: The Quiet Revolution," 24 Hastings L. J. 1087, 1125-26 (1973). Thus he favors a procedural due process right which courts could enforce (and which Dimond hopes would go far to avoid substantive maltreatment) without any commitment to judicially reviewable substantive duties. See id. at 1108 n. 89, 1110, 1119-20, 1121, 1122. But this is just what the *Roth* doctrine seems to rule out.

One might want to contend that assignment to any track below the highest is so stigmatizing as to affect the *reputational* entitlement

upheld, as a part of Fourteenth Amendment "liberty," in Wisconsin
v. Constantineau, 400 U.S. 433 (1971), and reaffirmed in the *Roth*
opinion, 408 U.S. at 573, (dictum), and in Goss v. Lopez, 419 U.S.
565 (1975). See, e.g., David Kirp, *supra* at 776-78. *But see* Paul v.
Davis, 96 S. Ct. 115 (1976); Bishop v. Wood 96 S. Ct. 2074 (1976).
But in terms of stigma, a distinction between assignment to an
intermediate or lower track and nonrenewal of a professional
teacher's contract seems fragile indeed. In fact, the high likelihood of
some stigma in the nonrenewal situation may be what moved the *Roth*
court to suggest (a suggestion implicitly confirmed by the opinion in
Goss v. Lopez) that the *Constantineau* reputational entitlement comes
into play only when the challenged official action involves an explicit
branding of an individual.

75. See note 46, *supra.*

76. See David Kirp, William Buss and Peter Kuriloff, *supra* note 71, at
   118-19; ". . . [I]f the complaint of the student and his parents is that
   reassignment to a special program deprives the child of 'regular'
   education, it is not clear that there is any deprivation of a vital,
   protectible interest. It is clear that the child is receiving something
   different. But is it more, or less, or is the change neutral?"

77. David Kirp, William Buss and Peter Kuriloff, *supra* note 71, at 122,
   say that "it is clear . . . that classification decisions at the present time
   are made by persons who have interests which often conflict with
   those of the child and which are likely to shape some decisions
   improperly." When that is true, it seems to offer a good reason for
   requiring impartial decision, though not for creation of a judicially
   enforceable entitlement. The reasons given for believing it true seem
   not to apply to "track" assignments within the range of programs
   provided for "normal" students. See id. at 47-48.

   Allowance must also be made for cases in which either the
   professed grounds of a given assignment, or the actual results of a
   series of assignments, indicate that a "suspect classification" is (or
   very likely is) at work. See, e.g., William Clune, "Wealth Discrimination in School Finance," 68 Northwestern L. Rev. 651, 653-57 (1973).
   When disfavored treatment is dealt out on the basis of membership in
   groups traditionally susceptible to political abuse and stigmatization,
   or its distribution suspiciously correlates with such membership,
   judges do have an institutional advantage over administrators
   precisely because of the judiciary's insulation from political accountability; and it may well be appropriate in such cases for judges to
   insist that the discriminatory treatment be abandoned unless it can be
   convincingly justified by noncontroversial considerations. See, gen-

erally, John Ely, "Legislative and Administration Motive in Constitutional Law," 79 Yale L. J. 1205 (1971). Moreover, I do not rule out that groups enjoying this form of special judicial protection might include, in addition racial and ethnic minorities, persons marked by certain forms of physical, emotional, or intellectual abnormality. See Note, "Mental Illness: A Suspect Classification?," 83 Yale L. J. 1237 (1974). Still, an important residue of cases will remain to which the statement in my text is fully applicable.

78. See David Kirp, William Buss and Peter Kuriloff, *supra* note 71, at 79-81.
79. Compare p. 145, *supra.*
80. E.g., Justice Powell dissenting in Goss v. Lopez, 419 U.S. 565, 594-97 (1975).
81. Compare Laurence Tribe, "Structural Due Process," *supra* note 68, at 312.
82. But compare O'Neil, "Of Justice Delayed," *supra* note 68, at 91-92, "Protests against the system and its policies may well be diverted into more constructive channels by creating an opportunity to confront one's accusers and vindicate one's interests in a presumably neutral forum."
83. Compare Ian Macneil, "The Many Futures of Contract," 47 So. Cal. L. Rev. 691, 723-25, 738-40 (1974).
84. See, generally, John Rawls, *A Theory of Justice* (Cambridge, Mass.: Harvard Univ. Press, 1971).
85. Compare Goldberg v. Kelly, 397 U.S. 254, 265 (1970): "Public assistance is not mere charity." See also Immanuel Kant, *The Metaphysical Principles of Virtue* secs. 23, 31 (J. Ellington trans. 1964).
86. See Laurence Tribe, "Ways Not to Think About Plastic Trees," 83 Yale L.J. at 1338-39.
87. See pp. 139-40, *supra.*
88. See pp. 139, *supra.*
89. See pp. 139, *supra.*

5

DUE PROCESS, FRATERNITY, AND A KANTIAN INJUNCTION

EDMUND L. PINCOFFS

It is impossible to legislate decency in human relations. Decency generally requires that a man seriously and adversely affected by an official's decision be told why the decision was made as it was, and that he be allowed to contest the reasoning that supposedly justifies the decision. Professor Michelman ably exhibits the difficulties that arise in the attempt to reduce these requirements of decency to a set of entitlements under the constitution. On the one hand, the requirements, tacitly acknowledged to be serious and central, cannot be located among constitutional entitlements; on the other hand, a "modest" court will not simply take the requirements as a basis for decision. The consequence is a Swiss cheese argument for heretofore undiscovered entitlements—an argument that masks the sub rosa invention of entitlements under the pretence of discovering them. Immodesty is not avoided, but only concealed.

In these brief comments, I will argue that the requirements of revelation to the person affected of reasons for the adverse decision, and of his participation in the decision by contesting, if he wants, the reasons given, have a recognizable and solid moral ground.

Michelman hints at what such a ground might be when he suggests that allowing officials to proceed without interchange "would have a meaning that clashes unbearably with a preferred conception of social and political life, in which self-respect is recognized as the fundamental human good which social life affects" (*Supra,* p. 148.) But Michelman does not (although he does a great deal else) analyze the conception of self-respect involved, nor attempt to show how and why it is fundamental.

To link my scattered remarks to Michelman's paper, I will focus on *Roth,*[1] and, in general, on problems of interchange between the administrator and the person adversely affected by the administrator's decision. I will assume for the sake of argument that Justice Douglas, in his minority opinion, is wrong in insisting on the relevance of the question whether Roth's freedom of speech has been infringed. The question I want to discuss is not whether it is possible to reconcile the demand for revelation and participation with the Constitution; but rather what can be said on moral grounds for the value of revelation and participation, whether the grounds that can be adduced are instrumental or noninstrumental ones. For simplicity, I will confine most of my remarks to participation, since whatever line of reasoning justifies participation (the opportunity to contest the official's reasoning) will justify revelation to the person affected of the official's reasons.

As I understand participation, it requires that a person who believes that he may be seriously and adversely affected by some adminstrative action be given a fair opportunity to examine critically the arguments by which the administrator justifies taking that action, and to present counterarguments intended to show that the action is unjustified. In examining the administrator's argument, he may, as Michelman notes, question the validity of the rule or maxim adduced as ground by the administrator, the applicability of the ground to himself, given the circumstances, and the administrator's understanding of the facts of the case that together make up the circumstances.

Now suppose that there is at present no likely way to show that Roth is constitutionally entitled to contest the administrator's decision. Suppose that what Michelman calls "judicial modesty" rules out attempts to include participation under the liberty or property provisions of the Fourteenth Amendment. Is there a well-founded argument that a less modest court might rightly accept; an argument that would avoid the arbitrary assumptions concerning the relative weights to be assigned to "interests" against which Justice Stewart rightly protests?

Let us go back to *Roth*. Assistant Professor Roth is not, admittedly, entitled to an extension of his contract. He does want reasons why his contract is not being extended, but the president refuses to give him reasons. Roth actually thought that the real reasons had to do with his political views and activities, and he wanted the grounds of this indefensible line of reasoning exposed. But that is irrelevant for the purposes of our discussion. For the purposes of our discussion, it does not matter what use Roth wants to make of the president's reasons, or whether he wants to make any use at all. Of course, Roth wants more than reasons; he wants the opportunity to contest the soundness of the argument which leads to the conclusion that he should not be continued in his post. ("Soundness" here has to do with more than the truth of the premises and the validity of the argument, since there is also the question whether the proffered argument is the real argument, the argument by which the president was in fact persuaded; and with whether that argument is a sound one.) Should Roth be given reasons and the opportunity to contest them, and if so why?

Michelman traces out some lines of argument that might seem to show that Roth is not entitled to reasons, but, as he holds, none of them seems very persuasive. A frequent argument, not mentioned, but ultimately unpersuasive too, is that to collect together and present to Roth the different reasons for which different colleagues and administrators were unwilling to continue him, would be gratuitously offensive and damaging to his self-image—gratuitously offensive and damaging because the collection of reasons taken together might seem to reflect a derogatory valuation not shared by any individual who had voted for noncontinuance for some of the reasons in the collection. Yet, if this danger were pointed out to Roth, and he insisted nevertheless that reasons be given, it would seem that this consideration would not provide adequate grounds for withholding the reasons which, together, have persuaded the president that Roth should not be continued. (The question whether the reasons should be given in writing gives rise to the additional, also ultimately unpersuasive, argument that such a list of reasons, becoming a part of the record to which administrators may in future refer in answering inquiries, may be professionally damaging. Here again, if Roth wants to take the risk, this consideration has little weight.)

But if there are no very persuasive arguments why Roth should not be given reasons, are there any arguments why he should—or are we to leave it that it is just intuitively obvious that he is morally (even if not legally) entitled to reasons? Are we to say that of course he should be given reasons—and a chance to contest them—out of simple decency? Or that in an ideal community he would be given reasons? Or that to refuse to give him reasons and an opportunity to contest them would be unthinkable? None of these remarks would be very helpful. None of them gives reasons for the giving of reasons; all seem like ways of avoiding the kind of account which must be given to those who are impressed with the need for official efficiency, for getting on with whatever the task may be.

Yet the president, like any public official, is a Janus-figure. He must speak not only to those whose interest is in the most effective use of his resources for the advancement of public education, but he must also speak to those who question the acceptability of his policies. The latter are the boundary makers, and, almost inevitably, the restrainers. They speak of justice and humanity and insist that effectiveness alone is not enough. Yet if anything is to be accomplished, it is clear that the president must not be too much restrained, must not be bound to attend to every cry of injustice or inhumanity no matter whose, no matter how unreasonable, no matter how publicized, no matter how prolonged. If entitlement seems the wrong handle on this problem it may be because entitlement ties too closely to property, and property is, as Michelman and the Court agree, not easily stretched to cover Roth's demand for reasons. Anyway, property rights are external in a way that Roth's rights—if he has rights—are not. If the university wants to take a man's home for a parking lot, he stands to suffer a loss at the hands of an organization and an enterprise of which he is no part. He has made no prior agreement that in any way qualifies the claim that he is being harmed. But Roth is a part of the enterprise, and he has entered into an employment agreement that explicitly says that he is hired for one year, and that offers him no assurance of consideration for continuance. How, then, is he harmed by the refusal—or failure—to renew his contract?

It could be argued that he is not, because his nonrenewal is an easily predictable outcome of an agreement into which Roth freely entered; an agreement in which there is nothing morally questionable, like the agreement to become an indentured servant. In agreeing to a one-year contract, Roth agreed that the contract would not be for more than one year. The harm lies not in nonrenewal but in the refusal to give reasons for nonrenewal. Roth knew that a renewal was a possibility—perhaps even a likelihood. Why, then, was he not renewed? The contract was, after all, probationary. Was the judgment that he was in some way deficient or at fault, or was it that he simply did not measure up to the talent available? Or did it have nothing to do with any of these matters, having to do, rather, with budgetary problems, or with the balancing of faculty between departments and colleges? Roth would seem to have a moral right to know whether his proposed nonrenewal implies that he is in some way at fault or deficient; and the president would seem to have a moral duty to make known to him, upon request, whether the nonrenewal implies fault, and if so, what the fault is supposed to be. But what is required is at least the sketch of an argument to show that the asserted right and duty do obtain, that they are not derivable from merely prudential grounds, and that they are nonetheless well founded on at least one moral principle that can lay claim to universal validity.

Somewhat to my own surprise, I find that I am driven, in my analysis of the moral rights and duties that obtain between Roth and his president to the second formulation of the Kantian categorical imperative; the formulation that commands us never to treat anyone—including ourselves—as a mere means. Think of the Kantian command as being justified and at the same time clarified by the examination of a number of varying paradigms of treating persons as mere means to some end. One paradigm that might be offered is precisely the case in hand. If the president is assessed—and assesses himself—solely on grounds of his efficiency in attaining the complex end of an adequate educational opportunity for those who are qualified to take advantage of it, then he regards himself as a mere means, and at the same time regards Roth and his colleagues as mere means to the attainment of educational opportunity. Now, suppose that the president fails to renew Roth because he believes that Roth is a poor teacher, but at the same time he refuses to give Roth any reason for his nonrenewal. He may attempt to justify his failure to provide reasons on grounds of efficiency. It would take a great deal of time for him or some dean or committee to give every discontinued professor who requested it a list of reasons—especially when the giving of reasons is likely to lead to a hearing, and possibly to a lawsuit. At the same time, he knows that Roth's conception of himself and of his own worth is tied up with Roth's conception of himself as a professional teacher. He also knows—or would be justified in assuming—that Roth is the product of a cultural tradition and an educational process in which by detecting and overcoming faults one improves one's performances. But if Roth is not informed of his fault, he is treated as a mere means; he is eliminated, like a faulty machine part, from an organization that will henceforth, supposedly, function better without him, and in that no further thought is given to Roth's interest in correcting his own performance.

There does not seem to be a good argument, on grounds of efficiency alone, why Roth should be given reasons. (There *would* be an argument for revealing to Roth the faultiness of his performance as a teacher if he were to be retained.) It might be held that the president should—on prudential grounds more widely conceived—inform Roth of his faults as a teacher, even if Roth is not to be renewed. It might be argued that the president's objective is to advance the interests of education, and that he would do so by offering Roth criticism and advice. But in this wide and nebulous responsibility very little leverage could be found for the claim that Roth had any moral claim on the president. The giving of reasons to Roth is then on a par with a hundred other things that the president can do that day to advance the general cause of educational opportunity. He may rightly believe that he can achieve more by tending to his duties on an accrediting committee, or by writing letters to foundations, than by passing the time of day with Roth.

Of course, Roth may have graver doubts. He may wonder

whether he has been found deficient in qualities that reach farther than his professional life. He may wonder if he has been judged lazy, intemperate, crude. What kind of fellow do they think that he is, anyway? He has been assessed, and he may have been found wanting. *Has* he been found wanting, and, if so, wanting what? Surely, if he is not to be treated as a mere means, he is owed the reasons that he requests.

But his being owed reasons is but a small distance—if it is any distance—from his being owed a hearing in which he can examine, and challenge, what is said by the president—in which he can participate in the decision that concerns himself. The president is not treating Roth as an end in himself if he gives reasons to the board of regents in executive session, or to an elected faculty committee pledged to secrecy. His reasons cannot be couched in an official jargon as unintelligible to Roth as Hindi. But the direct way to ascertain their intelligibility to Roth is to allow Roth to examine them. The reasons must not be vague or ambiguous beyond comprehension.

Here again, if the "reasons" are to count as reasons, Roth would seem to be the likely person to ask the questions that will allow them to qualify. The president can hardly be allowed to be the authority on whether the reasons he gives are vague, for he may believe it in the interest of efficiency or in his own interest to speak vaguely, and, thus, evasively, and in this way to slide by his obligation to Roth. Nor should the president be the authority on whether his reasons contradict one another, thus reducing reasons to nonreasons, nor on whether the conclusion that Roth should not be renewed follows from the reasons he gives. Even if the president were to decide what is a reason and whether the reasons given are consistent, and whether the conclusion follows, there would still be the possibility, in the absence of a hearing, that, given the circumstances, Roth was justified in teaching as he did, or that there was a valid excuse for his having taught badly.

It is not necessary, then, to suppose that there is value in sheer participation. Participation may be instrumentally valuable, but instrumental to the achievement of a moral purpose that is itself impossible to describe in instrumental terms, the purpose of treating a man not as a mere means but as an end in himself. This is not to say that there is no intrinsic value in participation. I would prefer to say that there may be, but that the moral value of participation turns on its relation to a moral end. This relationship of instrumentality is not the same kind as that between the president's raising money and educational opportunity for all. We might say that participation is an instrument by which the valuation of persons as ends in themselves is expressed. It is as if the Kantian principle were determinable in any number of ways, but participation is one of the ways in which it may become determinate. It does not follow that mere participation is of value (though it may have value), but rather follows that participation is morally valuable to the degree that it makes determinate the moral principle that we should never treat a man as a mere means.

If, with Michelman, we take self-respect to be the "fundamental human good," then the treating of persons as ends in themselves will, I suppose, be a psychologically necessary condition for the generation of self-respect. But I suspect that it would be better to say that the fundamental good, if there is one, is a state of affairs in which each person is respected as an end in himself. Then self-respect will not be delusory.

One way of making determinate the determinable Kantian injunction is through a contract theory, like John Rawls's, in which the social bargain is carefully drawn under conditions designed to guarantee, or at least make likely, that no individual will be a mere means to others' ends, and, positively, that he will be treated as an end in himself. Whether such a theory can be incorporated into the framework of law I have no idea; yet the theory just might, in its essentials, express a consensus as to the directions in which the Kantian principle should lead us. But it is quite conceivable to me that we should proceed less systematically, building up as we go along a set of paradigms for practices that should be avoided as treating persons as mere means, and not as ends in themselves.

Michelman has a good deal to say about the "fraternal" or "communal" value of revelation and participation. The Kantian principle suggests one formulation of what that value might consist in (expanded impressionistically in Kant's discussion of a "kingdom of ends"). Community consists in this: that no one can rightly complain of being *used* by another. This is a narrow and negative kind of definition of community, but for that very reason it may have considerable power as a shaper of the practices, legal or nonlegal, by which we live. It sets bounds on our treatment of each other, bounds to which we can appeal in different ways: by hints of moral insensitivity, by talk of rights, or by appeal to the law. It does not provide a positive goal—defined in attitudinal or institutional terms—but proceeds instead to refine our sense of what it is to *use* another person or oneself.

The obvious safeguard against such use is that the person enter meaningfully into the consultation about what is to be done to him, for him, with him. Revelation to him of the reasons for the proposed action, and his participation in the assessment of those reasons are then necessary conditions of meaningful consultation—consultation that is not merely a blind for action that takes no account of him, his interests, his desires.

Of course, none of this is much help in drawing a line between morally and legally impermissible use of a person. Yet one suggestion may be offered. The kinds of use on which legislative and judicial thought should focus are those in which, by the rules of a practice, allocations are made, by someone in authority, of what people desire, or what they want to avoid. It is this authoritative distribution that is the proper subject of legislation and of judicial review. I do not see why, given this context, the judge cannot make use, in reviewing administrative decisions, of a network of analogy with undisputed paradigms of *using* persons. One kind of paradigm may be provided in *Roth*, where reasons are not revealed, and no opportunity for consultation is provided.

Revelation to a person of the reasons for an adverse decision, and allowing him an opportunity to contest those reasons are ways, then, of showing forth, of exhibiting a principle on which community may be built. It is a rather special community in that its ties are not merely those of natural affection or concern, of loyalty, or of respect for authority. Fraternity and community will not, by themselves, be enough. Fraternity can be exclusionary and blind in its loyalty; communities can be frivolous in purpose or mean in their personal relations.

Decency requires that men who have a great deal to lose from an official decision be given an opportunity to contest it. But the decency in question is not a matter of small courtesy or of propriety. It is, rather, the decency that prevails when a community is so governed that no man need fear that he will be treated as a mere means.

NOTE
1. Board of Regents v. Roth, 408 U.S. 564 (1972).

6

PROCEDURAL FAIRNESS AND SUBSTANTIVE RIGHTS

THOMAS C. GREY

This essay is a rough attempt to sketch some of the general contours of the concept of procedural fairness. Procedural fairness is a concept in some respects broader and in others narrower than due process of law. On the one hand, norms of procedural fairness—a moral concept—apply to processes used in deciding nonlegal disputes. Thus a parent's decision of a dispute between children might violate notions of fair procedure if the parent listened to only one side of the dispute before deciding it. On the other hand, procedural fairness does not include those fundamental substantive rights which in our constitutional law are enforced in the name of due process—rights such as the freedoms of speech and religion insofar as they restrain state governments, or the rights of liberty and privacy usually characterized as aspects of substantive due process.

In general, however, it seems clear that the basic core of what lawyers call "procedural due process" is formed around the popular conceptions of procedural fairness manifested in the common judgments of conventional morality. Of course, the legal doctrines of due process are far more detailed, ramified and precise than are lay notions of fair procedure. But where the law of due process departs from the broad outlines of the morality of procedural fairness, producing results strongly contrary to widely shared intuitive judgments, it seems right to presume that it has gone astray.

I

Procedural fairness has both a loose and a strict sense. In its loose sense, the term includes certain rules and principles applicable to dispute-settling procedures that are designed to protect substantive rather than procedural values. I have in mind examples such as these: the criminal defendant's privilege not to testify; the rule excluding from evidence a priest's testimony about a penitent's confession; the rules prohibiting the use of evidence extracted by physical or psychological abuse; and rules prohibiting or restraining the use of evidence obtained by invasions of privacy or trespasses. These are not rules and principles of procedural fairness in the strict sense in which I shall use the term in this paper. They are procedural standards only in that their primary (or sole) application is to dispute-settling procedures. Unlike rules and principles of procedural fairness in the strict sense, they are not aimed at producing more accurate or fair *decisions* of those disputes. They are rather designed to protect various substantive rights and interests from the invasions to which they would be subject if the strictly procedural aims of correct fact-finding and rule-applying were pursued single-mindedly (or subject only to prudential constraints of cost).

These rules of due process (in the loose sense) may very often clash with values of strict procedural fairness. The point can perhaps be seen most clearly when a criminal defendant might be exculpated by a priest's testimony about matters revealed to him in someone else's confession. Here the principle that a defendant must have compulsory process to compel relevant testimony in his favor (a principle of procedural fairness in the strict sense) clashes with the priest-penitent privilege (a principle of due process in the loose sense—substantive due process, I should say, based on values of privacy and religious freedom).[1]

I believe that procedural fairness lends itself to coherent analysis as a single concept only if it is taken in the strict sense. This is so because in its looser sense it encompasses all the substantive rights which may be threatened in the pursuit of accurate and correct adjudication of disputes. Yet there is no limit in principle to the number and variety of such potentially threatened substantive rights. In the case of each of them, the considerations favoring their protection in the procedural context will be essentially the same as those favoring their protection generally. If procedural fairness were given so broad a sense, it would thus embrace all conceivable substantive moral and legal rights, and there could be no prospect of giving it intelligible consideration as a separate and finite concept on its own account.[2]

II

The rules and principles of procedural fairness (in the narrow sense) all are designed to promote the correct decision of disputes.[3] All of them tend to ensure that facts will be found more accurately or that evaluations will be made more reasonably and impartially than would be the case if they were not in force.

Consider, for example, the rules of fair procedure applicable in criminal trials. The judge must be impartial, judgment must be based on sworn testimony or other reliable evidence, the defendant must have counsel, he must be able to call witnesses in his favor and cross-examine the witnesses against him, and so on. These rules have as their object the prevention of the conviction of innocent defendants because of the malice, prejudice, carelessness, laziness, haste, or excessive zeal of law enforcement officials.[4] The similar rules of due process applicable in civil trials are likewise designed to lessen the likelihood of erroneous decisions, as are the less elaborate rules applicable in many administrative proceedings.

But the values of procedural fairness do not impose upon dispute-settling mechanisms an impossible counsel of perfection. Disputes should not be decided wrongly, but on the other hand they must be decided, and decided at a cost commensurate with what is at stake in the dispute. Accuracy-promoting mechanisms must not be imposed beyond the point at which the costs or delays they involve outweigh the benefits from the additional accuracy they secure. Recognition of this point introduces the balancing element inevitable in judgments of procedural fairness. Accuracy must be balanced against cost. Or, to put it more precisely, principles of fair procedure promote accuracy subject to the prudential constraints of cost.

A further qualification must be made. Principles of procedural fairness are not designed to promote accuracy in the abstract or to advance the pursuit of truth in general. For example, the rules of fair procedure applicable to criminal trials are all designed to reduce the likelihood of erroneous *convictions*. A criminal procedure which resulted in too many innocent defendants being convicted would on that account be unfair. But we would not condemn as violative of due process an apparatus of criminal procedure which resulted in too many acquittals of the guilty. We might say that it did not sufficiently advance the abstract cause of public justice, though we would more likely condemn it as lax or inefficient, bad as a matter of policy rather than unjust.

Consider a principle of fair criminal procedure that quite obviously retards rather than advances the overall accuracy of the criminal process. The requirement that guilt be proved beyond a reasonable doubt certainly produces more erroneous acquittals than it prevents erroneous convictions. Indeed, it is often paraphrased into a numerical form that dramatizes the point: "Better that ten (or five, or twenty) guilty men be acquitted than that one innocent man be convicted." The principle is clearly based on a relative assessment of the substantive interests at stake in a criminal trial: while it is important as a matter of public policy (or even of abstract justice) to punish the guilty, it is a very great and concrete injustice to punish the innocent.

In the normal civil law suit, there is no such asymmetry. The interests of fairness lie in seeing that the dispute is correctly decided according to accurately found facts, subject to the prudential constraints of cost. There is no greater injustice in an error one way than the other. Accordingly, procedural fairness requires that the facts be found by a preponderance of the evidence. A mild preference for the status quo dictates that the defendant shall win if the evidence is in equipoise. In respect to matters such as the right to counsel and the right to call witnesses, both parties have the same rights.

However, even outside the criminal process, judgments of procedural fairness may be asymmetrical. An example occurs in the administration of public assistance (or welfare) programs. For most of the history of welfare in this country, these programs have been administered subject to virtually no requirements of due process. Welfare authorities decided—often on an entirely informal basis—which applicants should be approved and how much they should receive. Only in the last few decades have legislatures and welfare bureaucracies established formal procedures designed to reduce the risk of erroneous denials of public assistance, though these same procedures have typically been at least equally well designed to prevent erroneous determinations of eligibility and overpayments.

A few years ago, the Supreme Court went beyond this and decided, as a matter of constitutional due process, that before a welfare recipient could have his grant discontinued on the ground that he had become ineligible, he must be offered the right to contest the finding of ineligibility at an administrative hearing.[5] This requirement went beyond the establishment of formal procedural equality between the state and the welfare recipient. As a dissenting opinion in the case noted, the state was forced to continue payments to recipients it had determined to be ineligible until it could establish their ineligibility at a hearing, even though there was very little practical likelihood that it could recover the payments made in the interim to ineligible recipients.[6] The majority of the Court did not deny that this would be a consequence of its decision, but argued that the particularly harsh consequences of erroneously denying welfare benefits to those who were eligible justified this special imposition on the state—in this context, unlike almost any other, temporary termination of benefits deprived the recipient of "the very means by which to live" and rendered his situation "immediately desperate."[7] Given this consideration, the Court concluded that it was necessary to depart from the normal procedure of requiring an alleged obligee to take affirmative action in order to compel payment from an alleged obligor who denies the obligation.

III

In the criminal prosecution, the typical civil suit, and the administrative determination of the eligibility of welfare recipients, the principles and values of procedural fairness are invoked only to protect the claims of individuals to correct decision of the dispute in question. "Individuals" here may include institutions when they are subject to the decisions of other, authoritative, institutions. Thus, a corporation may claim the protection of due process in a lawsuit, and even a nation may do so in a dispute before an international tribunal. But institutions—or even natural persons—may not invoke the values of fair procedure on their own behalf with respect to disputes that they have authority to decide: a state in a criminal prosecution; a corporation in the internal discipline of its employees; or a parent in his dealings with his children.

Principles of due process operate as an external moral or legal check upon the decision procedures adopted by authoritative deciders of disputes. They provide a counterweight to the natural interests of those decision makers. In the criminal process, the natural interests of the state tend toward the punishment of offenders and the avoidance of cost. Due process checks are thus required to safeguard the more fragile interest of the defendant in the assurance that he will not be punished unless guilty. In the typical civil lawsuit, the interest of the state as a neutral third-party adjudicator between private disputants is in minimizing the cost of decision. Thus, principles of due process are required to protect the interests of the disputants in the correct adjudication of their particular claims. In the welfare case, the courts have, in imposing special constraints of due process on the bureaucracy, revealed their judgment that administrative officials are naturally inclined to protect the public purse through summary procedures and substantive presumptions against eligibility. A parent deciding a dispute between children may unconsciously lean toward one child or may be too much influenced by his natural desire to have the dispute quickly settled to take sufficient care that it be settled right. In this context, the tugs of conscience provided by the extralegal principles of fair procedure tend toward restoration of the proper equilibrium of the competing factors.

IV

It is not always the case that when an institution makes a decision affecting the interests of an individual, principles of due process apply to the decision procedures adopted by the institution. The point is illustrated in the constitutional context by the Supreme Court's decision in the case of Board of Regents v. Roth.[8] In that case, a university teacher was employed under a one-year contract. The teacher was informed that his contract would not be renewed when it expired. He argued that due process required that he be told the reasons why his contract would not be renewed and given the opportunity to contest the validity and applicability of the grounds for the decision at a hearing.

The Supreme Court rejected his argument. The Court conceded that Roth had a strong interest in being continued in his employment, but nevertheless concluded that the decision to drop him could be made entirely unconstrained by any requirements of procedural due process. The Court reasoned that Roth had no claim of entitlement to renewal of his teaching contract. If Roth's original contract had provided that he would be rehired from year to year unless affirmative cause appeared to terminate his employment, he would have had a sufficient claim of entitlement to require the notice and hearing he sought. The same would have been the case if a state statute had required that university teachers, once hired, could not be let go except for cause. But in the absence of any such statutory or contractual provision, the expiration of Roth's contract left him with no legal claim to continued employment at the university—however strong his personal stake in retaining his job.

Implicit in the Court's decision in *Roth* is the premise that the Constitution permits the state to hire Roth in the first place without giving him any assurance of job tenure. Similarly implicit is the premise that a state university need not hire an applicant however well qualified he may be. The Constitution creates no substantive entitlement either to continuation of a job once the term of the employment contract runs out, or to the creation of an employment relationship at the behest of any particular applicant. If the Constitution did embody any such substantive entitlements, those entitlements would have supported Roth's claim to the benefits of procedural due process.

It is very often the case that an individual stands in Roth's situation. He has a strong stake or interest in a decision that a government official has authority to render favorably to him. Yet, because the individual has no claim of entitlement to a favorable decision, canons of procedural fairness are inapplicable to the decision-making process. As Roth's case shows, applicants for government jobs, or holders of government jobs whose contractual terms have run out, are typically in this position.

As another example, one might consider a prisoner who applies for executive clemency—pardon or commutation of sentence. It goes without saying that the applicant has a strong interest in the outcome of the decision on his application. Yet it seems certain that the courts would not require the decision to be made under any constraints of procedural fairness, and that they would give as their reason the absence of any plausible claim of entitlement to clemency on the prisoner's part.

In Roth's case and the prisoner's case, many of the conditions favoring application of principles of fair procedure suggested earlier do obtain. The officials with power to rehire Roth or pardon the prisoner may have inclinations natural to persons in their positions militating against the careful and individualized consideration of the factors supporting a decision favorable to the individual applicant. Such officials are busy people, and if left unchecked by special procedural restraints, are surely likely to take the path of least resistance and give relatively casual attention to the individual factors involved in each case—attention more casual than a postulated impartial ideal observer might think appropriate, given the intensity of the individual interests at stake. All these conditions are present, but what is lacking—and what the Supreme Court found present in the otherwise similar case of the welfare recipient's claim to continued public assistance—is a claim of entitlement on the part of the individual to the benefit he seeks.

In the welfare case, the Court found that the requisite claim of entitlement arose, not out of any substantive constitutional requirement guaranteeing welfare benefits, but out of statutes providing that public assistance payments should be made in defined amounts to applicants meeting defined conditions.[9] In the absence of a constitutional requirement of welfare, these statutes were adopted by legislatures which had very broad discretion over their substantive terms, and indeed had discretion to establish no welfare program at all.

Apparently, it is the establishment of substantive legal rules governing the bestowal of governmental benefits which creates entitlements to those benefits, and which thus trigger constitutional rights to procedural fairness in those applicants who can make colorable claims that under the rules they are eligible for the benefits. Thus if the official with authority to rehire Roth had been subject to rules setting forth the conditions on which probationary teachers were to be continued in employment, the courts would have imposed independent constitutional standards of procedural fairness on the procedure through which the decision applying those rules was made.[10] Similarly, if the exercise of the executive clemency power were subject to substantive rules, the procedures through which pardons were granted and denied would be subject to constitutional judicial review for fairness.

In my view, there is a paradox here. The Constitution is indifferent to the very intense and yet fragile interests of applicants for government jobs or for clemency as long as the officials in charge of deciding on those applications are left unguided by substantive rules governing those decisions. The Constitution is indifferent to whether those decisions are subject to substantive rules. If such rules are adopted, the Constitution is almost entirely indifferent to their content.[11] The Constitution is even indifferent to the question whether the benefits in question are available at all. But if the benefits are made available, and the conditions for bestowing them are defined by rules, the Constitution closely constrains the discretion of the rule-making authorities to design the procedures under which individual claims for the benefits in question are granted or rejected.

The paradox is this. Legislative procedural design responds to the same competing considerations of individual interest, cost and administrative flexibility which govern the substantive decision whether to provide benefits, at what level to provide them, and how closely to cabin administrative discretion by legislative rules. In the substantive design of programs, the political branches of government are left quite free to strike their own balance among these competing considerations. For instance, in Roth's case, the legislature was free to grant some job security to teachers in Roth's position or (as they decided in fact) to grant none. Presumably it was thought that the public interest in flexible and discretionary decisions with respect to probationary teachers outweighed the individual interest in job security.

On the other hand, the legislature might have decided to grant some substantive job security to teachers—requiring, for example, that their contracts should be renewed unless cause could be shown why they should not. At the same time, the legislature might have wanted to confine the effect of this standard to its restraining influence on the judgment of university officials, believing that the apparatus of formal hearings to determine whether cause was indeed present was not worth its cost in time, money, and loss of flexibility. As presently interpreted, constitutional due process would disable the legislature from adopting this combination of substantive entitlement with flexible administration, while leaving it free to dispense with the substantive entitlement altogether.[12] Why should this be so?

In explaining this paradox, it does not suffice to make reference to the importance and fragility of the individual interests at stake. By hypothesis, those interests are not sufficient to require the benefits to be granted at all. Nor does it suffice to advert to the inclinations of officials to slight those interests in their decisions whether or not to grant the benefits, when those inclinations are as much present when bestowal of the benefits is not governed by rules. Indeed, the rule-making authorities are left with full discretion to slight those interests as much as they wish in establishing the substantive terms of the rules governing the bestowal of benefits.

It is tempting to resolve the paradox legalistically; to argue that the Constitution requires fair procedure, but not clemency or job security or welfare. I think many lawyers and laymen alike would not press the inquiry beyond that response. But the temptation to rest on the constitutional text in justifying judicial review confined to the fairness of the *procedures* under which substantively optional benefit programs are administered should be resisted.

The truth is that nothing in the language or historical background of the constitutional due process clauses requires or even strongly suggests such review. The constitutional text forbids deprivation of "life, liberty or property without due process of law." Historically, the rights of life, liberty, and property were regarded as natural (and constitutional) rights which the legislatures could neither create nor destroy. The characterization of legislatively created benefits like job tenure or welfare payments as property— much less life or liberty—would not have occurred to the framers of our due process clause.

Traditionally, benefits such as these—benefits which governments can grant or withdraw in their discretion—have been described as "privileges" rather than rights, and as such outside the protection of the due process clauses. Where there was legislative discretion to create and define the substantive terms of a benefit program, there was equal legislative discretion to give structure to the procedures under which that program was administered. With respect to such discretionary programs, the process established by the authority with the discretion to define the program was the only process which was "due."

Modern courts have rejected this traditional position and the "right-privilege distinction" that underlies it. But their rejection cannot be based on the language or the historical meaning of the due process clauses. It must be justified by arguments from contemporary moral ideals implicit in the general concept of procedural fairness. And those arguments must confront the paradox presented by constitutional indifference to the substantive content and indeed to the very existence of benefit programs, combined with deep constitutional concern for the procedures through which those programs are administered once established.

V

As a first approach to the paradox, one might argue that it is not the content but the source of the programs which gives special force to the requirement that they be accurately enforced. Statutes such as those creating job security or establishing a welfare program may not themselves be required by justice or morality, but they have been passed by a democratically elected legislature, and as such represent the popular will. On this view, which stems from notions of the separation of powers, due process constraints are designed to prevent the circumvention of the legislative will by bureaucrats or executive officials through the kind of careless or intentional misapplication of statutes which can be caused or permitted by excessively informal procedures.

This attempt to justify review for procedural fairness as a device to protect legislators from bureaucrats cannot withstand analysis. Any procedure invalidated on grounds of due process has itself been either mandated directly by the legislature itself, or created by executive officials under express or implied legislative authority.

Procedures lacking such legislatively granted authority are unlawful without reference to constitutional due process; they are invalid because they violate statutory law. Due process—if it is to be the vital notion it has been in our constitutional law—must be a restraint on legislative as well as on executive procedural design.

Further, norms of due process are not applicable only to the enforcement of democratically promulgated substantive laws. Even a dictator may establish substantive laws the administration of which can be criticized as procedurally unfair. His substantive criminal code might not be very different from our own; but if in trials of alleged offenders, evidence was taken in secret, the judge was dependent on the executive, and the defendant was not allowed to be heard, the dictator would be subject to legitimate criticism for procedural injustice as well as for undemocratic rule. The same point can be made with respect to the application of norms of procedural fairness in the many situations where the applicable substantive norms are not legislated or promulgated at all; as, for example, when a parent decides a dispute between children or indeed whenever customary substantive norms are applied. It is, in short, simply not useful to regard procedural due process merely as an aspect of the theory of separation of powers, or as a protection of government by popular consent.

VI

A second approach would treat the special concern for procedural fairness as based on the morality of contractual obligation. Where substantive norms—whatever their source or status—govern a dispute, they generate in the parties to the dispute the legitimate expectation that these norms will be accurately applied. Even if the substantive rules are themselves only the product of a legislative balancing of conflicting interests, or indeed even if their content is quite arbitrary and devoid of any intrinsic moral force, the frustration of the expectation that they will be followed is felt as injustice. Morality does not require me to help my neighbor move his furniture, even though he would be happier if I did; but if I *promise* to help him and then do not (without adequate excuse), I have wronged him. Similarly, the constitution may not require governments to grant job tenure to their employees or welfare payments to their needy citizens, but statutes establishing such programs create expectations which if frustrated trigger a universal sense of injustice. Due process norms then operate to enforce a kind of "truth-in-lawmaking," to prevent frustration, through unduly inaccurate procedures, of expectations generated by substantive norms which by their terms guarantee benefits.

Here we have a plausible account of how it can be unjust to create a benefit program and then not implement it with sufficiently accurate procedures, even though it would not be unjust to have no such program at all. And the account meets the objections which defeated the "separation of powers" account of procedural fairness. It justifies due process as a restraint on legislative as well as executive power, since it can be invoked where a legislature creates a substantive entitlement but then mandates procedures inadequate to ensure its sufficiently accurate administration. It explains the applicability of standards of due process to substantive norms whose source confers on them no special legitimacy—a tyrant as well as a democratic legislature can create promiselike obligations by issuing a law establishing a welfare system or guaranteeing job security for employees.

Nevertheless, the promissory theory does not adequately resolve the paradox of due process. If we think of a benefit program established by law as a promise or set of promises establishing rights in the beneficiaries, why should we look only to the substantive provisions of the law defining the program as terms of the promise? The program establishes not only substantive entitlements, but also procedures for determining in individual cases whether the substantive terms are met. Government employees may not be fired except for cause—as determined by the following procedure. People meeting certain conditions are entitled to welfare—as determined by the following procedure.

Now imagine a due process attack charging that the procedures are error-prone, so that the expectations generated by the program will be unfairly frustrated, the promise will be broken. What is the promise? Is it that *every* claimant who in fact meets the terms of the program will receive the benefit? No one could sensibly read it that way; a procedure could not possibly be devised which would be wholly error-free. On the other hand, the terms of the program itself "promise" only that persons will receive the substantive benefits, subject to the error rate one would expect to result from application of the procedures established by the statute. Yet this promise will invariably be kept if the statute is enforced according to its terms. And if the statutorily prescribed procedures are not complied with, we again need no concept of due process or fairness to find them illegal—they violate the terms of the statute itself.

It might be argued that I have posed a false dilemma in describing a statute as promising either an (impossible) foolproof set of procedures or simply the enforcement of its own procedural terms. Perhaps popular expectations do not form around the actual, highly technical, procedural terms of statutory programs, although they do around the basic substantive terms. A benefit program might be thought to generate the expectation that its substantive terms will be enforced with a "normal" or "reasonable" degree of accuracy in application. The standard of normality would be determined by reference to the sorts of procedural safeguards commonly provided for already existing programs of a similar type. The moral force of that standard is again promissory—when a new statutory right is established, its beneficiaries can fairly expect that it will be enforced with the degree of accuracy and formality of procedure with which they have been accustomed in their similar previous dealings with the state. They cannot fairly be expected to look to "the fine print"—that is, the statute's own specifications of procedure—and to modify their general procedural expectations accordingly.

The difficulty with this suggestion appears when one probes more deeply into the factors that must be considered in making the judgment what is a "normal" level of procedural formality for the administration of a given statutory benefit. When one tries to assess how much and what kind of procedure would "normally" be attached to the adjudication of claims to a statutory benefit, one searches for some other benefit like it in relevant ways in order to establish a standard. What are the proper criteria of similarity? What other benefits would one compare, for instance, to those created by a statutory welfare program? Some might find the most relevant comparison in private or institutional charity programs, which are generally regarded as providing benefits as a matter of grace with virtually complete freedom of choice in the donor—a comparison which would suggest that very few or no procedural protections are required in welfare programs. Others might argue that the relevant comparison is to other economic subsidies established by law, such as those for farmers or the maritime industry. Still others would argue that because errors against welfare claimants, as distinguished from other subsidy beneficiaries, will lead to real misery and degradation, the relevant comparison is to the criminal law, where the most rigorous procedural safeguards are erected against the undeserved misery which results when a defendant is falsely convicted. Against this, it can be urged that the welfare program implicates a far more significant public interest than does the criminal process in simple, inexpensive and informal procedures—perhaps because of the great number of very similar claims, perhaps also because in welfare programs money spent on cumbersome procedures means less money to be spent directly on the needy recipients.

My point in listing these arguments is neither to be exhaustive nor to endorse any or all of them; but rather to point out that the quest for a "normal" level of procedural formality is by no means a simple factual inquiry. It is rather an exercise in evaluation; a search for the reasonable or appropriate level of procedure, which must take account of the values tugging in favor of greater or lesser procedural formality. Other things being equal, the stronger the substantive case for the benefit being provided to those claiming it, the stronger the case for procedures designed to prevent erroneous denials of the benefit. In the limiting case of a benefit which has behind it no independent claim of right—so that apart from the statute guaranteeing it, no one had any case for having it provided— it seems that it would be impossible to determine a "normal" or "reasonable" level of procedure which its recipients could properly expect. In the case of such a benefit, the only procedure that could reasonably be expected would be that procedure actually specified in the statute.

Such may actually be the law with respect to the procedure constitutionally required before an alien can be excluded from the United States. Postulating that admission of aliens to this country was a privilege to which the alien had no claim of right whatever—a pure matter of grace on the part of the United States government— the Supreme Court has held, in rejecting a constitutional challenge to the exclusion procedures, that "whatever the procedure authorized by Congress is, it is due process as far as an alien entry is concerned." [13] I repeat this passage not to endorse its soundness in context, for I believe that the alien seeking entry in the actual case in question—the alien bride of an American soldier—had a constitutional claim to entry behind her legal claim under the statute. But if we grant the Court's premise—that her only claim of right to entry arose from the substantive terms of the immigration statute—I can see no ground for disputing the Court's conclusion that the procedure provided in that same statute for adjudicating that very claim was the only procedure she could reasonably expect.

In general, the promissory theory of procedural fairness is, like the separation of powers theory, inadequate to resolve the paradox of due process. Upon analysis, it turns out that judgments of the appropriate level or procedure required in the administration of a benefit program must vary according to judicial evaluation of the force of the substantive case for providing the benefit in the first place. It thus remains a puzzle why special constitutional norms of justice should be applied to the procedures under which such benefits are provided, but the substance and even the existence of the benefit programs themselves are left to the discretion of the legislative authority.

VII

In my view, the paradox of procedural fairness as I have stated it is not resolvable. A decision to treat a legislatively created benefit program as subject to the constitutional-moral constraints of due process, while regarding the substance or existence of the program as a matter of legislative grace, would be simply an unjustifiable anomaly. To put the point another way, the old doctrine of the "right-privilege" distinction was in substance correct. It should (and covertly still does) control the application of norms of fair procedure to legislative benefit programs.

Using the example of welfare benefits, let me explain what I mean by this perhaps somewhat startling assertion. If I am correct in my thesis, the application of norms of procedural fairness to welfare decisions means that the courts regard claims to welfare benefits as claims of substantive right with a basis beyond the welfare statutes themselves. The overriding of legislative judgment as to the proper procedure for administering welfare programs means that the courts regard the *substance* of the welfare programs as no longer entirely a matter of legislative discretion, subject to legislative alteration at will and indeed to legislative withdrawal.

Surely this conclusion is contradicted by the emphatically proclaimed judical position that the substance of welfare programs is not subject to probing judicial review, and by the general understanding that there is no judicially enforceable "constitutional right to welfare." [14] Surely if a legislature repealed its welfare program altogether, the courts would not require it to reenact the program and enjoin it to raise tax moneys to support it. Surely, the objection continues, when the courts speak of an "entitlement" to welfare as the ground for judicial scrutiny of the procedures used in the program, they refer only to the fact that the legislature has chosen to structure the substance of existing welfare programs through reasonably definite rules governing eligibility and benefits provided.

Let me take the last point first, to explain what I mean by the existence of a substantive right to welfare. A right—as I mean the concept—is more than a legislatively created entitlement. To illustrate the point, consider the following example. Suppose that a legislature, unhappy with the procedural restraints placed upon its welfare program by the courts, sought to escape from those restraints by removing the entitlement element from its program.

As a first effort in this direction, the legislature might simply designate the welfare program as one designed only to express public charity or generosity, and not to confer any entitlement to benefits on the eligible recipients. Rules governing eligibility and amount of payment could be redefined—perhaps by way of a statutory preamble—as no more than internal directives from the legislature to the executive, designed to channel the public charity in the way most desired by its collective donors, the taxpayers.

I think most constitutional lawyers would agree that a legislature would not (and should not) be allowed to escape the constitutional requirements of due process in welfare administration by this kind of purely formal recasting of its welfare laws. But to reach this conclusion, one must abandon the premise that the legislature has plenary control over the substance of the program. There is nothing impossible in logic or unprecedented in practice about a legislatively created program, structured by internal directives to its administrators, which incidentally confers benefits on individuals who have no legally enforceable entitlement to those benefits.[15] If a legislature would not be allowed to recharacterize its welfare program into this mold and thereby escape the imposition of the restraints of fair procedure by the judiciary, a first substantive check on legislative discretion in the name of a right to welfare has been imposed.

Now suppose that the legislature—frustrated in its first attempt to escape the judicial requirements of due process—takes the further step of repealing the substantive provisions governing eligibility and benefit levels. The legislature might, for example, repose in a commissioner of welfare authority to dispense "to persons whom he in his absolute discretion determines to be needy and worthy of public assistance, such sums as he in his absolute discretion determines to be appropriate." Such legislation would remove any entitlement to welfare benefits by converting the state's welfare program into one ungoverned by substantive standards. In my view, it would not and should not work, any more than did the purely verbal attempt to legislate away the entitlement status of welfare benefits.

The most likely outcome of this statute would be that the commissioner would enact, in the form of administrative guidelines or regulations, rules to determine who should be eligible for welfare and for how much. These rules would perhaps closely resemble the preexisting statutory framework. But whether they did or not—and whatever efforts were made to label the rules "internal" or "administrative"—they would and should be treated as substantive standards defining the entitlement to welfare, and due process constraints would be imposed on their administration. The courts would, I think, say that the replacement of statutory standards by "internal" regulations was no less futile in destroying the entitlement status of the benefits than had been the formal statutory preamble.

In the unlikely event that no such regulations or guidelines were adopted, another aspect of due process doctrine would, I believe, be brought into play. If the decisions of the commissioner followed no standards, an applicant denied benefits could, I think, successfully challenge the denial on the basis that it was arbitrary. Such a challenge—which in our constitutional tradition would fall under the rubric of due process—would not be based on a claim of procedural unfairness in the relatively confined sense of that concept I have been developing. It would be a claim of substantive injustice—substantive due process—against the lawless administration of the welfare program. A court accepting the argument would order that the program be administered according to ascertainable standards—which then would themselves trigger the requirements of fair procedure in their application.

If I am right in my assessment of how courts would deal with these legislative attempts to remove the "entitlement" nature of welfare benefits, my argument reveals an important respect in which welfare benefits are a kind of constitutional "right" not entirely subject to the substantive control of the legislature. For it is by no means the case that every benefit—even every important benefit—bestowed by government would be treated in the same way. For instance, the power of executive clemency is almost invariably exercised without the guidance of substantive rules, under the virtually absolute discretion of the relevant authorities. Similarly, the hiring of public employees in the first instance need not as a matter of constitutional requirement be carried out according to rules and standards whose application is then subject to judicially imposed requirements of fair procedure. Conversely, even if public hiring *were* internally directed by guidelines stating criteria for personnel officials to use in hiring applicants, the courts would I think not treat these regulations as creating entitlements to be hired in those meeting the criteria set forth, entitlements enforceable in proceedings subject to the constraints of constitutional due process.[16]

On the other hand, it must be conceded that welfare is not a full-fledged, judicially enforceable, constitutional right. A legislature balked in its attempt to get free of procedural restrictions imposed on its welfare program would retain the power to reduce the cost of that program by cutting benefits across the board, reducing the number of recipients, or even eliminating the welfare program altogether. The courts would not closely scrutinize the steps taken and the lines drawn in such a substantive cost-cutting program—at least such is present constitutional doctrine.

The reasons for the courts' reluctance to intervene with the substance of welfare programs in this way lie, I believe, in the courts' present judgment of the proper limitations on their institutional competence and authority. Even if they considered that some guarantee of minimum material support for those unable to support themselves was a fundamental individual right—a right properly deserving of constitutional status—they might quite properly think it was a right beyond their power to enforce against infringement by direct legislative withdrawal of funds. At least—in the extreme case of total legislative withdrawal from public assistance—enforcement of the right to welfare would require the judiciary to order the disbursement of large sums of public money, to draft a complex scheme of social legislation, and to force the collection or diversion of massive tax revenues. None of these tasks are within our traditional conception of the judicial role, and that institutional consideration would probably prevent straightforward judicial protection of the right to welfare.

On the other hand, judicial enforcement of the requirements of the rule of law and of procedural fairness in the structure and the administration of welfare programs are quite reasonably within traditional conceptions of the judicial role. The difference is one of degree rather than kind—enforcement of formal procedures does cost public money—and it would be, I think, a mistake either to predict or inflexibly to prescribe that the courts never move on to scrutinize the substance of welfare programs. In the meantime, however, the right to welfare remains—with its partial judicial enforcement, confined to the procedural realm—as an obligation of government more stringent than a mere privilege, and indeed as a kind of "shadow constitutional right."[17]

VIII

Let me try to summarize the general conception of procedural fairness suggested and tentatively sketched in this essay. Procedural fairness involves a special moral concern for the correct and accurate decision of disputes which affect substantive rights. Its norms impinge from the outside on decisionmaking institutions, and require of those institutions more concern for the substantive rights which would be threatened or infringed by erroneous decisions than the institutions (or officials) would otherwise be inclined to show,

given the natural balance those institutions are likely to strike
between the competing claims of accurate decision, cost, and
institutional self-interest.

It makes sense to impose special procedural controls from outside
the authoritative decision-making institution—whether through the
moral check of conscience, or the external institutional check of
judicial review—only when the substantive right placed at hazard
has its source outside the decisionmaking institution itself. Thus
"entitlements" created only by the decisionmaking institution's own
rules should not be protected by external restraints of procedural
fairness. These, in the old terminology of the law, are "mere
privileges." The kinds of substantive rights which properly trigger
due process restraints are categorical moral rights or, in the legal
context, rights with a hierarchical status above the rules of the
decision-making institution. In the usual case—where the decision-
making institution's authority derives from the legislature—the only
substantive rights having this status are constitutional rights. Some
constitutional substantive rights may be judicially enforced largely
or only through procedural due process constraints, because institutional constraints on judicial power prevent their more direct
enforcement.

I have not here attempted to apply my analysis across the board
to all those interests which in recent years have been found to
trigger the constitutional protection of procedural due process.
Perhaps with respect to some of those interests it will turn out that
the characterization of them as constitutional rights—or at least as
"shadow" or nascent constitutional rights like the right to welfare—
is implausible. But if my suggested approach *is* misguided, what I
have described as the paradox of procedural fairness remains to be
resolved.

NOTES

1. Some principles of due process have a dual basis. Thus, coerced
   confessions are excluded from evidence in part because they are
   unreliable—a consideration based on values of procedural fairness in
   the strict sense. But even where reliable evidence corroborates the
   accuracy of a coerced confession, it is still excluded as the illicit fruit
   of police conduct violating the substantive rights of the defendant—

rights which were violated before, and independent of, the attempt to use the confession in evidence.

2. It seems to me that Professor Michelman, in his stimulating paper in this volume, may be urging the recognition of a substantive right when he suggests that where an official decision injures an individual's vital interests, minimum standards of courtesy and decency should require that the official discuss the decision with the individual before it is made—even where such discussion could not serve procedural values because there exist no external standards to distinguish a "correct" from an "incorrect" decision. On the other hand, some of the examples he adduces of non-instrumental procedural rights seem to me better analyzed as procedural protections of inchoate substantive constitutional rights. See Section VII and note 17, infra.

3. I confine myself in this paper to the norms of fairness governing adjudicative dispute-settling—instances where an authoritative decision-maker applies preexisting norms to the facts of a disputed situation in order to determine who is right and who is wrong. For a useful discussion of this and other forms of dispute settling, see M. Golding, *Philosophy of Law* (Englewood Cliffs, N.J.: Prentice-Hall, 1975), pp. 105-25.

4. Cf. Stanley v. Illinois, 405 U.S. 645, 656 (1972): "One might fairly say of the Bill of Rights in general, and the Due Process Clause in particular, that they were designed to protect the fragile values of a vulnerable citizenry from the overbearing concern for efficiency and efficacy that may characterize praiseworthy government officials no less, and perhaps more, than mediocre ones."

5. Goldberg v. Kelly, 397 U.S. 254 (1970).

6. Id. at 277-78 (Black, J., dissenting).

7. Id. at 264.

8. Board of Regents v. Roth, 408 U.S. 564 (1972).

9. Goldberg v. Kelly, supra, note 5, at 562.

10. Cf. Perry v. Sindermann, 408 U.S. 593 (1972); Arnett v. Kennedy, 416 U.S. 134 (1974).

11. One must say "almost indifferent" because there are some constitutional restraints on the substantive provisions governing even the most discretionary benefit programs. Thus they may not discriminate on grounds of race or religion. Perhaps in general benefits may not be denied on grounds which are wholly whimsical and arbitrary. However, these programs need not be administered according to stated and definite standards or rules.

12. This is essentially the holding of Arnett v. Kennedy, 416 U.S. 134

(1974). The doctrine is reaffirmed in Bishop v. Wood, 96 S.Ct. 2074 (1976), though it seems to me to have been seriously misapplied in that case for the reasons set forth in the dissenting opinions of Mr. Justice Brennan and Mr. Justice White.

13. U.S. ex rel Knauff v. Shaughnessy, 338 U.S. 537, 544 (1950).

14. On the refusal to give substantive scrutiny to the provisions of welfare laws, the leading case is Dandridge v. Williams, 397 U.S. 471 (1970).

15. Welfare programs themselves were until very recently regarded in this light. For a recent recognition that rules structuring benefits do not necessarily confer entitlements on those who would receive the benefits if the rules were correctly applied, see Paramount Convalescent Center v. Department of Health Care Services, 125 Cal. Rptr. 265 (1975). In that case, applicable state law provided that the state Department of Health Care Services "shall" enter into a contract for extended care services under the Medicare program with every nursing home which seeks such an arrangement and which meets certain quality standards. The department refused to renew a contract, and did not provide a hearing on the question of whether the nursing home met the standards. The California Supreme Court rejected the nursing home's argument that this violated procedural due process, holding that the purpose of the mandatory provisions was not to create an entitlement in the nursing homes, but rather was to protect patients by assuring them of financial assistance.

16. The courts would treat "internal" guidelines as not intended to create entitlements in the recipients and hence not triggering due process constraints; cf. Paramount Convalescent Center v. Department of Health Care Services, 125 Cal. Rptr. 265 (1975).

17. Compare the discussion in this section with Professor Michelman's analysis of due process as applied to public housing in Sections V and VII of his paper in this volume. Our approaches to these analogous problems are similar in important respects, and our conclusions are very much the same.

We do remain in disagreement on an important point—whether principles of fair procedure are invariably meant to protect substantive rights. I believe that they are; see Section I, supra. Professor Michelman argues that the requirements of due process rest at crucial points not on their tendency to prevent errors violating substantive rights, but on intrinsically procedural values of revelation and participation, founded ultimately in fraternal ideals. The central example he adduces in favor of his position—the requirement of fair procedures for making tracking decisions in the school—seems to me better explained as another instance of an inchoate or nascent substantive constitutional right, here the right to an adequate education. See San Antonio Independent School District v. Rodriguez, 411 U.S. 1, 25 n. 60 (1973); and cf. id. at 110-117 (dissenting opinion of Marshall, J.). In my view, ideals of fraternity or community have a place in the argument, but that place comes in the important support they offer to the substantive rights in question. See Grey, *Property and Need: The Welfare State and Theories of Distributive Justice*, 28 STAN. L. REV. 877, 894-897 (1976).

7

DUE PROCESS AND PROCEDURAL JUSTICE

DAVID RESNICK

Due process is a fundamental constitutional principle in American jurisprudence. It appears in criminal law, civil law, and administrative law; it applies to the actions of such diverse groups as the police, administrative agencies, legislative bodies, and courts of law. As a descriptive concept, it has been used to explain and organize a great variety of existing legal rules and procedures; as a normative principle, it has been used to justify existing rules and procedures and to generate new ones. As part of our Constitution, it has been responsible for the creation of new legal rights. In the name of due process, courts have recently forbidden a number of customary practices in the field of criminal law; in the past, they have employed the concept to nullify social and economic legislation.

Due process is an extraordinarily rich and intricate legal concept; as such we would expect that an adequate analysis would be a difficult task. The inherent difficulty is compounded by the fact that due process is a peculiarly American phenomenon: no other legal system has anything quite like it. Due process is a legal principle which has been shaped and developed through the process of applying and interpreting a written constitution. An explanation of the centrality and pervasiveness of due process in American jurisprudence involves complicated issues in the history of American constitutional law. Despite its complexity (or perhaps because of it) due process is a fit subject for philosophical analysis. The question I explore in this paper is: why does our sense of justice require due process? To answer it I treat due process as a special notion of justice that arises from the application of general principles of justice to the exercise of political authority.

Because of our political tradition, it is natural to think of due process as a right guaranteed to individuals by the Constitition. But what is it a right to? It seems to be a right to a procedure, a right to have one's treatment determined according to some prescribed method; and the moral basis of such a legal or constitutional right would appear to rest on the idea that citizens have a right to be treated justly by the state. But such an analysis is in itself confusing. What is the relationship between a right to a procedure and a right to be treated justly; how can the fact that a prescribed procedure was followed in a particular case effect the justice of its outcome?

I take it that the right to a procedure is puzzling because what we have a right to is certain states of affairs; we have a right to just treatment by the state, and the process by which such treatment is accorded individuals would seem to possess no independent moral value. The concept of due process provides criteria for assessing the justice of a procedure, but what seems to matter is the results. How can injustice be less unjust merely because certain procedural rules have been followed? If I find myself rotting in prison, totally innocent, yet duly convicted and sentenced for a crime I did not commit, how can the fact that I have been accorded all my procedural rights make any difference to me? I have been deprived of my liberty; whether or not this has been done with all the niceties of due process seems irrelevant. The state has treated me unjustly; by imprisoning me it has violated my right to liberty.

Thus an assertion of an individual right to a procedure must in some sense be a demand for just treatment by the state. If, in addition to the traditional individual rights of life, liberty, and property, we assert the right to a procedure, the justification for asserting the right to it should be that its recognition by the state prevents yet another form of unjust individual treatment. The interesting feature of such an explanation is that it interprets unjust treatment by the state as the violation of a personal or individual right; if my right had not been violated, then I would not have been treated unjustly.

Yet if we reflect on why the violation of an individual right by the state is a type of unjust treatment, it appears that the right to due process is rather different from the rights to life, liberty, and property. The right to liberty, for instance, does not entail that every deprivation of personal liberty by the state is unjust; imprisonment as a criminal penalty is certainly permissible. The right to liberty limits the actions of the state; in effect, it divides all possible deprivation of liberty by the state into just deprivations and unjust deprivations. Only unjust deprivations are instances of unjust treatment, and only these deprivations are referred to as violations of the right to personal liberty. The assertion of the right to liberty entails that every deprivation of liberty stands in need of justification; but the crucial point is that there are standard, familiar, established ways in which such justifications are obtained.

In the case of the right to due process, something rather different seems to be going on; there is no just way in which the state can deprive a person of due process; every deprivation of due process is by definition a violation of the right to due process. This is not to deny that we can imagine circumstances which would justify such deprivation—say, during wartime emergencies—but it would be best to describe such cases as justifiable unjust treatment. There are, of course, analogous arguments in respect to other rights, yet there are a great number of perfectly ordinary circumstances in which the state deprives persons of life, liberty and property without treating them unjustly. The right to due process as a principle rather than a right; a principle which is used to generate a number of specific rights, procedures, and practices. This principle is grounded in a common and public sense of justice which itself is open to philosophic reflection and analysis. The warrant for such an approach arises directly from an analysis of due process as a legal principle. Justice Frankfurter provided a very illuminating analysis along these lines:

> But "due process," unlike some legal rules, is not a technical conception with a fixed content unrelated to time, place and

circumstances. Expressing as it does in its ultimate analysis respect enforced by law for that feeling of just treatment which has been evolved through centuries of Anglo-American constitutional history and civilization, "due process" cannot be imprisoned within the treacherous limits of any formula. Representing a profound attitude of fairness between man and man, and more particularly between the individual and government, "due process" is compounded of history, reason, the past course of decisions, and stout confidence in the strength of the democratic faith which we profess.[1]

In Rochin v. California, Frankfurter presented his most complete account of the due process clause of the Fourteenth Amendment. He argued that due process restricts the manner in which states may enforce their penal codes. Convictions cannot be obtained by means which

> ... offend those canons of decency and fairness which express the notions of justice of English-speaking peoples even toward those charged with the most heinous offenses. These standards of justice are not authoritatively formulated anywhere as though they were specifics. ... Due process of law, as a historic and generative principle precludes defining, and thereby confining, these standards of conduct more precisely than to say that convictions cannot be brought about by methods that

Perhaps our sense of justice requires due process because due process is a means for achieving the purposes of a just legal system. Due process may be thought of as a demand that a procedure conform to the requirements of formal justice, and formal justice is a basic feature of our idea of the rule of law. John Rawls defines a legal system as "a coercive order of public rules addressed to rational persons for the purpose of regulating their conduct and providing the framework for social cooperation."[3] He suggests that the idea of the rule of law links up with our sense of justice because the concept of formal justice, understood as the regular and impartial administration of public rules, when applied to a legal system, becomes the rule of law. He argues that we can account for various precepts of justice associated with the rule of law by referring to the idea of a legal order:

> If laws are directives addressed to rational persons for their guidance, courts must be concerned to apply and to enforce these rules in an appropriate way. A conscientious effort must be made to determine whether an infraction has taken place and to impose the correct penalty. Thus a legal system must make provisions for conducting orderly trials and hearings; it must contain rules of evidence that guarantee rational procedures of inquiry. While there are variations in these procedures, the rule of law requires some form of due process: that is, a process reasonably designed to ascertain the truth, in ways consistent with the other ends of the legal system, as to whether a violation has taken place and under what circumstances. For example, judges must be independent and impartial, and no man may judge his own case. Trials must be fair and open, but not prejudiced by public clamor. The precepts of natural justice are to insure that the legal order will be impartially and regularly maintained.[4]

Rawls also refers to the precepts of natural justice as "guidelines intended to preserve the integrity of the judicial process." Thus it would seem that a judicial process which is administered in accordance with the precepts of natural justice would have the virtues of impartiality and regularity; in effect, it would conform to the requirements of formal justice. Yet the criteria of formal justice are not the only ones which we apply to a judicial process. It is perfectly intelligible to ask whether particular outcomes of a judicial procedure are just. We feel that formal justice is not always equivalent to substantive justice, an impartial outcome is not the same thing as a correct outcome. If we try to explain due process simply in terms of formal justice we are right back where we started from. How can the fact that an outcome is formally just make an unjust outcome less unjust?

In another section of *A Theory of Justice*, Rawls provides a very illuminating discussion of various types of procedural justice and clearly brings out the limitations of the concept of formal justice. He defines two main types of procedural justice in terms of the way in which they employ criteria for just outcomes. A procedure conforms to the notion of pure procedural justice when there is no criterion for the right or just outcome independent of applying the procedure itself; if the procedure has been properly followed, any outcome is just. An example is a number of persons engaging in a series of fair bets in which the distribution of money after the last bet is made is considered fair whatever it happens to be. Pure procedural justice requires that the background conditions be fair, and the procedure for determining results must actually be carried out. Rawls contrasts pure procedural justice with two other notions of procedural justice which he calls perfect procedural justice and imperfect procedural justice; both entail the existence of an independent criterion for determining outcomes. They differ in that perfect procedural justice is a procedure which always achieves the just outcome, whereas imperfect procedural justice obtains when there is no feasible means for guaranteeing such a desirable state of affairs. The example he uses to illustrate the concept of imperfect procedural justice has very obvious implications for understanding due process:

> Imperfect procedural justice is exemplified by a criminal trial. The desired outcome is that the defendant should be declared guilty if and only if he has committed the offense with which he is charged. The trial procedure is framed to search for and to establish the truth in this regard. But it seems impossible to design the legal rules so that they always lead to the correct result. The theory of trials examines which procedures and rules of evidence, and the like, are best calculated to advance this purpose consistent with the other ends of the law. Different arrangements for hearing cases may reasonably be expected in different circumstances to yield the right results, not always but at least most of the time. A trial, then, is an instance of imperfect procedural justice. Even though the law is carefully followed, and the proceedings fairly and properly conducted, it may reach the wrong outcome. An innocent man may be found guilty, a guilty man may be set free. In such cases we speak of a miscarriage of justice: the injustice springs from no human fault but a fortuitous combination of circumstances which defeats the purpose of the legal rules.[5]

Since a trial is a case of imperfect procedural justice, we have a way of accounting for the fact that according an individual all his due process rights can still lead to an unjust result; due process of law is not a perfect process. Since we have an independent criterion for outcomes, we can explain why an outcome that meets all the requirements of formal justice is not necessarily actually just. But this raises another problem; since we have an independent criterion for just outcomes, it is certainly possible that a just outcome could be achieved by means of a procedure which violates due process: a person could receive an unfair trial, be declared guilty, and in fact actually be guilty. Now we are faced with the opposite difficulty; why should we consider an outcome unjust because it has not been achieved by means of due process?

Before proceeding, I should like to clarify an ambiguity in the meaning of outcomes which stands in the way of an adequate solution. Rawls describes a wrong outcome in the following way; ". . . an innocent man may be found guilty, a guilty man may be set free. In such cases we speak of a miscarriage of justice. . . ." The ambiguity turns on whether by "outcome" we mean an assertion or an action; whether what we have in mind are verdicts of guilt or innocence, or actions taken by the state such as imprisoning a person or setting him free. It would seem more appropriate to label actions as true miscarriages of justice.

We may tend to ignore such a distinction because we simply assume that the appropriate actions follow automatically upon a verdict. Yet it is certainly possible that a jury may reach the right verdict and the state take the wrong actions; punishing a person despite an acquittal, and vice versa. This, of course, introduces another type of injustice. In any case, in order to remove this ambiguity, when I refer to actions taken by the state such as depriving particular persons of life, liberty or property, I shall call such actions "treatments." I shall use "findings" to refer to outcomes in the narrower sense of verdicts, judgments, and the like.

The plausibility of using a trial as an example of imperfect procedural justice and claiming that the criterion for a just or correct outcome is independent of applying the procedure itself, and thus sharply distinguishing it from pure procedural justice, turns on taking outcomes in the narrow sense of "findings." To say that the desired outcome is a declaration of guilt if and only if the defendant committed the offense with which he is charged, assumes that by outcome we mean the assertion of a proposition that is either true or false. A finding does not become true or correct by virtue of the operation of a procedure; if it is true, it is true independent of the procedure itself.

If we use "outcome" in the broad sense of harmful treatments that the state intentionally inflicts on individual citizens, it is clearly not the case that such treatments are just treatments independent of procedure. Due process of law requires that the procedure for determining outcomes must actually be carried out, and that the procedure itself must contain certain basic features. Due process is a necessary, but not sufficient condition for just treatments. The fact that due process is a necessary condition for just treatments entails that the absence of due process is a sufficient condition for unjust treatment. We might say that any treatment that would have been just according to an independent criterion for assessing outcomes, is in fact unjust if performed without employing an appropriate judicial process. It is not the case that following a certain procedure transforms what would otherwise have been an unjust treatment into a just treatment. Such an error arises from a mistaken belief in the efficacy of the concept of formal justice itself. It is the absence of formal justice that transforms what would otherwise have been just treatment into unjust treatment.

If the foregoing account is plausible, then the way to uncover the moral value of following a procedure is not to ask how following procedure can make some palpably unjust treatment less unjust; rather, we ought to inquire why not following or violating a procedure makes a treatment unjust.

We can see that due process is a necessary but not sufficient condition for just treatment by analyzing the way in which we employ a judicial procedure that meets the criteria for due process in order to provide a justification for the intentional harmful treatment of individual persons by the state. It is prima facie wrong to deprive a person of life, liberty, or property, and such deprivations must be justified in every particular case; if due process of law is absent, then there is no good reason—or good enough reason—for believing that a particular individual actually deserves such treatment. The need for a justification helps to explain why due process requires a procedure which combines aspects of both pure pro-

cedural justice and imperfect procedural justice: a procedure
provides a justification or good reason for asserting that a particular
treatment is just if and only if it is actually performed in the proper
manner.

Procedural justice as justification is analogous to the old analysis
of knowledge as justified true belief; in cases of intentional harmful
treatment of individuals by the state, to assert that a person has
been treated justly is like asserting correctly "I know that p is the
case." In order to know p, it is necessary that p is true, that I believe
p, and that I have some justification for holding this belief. To say
"I know the cat is on the mat," it must be true that the cat is indeed
on the mat; but the mere fact that it is, is not sufficient for a first
person assertion of knowledge since all sorts of things are true about
the world of which I have no knowledge whatsoever. I must believe
that the cat is on the mat, but a true belief is not yet knowledge. I
must have a justification for holding such a belief; I must be able to
provide reasons, and these reasons must be of the right sort and
must relate to the truth of the belief I am asserting.

Leaving aside all the standard objections to the analysis of
knowledge as justified true belief, I think it is still fruitful to suggest
an analogous analysis of just treatment, in the sense of intentional
harmful treatment of an individual by the state. Just treatment can
be analyzed as justified deserving treatment; the concept of desert
corresponds to the truth value of propositions about the world. In
respect to punishment, the criterion for desert is that a person
committed an offense against the criminal code. Of course, we are
assuming a just legal system that incorporates the precepts of justice
in respect to punishment. The notion of desert in this sense reflects
the independent criterion for correct outcomes that characterizes
imperfect procedural justice. Due process describes a procedure that
justifies outcome; it provides reasons for asserting that the treatment
a person receives is the treatment he deserves. The notion of
justification accounts for the way in which due process is a form of
pure procedural justice. The procedure must be carried out in order
to provide a justification, and all outcomes of such a procedure are
equally justified. But such justifications are not absolute since the
procedure is not infallible; at best, such justification provides a high
degree of certainty.

In describing how we acquire empirical knowledge we sometimes refer to formulating a hypothesis and testing it; testing describes the procedure we employ in order to verify or falsify any hypothesis, the test provides a justification for asserting that the hypothesis is probably true or probably false. Though we may loosely speak of falsification as if the test or crucial experiment makes a hypothesis false, what makes it either true or false are the facts of the world. Other things being equal, the better the falsification procedure, the greater warrant we have for believing that a hypothesis is false. We might think of accusation as a hypothesis about desert and a judicial procedure as a way of verifying or falsifying it. The outcome of a procedure in the narrow sense is a finding; in the case of a criminal trial a finding of guilty is equivalent to asserting that an hypothesis is true "beyond a reasonable doubt." Since an appropriate action follows automatically from the finding according to a simple description of a judicial procedure, we could say that a person punished after being duly tried and convicted is being treated justly "beyond a reasonable doubt."

Such an analysis points to the crucial role of procedure in providing a high degree of confidence in the justice of outcomes; other things being equal, the higher the standards of proof the greater the confidence we may place in guilty verdicts or negative findings. Yet since a procedure itself is an institution or system of public rules we might say that formal justice understood as the regular and impartial administration of these rules, must also be taken into account when assessing the effectiveness of a procedure in terms of its role as providing justification for inflicting harm. The standards of proof together with formal justice determine the subjective probability, or degree of confidence, that we may place in the correctness of each outcome. One basic moral justification for employing a procedure is that it must be the case that a person who is deprived of life, liberty or property by the state is very likely to deserve such treatment. Thus our concern with the subjective probability of correct outcomes reflects a requirement of morality and not simply efficiency or rationality.

To think of due process merely in terms of justification ties it too closely to the notion of moral certainty. It obscures the way in which we employ a procedure as a means for applying rules correctly, and not simply to provide a reason for believing that rules have been applied correctly. For example, we might hold that any judicial process that is applied properly serves to provide good reasons for believing that a particular action taken by the state is correct; yet judicial processes might function very differently in respect to the way in which they assure that rules are applied correctly. We might draw a distinction between two types of judicial procedure; a due process procedure and a judicial review procedure. (I trust such a distinction is at least at home in administrative law if not in criminal law.) A due process procedure is one that requires fair notice and a fair hearing before an action is taken; a judicial review is an appeal procedure that occurs after a determination is made. If applied correctly, both types of procedures can serve to justify actions in the sense that they provide good reasons for believing that a particular harmful action is justified. Although they both attempt to minimize errors, they operate very differently; a due process procedure attempts to avoid errors, while judicial review attempts to correct them. Needless to say, the real world effects of adopting a procedure that is applied before an action is performed differ sharply from the effects of a procedure that is applied after the action.

In order to clarify the way a procedure operates as a means for applying rules correctly, we might think of the justification for employing a procedure as analogous to the justification for using a postal scale. Assume that we want to affix the correct postage on a number of letters; the rules for correct postage require that a letter that weighs more than one ounce have a blue stamp, and one that weighs less than one ounce have a red stamp. Consider the following description of the practice of affixing postage stamps: we first put a letter on a scale, then read the scale in order to find out whether it weighs more or less than one ounce: if it weighs more, we put on a blue stamp; if less, a red stamp. Before weighing a letter, it is either true or false that it weighs more than one ounce, and it is either true or false that it requires a blue stamp. Putting a letter on a scale does not make it weigh more than one ounce, nor does it require a blue stamp because the scale reads more than one ounce. The weight of a letter depends on what is put inside, the postage on the regulations of the postal service. Similarly, what makes a person guilty of committing an offense is his actions; the rules of a criminal code are what makes him deserve punishment. More precisely, a criminal code defines what actions are to count as offense and the penalty appropriate to various offenses.

If we were asked to justify the use of a scale in the practice of affixing postage stamps, we might reply that it is obviously necessary to weigh a letter in order to affix the correct stamp. Similarly, we might say that a judicial process is necessary in order to apply a code of criminal justice. Yet in both cases this necessity is not a logical necessity. We do not mean that it is impossible to put on the correct stamp without weighing the letter. If we dispense with the scale entirely and affix stamps randomly, it is still the case that a letter that weighs more than one ounce and has a blue stamp on it has the correct postage. We employ a scale in order to maximize the number of letters with correct postage: we attempt to minimize or eliminate errors. Since the purpose of determining the weight of a letter before affixing a stamp is to eliminate errors, we would prefer a more accurate weighing device to a less accurate one. Though picking a letter up in your hand and estimating its weight is better than randomly affixing stamps, it would be preferable to employ a scale. Yet the degree of accuracy need not be greater than that required for our purpose.

I have tried to suggest that one fundamental moral justification for requiring due process is that due process minimizes the number of unjust treatments; it is not simply a just or humane way of depriving persons of life, liberty or property. To the extent that due process requires an accurate judicial process, it fulfills two morally valuable functions: in terms of subjective probabilities, it maximizes correct outcomes and minimizes errors. The fact that intentional harmful treatments are the outcomes of a procedure that accords with due process gives us both an assurance that the number of unjust treatments will be as few as possible and warrants confidence that those who are harmed actually deserve to be.

But due process also involves the justice of the procedure itself. Accuracy is not the only value that we wish to maximize; we do not evaluate the justice of a procedure merely in terms of its ability to achieve correct outcomes. Due process is supposed to express our feeling that convictions ought not to be obtained in ways that offend our sense of justice; fidelity to the ideal of due process shows our deep commitment to the values of fair play and fair treatment, and so forth.

We might try to account for such intuitions by thinking of them as an appeal to the old maxim that the ends do not justify the means. The traditional way of posing the means/ends problem that leads to a conclusion in accord with the maxim, entails an argument to the effect that certain efficacious means for achieving desirable or morally desirable ends ought not to be employed on moral grounds. For example, assume that we wish to choose between two procedures A and B, each of which provides the same high degree of reliability in the sense that they both minimize the number of innocent people declared guilty. B is a more accurate procedure because it convicts a greater proportion of those who actually commit offenses. Other things being equal, it would be rational to prefer B to A; but if B achieves this result by employing certain morally undesirable means, then other things are not equal. If it employes torture, coerced confessions, illegally seized evidence, and the like, then we ought to choose A.

It is possible for the state to increase the number of convictions by employing methods that entail morally or legally undesirable consequences. These methods do not affect the reliability of the outcome; we do not think that a person convicted by means of illegally seized evidence is less likely to have committed an offense because the state employed such evidence to obtain conviction. We feel that the moral costs of such practices far outweigh any possible benefits; all sorts of practices far outweigh any possible benefits; all sorts of practices that we consider violations of due process seem to be of this sort. We might think of double jeopardy, privileged communications, the right not to be compelled to testify against yourself, or your spouse, exclusionary evidentiary rules, and so forth.

The moral costs of practices prohibited by the concept of due process may be analyzed and explained in numerous ways. We sometimes refer to due process in terms of procedural safeguards; to the extent that these safeguards are distinct from those that protect the integrity and reliability of the judicial process itself, they protect other moral values and prevent or discourage agents of the state from engaging in practices that have morally undesirable consequences or effects.

Since no just procedure would contain these practices, we can consider them as constraints; in this sense, due process requires judicial procedure consistent with the other ends of the legal system. We might lump these morally objectionable practices together under the notion of unjust procedural practices. Unjust procedural practices are those with morally undesirable consequences; the justification for excluding them from any just procedure is independent of their effects on outcomes. Though the criterion for determining whether a particular procedural practice is unjust is distinct from those entailed by the concept of a just outcome, we might still feel that they affect the moral value of outcomes. Since we feel that just results ought to be achieved by just means, we will say that if unjust means are employed an outcome becomes tainted with injustice.

In contrast to unjust procedural practices, there is another large category of practices related to procedures that offend our sense of justice. These depend upon the structural features of the procedure itself and relate to the criteria for just outcomes. For example, it is a violation of due process for a judge to have a pecuniary interest in the outcome of the case; if a judge's salary depends directly on the conviction rate of those who are tried in his court, then it is reasonable to assume that correct outcomes are less likely. Similarly, if a defendant is not allowed sufficient time to prepare a defense, given the nature of our adversary system of criminal justice, if he is found guilty, we feel less than fully confident in such a verdict. It is reasonable to assume that he might have been found innocent were it not for the fact that he could not put up a good defense. We demand a public trial because we fear a secret trial might very well be used by the state as a means for convicting innocent persons. We want a public trial to assure us that the outcomes are not an expression of the private passions and prejudices of those entrusted with the administration of the criminal justice system. Yet we also want to assure that a trial is insulated from public prejudice and passions; thus we have rules about pretrial publicity, change of venue, selections of juries, and the like.

A person convicted of committing an offense against the criminal code is supposed to be guilty beyond a reasonable doubt. Yet the presence of certain practices in a judicial process are sufficient to raise reasonable doubts; these practices are themselves grounds for doubt. They offend our sense of justice because they affect the degree of certainty which we feel is required in order to inflict harmful treatment on individuals. We might call such practices unfair procedural practices; they differ from unjust procedural practices because the criteria for fairness are not independent of the effect such practices are thought to have on outcomes. If unjust procedural practices make outcomes undeserving, we might say the unfair procedural practices make an outcome unjustified.

We may note that the notions of unfair procedural practices and unjust procedural practices are not mutually exclusive categories; they refer to the types of arguments and considerations which are appealed. A particular practice may be thought violative of due process on both grounds. For example, we can argue that torture is a practice which cannot be tolerated in any civilized system of criminal justice; it is a morally abhorrent way of collecting evidence, it violates the sanctity of the person, it degrades both the victim and torturer, and so on. In this sense, torture is an unjust procedural practice. Yet it can also be argued that the evidence received through torture is likely to be biased and unreliable; if we appeal to such considerations, then we are conceiving of torture as an unfair procedural practice. Thus, if due process expresses our sense of justice, then a particular practice may very well be offensive in two essentially distinct ways.

What counts as an unfair practice depends upon the type of procedure we employ and the assumptions we make about the way in which it operates. I tried to distinguish such practices from those I have called unjust procedural practices because in the latter case, we feel that any gain in efficiency, in terms of monetary cost, increase of conviction rates and the like is not a sufficient justification for employing them. To say they offend our sense of justice is to say they are somehow wrong in themselves and trade-offs in terms of other benefits are impermissible. In the case of unfair practices, the justification for prohibiting them is in terms of their effect on the reliability of outcomes. I should like to argue that they do not have the same status, or rather ought not to have. Especially when it comes to unfair procedural practices our sense of justice may not be the most reliable guide.

The maxim that justice requires the appearance of justice is perfectly rational because given what we know about human nature and our experience of the world the outcomes of a procedure that appears to be unfair is less reliable, it is more open to doubt; if it is the case that a trial doesn't look fair, or a judge appears to be partial to one side, and the like, this creates a reasonable presumption that the outcome may not be correct, or even warrants the belief that it is probably incorrect. To some extent our sense of justice is historical; the fact that certain features of a procedure offend our sense of justice may be merely a reflection of our familiarity with procedures of a certain type.

At this point we may summarize the results of our discussion and relate the analysis of just treatment as justified deserving treatment and the analysis of due process as excluding unjust procedural practices and unfair procedural practices. This enables us to present in somewhat abstract form a moral theory of due process that shows that when the state inflicts harm upon an individual by depriving him of life, liberty or property due process is required in order for such treatments to be just.

1. Procedures are in accord with due process if and only if, they are not unjust and not unfair.
2. Just harmful treatment is justified deserving harmful treatment.
3. If some procedure used in obtaining a harmful treatment is unfair, then that harmful treatment is undeserved.
4. If some procedure used in obtaining a harmful treatment is unfair, then that harmful treatment is not justified.
5. If due process does not obtain with respect to some harmful treatment, then some procedure used in obtaining that harmful treatment is either unjust or unfair (by 1).
6. If due process does not obtain with respect to some harmful treatment, then that harmful treatment is unjust (by 2, 3, 4, 5).
7. If a harmful treatment is just, then due process obtains with respect to that harmful treatment (by 6).

After setting forth the above theory of due process that is intended to describe and account for our moral intentions about procedural justice, I now turn to a discussion of a specific type of procedural fairness. I do so in order to show how we can proceed beyond the observation that due process requires that a procedure be accurate and that fairness is tied to accuracy. Once we think of fairness as itself open to reflection and investigation, we can see how the concept of due process is related to other moral and legal problems.

By labeling as unfair practices that affect the reliability of outcomes in the sense that they increase the likelihood of errors, I suggest that a procedure composed exclusively of fair practices is thought to be an accurate procedure. Part of the reason that accuracy is tied to fairness can be explained by the fact that we employ an adversary system. An adversary procedure is one type of competitve zero-sum game in which fairness is a fundamental condition for achieving correct outcomes. We might think of a prize fight, or a race, or a chess game, and the like. The rules of the game define one type of fairness; a violation of the rules gives one side an unfair advantage. There are also background conditions that require that the participants are roughly equal in ways relevant to the game; it is unfair, in this sense, to match a heavyweight with a lightweight, a chess master with a novice, and so on. If the background conditions of fairness are not met, there is no contest. The outcome is a foregone conclusion; the competition does not achieve its purpose. If we assume the purpose of a prizefight is to discover who is the better boxer, then if we pit a heavyweight against a lightweight and he wins by a knockout, this does not really prove anything; similarly, if two heavyweights fight and one has a horseshoe concealed in his glove, then the outcome is equally worthless. Another basic assumption is that the outcome is achieved through competition, not cooperation; that the fight is not fixed; that both sides try as hard as possible to win within the rules.

Fairness is a structural requirement for such contests; in order to achieve their purposes the rules themselves must be fair, the contestants equally matched, and both sides must put up a fair fight. Our system of criminal justice requires fairness in order to achieve its purpose:

> In the Anglo-American tradition we employ an adversary system—a system based upon the idea that truth will emerge out of the struggle between two contesting parties presenting their case to an impartial tribunal. Each man's lawyer will do his best to establish a case for his client and destroy the case

that his opponent is trying to make. The system is a commitment to the notion that the right result will emerge out of conflict. Such a system will work only if the two contesting parties are relatively equal. Obviously, if one side is much stronger than the other, a correct determination will not come out of the conflict, but only the answer that power can impose. It is fundamentally important to keep the sides in the criminal case equal if the system is to work. Anything that tends to build up one side as opposed to the other, or anything that tends to weaken one side, is detrimental to the adversary system.[6]

We might consider the right to counsel in this fashion, as an emerging historical awareness that fairness is required for the reliable operation of our adversary system of criminal justice. Consider the following explanation for the inclusion of the right to counsel in our Constitution:

Originally in England, a prisoner was not permitted to be heard by counsel upon the general issue of not guilty on any indictment for treason or felony. The practice of English judges, however, was to permit counsel to advise with a defendant as to the conduct of his case and to represent him in collateral matters and as respects questions of law arising upon the trial. In 1695 the rule was relaxed by statute to the extent of permitting one accused of treason the privilege of being heard by counsel. . . . In the light of this common law practice, it is evident that the constitutional provisions to the effect that a defendant should be "allowed" counsel or should have a right "to be heard by himself and his counsel," or that he might be heard by "either or both," at his election, were intended to do away with the rules which denied representation, in whole or in part, by counsel in criminal prosecutions, but were not aimed to compel the State to provide counsel for a defendant.[7]

Gradually this right has been expanded into a duty to provide counsel in criminal cases if a person lacks sufficient means to employ his own. In recent times the rights of the indigent have greatly increased as due process has become linked with equal protection. In Griffin v. Illinois, Mr. Justice Black has argued:

Providing equal justice for poor and rich, weak and powerful alike is an age-old problem. People have never ceased to hope and strive to move closer to that goal. This hope, at least in part, brought about in 1215 the royal concessions of Magna Carta: "To no one will we sell, to no one will we refuse, or delay, right or justice. . . . No free man shall be taken or imprisoned, or disseised, or outlawed, or exiled or anywise destroyed; nor shall we go upon him or send upon him, but by the lawful judgment of his peers or by the law of the land." These pledges were unquestionably steps toward a fairer and more nearly equal application of criminal justice. In this tradition, our own constitutional guarantees of due process and equal protection both call for procedures in criminal trials which allow no invidious discriminations between persons and different groups of persons. Both equal protection and due process emphasize the central aim of our entire judicial system—all people charged with crime must, so far as the law is concerned, "stand on an equality before the bar of justice in every American court.[8]

This argument also appeals to fairness, but a different sense of fairness. The rich can afford a lawyer; therefore they can provide themselves with a fair trial. But the poor cannot. A fair trial ought to be available to everybody, rich and poor alike; it's not fair that the poor cannot get a fair trial. We ought to aid the indigent defendant in order to overcome the morally undesirable consequences of economic inequalities. The duty to provide counsel for those in need might be defended in humanitarian terms; it would be similar to an argument that the state ought to provide medical services to the poor in order to prevent needless suffering. We feel that no one should be deprived of the services of a physician merely because he is too poor to afford one. We might provide similar arguments for aid to dependent children, housing, food, and the like. The claim is that there are certain basic goods and services which everyone is entitled to; such claims appeal to the concept of distributive justice. It is the moral duty of society to provide some minimal amount of these goods to those who cannot afford to purchase them on the free market; all others are expected to expend their own resources and provide themselves with whatever amount of these goods they desire and can afford.

Yet if we take seriously the claim that an adversary procedure is the most accurate and reliable one, rather than seeing the provision of aid to the indigent as a requirement of distributive justice or as a goal of equal treatment for the rich and poor alike, we can argue that the basic reason for the state providing such services follows directly from the justification for a system of criminal justice. Assume a society of rational self-interested egoistic individuals who wish to maximize the value of their individual life, liberty, and property. All they desire from the state is security; their criminal code reflects this basic aim. It forbids actions that deprive persons of these basic goods. Punishments are conceived of as rational deterrents; the more severe penalties are reserved for more serious offenses. There are two ways a person may be deprived of these basic goods; as the victim of a crime or as the recipient of punishment. If we define unjust actions as the wrongful taking of life, liberty, or property, there are two types of injustice; crimes and mistaken punishments.

If I am a random person living in such a society; I am interested only in security and do not particularly mind gaining from injustice. Yet it would seem that it is in my interest to minimize the number of unjust acts. If I am concerned with the value of my individual life, liberty, and property, then I am harmed by every unjust conviction; there is a finite probability that I myself may be the innocent victim. Furthermore, unjust convictions increase the rate of crimes; if an innocent person is convicted and punished, then there must be some guilty person who is not, and he will probably go on to commit further crimes. As a rational, self-interested person I have no more desire to convict an innocent man than to see a guilty one go free; I have an interest in accurate punishments.

Since I believe in rational deterrence theory as a justification for punishment I am also opposed to one person or class of persons getting a harsher or lighter punishment than that provided for by a rational criminal code. The reason I would choose a system in which a more severe penalty is provided for a more serious offense depends upon the following argument: if two crimes of differing seriousness such as murder and robbery received the same penalty, then there would be no incentive for a criminal to choose the lesser crime rather than the greater. If a person wants to steal something, and it's somewhat easier to shoot his victim, then there is no reason not to. If one class of persons—say, the poor—always get a more severe penalty, if they receive the penalty for murder though they merely commit robbery then they may as well murder. Similarly, if another class—the rich—always get a lighter penalty, if they receive the robbery penalty for murder, then similar consequences follow.

Thus in respect to a person accused of committing a crime, my interest certainly does not lie exclusively on the side of the prosecution; I want to convict him only if he's guilty as charged, and I do not wish him to receive a harsher penalty than he deserves. If it is the case that the adversary system is the most reliable one, it would seem that the interests of the people lie on both sides—or rather neither side.

This argument provides a justification for providing counsel to indigent defendants, but it does more than that. Assuredly attorneys differ in skill; the time and resources they can devote to a case certainly affect the outcomes. Other things being equal, it would seem that a highly skilled attorney backed with resources for investigating cases, calling expert witnesses, and the like, greatly increases the probability of someone who is guilty getting an innocent verdict or a less severe sentence than he would deserve given the seriousness of his offense. But certainly no social benefit is achieved by allowing wealthy criminals to have such advantages; if the rich always or very often get lighter sentences than those required by a rational system of deterrents, then there would seem to be very good reason for depriving them of the benefits of their wealth by insulating the system of criminal justice from such disturbing influences. From the viewpoint of society, there is such a thing as permitting individuals to provide themselves with too much legal talent and services; since the rules of criminal procedure are constructed in such a way that correct results emerge only when the sides are roughly equally matched, and the rules are drawn for the average case, then the rich can easily take unfair advantage of such a legal system.

If justice ought not to be for sale to the highest bidder, it would seem to follow that we ought to abolish the private practice of criminal law as we know it; the private practice of criminal law not only provides less than equal justice for the poor, it provides more than equal justice for the rich. If we believe in the adversary system of justice, why not have two district attorneys; one for the prosecution and one for the defense? If I trust a public official to prosecute cases in my name, why shouldn't I trust one to defend cases? If public prosecutors can be vigorous and skilled advocates for one side, what prevents public defenders from performing similarly for the other side? It certainly cannot depend merely on who pays their salaries; judges can be fair and independent arbiters and yet draw their salary from the state. We already fund two out of the three actors in a public trial—why not fund the third? If we adopt such a scheme the innocent would not be impoverished by the cost of defending themselves; the rich would get a slightly less competent defense and the poor a slightly better one. Justice would be better served, and the only losers would seem to be criminal lawyers and rich criminals. Why not prohibit the private acquisition of the services of a criminal lawyer; in the name of due process, fairness, and equal protection of the laws, I call for the abolition of the private ownership of the means of protection.

Yet prohibiting the private acquisition of the services of criminal lawyers need not entail ending the private practice of criminal law. There is a difference between the public provision of a service and public funding; it may be more desirable to employ a system of assigned counsel in all criminal cases, thus avoiding the evils of bureaucracy, careerism, political pressure, civil service mentality, and the like. These considerations might also tell against having a public prosecutor; perhaps it would be best to rely on the private sector exclusively, and employ a system of assigned counsel for both sides in all cases. These questions raise issues of public policy and economics that cannot be dealt with here. In any case, the concept of equal justice and due process provides good reasons for withdrawing the services of defense attorneys from the free market, for not permitting differences of wealth to affect the quality of justice.

NOTES

1. Joint Anti-Fascist Refugee Committee v. McGrath, 341 U.S. 123 (1951).
2. Rochin v. California, 342 U.S. 432 (1957). For an account of Frankfurter's views on due process, see Clyde Jacobs, *Justice Frankfurter and Civil Liberties* (Berkeley: University of California Press, 1961).
3. John Rawls, *A Theory of Justice* (Cambridge: Harvard University Press, 1971), p. 235.

4. Ibid., pp. 238-39.
5. Ibid., pp. 85-86.
6. Steinberg and Paulsen, "A Conversation with Defense Counsel on Problems of Criminal Defense," 7 Prac. Law 25, 26 (1961), cited in Monrad G. Paulsen and Sanford H. Kadish, *Criminal Law and its Processes* (Boston: Little, Brown and Company, 1962).
7. Betts v. Brady, 316 U.S. 455 (1942).
8. Griffin v. Illinois, 351 U.S. 12 (1955).

8

ON DE-MORALIZING DUE PROCESS

THOMAS R. KEARNS

I. INTRODUCTION

We are inclined to believe that many legal doctrines originate in morality; that they are, more specifically, simply the result of applying the demands of morality to the legal context. This supposition probably has a certain historical validity. It seems likely that in fashioning certain legal doctrines, legislators, judges and legal scholars actually set about to discern the requirements of morality as they pertain to the law. There is, in any case, considerable evidence of this kind of effort in connection with due process, the doctrine whose relation with morality is the main subject of this paper. But the historical point is not my concern. What interests me is a conceptual matter; specifically, whether due process is best understood—as is commonly supposed—in terms of certain moral requirements applied to the law.

How due process is best understood obviously depends on the kind of understanding one seeks. Thus, an account of the *origins* of due process would surely be closely tied to certain moral concerns, far more so than a legal account capable of explaining and predicting today's requirements in detail. So I am obliged to say

229

what kind of an account I seek, and that is not easy. Roughly, what I want is a statement of the basic or underlying theme or concern of due process. Such a statement would provide an answer to the almost philosophical-sounding question, "What, finally (ultimately, really), is due process all about?" It would also comport with the general contours of due process as they appear in Anglo-American law; but, unlike a strictly legal account, it would not, as regards details, have to be predictively powerful. Far more important is that it be persuasive or normative in character, indicating a path along which due process might be developed, providing a basis for deciding so-called hard or open cases, even identifying areas for gradual revision. All of this is vague, but it succeeds in placing the account in the right conceptual domain, the one in which it seems quite intelligible to assert (or deny) that due process is mainly or essentially a moral doctrine.

Perhaps it is appropriate to ask now, in a preliminary way, why anyone might take exception to, might doubt, this seemingly innocuous thesis linking the core of due process with morality. Disagreement about the pertinent requirements of morality aside, applying moral precepts to anything as complicated as a legal system is almost never a simple matter. And part of the reason for this is that our moral rules and principles apply, in the first instance, not to normative systems, but to persons. Between the law, one kind of normative system, and persons, there obviously are substantial differences. But the moral import of these differences—and so the way our standard moral concerns should be asserted or secured in connection with social structures like the law—is by no means obvious. Indeed, it might well be that the picture of applying our usual moral commitments directly to normative systems actually tends to imperil the moral ends we hope to achieve.

In the present study, I sketch three "moral" models of due process, three possible accounts that derive from different ways of applying certain fundamental moral concerns to the law's activities, especially where unfavorable action against assignable members is contemplated. But along the way I also propose an "amoral" model, one that purports to discover the underlying theme of legal due process in certain qualities of normative systems generally, qualities having to do with these structures' special virtues and vulnerabilities as vehicles for effective collective action. I conclude with a brief assessment of the moral implications of such an account.

II. MORALLY RESPONSIVE SYSTEMS

Collective action, suitably directed by a system of standing rules, is often more efficient and in other ways more rational, even more satisfying, than isolated, individual effort. But participation in normative systems involves conspicuous dangers. By definition such systems require authorities to make, interpret and enforce rules. They thus involve a concentration of power capable of abuse, easily capable of inflicting considerable harm on assignable individuals. Normative systems are morally worrisome.

Presumably, substantive harms—harms flowing from a system's decisions to seek this or that end—are to be guarded against mainly by procedural strictures determining how decisions shall be taken and who shall be a party to them. But there are also procedural harms, injuries a normative system can inflict on assignable individuals by the way it implements decisions unfavorable to its members. From this perspective, an account of due process would characterize the procedural harms against which a system's members should be protected.

The task may not seem particularly demanding, especially in light of the relatively weak constraints I have placed on what shall count as an acceptable account of due process. One proposal readily comes to mind. It is a familiar imperative of interpersonal morality that actions known or believed to be harmful to others—even if finally justified—must be undertaken with special sensitivity and care. For example, if, for what I believe is a greater good, I contemplate breaking a promise, I must be especially careful that the facts are as I suppose, that I understand the impact of my breach on my promisee, and so on. Moreover, I may even be obliged to discuss the matter with that person, to explain what is at stake and, where appropriate, issue an apology or in some other way made amends. Why not straightaway apply the analogues of this requirement to the conduct of normative systems? Here, surely, is the beginning of a promising statement of the rationale underlying due process of law.

But the matter is not quite this simple. As between persons, it is tolerably clear who are the intended beneficiaries of this imperative, and it is tolerably clear what kind –if not the degree—of care is contemplated. These things are decidedly unclear when the imperative is applied to normative systems. First, many of the slights and insensitivities against which the parent imperative is directed presuppose certain kinds of relationships between persons, certain kinds of intimacy and knowledge, that are largely and understandably lacking in connection with normative systems. For example, these systems are by definition rule-governed enterprises and tend to be inherently distant and impersonal. The possibility of suffering certain kinds of harms at the hands of these systems is therefore minimal or nonexistent.

What harms *does* this "transplanted" imperative pick out? Conceivably, one of them is the impersonality of normative systems; this, after all, is a familiar defect of many interpersonal relations and surely it can be overdone in connection with normative systems. But this only brings to mind a second unclarity; the extent to which essentially private sensibilities should be set aside in favor of a collective good, a good in which everyone presumably has hopes of sharing but which might be impeded or might not materialize at all if the procedural strictures are too tight.

The obvious point of the foregoing remarks is that normative systems involve complexities not present at the interpersonal level, complexities regarding the identity of the parties to whom moral constraints are supposed to apply and the way in which the several parties and their several interwoven interests should be disentangled and assessed. A call (modeled on interpersonal relations) for special sensitivity and care where a normative system contemplates or takes unfavorable action against assignable members, is just not very illuminating.

III. THE MORAL INTEGRITY OF SUBJECTS

A simple adjustment might substantially improve the suggestion. Thus, however complex normative systems are, no matter how many parties are involved and however intricate their interactions, we are always dealing finally with persons. And even though normative systems are not persons and so, perhaps, are not the immediate subjects of morality, and even if, what has not been shown, normative systems somehow have protectible interests not reducible without remainder to the merely aggregated interests of their members, it is certain that a system's procedures should not compromise the status of its members as moral agents. Thus, the moral integrity of persons, even of persons who are members of normative systems, is something that cannot be overriden by or sacrificed to some collective good, for on the existence of that integrity every other value surely depends. Perhaps here, then, is a way to hold the complexities of normative systems at bay, to indicate a kind of moral minimum which is neither obscured by the previous problems nor susceptible to their corrosive powers.

Here the tie between due process and morality is made at a very elemental level, conceptually prior to the appearance of such complicating things as the shared ends and complex strategies underlying some normative systems. For this view reminds us that persons are the immediate subjects of morality and unless their status as moral agents is protected, further moral concerns are largely idle. Thus, before encountering the complexities that troubled us with the first formulation, it may be possible to mark off a domain of essentially private interests that can plausibly lay claim to moral primacy. The interests suggested by the notion of a moral agent are sufficiently well defined to indicate a number of procedural imperatives for the conduct of normative systems. Moreover, this perspective respects the distinction between a system's procedural and substantive qualities. Just as moral agents have a capacity to do evil as well as good, a normative system that is procedurally impeccable—even from the proposed point of view—might nonetheless be substantively reprehensible. Enough has been said to warrant developing the view somewhat more fully.

How a normative system must conduct its affairs if it is to respect and protect its members as moral agents is indicated reasonably well by reflecting on what is involved in being a moral agent. To begin with, moral agents are in some sense rational, they are capable of perceiving their actions as being of this kind or that, and they are concerned to make sense of their lives, to plan and organize their activities and efforts in ways they judge to be sensible and satisfying. They also have a certain amount of self-respect—a sense of personal worth or dignity—and they have at least a minimal regard for others, including, I should think, a disposition to honor or respect what they take to be the equal worth of all other moral agents. There is no need to insist on exactly these elements, for we are concerned here simply to sketch a basic perspective or theme for due process. Surely, at this level, considerable variation is compatible with what I propose to call the Moral Integrity view of due process (hereafter, MI).

Some of the implications of MI in terms of specific due process requirements are fairly clear. It is, I think, apparent that MI would require normative systems to conduct their business, at least for the most part, by means of rules, rules that are not changed too frequently, are generally prospective (not retroactive), intelligible, properly "noticed," consistent, performable—in a word, by means of *followable* rules.[1] In no other way can the rationality of moral agents be respected. It is also tolerably clear that considerations of dignity and rationality would—to mention a few items—require a hearing where assignable individuals are to suffer deprivations of life, liberty or property, especially where these are allegedly justified in terms of some collective good, enjoin the use of stomach pumps to obtain evidence, direct public housing officials to give reasons for evictions, bar unreasonable searches and seizures, and reject nearly all forms of compulsory self-incrimination. Nor is it difficult to see that MI would issue in proscriptions against double jeopardy and suggest the importance of providing legal services for indigent criminal defendants. In sum, it appears that by reference to concerns of dignity and rationality, the Moral Integrity view is entirely capable of reproducing or accommodating the familiar contours of procedural due process.

I should emphasize that MI indicates that due process is to be thought of as the protector of a certain domain of inviolable, essentially personal, private, but still profoundly moral, values. The values in question are personal because they link up in obvious ways with each person's own status as a moral agent; they are moral because they are elements of what is involved in being a moral agent and also because they express values that persons must, as moral agents, respect in one another; finally, the values are private because unlike, say, friendship or truth telling, they make no essential reference to others nor to any collective good.

Aspects of MI were adumbrated almost twenty years ago in

Sanford Kadish's helpful study of due process.[2] There Kadish maintained that due process is "more a moral command than a strictly jural precept"[3] and its object is to restrict "the manner in which governmental power is exercised upon the individual, even in an area of legitimate concern. . . ."[4] Even more specifically, Kadish insisted that due process is concerned to preserve "the intrinsic dignity of the individual."[5] Though he isolates for separate treatment a concern to maximize the reliability of guilt-determination processes, it is easy to see how this concern might be viewed as merely a part of the larger concern to protect individual dignity. And from here it obviously is not far to MI.

These brief remarks are intended to indicate that the Moral Integrity view gives ample expression to our deep moral concern that individuals not be overrun in the pursuit of collective goods, that protections against certain kinds of intrusions on the human spirit, on an individual's moral integrity, are of utmost importance, almost no matter what their cost in terms of external goods or the common welfare. The view also seems to be consonant with much legal rhetoric and with the law's general requirements and it enjoys the support of at least one prominent legal theorist. Moreover, MI indicates that the concerns underlying due process are not confined to the law, that, in fact, they surface wherever collective goods are sought by means of rule-governed activity and a system's procedures create a risk of moral harm to assignable individuals. The notion is thus made available to those who, like myself, would contend for due process in nonlegal settings, but would insist, of course, that the law's particular requirements are often inappropriate elsewhere.

IV. OBJECTIONS TO MI

Despite this support for MI, the view is finally unacceptable, perhaps especially from the moral point of view. The primary object of social morality is to guide and harmonize human interests and efforts, particularly to eliminate needless and self-destructive conflict in the interactions of persons in social settings. Normative systems, perhaps more so than the unhelpfully general and generally inelastic edicts of a shared social morality, are the major mechanism we have for achieving this direction, this integration of human activity. They are, therefore, much too important to be left outside of our moral reckoning, though how they are to be taken into account is not at all certain. But we should resist the suggestion implicit in MI that, as regards their manner of conduct, normative systems can and should be thought of as persons to whom the requirements of interpersonal morality might be applied directly.

First, this perspective is likely to encourage sensitivity to a system's way of proceeding which might be morally offensive as between persons but which is quite unobjectionable at the level of normative systems. Tact, for example, is generally required of persons in their dealings with one another, but not of normative systems. Similarly, but more importantly, as between persons, impersonality, that is, a refusal to attend to, to take into account, what is special or idiosyncratic about this or that person, is often quite objectionable. But in certain contexts and in certain respects, this is a decided virtue of normative systems.

Second, the perspective is starkly silent about problems peculiar to normative systems, problems whose resolution might sometimes best be accomplished procedurally and in ways that at first glance might seem patently unacceptable in terms of human dignity and moral agency. For example, persons who, relative to their respective preference-rankings, are equally committed to a certain end and who are thereby drawn into membership in a system that promises to advance that end, may discover to their collective dismay irreconcilable commitments and views about *how* the shared end should be pursued. And—at least sometimes—this problem of aggregating individual preferences compels normative systems to impose requirements that in some relatively clear sense are irrational for everyone involved.[6] In sum, the sensible identification of the requirements of moral agency may depend substantially on familiarity with various qualities and problems peculiar to normative systems. It therefore may not be possible, as MI casually suggests, to discover the morally appropriate procedural constraints on normative systems by attending exclusively to the notion of a moral agent. But what else should be taken into account MI does not say.

Third, MI must be faulted because it seeks to ground respect or support for the requirements of due process either in the risk each person runs as a member of a normative system of suffering an unacceptable private harm (publicly inflicted) or in whatever empathy can be engendered for other members who stand to suffer such harms. And this is lamentable because it tends to emphasize the contrast between collective and essentially private matters, between various joint goals and the merely "shared" concern that each person has for his own moral integrity. And it emphasizes this contrast without identifying the tensions it may reflect or give rise to, and without indicating how, if at all, those tensions might be averted or ameliorated. From the perspective MI provides, the requirements of due process have more the feel of minimal laws of warfare than the procedural framework of a constructive undertaking. Moreover, implicit in the view is the entirely gratuitous assumption that the moral status of persons is tolerably well defined without any reference at all to normative systems, without reference to the extension of rational behavior made possible by such systems,[7] without reference to the pleasures of trust and participation and the adjustment of aims and means that this may entail. Here, obviously, the second and third objections join forces to challenge MI's easy supposition that the notion of a moral agent is entirely separable from the notion of a normative system.

V. AN AMORAL ALTERNATIVE

To introduce a radical alternative to the Moral Integrity view, it is helpful to return briefly to Kadish's paper and to note that he, too, finally rejected this essentially individualistic, private perspective. For him, due process controversy emerges mainly at the juncture of opposing values, two values in particular, individual dignity and maximally reliable determinations of guilt.[8] He would, it seems, firmly resist my casual suggestion that the two values might be merged under a slightly enlarged conception of individual dignity. The basis for that resistance is evidently to be gleaned from two examples, the first of which, however, is quite weak. It consists of the observation that a full complement of procedural safeguards in connection with juvenile offenders or the mentally ill may tend to undermine rehabilitative interests.[9] I am not satisfied that the latter interests clash with a concern for human dignity—at worst, there is here only an uncertaintly about the best way to protect that dignity, but possibly I have misunderstood. In any case, Kadish's second example makes what I take to be the stronger point, for he notes that, though the reliability of governmental discharges on grounds of disloyalty would doubtless improve if judicial hearings were required, at stake, too, are important interests of the government, for example to be rid of harmful employees and to protect the identity of valuable informers.[10]

These two examples capture the core of Kadish's vague but still suggestive remarks that "the ultimate nature of the impasse of all procedural due process issues may be the same: preserving the integrity of a democratic community without imperiling other legitimate values." [11] The different kinds of values are not identified, their possible relationships are not detailed and the main concern is to characterize due process controversies rather than to illuminate directly the nature of due process itself. But if governmental interests of the kind referred to in the second of Kadish's examples are indeed the proper concern of due process, then it is certain that the Moral Integrity view is unacceptably narrow. That MI *is* too narrow, is, I believe, a conclusion Kadish would staunchly support.

Unfortunately, Kadish's study is not very helpful about what should be done, about the considerations that should come into play, when dignity and reliability clash. He observes that the personal and social impact of a proceeding's determinations (or misdeterminations) can be more or less serious, more or less important or harmful, and he offers the sensible suggestion that the process that is due or appropriate might vary accordingly.[12] But such observations do not amount to an account of due process, not even on my lenient description of what might qualify as an account. There is, for example, nothing here that approaches a unified rationale of due process in terms of which the relevant variations among various proceedings might be identified, the relevant parties and interests distinguished and related, and a general but still informative analysis generated of the interactions between parties and between apparently competing values. Moreover, the blanket contrast between personal and social concerns contains no suggestion at all that due process might be peculiarly tied to the special ways that normative systems (in this case, the law) serve and threaten both personal and social values and the interactions between them. The aim of much of the subsequent discussion is to present and argue for just such a view.

VI. THE IDEA OF SYSTEM

Normative systems manage to extend the possibility of rational action mainly by coordinating human effort and by (at least partially) tying down the future.[13] For the most part, this structuring of present activities and dispositions and future states of affairs is accomplished by promulgating and publicizing and in other ways supporting a system of rules. The effort is also promoted by anticipating and responding resourcefully to changes in interests, needs or circumstances affecting the system's primary aims. Not infrequently this requires that rules be changed, sometimes abruptly, sometimes without proper notice. Plainly, these strategies, these contributions to a rational collective undertaking, interact with one another, sometimes in wrenching opposition—a natural upshot of the quest for coordinated stability which is somehow flexible as well.

Moreover, each of these elements singly contains the seeds of additional tensions. Thus, members of every normative system have substantially differing sets of interests, aims, or needs, so it is practically unavoidable that human activities coordinated by standing rules will not display an entirely fair or just allocation of benefits and burdens. Similarly, the future can be tied down and reliable expectations created only if at least some relatively minor, incidental adjustments or corrections are foregone; rules that are altered too much or too rapidly lose their capacity to guide conduct and to promote the general ends of stability, predictability and reasonable confidence about some of the spatially and temporally distant doings of others.[14] Finally, anticipatory, resourceful responses to changes affecting a normative system's primary ends require authorities who are not mere caretakers but who are, instead, wielders of considerable discretionary power.

Here, then, on the very surface of normative systems, are some powerful indications that we are obliged to tolerate, for example, some disagreeably disparate treatment of a system's members, some individuals' losses recouped by no one, though suffered in the name of the collective effort, and some intrinsically uncontrollable power in the hands of every system's authorities.[15] Moreover, notorious problems associated with aggregating personal preferences raise serious doubts about the underlying notion of collective rationality.

And, what is not an entirely separate point, it is almost inevitable that a system's primary ends tend to function to some extent as ideals, creating, in the presence of discretionary powers, special danger of selective enforcement of the system's rules and other abuses of authority not easily detected nor convincingly demonstrated in particular cases.

The foregoing is meant to suggest that there are inherent or natural proclivities of normative systems which, if not carefully curtailed will destroy what I propose to call *system,* namely, that ensemble of properties of normative systems that tends to make such structures reasonable and effective mechanisms to obtain the special benefits of relatively long-term collective effort. I have in mind, as a prominent (but by no means) sole constituent of this ensemble, the sizable discretion at the disposal of every system's officials. Even if this discretion could be eliminated, it would be a mistake to do so; it would cripple a system's capacity for adaptive, resourceful pursuit and development of its basic ends and so deprive it of a primary virtue of normative systems generally.[16] Of course, officials' discretion remains a familiar and reasonable basis for concern, since it is, experience shows, a powerful temptation to wrongdoing. But the crucial point is this: there is no way to eliminate the danger or even to monitor it effectively, without destroying it, for discretion is most valuable in connection with matters that are not easily or wisely subjected to rules.

Discretion is thus an essential feature of system. It contributes substantially to the capacity of normative systems to respond effectively to the unexpected, to smooth out and to allocate sensibly unanticipated benefits and burdens, and so on. But the risks are rampant. In sum, discretion is a dangerous virtue, confronting us with the frustrating task of defending against it without doing it harm.

At a more general level, governance by standing rules (as opposed, say, to short-lived edicts or momentary directives) is another crucial feature of system. Through rules, members of a normative system can maximally contribute to and participate in the upshot of coordinated, collective effort and they can enjoy as well the important benefit of reasonable foreknowledge about certain of their own activities and the activities of others. Plainly, not all structures for coordinating human activity can be counted on for such virtues (the erratic directives of a despot, for example).[17] Of course, there is a certain tension in all of this, for it has already been contended that flexibility is a virtue of normative systems. So, without pretending to solve the problem, it should be noted in passing that—to the extent that the development or evolution of a rule or set of rules can be anticipated by its addressees—the possibility of effective, nondisruptive compliance is enhanced.

It should also be noted that the benefits of governance by rule tend to be maximized where individual members comply in the belief that they and others stand to gain thereby and each is confident that others share this view. In fact, in all of these matters, second-order effects are of special importance.[18] Thus, it is not enough that, in fact, a system is impeccably rulish or has exemplary (say, easily anticipated) developmental patterns. Members must themselves have confidence that this is so and they must believe that one another believes it as well. Finally, and most importantly, with respect to the entire ensemble of qualities, members must be confident they will receive an early warning of any serious erosion of system—ideally, early enough to permit withdrawal, to minimize private losses, to avoid the risk of special, disproportionate harms to themselves.

VII. THE MAINTENANCE OF SYSTEM

The purpose of introducing the idea of system and of discussing a few of its constituents has been to draw attention to some of the dominant strategies, virtues and dangers peculiar to normative systems and to indicate that the achievement of system is both the means by which the special benefits of collective effort can be realized and the source of special dangers against which adequate provision is not only advisable but is positively promotive of a system's undertaking. This complex of considerations provides, I believe, the material for a genuine alternative to the Moral Integrity view of due process.

Boldy stated, the primary concern of due process is the maintenance of system (to be distinguished from, though related to, the overall success of this or that normative system). It consists largely of a set of procedures designed to assure members that they will be amply informed about the condition of system, that, for example, officials and others will be suitably compelled to confront openly and publicly the troublesome implications of a system's operations, including, among other things, its level of effectiveness relative to stated aims, the occurrence of unauthorized changes in those aims, dangerous accumulations of power, and unacceptable harms to assignable individuals. Obviously, there are many good reasons for insisting on procedures such as these, but from the perspective of the view of due process being developed here, the overriding consideration is this: only if such provisions are made can members reasonably and confidently suppose that their collective aims are being pursued through the use of system, that the potential advantages of this mode of group action are indeed in the offing (or that they are at least being actively pursued), and that there exist suitable safeguards against the considerable risks involved. Where reasonable grounds for this confidence are lacking, members can safely assume that the primary advantages of normative systems are not in fact available. And, as was indicated above, this assumption tends to be powerfully self-fulfilling.

This account of due process, what I shall call the Maintenance of System view (hereafter, MS), presupposes that we have at our disposal satisfactory ways of detecting in advance any threatening inroads against system and, as a related matter, that there are persons suitably motivated and properly informed to issue reliable warnings about the condition of system. Fortunately, there are, it seems, few difficulties here. First, a full study of normative systems—something going well beyond these sketchy efforts—would amply detail numerous points of primary concern or interest, points of special danger, or special value, or both. Even the present effort has indicated enough about normative systems to make it obvious that they (especially legal systems) tend to involve an accumulation of power the abuse of which could easily be masked if, say, certain forms of compulsory self-incrimination were in any way tolerated. Similarly, it is clear that an important defense against abuse of this power is assurance that official direction is mainly by means of rules—as opposed to momentary directives—for the latter are not so easily assimilated by the private plans of addressees and they thus tend to be disruptive and to stand in greater need of coercive support. The ways this tends to increase the dangers of life in a normative system need not be rehearsed.

Second, as regards the availability of motivated and informed parties to activate the appropriate warnings, the answer seems to be relatively simple: at the points judged especially precarious for system, there will invariably be persons who deem themselves seriously aggrieved and who will therefore be amply motivated to invoke whatever procedures are made available to challenge and publicize worrisome or otherwise important aspects of the collective undertaking. Persons who meet this description can safely be relied on to elicit steady disclosures regarding the condition of system. At the same time, of course, they can be relied on to promote the well-being of system. It should be noted in passing that MS makes it quite understandable why due process might come to be thought of as procedures for the protection of assignable individuals against whom the system contemplates some harm, for, according to MS, aggrieved persons are relied on to process the system. This sharpens the issue between MS and other accounts of due process: from the perspective of due process, *which* should be adopted as basic: (a) the protection of persons in the face of (perhaps finally justified) harm, or (b) the maintenance of system, which for the most part only relies on the threat of personal harm to promote enforcement of rules that are themselves designed, as their first function, to service system? Additional reasons for preferring (b) are detailed below.

Our discussion to this point makes it reasonable to believe that MS would reproduce many of the rules familiarly thought of as the protections of procedural due process. It is easy enough to see, for example, that the protection of system requires various forms of participation, revelation, and justification; demands proper notice of official action; precludes compulsory self-incrimination, and so on. In fact, at this level of generality, and especially in connection with the law, the Maintenance of System and Moral Integrity views of due process are not easily distinguished by pointing to specific differences in their respective requirements. But the difference in underlying rationales is nonetheless pronounced. For example, the importance of conformity between official action and announced rule would be explained on MI in terms of an alleged connection between rules, reasons, and morality. By contrast, MS would simply point to the logical connection between rules and system. The conceptual gulf between the two views is thus substantial. But there are also some very important practical differences, especially at what might be termed the motivational level.

The Moral Integrity view takes as its point of departure an

assumed antagonism between collective undertakings and the preservation of one's status as a moral being. It is thus concerned to identify unacceptable harms and to adopt procedures to guard against them. On this view, the process a system owes its members is what is required to protect them as moral agents from harms the system might otherwise inflict. The perspective would seem to encourage a relatively static regard for essentially private worth, shared in by a system's members only in that each person insists on it in his own case.

By contrast, MS emerges from the qualities of system that make collective effort attractive but are themselves peculiarly liable to degeneration and abuse. Due process is thus conceptually tied to normative systems and what is due is to be discerned by attending to the special requirements of system. The dominant concern, then, is to process system, to institute procedures that will attend to the special vulnerabilities of system while preserving its valuable capacity to coordinate action, to reinforce or amplify the efficacy of individual effort, to respond adaptively and resourcefully in the face of changing circumstances, interests or needs. Of course, the view is by no means oblivious to the several ways that persons are at risk as members of a normative system; indeed, the view explicitly seeks to identify those risks and to gain members' confidence regarding the condition of system by various procedural devices, devices that simultaneously enhance the system's prospects as regards its basic aims.

Implicit in the foregoing is the deep motivational contrast between the two views that I alluded to above: the Moral Integrity view points to the possibility of harms to oneself or else relies on a degree of empathy for the harms others might suffer, whereas MS emphasizes the direct interest each member has in the concerns of due process, for it shows how these concerns are related to the well-being of members and of system and to the overall success of the collective undertaking. More pointedly, MS makes it possible to see demands for due process, one's own as well as others', as something other than a charge on the common good, or something other than what must be tolerated so that essentially private harms can be avoided or redressed. In sum, it appears that the latter view does a superior job of conceptually linking due process and normative systems, of identifying at least some relatively objective considerations indicating the appropriate content of due process, and of making available motivational support for the concerns of due process that is both privately compelling and properly supportive of the collective enterprise.

Against MS it is likely to be objected that by focusing on system, justice is not done the commonplace belief that due process is predominantly a moral precept; and failure in this regard is surely objectionable, perhaps calling into question whether the view is genuinely about due process at all. Moreover, even if the objections against the Moral Integrity view are well taken, there are other ways to link due process and morality. I propose briefly to examine two such alternatives before confronting the suggestion that MS seriously de-moralizes due process.

VIII. THE INTERACTIONAL VIEW

It might be thought that the notion of system is entirely superfluous, that a morally compelling picture of due process might be drawn directly from some fairly simple presuppositions pertaining to certain essential interactions between a system's officials and its subjects. The required interactions occur in two ways: one objectively, by means of rules, and the other subjectively, by means of certain shared intentions, purposes or goals. Plainly, interaction by rule is possible, as was noted before, only if the rules are by and large followable; if they are publicized, not changed too frequently, not impossible to perform, consistent with one another, intelligible, prospective rather than retroactive, and so on. Unless the condition of followability is met, conduct cannot be subjected to the governance of rules; subjects cannot guide their conduct by reference to what is not followable. Of course, followable rules need not be followed. Some motive must be at hand, and, except for dominantly coercive systems, this will usually take the form of a second interaction between officials, namely, a commitment to certain shared aims or goals which officials seek to promote by means of the rules they formulate.

At this point, all that is needed is the confidence of the pertinent parties that the announced rules will indeed be applied in the manner indicated and that those rules will by and large be observed by the persons to whom they are addressed. Presumably, one element of the needed confidence depends on the fact that the act of promulgating a public rule has a social meaning; that its addressees can depend on it, that it is—in effect—an invitation to them to order pertinent aspects of their lives in accord with its direction. As regards the other side of the relationship, perhaps the following observation suffices: by participating in a system, by sharing in its benefits or by indicating a claim to those benefits, subjects express to officials and to one another their commitment to the system's underlying aims; they thus indicate a preparedness to subject pertinent aspects of their conduct to the governance of rules.[19]

Surely it is not farfetched to suggest that these interactions between and among subjects and officials yield a network of interlocking expectations having all of the moral import of the promissory configurations they closely resemble. Moreover, some of these interactions quite obviously presuppose that certain basic requirements of due process are satisfied; the implications of "governance by rule" are alone enough to ensure this result. It would seem, then, that the Interactional View, as I shall call it (hereafter, IV), holds promise of providing a compelling moral foundation of due process.

But IV is not without its defects. Perhaps the most serious one is that it appears to limit the protections of due process to what can be gleaned from the presuppositions or implications of the notion of governance by rule. And in this there seems to be nothing that would, for example, bar the use of stomach pumps as a way to obtain evidence, preclude other objectionable kinds of compulsory self-incrimination, including outrageous searches and seizures, or entitle one to a hearing when property is to be taken for the public good. The problem is this: IV sketches the basis for reciprocal restrictions on subjects and officials, but those restrictions pertain mainly and only generally to the need to observe announced rules. They are, therefore, almost completely uninformative about the special ways in which a system, even by rule, might, but should not, impinge on its members. In sum, IV seems to be more promising as an account of the principles of legality than as an account of due process. For the latter purposes, IV is just too limited.[20]

I can imagine, however, a slightly less literal understanding of the Interactional View, emphasizing the fact that the view dispenses with all references to system, that it focuses instead on identifying and attaching moral significance to the several important ways that officials and subjects must interact in normative systems. This characterization has the appealing quality of reminding us that normative systems are comprised of persons, but it should also remind us of the considerable perplexity that officials and subjects themselves have about their respective responsibilities and rightful expectations. For example, most participants in normative systems—officials and subjects alike—understand that subjects may appropriately be required to suffer certain kinds of official conduct the private analogues of which would almost certainly be morally objectionable. But there is much dispute, much uncertainty, about particular cases and about kinds of harms. By eliminating all reference to system and by representing officials and subjects as morally interchangeable units who just happen to be differently situated in the background structure, IV would seem to be unilluminating as regards moral issues that are peculiar to normative systems, for example, as regards whether a consistent, morally defensible system might in special cases place officials and subjects under contrary directives, say, confer a right on subjects to do X but mandate officials to take some unfavorable action against those who do X.[21] Though such an issue surely has bearing on matters of due process (even on IV's narrow characterization of this domain), IV is totally uninformative.

The perspective provided by the Interactional View does make it relatively easy to see that serious tensions might arise between essentially private concerns and the achievement of the shared ends out of which a given normative system emerges. But the view seems to be far more informative about the existence conditions of such systems than it is helpful about the ongoing problems involved in understanding and effectively resolving the tensions alluded to above. It seems better suited to explaining the basis of officials' and subjects' interlocking obligations in some properly processed system than in identifying and accounting for the restrictions that such a system would observe. Moreover, IV is misleading. It simply ignores the important fact that the idea of an official is conceptually tied to the idea of a normative system and to the achievement of shared goals in a very special way. That way includes, of course, the idea of governance by rule, but by flexible rule, and sometimes unrulishly, as MS rightly emphasizes. In brief, it seems that the situation is far more complicated than the Interactional View can accommodate.

IX. THE MORAL AGENT VIEW

In search of an underlying rationale for due process, and as an alternative to MS, we have considered two ways of linking due process and morality. One way treated due process as the procedures a normative system must observe if the moral agency or moral integrity of its members is to be respected. The other way focused on certain quasi-promissory configurations (associated with the attempt to realize certain shared ends by means of rules) that emerge from the essential interactions of a system's officials and subjects. In both of these efforts, the directives of interpersonal morality were applied directly to persons and to normative systems in an attempt to discover how the latter should be required to behave. But possibly there is another way to make this determination, nonetheless preserving some interesting link with morality.

It is undeniable that normative systems are not persons and it might be contended, contrary to the previous efforts, that the substantive provisions of interpersonal morality cannot be applied directly to normative systems. However, granting this does not foreclose the possibility of linking due process and morality, for even if the only morality we have is interpersonal in character, we are not restricted to using its *substantive* provisions. Thus, the differences between normative systems and persons are not so great as to make the following question absurd: what qualities—presumably expressed in terms of various ways of conducting business—would normative systems have to have if they were to maximize their resemblance to moral agents? The answer, derived from our standard notion of a moral agent, would describe the requirements of due process, or so the Moral Agent view (hereafter, MA) would propose.

In connection with MI, in our effort to determine what is required of normative systems to respect the moral status of their members, we had occasion to consider the nature of a moral agent. The elements identified there can be cited again, this time to lay the foundation for a brief sketch of the qualities that a normative system would have if its resemblance to moral agents of a kind were to be maximized. It was proposed that moral agents are in some sense rational, that they are capable of perceiving their actions as being of this kind or that, and that they are concerned to make sense of their lives, to plan and organize their activities and efforts in ways thought to be sensible and satisfying. They also have a certain amount of self-respect, a sense of personal worth or dignity and they have at least a minimal regard for others, including, probably, a disposition to honor or respect what they take to be the equal worth of all other moral agents. As before, there is no need to insist on exactly these elements. What we seek now is some indication of the form these qualities would take in connection with normative systems.

Presumably, respect for other moral agents would appear as a high degree of congruence between official action and announced rules and would include various mechanisms for ensuring members an appropriate level of participating in the system's activities and providing explanations of and justifications for actions proposed or taken. The concern to understand self and others would probably also be reflected in systematic and pervasive efforts to gather information regarding circumstances, needs and interests of a system's members, and to fashion, on an ongoing basis, a public statement of the system's dominant aims. Of special importance— also strongly associated with the requirement of respect for others— would be a pervasive, probing effort to detect a system's interactions with other systems, and an effort to understand and to take into account their implications for a system's own members and for the members of other systems. MA appears to be especially effective at focusing attention on the clashing obligations and tangled loyalties that interacting systems can create for their members. The Moral Agent view would no doubt issue in procedures to scrutinize this interplay, requiring, perhaps, the development of a fairly comprehensive view about the relative importance of the ends of various normative systems and about the ways important conflicts should be resolved. Efforts to comply with this requirement can, I think, be counted on to generate many of the familiar provisions of procedural due process. Finally, a system might be thought of as rational (though not necessarily reasonable) to the extent that it acts purposively, with an end-in-view, and a commitment to some degree of efficiency in connection with selected ends.

All of this is admittedly quite vague, but it illustrates well enough the procedural patterns that a normative system would have to exhibit were it, as MA requires, to maximize its resemblance to moral agents. To the extent that these patterns overlap with the standard requirements of due process, there is support for the contention that MA provides a suitably "moralized" account of due process.

What can be said about this view of due process? Its strength, I think, revolves around the attention it directly accords normative systems as morally significant units on the social scene. It does this primarily in two related ways. First, it reminds us that although normative systems are not persons, they are managed by persons; they are susceptible to strikingly similar kinds of moral deficiencies (a narrow egoism, for example), and they are entirely capable of inflicting serious moral harm on others. Second, the view supports our firm conviction that anything that affects our lives so directly, powerfully and purposively as normative systems, must somehow be held responsible for its activities and their consequences. It must be subject to moral assessment, even if, as MA suggests, some kind of elaborate analogy is required to prepare it for our moral apparatus, to make that system of considerations applicable to these complex social structures.

But the view's strength is also its weakness, or so it seems to me. When we speak of holding a normative system responsible for its activities, we mean—or should mean—that we shall reject efforts on the part of a system's officials to escape responsibility for their actions by making uncritical reference to the system's ends. There is, however, no need to hold normative systems responsible directly, whatever that might mean; indeed, the attempt to do so by perceiving systems as moral agents of a kind is quite likely to have the untoward consequence that normative systems will themselves come to be regarded as rightholders, as claimants against their members, in something other than the fiduciary capacity we normally attribute to them. And what is true in this regard holds overall in connection with the effort to conceive of normative systems as moral agents of a kind. These systems are dangerous enough without straining to see them in this light, as entities that may compete on equal moral footing with persons.

Arguably, my suggestion that MA would place persons and system on equal moral footing is entirely gratuitous. It is fair to note, however, that MA provides no grounds for any other assumption. Having prepared normative systems as moral agents, the view would appear to stop disappointingly short of providing any guidance regarding the interactions of systems and subjects, evidently leaving to some region of morality, or to some moral doctrine other than due process, the entire task of unraveling, assessing and integrating the tangled interests that typify life in a rule-governed enterprise. If so, MA manages to fashion a link between due process and morality only by leaving in utter darkness the moral issues that probably matter most in normative systems; for example, how the sometimes clashing interests of assignable members and the system's declared ends are to be resolved. Finally, embedded in MA's basic strategy is the amiable but disputable assumption that substantive and procedural issues are neatly separable: that the assignment of values to conflicting interests can be made without reference to procedural provisions, and that the adequacy of procedures can be determined without attention to the way conflicting values are assessed.

X. CONCLUSION

The foregoing materials explored three ways of understanding due process in terms of morality: by conceiving of its requirements as designed to respect the moral integrity of a system's members (MI); to fulfill the quasi-promissory implications of seeking shared ends by means of rules (IV); and to qualify normative systems themselves as moral agents of a kind (MA). The views have been faulted on a variety of grounds: for relying too strongly on the separability of substance and process; for inadequately motivating support for due process claims; for distorting the identity, nature, and interactions of the parties involved in normative systems; and for failing to direct attention to and illuminate those special qualities of normative systems that make them of such great practical and moral importance. But I suspect that none of these objections is conclusive against the proposals at which they have been levelled. It might well be that at any given time the requirements of due process are indeed the outcome of an ongoing battle between private and collective interests and that it is a virtue—not a defect—of the Moral Integrity view that it highlights this fact, reminding us, perhaps, that the protections due process affords depend finally on the power and persistence of personal vigilance and concern. Moreover, I have no doubt that far more than three ways could be found to moralize due process. Still, the problems discussed in connection with these three views provide some reason for thinking that the underlying effort, the attempt to explicate due process as a direct derivative of morality, is misdirected. This, anyway, is the dominant theme of these concluding remarks.

It is, I think, quite understandable that we should turn to morality in hopes of finding the basic theme or task of due process. Normative systems, the only kind of entity to which the notion of due process has application, are capable of causing great harm, a capacity, experience shows, that has been realized all too frequently. Fortunately, however, they are managed by persons and, like persons, they are amenable to human regulation and control, though most easily, perhaps, in connection with the ways decisions are made and implemented. It would be foolish, then, to allow these powerful structures to exert their force with moral abandon. Like persons, they must be brought under the strictures of morality, at least as regards basic operating procedures.

If the foregoing sketch has any validity, the demand for a moral explication of due process trades heavily on an analogy between normative systems and persons, an analogy that is quite compelling until the attempt is made to discern in any detail just what morality requires of a system's procedures. Then, as was remarked at the outset of the present investigations, the differences between persons and systems loom large: unlike persons, normative systems are comprised of persons; unlike persons, normative systems have no value aside from their contributions to the well-being or happiness of persons, and so on. Surely these and other differences are among the things that imperil, at the very outset, any effort to provide what I have called a "moral" account of due process.

But I suspect there is a further and deeper difficulty confronting such efforts. It has to do with the fact that, though normative systems are not persons, they are nonetheless a functional unit of dominant importance on the social scene. In fact, they are the primary mechanism we have for advancing a central concern of morality, the coordination and harmonization of human energies, efforts and plans. Issues of metaphysical reductionism aside, we shall, I suspect, lose touch with what is morally most important about normative systems if we insist on thinking of them as persons of a kind or as mere complexes of variously situated persons, some of them officials, others subjects. Only when they are perceived as systems of flexible rules—much in need of resourceful management and development and greatly dependent on a fragile network of confidences linking subjects and officials—is it possible to discern the special causal and conceptual ties between procedural due process and the central aims of morality generally. If I am right about this, then what seems both more pressing and more promising than a moralized account of due process, is a deepened understanding of the workings of normative systems, especially of the nature of *system* and the conditions required for its emergence and maintenance. Presumably, that understanding would indicate the kinds of procedures normative systems should observe. It would also provide the basis for informed, particular moral jdugments about the impact of a particular system's procedures.

As I have argued throughout this paper, the Maintenance of System account is thus properly intent on understanding the special strategies, virtues and vulnerabilities typically associated with normative systems and to indicate thereby the procedures needed to maintain and promote system. It is clear, though, that MS thus forgoes the idea of shaping a system's procedures so as to bring it directly under morality's rule. Does it also de-moralize due process? Only, I think, conceptually, for its contribution to the moral virtues of normative systems and to the quality of lives lived therein promises to be greater than what could be expected were we to accept the guidance of the moralized accounts. And it is a good thing to improve the moral quality of normative systems, even if that involves de-moralizing a concept.

NOTES

1. The list is borrowed from Lon Fuller's specification of the principles of legality in *The Morality of Law* (New Haven: Yale University Press, 1964), p. 39. The suggestion that most of the entries pertain to

followability comes from David Lyons's paper, "The Internal Morality of Law," Aristotelian Society Proceedings 1970-71, 105, 109.

2. Sanford Kadish, "Methodology and Criteria in Due Process Adjudication—A Survey and Criticism," 66 Yale Law Journal (1957), 319-63.

3. Ibid., p. 341.

4. Ibid., p. 340.

5. Ibid.

6. See Kenneth J. Arrow, *The Limits of Organization* (New York: W.W. Norton & Co., Inc., 1974), Chapter I, especially pp. 24-25.

7. Ibid., p. 16.

8. Kadish, "Methodology and Criteria," p. 347.

9. Ibid., p. 348-49.

10. Ibid., p. 347.

11. Ibid., p. 343.

12. Ibid., p. 350 ff.

13. Arrow, *The Limits of Organization,* Chapters I and IV.

14. Fuller, *The Morality of Law,* pp. 79-81.

15. On the eliminability of discretion see, generally, Kenneth Culp Davis, *Discretionary Justice* (Illini Books, 1971); Kadish and Kadish, *Discretion to Disobey* (Stanford: Stanford University Press, 1973), and Duncan Kennedy, "Legal Formality," 2 J. Legal Studies (1973) 351.

16. Kadish and Kadish, *Discretion to Disobey,* Chapters 1 and 4.

17. See Fuller, *The Morality of Law,* Chapter II.

18. See David K. Lewis, *Convention: A Philosophical Study* (Cambridge, Mass.: Harvard University Press, 1969).

19. This discussion is largely a new application of Fuller's treatment of the principles of legality. His purposes are different from those being attributed to the Interactional View and the criticisms of that view, adduced subsequently in the text, do not apply to Fuller's efforts.

20. Again, Professor Fuller bears no responsibility for this novel application of his work on the principles of legality.

21. We often suppose that "when an individual has correctly decided that he ought to do X, then any higher-order judgment about his decision to do X or his act of actually doing it ought to license or approve of, rather than disapprove of or penalize, the decision and/or the act itself." This, what might be called the "reflection principle," has been challenged by Rolf Sartorius in "Individual Conduct and Social Norms," Ethics Vol. 82 (1972), 200-218, principle stated at p. 204.

PART III

9

DUE PROCESS IN A NONLEGAL
SETTING: AN OMBUDSMAN'S
EXPERIENCE

DAVID J. DANELSKI

As a university ombudsman, I was especially interested in Frank Michelman's and Edmund Pincoffs's discussion of the moral and legal requirements of due process in cases like Roth v. Board of Regents.[1] Several persons in Roth's position have sought my help as ombudsman in the past two years, and although only a few of them had their contracts renewed, all of them were given reasons for their terminations. This indicates that the standards of due process in some nonlegal settings differ from judicial due process. For academic ombudsmen, those standards are much like the standards discussed by Michelman and Pincoffs. The observations that follow are based on my experience as an ombudsman.

(1) It is a mistake to dwell solely on the legal aspects of due process, particularly in cases like Roth's, for seldom are such disputes settled in courts. In fact, the lesson of *Roth* is that in such cases the judicial route is a dead end. Even if *Roth* had offered hope of legal redress, few professors in Roth's position would go to court because of the costs involved. Typically they would go to nonjudicial agencies for help—faculty academic freedom committees, the American Association of University Professors, or an ombudsman's

office—because those agencies are more likely than courts to settle such matters quickly and economically. That is one of the reasons for the dramatic increase in the number of ombudsmen's offices in American colleges and universities in recent years.[2]

Another reason is that the vast majority of complaints about institutional injustice are not susceptible to judicial resolution. Although ombudsmen's procedures are extralegal, they are influenced by legal notions of due process. This is due in large part to the facts that due process is a legal concept and that many ombudsmen are trained in the law. When a due process question is raised with them, the initial questions they are apt to ask are: Do I have jurisdiction? Has notice been given? Has there been an opportunity for a hearing? Then they ask: Even if all the legal requirements of due process have been met, is the procedure fair? The question of fairness rather than legality is crucial in everything an ombudsman does. But what are the standards of fairness? In seeking to answer this question, Michelman's and Pincoffs's ideas are very useful.

(2) Most ombudsmen would readily accept Michelman's paradigm of due process. My own procedure includes its basic elements of revelation, participation, and justification. In some ways, ombudsmen are in a better position than judges to guarantee this conception of due process. Like judges, they are independent and impartial. But—unlike judges—they do not have the power of binding decision; their power is based on moral authority and persuasion. And unlike judges, they participate actively in the settlement process; they act as investigators, mediators, and counselors. They cannot control the outcome of the settlement process, but they can insist that it be fair.

The general procedure in my office is as follows:

(a) *Complaint.* The typical case begins with a complaint. Any person who feels that he or she has been treated unfairly by anyone in the university community may make a complaint. The right to complain is in my opinion essential to due process. The complaint procedure in my office differs from the complaint procedure in courts in the following respects: First, it is informal and virtually costless. No trained intermediary—e.g., a lawyer—is necessary, and no formal statement need be made. Second, complaints are made confidentially and the identity of persons making them is not disclosed unless they consent. Third, sometimes I initiate the complaint process. I may read about some university action that on its face seems unfair, or hear about it from a third party and ask to see the parties involved. Fourth, in some cases, the principal effect of making a complaint is catharsis. In discussing their complaints, it is not uncommon for complainants to show anger or other emotion. For some of them, the matter ends there, and they ask that no action be taken on their complaints. Usually all of the elements of Michelman's due process paradigm are present—at least incipiently—at the complaint stage. Revelation (though often incomplete) usually occurs prior to complaint, the ombudsman's interview with the complainant involves participation, and justification is usually discussed in the interview. Sometimes I provide the university's justification for an action or rule, illustrate it by discussing similar cases, and, if asked, give my opinion about the matter. After the initial interview, occasionally a complaint will be withdrawn because the complainant is persuaded that the university is justified in its action.

(b) *Investigation.* The purpose of investigation is to determine the facts underlying the complaint and if possible to settle the matter at this stage. Frequently investigation discloses facts not given by the complainant, and typically the same facts are seen differently by the parties to a dispute. Usually I conduct the investigation myself, and if there are documents relevant to the dispute, I start with them. I have access to virtually all records and persons in the university. Two elements of Michelman's paradigm are uppermost in my mind during investigations: revelation and justification. I seek facts to communicate to the complainant so that revelation can be as complete as possible, and I seek justification for the action taken or contemplated by the university. In a case of nonrenewal of an appointment of a professor, I ask the department chairman or dean why the action was taken. If the complainant suspects that his or her contract is not being renewed for a specific reason—e.g., political views, poor teaching, or a personality conflict—I ask whether there is any basis for the suspicion. Generally I use the complainant's statements to me as hypotheses to be verified. Occasionally the person or office against whom a complaint is made concedes that it is valid or at least partially valid. In such cases, the complaint is easily settled. Although facts can be ascertained more or less objectively, justification tends to be subjective. Parties to disputes usually understand this. In disputes between students and instructors, the faculty sometimes asks me what I think is fair, saying beforehand that he or she will abide by my determination. In some cases, investigation shows that no facts support the complaint or that the university's action is justified. In those cases complaints are usually withdrawn.

(c) *Participation.* I encourage complainants to participate in the settlement of their own complaints. One of the main purposes of participation, in my view, is the restoration of relations that make the university a community. Face-to-face discussion of complaints by parties—with an ombudsman acting as mediator or observer—often establishes a factual basis for settlement, as well as the rules or principles governing the matter. Conflict is common in this phase of the settlement process, for cases in which the complaint is conceded to be valid or partly valid are normally settled during investigation. In my view, such conflict is useful in restoring relations because it often brings repressed feelings and grievances into the open so that they can be dealt with objectively. It also permits the persons involved to know and understand each other better. In cases in which one or more of the parties refuse to meet—or cases in which such meetings are unnecessary—complainant participation is vicarious, and I act as a go-between. If initial participation does not lead to settlement, sometimes others are brought into the process, and resolution of the dispute is attempted at a higher level of the university administration. Participation is usually informal, but in some cases formal resolution is sought by resorting to an established grievance procedure or arbitration.

(d) *Settlement.* Justification is crucial to settlement. If the university cannot justify action regarded as unfair by a complainant, settlement invariably favors the complainant. When the university clearly justifies its action, settlement seldom favors the complainant. If I believe that justification is clear, the complainant usually accepts it. In cases where the proffered justification is unclear or arguable, I attempt to work out a compromise settlement. In seeking common ground on which all can stand, I take into account the emotional dimensions of the dispute. I assume that the parties have throughout acted in good faith. Where possible, I view the dispute as based on mistake and misunderstanding, and I avoid assignments of blame. I do my best to present settlements so that they are face-saving. If I do not think the justification proffered is adequate, I advise against settlement and seek to move the dispute to another level of the university, and in some cases even out of the university. In other words, I seek another round of participation but with additional persons participating. When all procedures are exhausted and the complaint is rejected, I do my best to get the complainant to accept the outcome. I offer what emotional support I can and suggest ways of coping with the outcome. I regard acceptance of a settlement as important so that the dispute ends and the persons involved can go on working and living with each other. The guarantee of full due process—revelation, participation, and justification—makes it easier for the complainant and the university to accept an adverse settlement. A person whose complaint is rejected knows at least that he or she had a chance to learn in detail the reasons for adverse action, that there was an opportunity to participate in the resolution of the dispute, and that an ombudsman was willing to help at every stage of the process. Cases of complete rejection of a complaint occur, but not frequently. The vast majority of complaints result in settlements that the parties can accept.

(e) *Review.* The investigation, attempts at settlement, and settlement of each complaint are recorded and later reviewed systematically to determine the causes of complaints, particularly recurring complaints. That often requires further investigation, and that investigation usually results in recommendations to persons and groups in the university who have policy-making responsibility. The main purpose of this stage of the procedure is to use constructively the knowledge obtained in settling complaints, to reduce the number of complaints by eliminating their causes, and to make the university a more effective and more just institution.

(3) Pincoffs's discussion of the Kantian principle that one should never treat humanity—whether in oneself or another—as a mere means is central to my work. I use the principle in making arguments that I hope will be the basis of a settlement. In cases like *Roth,* I appeal to the principle precisely as Pincoffs did. I regard it as the basic norm for my behavior as an ombudsman. Not only is the principle the best moral basis for action, it is in my opinion also the best practical basis for effective dispute settlement. It is perhaps easier to settle disputes politically—by influencing the behavior of

parties to them. But the line between such influence and manipulation is thin or nonexistent. If a settlement is manipulated, it is not likely to be as enduring as one chosen freely by the parties to a dispute. Further, I feel that trust and confidence in me as an ombudsman are crucial in settling disputes, for they enhance the moral authority of my office. The best way to earn the trust and confidence of parties to disputes is to help them but not to make decisions for them. The principle operates in cases in which I cannot obtain what the complainant wants. In cases like *Roth,* I can obtain due process for the professor, but what he or she really wants is a job. If the university's decision is negative after investigation and settlement, I do not feel my responsibility is discharged. I do what I can for the professor, not only to help him or her accept the settlement, but even to find a new job. Some might say that goes beyond the scope of my office, but if one accepts the Kantian principle, there is no convenient stopping place. Moral considerations may require behavior that goes beyond the requirements of one's office.

I stress that I am describing my work in ideal terms. I admit that my behavior as ombudsman does not measure up to this ideal, but insofar as it does not, my procedure fails to attain the high level of fairness that it should, and thus I am not as effective as I could be.

(4) Although I agree with Pincoffs's statement that a college or university president is not morally bound to attend to every cry of injustice in his or her institution, the question remains: does the institution have an obligation to see that somehow the cries for justice receive attention? Before the judicial specialists emerged in the West, cries of injustice were heard by kings. This was a time-consuming task that could have been handled more efficiently by others, and eventually this governmental function was delegated to persons we know now as judges. There has been a parallel development in recent years in the establishment of ombudsmen's offices in both public and private institutions. The reasons for their establishment are both practical and moral. One of the reasons for the importance of ombudsmen is that they are guarantors of due process. It is true, as Pincoffs points out, that Roth had a contract of employment for one year; but if his university had an ombudsman, he had a right under his employment contract to avail himself of

that ombudsman's services, which means that very likely he would have received all elements of Michelman's due process paradigm. He may or may not have had his contract renewed, but it is quite likely he would have been given the reasons for the university's action.

NOTES

1. 408 U.S. 564 (1972).
2. In 1974 there were ombudsmen's offices in more than 100 colleges and universities in the United States.

10

SOME PROCEDURAL ASPECTS OF
MAJORITY RULE

GERALD H. KRAMER

I. INTRODUCTION

The idea of due process in the broadest sense entails some notion of procedural fairness or appropriateness; or—perhaps more accurately—of appropriate procedures and safeguards, properly applied, having been used in the process of reaching a decision or outcome. These safeguards and principles range from broad principles to quite specific and technical procedural rules. The particular body of rules embodied in our present understanding of the concept is the product of an historical evolutionary process in which it has undergone successive modification and refinement.

A somewhat analogous body of principles and customs exists in the political domain, where the rules of order of parliamentary procedure have become the established basis for the conduct of deliberative assemblies, in which the clash of divergent individual views and interests must be somehow reconciled and translated into a collective decision. These rules, too, are the result of a long evolution, in which judicial review has played an important role. The roots of the modern rules of order go back to eighteenth-century codifications of the customs and practices which had evolved in the British House of Commons. However, the subsequent common law of parliamentary procedure for voluntary nongovernmental assemblies has developed into a set of procedures which differ in many essential respects from those of official parliamentary or legislative bodies. We shall be exclusively concerned here with the rules for voluntary groups, as codified in various handbooks of parliamentary procedure.

The paper is organized into three parts. In the first, we examine the somewhat elusive concept of the majority principle. In this, we can imagine ourselves in the position of a benevolent despot, who wishes to respect the majority principle; or, alternatively, of a court reviewing the decision of some assembly, to ensure it does indeed reflect the will of the majority. In either case we suppose complete and accurate knowledge of every citizen's preferences for the alternatives is available and focus on the question of what choice accords with the majority principle. The answer is not obvious, and despite the importance of this issue for democratic theory and for legal review based on the principle of majority rule, the question is one which has not received a great deal of attention by political philosophers. We shall review several possible formalizations of the majority principle and consider some broader aspects and implications of these different formulations.

In a democratic assembly, decisions are made by the members themselves, not by a benevolent despot acting in their behalf. To make these decisions a particular *voting procedure* must be employed, whereby individuals may register their own preferences, and these votes are aggregated into a collective decision. There are many possible such methods of voting which use some form of majority rule in counting votes to arrive at a decision. In Part III we shall review several common ones, including those presently favored by current parliamentary practice (the "admissible" procedures), and some others which have been explicitly or implicitly abandoned during the evolution of the modern rules of order. In the final Part IV, we examine how these different voting procedures function in practice, and particularly, whether they lead to decisions consistent with the majority principle.

II. THE MAJORITY PRINCIPLE

The majority principle has played a central role in the development of current parliamentary procedure, a fundamental test of any practice being whether it facilitates, or frustrates, realization of the majority will in the course of an assembly's deliberations. But this general premise, though often invoked in parliamentary law, is not a self-evident or precise test. To make it usable for our purposes, we first need a careful characterization of the somewhat subtle concept of "the majority will."

The general idea of the majority's will is clear enough when there are only two alternatives: if the assembly is unable to achieve a complete consensus after reasoned consideration of the two courses of action, then whichever course is favored by the larger number is the will of the majority. In this case the concept is unambiguous.[1]

The notion is much less clear when the choice involves three or more alternatives. To illustrate some of the problems and ambiguities surrounding it, consider a simple example of an assembly confronted with three alternatives: A, B, C (which might be three candidates competing for a single office, or three mutually inconsistent proposed courses of action). Let us suppose that after discussion and consideration of their merits, attitudes towards the alternatives crystallize into three main patterns: there is one faction which favors A over B, and B over C; another group which considers C best and B second best; and finally a contingent which ranks them B, C, A. We can summarize these three preference orderings thus:

Ranking of Alternatives:	A	C	B
	B	B	C
	C	A	A
Faction:	I	II	III
Size:	40	35	25

Figure 1

What is the majority will here? This evidently depends on the relative sizes of the factions. If one of them—say, group I—contained more than half the membership, then its preferences would constitute the majority will. In that case, its highest ranking alternative (A in the example) should be adopted. To put this idea in more general terms, if there is some single alternative which is ranked first by a majority of voters, we shall say there exists a majority will in favor of that alternative, according to the *absolute majority* (AM) criterion.

The Condorcet Criterion

The difficulty with the absolute majority criterion is that quite often no alternative will satisfy it. This will be so in the example above, unless one of the factions happens to contain over half the membership. As the number of alternatives and factions increases, it is increasingly unlikely that any single alternative will be ranked first by a majority. The AM criterion is thus a fundamentally conservative one, which in many situations will not yield a majority will.

A less conservative principle can be described as follows. In the above example, alternative B is preferred to A by factions II and III; hence (if the sizes of the factions are as given in Figure 1) B would defeat A in a direct pairwise vote. B would also defeat C in a direct vote (via factions I and III), and C in turn would defeat A (via factions II and III). The pattern of pairwise votes can be summarized thus:

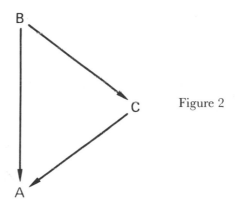

Figure 2

The pairwise votes here lead to a consistent ranking of the alternatives (B over C, C over A). The highest-ranking alternative, B, can defeat each of the other alternatives in pairwise votes, and in that sense there exists a majority will in favor of it. If there exists such an alternative which cannot be defeated in any pairwise vote, we shall say there exists a majority will for it, according to the

Condorcet criterion (C). When an alternative satisfies the Condorcet criterion, we can speak of the *majority* will, but not of the *majority's* will; since different majorities will form (II and III or I and III, in the example above) to defend it against its possible rivals. Note also that this criterion requires only that there be an alternative which can defeat all others in pairwise votes, and hence can be satisfied even if the pairwise votes fail to yield a consistent ranking of the remaining alternative.

It is clear that an alternative which satisfies the absolute majority criterion necessarily also satisfies the Condorcet criterion, and that the converse need not be true, as the example of Figure 2 shows. The Condorcet criterion is thus less conservative than the Absolute Majority principle. Nevertheless, it shares with the AM criterion the same basic shortcoming; that in some situations, it will fail to yield any clear majority will. We can show this with the following example, again involving three alternatives and three factions:

Ranking of Alternatives:	A	C	B
	B	A	C
	C	B	A
Faction:	I	II	III
Size:	40	30	30

Figure 3

Here we find A preferred to B by I and II; B to C by I and III; and C preferred to A by factions II and III. Thus the pairwise votes will yield this pattern:

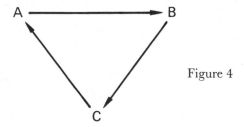

Figure 4

The pairwise votes lead to an inconsistency, or *cycle;* and there is *no* alternative which satisfies the Condorcet criterion, since each can be defeated in some pairwise vote.

Cyclical Majorities and the Majority Principle

Such "cyclical majorities" are not mere logical possibilities, of infrequent occurrence and little consequence. They do occur empirically, have been observed in such areas as the U.S. Congress, university senate elections, and committees of various kinds. It is difficult to get accurate quantitative estimates of their empirical frequency, since many potential cycles will go unnoticed simply because the usual voting methods do not involve enough paired comparisons to reveal their existence. In the example of Figure 3, for example, any two votes are consistent, and the cycle is revealed only by introducing a previously defeated alternative again and taking a final vote. For k alternatives, a succession of k-1 pairwise votes will permit them all to be considered, and the surviving alternative will be an apparent winner; yet at least one—and perhaps as many as k-2—additional votes (depending on the order of voting) would be needed to ensure that this alternative satisfied the Condorcet criterion. Most common voting procedures do not require these additional votes to be taken, and hence will conceal any cycles that may be present. There have been attempts to assess, on a priori theoretical grounds, the "probability" of a cyclical majority for varying numbers of voters and alternatives. These calculations assume that every possible individual ranking is equally likely for each voter, and that there is no correlation among voters' preferences. They indicate that the probability of fulfilling the Condorcet criterion ranges from .80 for five alternatives and five voters, to .5 for ten alternatives and many voters, and approaches zero as the number of alternatives increases. No doubt these results exaggerate the prevalence of cycles, since some consensus will generally exist (i.e., there will be some correlation among voter preferences), and on many issues preferences will be structured to some degree (i.e. all orderings will not be equally likely). Nevertheless, the probabilistic calculations—other theoretical considerations—and the scanty empirical evidence currently available all suggest that cyclical majorities are by no means uncommon.

When they are present, they may have serious practical and strategic ramifications. Equally important, they have important normative implications. The AM and Condorcet formalizations of the majority principle are *incomplete,* for in cyclical majority situations such as that described in Figure 3, they will fail to yield a majority will. In such cases, the majority principle becomes inapplicable, and provides no guidance for collective decision.

A conservative who believes collective action ought to be taken only when there is a clear and compelling mandate to abandon the status quo should find this incompleteness of the majority principle attractive, and argue that in situations where no majority will exist the presumption should be for inaction and the status quo. (On this basis, he might even argue for the more restrictive absolute majority principle over the less restrictive Condorcet formulation.) The consequences for judicial review of parliamentary proceedings are more ambiguous, though equally important. If an assembly's decision was challenged on the grounds that it did not represent the majority will, a court might interpret this broadly to mean that the decision is invalid unless it can be shown to satisfy the majority principle. In this case, the incompleteness of the above criteria clearly produces the same conservative bias in favor of inaction in cases where no majority will exists. A narrower interpretation of the challenge, however, might permit the decision to stand unless it can be shown that it fails to satisfy the majority principle, and that some other action or decision does. On this interpretation, the incompleteness of the majority principle creates a presumption in favor of the challenged decision. As we shall see, in cases where no majority will exists, the nature of the decision under most procedures depends to a large extent on the order of voting—or agenda—which was used to reach it; so, in these cases, the narrower interpretation of review is in effect biased in favor of those individuals or groups responsible for the agenda. In that sense, incompleteness still produces a conservative bias, though of a somewhat different sort.

For a democrat of more reformist or activist persuasion, the incompleteness of the criteria considered so far may seem a serious defect. For on this view, the purpose of majority rule is to choose that course which best accords with majority sentiment—without any presumption in favor of the status quo, or of imposed or manipulated decisions controlled by a few. Thus a proper formulation of the majority principle—on this view—ought to be completely decisive, in the sense of always yielding a majority will, and not permitting the status quo or other actions to prevail by default.

Some Less Conservative Criteria

Let us therefore examine some possible extensions of the majority principle. One possible—though partial—extension can be based on the pattern of pairwise votes. With four or more alternatives, the majority preference relations might fall into various patterns:

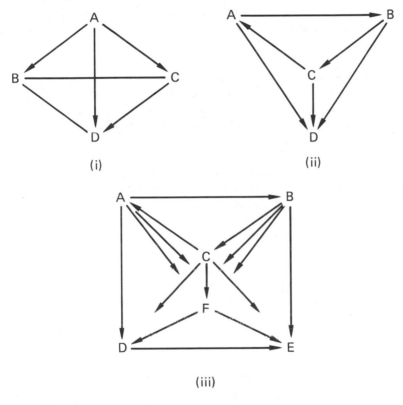

(i)

(ii)

(iii)

Figure 5

In (i), A is a majority winner and satisfies the Condorcet criterion, even though there is a cycle among the lower-ranking alternatives. The situation is different in (ii), where there is a clear majority *loser*—D—but no majority ranking of the other alternatives. In (iii) there is a subset of alternatives, {A, B, C}, each of which can defeat every alternative not belonging to the subset, but again, there is no clear majority will among the members of this set. In these last two cases, the majority preference relation provides a *partial*—but incomplete—resolution to the choice; and a plausible extension of the majority principle is to require that the choice be consistent with this partial structure. We can make this requirement precise as follows. Suppose there exists a subset M of the outcomes, with the following three properties:

(a) M contains at least one outcome;
(b) at least one outcome is not contained in M;
(c) any outcome in M defeats any outcome not in M.

Then we shall say there exists a majority will for M, according to the *Cyclical Condorcet* (CyC) criterion.

Though the Cyclical Condorcet criterion is a generalization of the C and AM principles, there are still situations, such as those of Figures 3 and 4 above, in which there is no majority will under any of these three criteria. Thus the CyC principle, though more general than the other two, is still incomplete and in that sense conservative.

A common voting principle which is not conservative in this sense is that of *relative* majority—or plurality—rule. According to this *relative majority* principle (RM), the alternative which is ranked first by the greatest number of voters is the majority will, even if the number favoring it is less than an absolute majority. In the cyclical majority example of Figure 3, alternative A would be chosen under this criterion, since it is favored by more voters (40) than is B (30) or C (30). Clearly the RM principle always yields a majority will (ties are possible, though unlikely if the number of voters is large), so it is indeed complete. Elections to governmental offices and positions of various kinds are often based on plurality or relative majority electoral rules; but in parliamentary proceedings, courts have consistently held plurality-type election rules to be invalid, on the grounds that they permit a minority to decide the issue and thus violate the fundamental principle of majority rule.

A rather different extension of the Condorcet criterion—which might well satisfy legal interpretation of the majority principle—can be formulated in terms of "special" majority rule. By a *special* majority we mean a majority of size greater than a certain fraction of the assembly, such as two-thirds, three-quarters, or whatever.

Any number λ which lies between ½ and 1 defines a particular type of special majority. Special majority rule does not in itself circumvent the cycling problem, for it can be shown that for any λ<1, there will exist situations in which every alternative is defeated by some other alternative. For an example with the (rather large) value λ = ¾ (rule by three-fourths majorities) consider the following situation:

Ranking	B	C	D	E	F	A
	C	D	E	F	A	B
	D	E	F	A	B	C
	E	F	A	B	C	D
	F	A	B	C	D	E
	A	B	C	D	E	F
Faction	I	II	III	IV	V	VI

Figure 6

All factions are of equal size, each containing ⅙ of the membership. If we examine the various pairwise votes, we find that A is preferred to B by factions II through VI, and hence by ⅚ of the voters. Thus A defeats B. In the comparison between A and C, A is preferred by factions III through VI, which contain only ⅔ of the membership. Since this is less than the required majority of ¾, A does not defeat C, nor does C defeat A. Thus some of the pairwise contests will be indecisive under special majority rule. If we proceed through all the other pairwise comparisons, we find the ¾ majority preference relation is as follows:

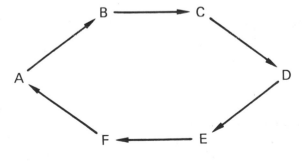

Figure 7

Thus every alternative is defeated by some other alternative, and the special majority relation cycles. Such cycles are possible for any value of λ less than 1.0.

On the other hand, for any given situation there will be *some* special majority rule which does not cycle. As an illustration, consider again the situation of Figures 3 and 4. Simple majority rule ($\lambda = \frac{1}{2}$) cycles there, but if we choose the value $\lambda = \frac{2}{3}$, we find the following:

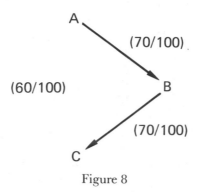

Figure 8

Here in the comparison between A and C, neither defeats the other by the required $\frac{2}{3}$ majority. Thus there is no cycle, and the alternative A satisfies a Condorcet-like condition, of not being defeated by any other alternative. If we chose a larger value—say $\lambda = \frac{3}{4}$—*none* of the alternatives would defeat—or be defeated by—any other: hence, every alternative would satisfy the condition of being undefeated, so this special majority rule would permit too many "ties" to be of much help.

However, a sharper—yet still complete—criterion can be obtained by choosing, in any situation, λ^*, the *smallest* value of λ at which one of the alternatives is undefeated. We shall say there exists a majority will in favor of that alternative, by the *special majority* (SM) criterion. If the situation is such that the ordinary Condorcet criterion is satisfied, this value will turn out to be $\frac{1}{2}$, so the SM and Condorcet criteria agree. If $\lambda^* < \frac{1}{2}$, then any smaller value $\lambda < \lambda^*$ will yield a cycle, so the SM criterion will be based on the voting rule which comes closest to majority rule, while still giving a majority will. (It is easily shown that such a λ^* always exists, so the SM criterion is indeed complete.)

Relations between the Different Criteria

The relationships between the various formulations of the majority principle are summarized in Figure 9 below,

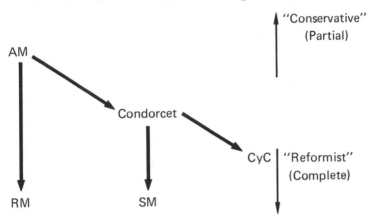

Figure 9

where "AM→RM," for example, signifies that the AM criterion implies (or is a special case of) the RM criterion; or, equivalently, that the latter is a generalization of, and subsumes, the former. It is clear from the definitions that the RM and Condorcet criteria generalize the Absolute Majority principle and that the SM and CyC are in turn generalizations of the Condorcet principle (and hence also of AM).

The three "reformist" criteria (RM, SM, CyC) are inequivalent, since none is a generalization of any other. To see this, consider first the example of Figures 1 and 2. Here the relative majority will is A (being favored by 40 members), while the SM and CyC criteria lead to the Condorcet winner, B. To show the inequivalence of the CyC and SM criteria we can consider the following example:

Ranking	P	Q	S	R	S
	Q	S	P	Q	R
	R	R	R	S	P
	S	P	Q	P	Q
Faction	I	II	III	IV	V
Size	33	25	20	12	10

Figure 10

If we work out the votes on the possible pairwise votes, they are as follows (sizes of the various majorities being indicated in parentheses):

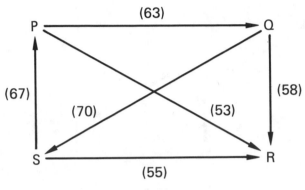

Figure 11

There is no Condorcet winner, but by the Cyclical Condorcet criterion, there is a majority will for the set {P, Q, S}. By the SM criterion, however, λ^* will be .58 (with any smaller λ there will be a cycle), and R the preferred alternative. Clearly, therefore, the CyC and SM criteria do not coincide.

Independence of Irrelevant Alternatives

Let us now consider an important procedural condition which a usable notion of majority rule should satisfy. Suppose an assembly were faced with a given set S of alternatives, and that (by some criterion) there exists a majority will in favor of one of them, say a. If a suitable voting procedure were employed (and if all voters were well informed of the issue, and voted honestly), the alternative a would be adopted, or candidate elected. Suppose now that after the decision, it was discovered that one of the alternatives in S was not really eligible for consideration—it was an unconstitutional proposal, or a candidate who did not meet the organization's eligibility requirements. If the chosen alternative a were itself the ineligible one, then of course the current decision would be invalid and the choice would have to be considered anew. But if the ineligible option is one that was not chosen anyway, its presence or absence should not alter the existence of a majority will in favor of *a*. The ineligible alternative is *irrelevant*, and the choice itself should be *independent* of such irrelevant alternatives.

If it were not, democracy could easily become unworkable. Any election could be voided if one of the losing candidates were subsequently discovered to be ineligible (or conceivably even if he subsequently died or left the organization). A decision to adopt a certain proposal would not be a valid reflection of the majority will, if some technically ineligible or unconstitutional proposal were introduced into the voting at some point, even if it received no support and was immediately voted down. A court, in reviewing such a decision, would have to verify the eligibility of *all* of the alternatives, not just the winning one. Even worse, it would also have to ensure that *all* eligible alternatives had been considered, and none omitted from explicit consideration.

In most deliberations only a few of the many conceivable and eligible proposals or candidates are actively considered. Indeed, the purpose of nomination and agenda committees is precisely to narrow the choice in this fashion, by eliminating unpopular alternatives which have little support and no chance of winning, to save time and ensure careful consideration of the major alternatives. Yet if the majority principle does not satisfy the independence of irrelevant alternatives condition, such screening could result in adoption of an alternative which does not accord with the majority principle, and no decision could be taken as valid unless every conceivable alternative had been considered and voted on.

Clearly this would hardly be feasible in practice. It is conceivable that a concerned citizenry or assembly might regularly inform itself and vote intelligently on relatively delimited sets of alternatives; it is hardly likely, or indeed possible, that any sizable body could or would, as a matter of standard practice, carefully examine and vote on all the logically conceivable alternatives entailed in any complex issue. To be workable, a notion of democratic choice must involve some type of informational decentralization akin to that expressed by the independence of irrelevance alternatives condition.

It is thus important to consider whether the various criteria proposed above satisfy this independence condition. To do this, let us first define the condition more carefully. Let S be a set of alternatives, and C(S) the set chosen under some particular criterion. An alternative which belongs to S—but not to C(S)—is *irrelevant*. Let S′ be a subset of S obtained by deleting some or all of the irrelevant alternatives. If the alternatives chosen in the original situation still satisfy the criterion with respect to the reduced set (i.e. if C(S) ⊂ C(S′)), then we shall say the criterion in question is *independent of irrelevant alternatives* (IIA).

It is clear that the absolute majority principle satisfies the IIA condition, for an alternative which is ranked first by over half the voters will still be so ranked if other alternatives are deleted. The Condorcet criterion also satisfies IIA, since an alternative which defeats every other alternative can also defeat every subset of the other alternatives. By the same reasoning, the Cyclical Condorcet does also—except in the degenerate case where *all* the irrelevant alternatives are deleted, and no CyC majority will exists in the reduced set.

However the two "reformist" criteria are not independent of irrelevant alternatives. In Figure 1, for example, S = {A, B, C}, and the chosen alternative is A under RM. Yet if B is deleted, C will have a majority, so the original relative majority choice—A—is dependent on the irrelevant alternative B. For the special majority principle, consider the example in Figure 11. In the initial situation, R is chosen from the set {P,Q,R,S} on the SM criterion. Yet if the irrelevant alternative P is deleted, R no longer satisfies SM, and a different alternative—Q—will become the majority will (on the Condorcet and hence the SM criterion), again violating IIA.

Thus both of the "reformist" criteria are—in an important sense— unworkable. Because of their dependence on irrelevant or obscure but potentially eligible alternatives, it is difficult to imagine that either principle could be a useful criterion as a basis for designing practical voting procedures or for assessing their consonance with the fundamental principle of "majority rule." Whether a plausible "reformist" formulation of the majority principle can be devised, which does not make the choice dependent on irrelevant alternatives, is an interesting and still unresolved question.

III. PROCEDURES

The discussion so far has been concerned with norms and principles, not with practical matters of implementation. The majority principle is an ideal which might be a useful guideline for a court, or for a benevolent dictator who knows his subjects' preferences and wants to act in accord with the majority will. In a democracy, however, decisions are made by the citizens themselves, acting through some well-defined voting procedure, not by a benevolent despot with perfect knowledge of everyone's preferences. This raises the question of whether a given, apparently democratic voting procedure will in fact result in a decision which satisfies the majority principle. To obtain an answer, we must characterize voting procedures more precisely.

A voting procedure prescribes a particular form of balloting—or possible ways each individual may vote—and a vote-counting rule which aggregates individual ballots into a collective decision. A person's *vote* is an overt act, or behavior, logically distinct from his *preference*, which is a private, more or less psychological entity. Though in ordinary usage we often interpret a person's vote as indicating his preference, in fact it need not do so; since inadvertence or strategic considerations may lead him to vote in ways that do not accurately represent his underlying preferences. The majority principle specifies how the (true) underlying preferences of all citizens are to be aggregated into a (true) majority will; a voting procedure, by contrast, specifies how the overt *votes* are to be aggregated into a *decision* or outcome, without respect to the notion of preference.

More precisely, then, for any given set of possible outcomes or alternatives $\alpha = \{a,b,c \ldots\}$, a voting procedure must specify for each voter i his possible way of voting or *strategies* $S_i = \{s_i, s'_i \ldots\}$ (normally these are the same for every voter i), and a rule that determines which alternative is chosen under each possible combination of individual voting choices. (This rule is technically a *function* $f(s)$ which assigns to each combination of choices $s = (s_1, s_2, \ldots s_n)$ a unique alternative $a \, \varepsilon \, \alpha$.)

A procedure is *majoritarian* if it enables any majority of voters to prevail over the opposing minority, and secure whatever outcome it chooses. More precisely, a majoritarian procedure is one such that for any alternative $a \, \varepsilon \, \alpha$, there is a designated set $\{s^*_1, s^*_2, \ldots s^*_n\}$ of strategies, one for each voter, with the following property: let $s = (s_1 \ldots s_n)$ be any combination of individual strategy choices, and let C be the set of voters whose choices s_1 correspond to the designated

s^*_1 strategies (i.e., C is the set of i EN for whom $s_i = s^*_i$). Then if C constitutes a majority (i.e., contains more than $\frac{1}{2}n$ voters), the actions $(s_1, s_2, \ldots s_n)$ must necessarily lead to a (i.e., $f(s) = a$).

Thus, under a majoritarian procedure, a majority can always prevail and obtain any outcome it desires, irrespective of the actions of the minority. (This does not preclude the possibility that a minority may sometimes also prevail, for example if the opposing majority happens not to choose their s^*_i strategies). The definition given above is quite general, and characterizes a large class of specific voting methods. We shall examine several such methods in detail below.

A majoritarian procedure need not lead to majority rule. This fact, which may not be entirely obvious, is a central point of our analysis. In Part IV we shall show that perfectly plausible majoritarian procedures can lead to outcomes which violate the majority principle in any of its formulations. To do this, let us first describe some common majoritarian procedures.

Some Specific Procedures

Under *plurality* voting, each voter casts a single vote for one alternative, and whichever alternative receives the most votes is adopted. If we suppose there is some consistent method for resolving ties, this voting method constitutes a procedure and is majoritarian: for although a minority may sometimes prevail over other, smaller minorities under this rule, it is clear that a majority of voters can always prevail, by all voting for the same outcome. The plurality rule—though still used in large-scale political elections and primaries—is not favored in current parliamentary practice, where an absolute majority of votes is required to elect. If in an election for some parliamentary office, no candidate receives a majority, the election is indecisive and a new election held, the balloting continuing until someone receives a majority. (Since this method can thus be indecisive, however, it is not technically a procedure in the sense of our definition.)

A somewhat different procedure is occasionally proposed for choosing among alternative proposals. Each of the proposals is voted on in turn. If none receives a majority, none is adopted; while if one or more does, the one with the largest majority is adopted. We shall refer to this as the *separate votes* procedure. (Clearly it is majoritarian.)

Sequential Procedures

For voting on proposals (as distinct from electing candidates) current practice does not favor any of these procedures. Instead, procedures are prescribed in which the various proposals and amendments are voted on separately and sequentially. Such methods are instances of a general class of procedures which have recently been characterized and analyzed in some detail by Farquharson[2]. This class of procedures can be described as follows. There is an initial set of outcomes, from which one must be selected, by a sequence of yes-or-no (or "binary") individual votes. Each round of voting (or "division") is of the following form: there is a set B of alternatives still under consideration (having survived the votes so far). The vote in question is a choice between two subsets, B_1 and B_2, of the parent set B. These subsets have the following properties: first, every alternative in B belongs to one or both subsets; i.e., $B_1 \cup B_2 = B$ (alternatives remain in contention until they are voted out). Second, neither subset is identical to the parent set, i.e. $B_1 \neq B$, $B_2 \neq B$ (each division must make some progress toward a final decision, by eliminating some alternatives from further consideration). And third, the subsets must be distinct; i.e., $B_1 \neq B_2$ (the division must constitute a real choice). Each voter votes for one or the other of the subsets, and whichever set receives a majority is adopted, and becomes the parent set for the next division. A *binary procedure* is a hierarchy of such divisions in which the entire set of alternatives is the parent set of the first division, and the outcome of each division leads to a predetermined next division, until eventually only a single outcome is left.

To illustrate such a procedure, consider the example of an assembly sitting as a judicial tribunal, with responsibility for both determination of guilt, and sentencing, of a defendant. A natural way of proceeding after hearing the case would be to first decide the question of guilt, and then consider the issue of sentencing in the event of a guilty finding. The relevant final outcomes, let us suppose, are a finding of Innocent (I); a verdict of "guilty" with a Severe sentence (S); or one of guilt with a Lenient sentence (L). The sequential voting procedure described above can be characterized by a tree, the nodes corresponding to the successive decisions

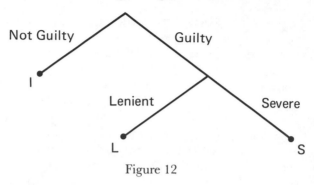

Figure 12

which must be voted on. The set of outcomes is {I,L,S}, while the first division is between the subsets {I}, {L,S}, which satisfy the three properties required of a division. If {I} is chosen, the outcome is I, while if {L,S} wins the initial vote, there is a second division between {L} and {S}, which determines the outcome.

Parliamentary Procedures

The order of voting would be somewhat different if the tribunal followed normal parliamentary procedure. After hearing the case, a specific motion would presumably be introduced; for example, that the defendant be found guilty and sentenced severely (S). During discussion of the motion, an amendment might be moved, that the sentence be changed to a lenient one (L). After debate, the amendment would be voted on first, then the main motion. Adoption of the amended or original main motion would yield the outcomes L or S, respectively, while its rejection would (let us suppose) be equivalent to a finding of innocence. This somewhat different sequential procedure can be represented as follows:

Here the initial choice is between the sets {I,S} and {I,L}. This satisfies the conditions for a binary division (even though the two sets are not disjoint, since both contain I), and the overall process constitutes a binary procedure.

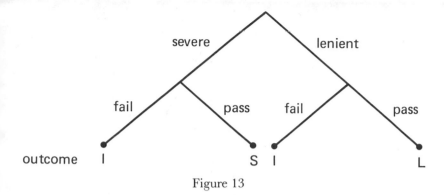

Figure 13

In general, the prescribed parliamentary procedures for deciding among competing proposals require that one of them (e.g., A) be moved (and seconded) for adoption. The alternative proposal A′ may then be moved as a substitute motion, to be treated as an amendment. If there is another competing proposal (or proposals) A″, it may be moved as a secondary amendment (that is, an amendment to the amendment) if it is in the nature of a refinement or modification of the pending amendment; but if A″ is simply another substitute motion, not germane to A′, it must be moved as a separate (primary) amendment, after the pending amendment A′ is voted on. Secondary amendments are voted on before the primary amendments to which they apply; and all primary amendments are voted before a final vote or the motion (as amended) is taken. If the motion is defeated, the outcome is preservation of the status quo, X.

The possible voting procedures under the rules of order are thus: The set of outcomes in (ii) and (iii) is {X,A,A′,A″}, while in (i) there are only two proposals: A and A′. In every case, the amendment A′ is introduced first. In (i) and (iii), the first vote is on it versus the initial proposal A, yielding the divisions {X,A}, {X,A′} in (i), and {X,A,A″} and {X,A′,A″} in (iii). With the procedure (ii), however, the secondary amendment A″ is voted on first; so the initial vote is between A″ versus A′, yielding the division {X,A,A′}, {X,A,A″}. If A″ is defeated, the next division in (ii) is between the original amendment A′ and the initial proposal; i.e., {X,A} and {X,A′}; while if A″ wins, the subsequent division is on it versus A, i.e., {X,A}, {X,A′}. (In procedure (iii) with two primary amendments,

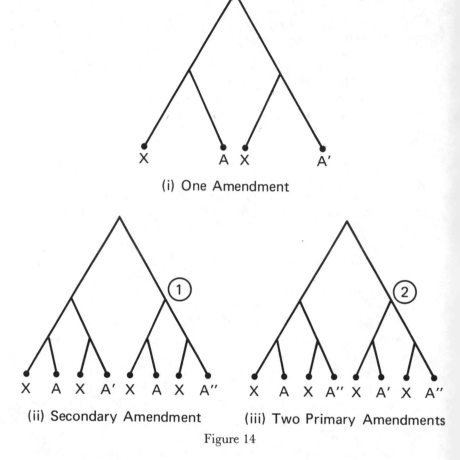

(i) One Amendment

(ii) Secondary Amendment   (iii) Two Primary Amendments

Figure 14

by contrast, the second divisions are between the second primary amendment, A'', and the pending proposal as amended; i.e., between A'' and A' (if the first amendment was adopted) or A and A' (if defeated), yielding the divisions $\{X,A''\}$, $\{X,A''\}$ and $\{X,A\}$, $\{X,A''\}$ respectively.)

Clearly, these are not the only admissible procedures; for if some other alternative had been moved initially, and/or the order of the amendments were varied, other admissible procedures would be generated. Nevertheless, all admissible procedures have the following properties:

First, every last division is between the status quo X and some proposal; i.e., is of the form {X}, {A}.

Second, every earlier division is a comparison between two proposals; i.e. is of the form {A,B,B'...}, {A',B,B'...}, where A and A' are the two proposals being compared, and all other alternatives B, B', ... are contained in both of the sets which constitute the division.

We shall say that a binary procedure with these properties is *admissible*. These two properties above do not completely characterize the admissible procedures (e.g., they take no account of the germaneness requirement for secondary amendments, or of the fact that tertiary and higher-order amendments cannot be moved). However, these two necessary conditions will suffice for our purposes.

It should be clear that there are many perfectly plausible binary procedures which are not admissible. For example if amendments were voted after—rather than before—the main motion, we would have procedures like (i) in Figure 15:

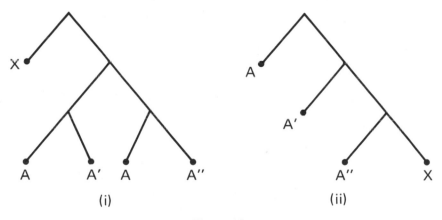

Figure 15

Procedure (ii) is a *successive elimination* one, with each proposal being considered in turn, and either adopted forthwith, or eliminated from further consideration. Neither of these apparently reasonable procedures (and there are many others as well) is admissible, however, since (i) does not satisfy the second admissibility condition, and (ii) violates the first.

IV. MAJORITARIAN PROCEDURES AND THE MAJORITY PRINCIPLE

Whether the various procedures described above lead to decisions consistent with the majority principle will depend, in part, on how the members of the assembly act or vote. Let us consider how to characterize this behavior.

By a "sincere" or "honest" voter we mean one who "votes his true preferences," without worrying about how others might vote, or how their actions might affect the final outcome. Under certain procedures, however, some voters may find it advantageous to act differently and vote "insincerely" or "strategically." We can illustrate this with the example of Figure 1, using the plurality voting procedure. Under sincere voting, each individual would vote for his highest-ranking alternative, and the result would be outcome A. If the members of faction II voted for alternative B, however, it would be the outcome; and since they all prefer this outcome to the sincere-voting result A, clearly they have an incentive to abandon their sincere strategies and vote "strategically" for B. Similar examples can be devised for each of the other voting procedures described above: under any voting procedure, there will be situations in which some voters have incentives to vote strategically, in ways that do not directly reflect their true preferences for the alternatives.

However, we shall regard these strategic distortions as second-order effects and concentrate our analysis on the sincere voting case. There are several reasons for this. In many assemblies and informal associations these are effective—if informal—norms against overtly strategic or collusive voting. Moreover, in order to obtain strategic advantage, a voter must possess a great deal of information about the preferences and strategic inclinations of the other members of the assembly, and must have the sophistication to use this information properly. (The strategic calculations can become quite complex as the number of issues and voters increases, particularly with sequential voting procedures.) For most issues—most of the time—few individuals will be willing or able to make the necessary effort. Strategic voting may be important in highly politicized bodies, or in certain types of situations (such as multi-candidate elections under plurality voting, where the strategic considerations are particularly transparent), but such empirical evidence as is available suggests that it is quite rare for the types of issues and voluntary, informal assemblies we are considering here. And in any event, since we are primarily concerned with normative issues, it seems appropriate to focus on the fundamental question of whether sincere voting satisfies the majority principle.

Sincere Voting

Let us thus consider in more detail just what might be meant by "sincere" behavior, or "honest" voting. Evidently there is one situation in which we would expect a person's actions to always reflect his (true) preferences: where he can control the outcome by himself, without having to consider the effects of possible actions of others. In such a situation, the individual would try to act so as to secure the best possible outcome (from his point of view); by doing otherwise, he could only hurt himself. There is no incentive in this case toward deviousness, and only stupidity or misinformation—but not self-interest—could lead him to act dishonestly. Thus we shall say a voter is acting honestly—or *sincerely*—if he behaves as though his actions alone determined the final outcome.

This characterization is still not entirely precise, and it requires some additional interpretation for specific voting procedures. Clearly, under the plurality voting procedure, a sincere voter votes for his most-preferred alternative. Under the separate votes procedure, we shall interpret sincere voting as voting "for" the alternatives the individual prefers to the status quo, and against the others.

The situation is a bit more complicated with sequential procedures. For example, with the procedure described in Figure 12, the initial choice is between the sets {I} and {L,S}, while the final division is between {L} and {S}. How would a sincere voter choose here?

His choice is clear enough in the bottom node, since each of the two choices corresponds to a single outcome; hence the voter votes for whichever outcome—S or L—he prefers. The first vote—on guilt or innocence—is a choice between a single outcome, I, and a *set* of outcomes, {S,L}, either member of which may be the ultimate result (depending on how the subsequent vote turns out). This is characteristic of all sequential procedures: certain choices are between pairs of *sets* of outcomes, rather than of single outcomes.

A sincere voter—acting as though he were the only voter—will choose that set which contains the outcome he prefers: thus one who believes the defendant guilty and deserving a severe sentence will choose the set {S,L}, for example; while one who believes him innocent will vote for the other set.

If the admissible amendment-type procedure of Figure 13 has been used instead, the initial division would be between {I,S} and {I,L}. A sincere voter who believes the defendant guilty will find his preferred outcome (S or L) contained in only one of these sets, so his behavior is clear enough. A voter who believes him innocent, however, finds his preferred outcome—I—is common to both sets. How should he vote? We shall interpret honest or sincere voting as behavior which reflects his preferences for the lower-ranking outcomes which differentiate the sets; assuming the voter prefers a lenient sentence to a severe one, a sincere vote in this case would be a choice of the set {I,L}.

Thus, to collect these comments and observations into a summary statement, we shall say a *sincere voter* is one who, when confronted with a choice between two sets of outcomes, acts as follows: If one of the sets contains his top-ranked outcome and the other does not, he votes for the former; or if both contain his first choice, but one contains his second choice and the other does not, for the former; or if both contain his two top-ranking outcomes, he votes for whichever set contains his third choice; and so on.

Effects of the Various Procedures

Having defined sincere voting, let us now examine the operation of the various procedures, under the assumption that all voters behave sincerely.

Consider the following example:

Ranking		A	C	B
		B	X	X
		C	B	C
		X	A	A
Factions		I	II	III
Size		40	35	25

Figure 16

If all the pairwise comparisons are analyzed in terms of each faction's true preferences, we find the following:

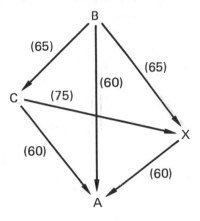

Figure 17

Thus the Condorcet condition is satisfied, and B is the majority will by the C, CyC, and SM criteria. (There is no majority will by the AM criterion.)

Under *plurality* voting, the result of sincere voting will be A, favored by the largest number. This is not the Condorcet winner, so clearly the majority principle is not satisfied. In fact, it is very badly violated, since in this example the pairwise votes lead to a consistent ranking of all the alternatives (B over C, C over X, X over A), and plurality voting yields the worst possible outcome by this majority ranking. The current disrepute of plurality voting in parliamentary law is well founded.

The separate votes procedure, however, is apparently regarded as legally consistent with the principle of majority rule, and in fact is still recommended in some handbooks of parliamentary procedure (where it is generally referred to as the method of "filling the blanks"). Yet it is even worse than the plurality procedure. In the example above, if the three motions are voted separately, both B and C will defeat the status quo. C will do so by a greater margin, however (75 vs. 65 votes), so it—rather than the Condorcet winner B—will be adopted. But the separate votes procedure violates not only the Condorcet criterion, but also violates the ultra-conservative absolute majority principle. To see this, suppose alternative A were deleted from the above example. Then there would be an absolute majority for B (factions I and III, comprising 65 voters). Yet the separate vote method would still lead to the outcome C, and thus would fail to enact the absolute majority winner.

For the sequential procedures, consider the following example with two proposals and three voters:

Ranking	A	B	X
	X	X	A
	B	A	B
Voter	1	2	3

Figure 18

If the pairwise votes are taken, we find

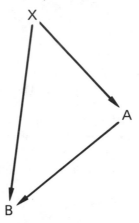

Figure 19

The Condorcet criterion is satisfied, and the status quo X is the majority will. Consider now the following binary procedure, in which B is a substitute motion for A, but the amendment is voted on after—rather than before—the main motion:

(If the outcomes A and B are Severe and Lenient sentences, and X the finding of Innocence, this is the first procedure for the judicial tribunal described earlier in Figure 12.

In the initial division the choice is between {X} and {A,B}. Under sincere voting, voter 3 will vote for {X}, while voters 1 and 2 will vote for {A,B}. On the second division, 1 and 3 will vote for

{A}, leading to its adoption. However, the Condorcet winner in this example is B, not A. Thus a sequential procedure need not—in general—satisfy the majority principle.

Now consider the admissible procedure, under which the amendment is voted before—rather than after—the main motion:

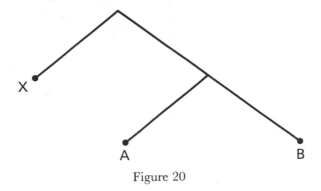

Figure 20

In this the initial choice is between {X,A} and {X,B}, so under sincere voting, voters 1 and 3 will vote for {X,A}. On the final vote between {X} and {A}, voters 2 and 3 will vote for {X}, leading to rejection of A and preservation of the status quo X. Hence, in this case, the admissible procedure satisfies the majority principle.

Let us now try the more complicated example described in Figures 16 and 17, with the three substitute motions to be voted on by the following admissible procedure:

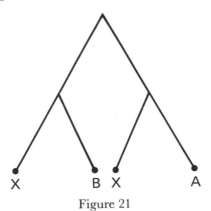

Figure 21

Here the initial vote is on the original motion A versus the first substitute B; i.e., between the sets {X,A,C} vs. {X,B,C}. Under sincere voting, factions II and III will vote for {X,B,C}, and it will win by a vote of 60 to 40. The subsequent divisions is between A and the second substitute C; i.e., {X,B} vs. {X,C}, and factions I and III will vote for {X,B}, leading to its adoption. On the final vote, {B} will defeat {X} by a vote of 67 to 33 (factions II-V), so the final outcome is again the Condorcet winner, B.

We could try other admissible procedures as well; for example, by varying the order of introduction, or using a secondary amendment procedure:

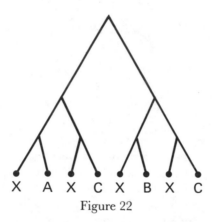

X   A   X   C   X   B   X   C

Figure 22

In all of these cases, the outcome will still be the Condorcet winner, B. This is true quite generally; for it can be shown that with any admissible procedure, if a Condorcet winner exists, it will be the sincere voting result. It follows from this that the admissible procedures—in contrast to others—do satisfy the Condorcet formulation of the majority principle.

As we noted earlier, however, the Condorcet criterion itself is a conservative one, which fails to yield a majority will in some situations. Thus it is of interest to ask how the admissible procedures act when there is no Condorcet winner, and in particular, whether they ensure satisfaction of a less conservative, "reformist" version of the majority principle. To explore this, consider the example of Figures 10 and 11, with the admissible procedure of Figure 22. If the

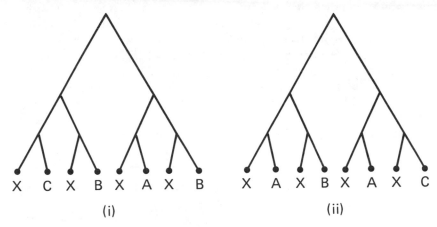

Figure 23

alternative S is identified with the status quo X, and P, Q, and R are identified with A, B, and C, respectively, then P (A) will defeat Q (B) on the first vote, and will defeat R (C) on the second division. On the final vote (at the lower left-hand node of the tree) the status quo S (X) will prevail, and it will be the final outcome. Since (from Figure 11) P is the Relative Majority winner and R is the Special Majority winner, it follows that neither of these "reformist" criteria are satisfied by admissible procedures.

The outcome S does satisfy the Cyclical Condorcet criterion, however. If other admissible procedures are tried (for example, those of Figure 23, and the other procedures obtained by varying the identification of P, Q, R, S with A, B, C, X) it will be found that P and Q, as well as S, will sometimes be the result. This suggests a general result that can in fact be shown to hold in general (not just for the example of Figure 10): the outcome under an admissible procedure necessarily satisfies the Cyclical Condorcet criterion.

V. CONCLUSIONS

In broad outline, we have proceeded in this paper by first attempting to formulate a precise "substantive" characterization of the majority principle, and then investigating (in a nontechnical fashion) a variety of commonly used procedural devices to assess the degree to which they lead to outcomes which are consonant with that principle. This general approach to the normative evaluation of alternative institutional arrangements is one which has been used in other areas such as welfare economics, where a central goal of theoretical analysis is to assess the consequences of alternative policies or institutions in terms of such "substantive" criteria as Pareto-efficiency, or equity. The general approach might also be useful for exploring comparable issues arising in the due process area.

In welfare economics, there are widely accepted, precise formulations of such fundamental normative standards as efficiency and optimality. This is not so in the domain of political theory. In particular, the key concept of the majority will is by no means an elementary or self-evident one; and we have noted a number of ambiguities and difficulties which arise when one attempts to formulate a formal and general explication of the concept. Much of our analysis of procedures has been in terms of the Condorcet formulation of the majority principle. A central finding emerging from this analysis is that the "admissible" amendment-type procedures developed during the course of parliamentary evolution satisfy the majority principle. They differ in this respect from other plausible majoritarian procedures which, though based on majority voting, need not result in enactment of the majority's will. The relation between substantive and procedural approaches as to majority rule is thus a complex one, and the ultimate substantive import of given procedural provisions is by no means self-evident. Indeed, some procedures which are sometimes advocated in parliamentary handbooks and legal review (such as the method of "filling the blanks," and other which we have not described in this paper) in fact violate the majority principle, and thus, on our analysis, stand in serious need of revision.

The Condorcet Criterion, on which our analysis has been largely based, implicitly defines what is in many respects a fundamentally conservative view of the nature of majority rule. The question of whether it is possible to give a satisfactory formulation of a more activist or "reformist" characterization of the majority principle is a significant and difficult one, deserving of serious attention by democratic theorists; and the question of whether procedural or institutional means can be devised to implement such an ideal as one which should prove equally challenging to political scientists.

NOTES

1. Some minor potential ambiguities should be noted and disposed of. One concerns the possibility of ties: here, we shall suppose (following normal practice) that there is a presiding officer who can vote to break ties, but not to create them, thus making a tied vote impossible. Another concerns the question of how to treat individuals who are indifferent between the two alternatives, and how abstentions are counted. We shall assume throughout the paper that all voters have (strict) preferences for all alternatives (i.e., that there are no ties in any voter's preference ranking), and that they never abstain; hence no such ambiguities can arise.
2. Robin Farquharson, *Theory of Voting* (New Haven: Yale University Press, 1969).

11

MAJORITY RULE PROCEDURE

ARTHUR KUFLIK

I. INTRODUCTION [1]

In "Some Procedural Aspects of Majority Rule," Gerald Kramer formulates several conditions which it might be reasonable to expect a collective decision-making procedure to satisfy. For example, it is desirable that a procedure be (1) *decisive* (i.e., "sufficiently well-defined and structured to ensure that some decision is finally reached"); (2) *impartial* (the result should "not depend on the order of the voting or on the labeling of the alternatives"); (3) *robust against devious voting* (i.e., the procedure should provide no incentive to vote for any proposal or candidate which one would not vote for were the outcome determined solely by one's own vote); (4) *majoritarian* (what results from following the procedure should reflect the will of the majority).

Professor Kramer suggests that these conditions can be regarded as canons of parliamentary procedure which are analogous (if not on a one-to-one basis, then taken as a set) to the requirements of due process encountered in the judicial sphere. In addition, he maintains that "the most important of these, firmly established in parliamentary law, is the principle that the majority shall prevail."

In fact, "the fundamental purpose of proper parliamentary procedure is to facilitate—and not frustrate—rule of the majority. Such procedures, we shall say, satisfy the *majority principle*." [2]

Is majority rule in some sense a matter of parliamentary "due process"? *Does* the "majority principle" express a fitting constraint on collective decision-making procedure?

It is remarkable how many and varied are the contexts in which rule by a majority is thought to be appropriate.[3] The "deliberative bodies" which adhere to some version of the majority principle range from formal judicial tribunals to informal gatherings of friends trying to decide where to dine out for the evening. In the discussion which follows, I believe it will become apparent that no single line of argument is adequate to support the majority principle throughout the full range of situations in which "rule by majority" nevertheless seems to make some sense. In the end, we do better, perhaps, not to speak of *the* majority principle at all; for both the nature of and justification for majority rule procedure vary so considerably from context to context.

Professor Kramer has already discussed three different ways of construing "majority winner." [4] But, of course, there are yet other respects in which talk about "rule by majority" is not unequivocal (however we resolve the ambiguity to which Professor Kramer calls attention). For in addition to asking:

(a) What shall count as being in accordance with the will of a majority?

we might also ask:

(b) Who shall have a vote? (i.e., rule by a majority of whom?) [5]

(c) On what basis should voters decide how to vote? (e.g., from the point of view of their own interests? from the point of view of the public interest?)

(d) Which matters are appropriately decided on a majority rule basis?

How these questions are answered bears directly on our understanding and assessment of the majority principle. I shall not attempt to deal with the complications which they raise one by one.

Instead, I shall try to suggest different reasons for insisting on "majority rule" (appealing only to a vague and intuitive understanding of what could be meant by these words). In the process, it will become apparent that each case for "majority rule" carries along with it its own set of answers to the questions posed above.

Finally, I shall try to show how different lines of argument on behalf of majority rule entail (or at least suggest) rather different answers to what may well be the most important question of all:

(e) When, why, and to what extent, should persons who find themselves in the minority be "reconciled" to the rule of the majority?

II. ARGUMENTS FROM "PRACTICAL NECESSITY"

Perhaps an argument for majority rule can be constructed along roughly the following lines. If a majority of individuals who are involved in a certain matter do agree about what ought to be done, their will *is* going to prevail. But everyone is better off if what will happen in any event happens without violence and without bloodshed. Majority rule merely institutionalizes the inevitable (with evident benefit to all).

Obviously there are problems with this argument. The majority (when there is a majority) does not always manage to get its way. A militant minority—well organized and intensely committed—can sometimes prevail against a much larger but less well-organized majority group, whose members may also be much less keenly aware of common interests.

Even when it is reasonable to expect that the majority *will* prevail, it can hardly be inferred that the majority *ought* to prevail. Right is not made by a greater numerical presence any more than by might. At best, there is an argument here to support the claim that *sometimes* persons who find themselves in the minority ought to acquiesce in the rule of the majority but *not* the quite different claim that rule by majority is a morally legitimate procedure. From the perspective of this argument, persons who find themselves in the minority have more reason to be *resigned* to the rule of the majority than genuinely *reconciled* to it.

A related argument relies on slightly weaker assumptions. Peace is a condition of almost all that persons might hope to accomplish. If there are circumstances in which no matter what is decided (or not decided), a certain proportion of the population is going to be seriously disaffected, it is best that the number of disgruntled persons be as small as possible. The fewer such persons there are, the less likely is resort to violence and the more likely it is that, even if violence does occur, peace could be restored with a minimum of strife. (With respect to limited purpose, voluntary associations, the analogous problem is to find a procedure whose decisions alienate as few of the members as possible. For otherwise, the membership may shrink to the point that the association will no longer be able to serve either whatever purpose(s) it was originally intended to serve or even the purposes of the members who remain.)

It is not assumed here that one group is destined to prevail over the others in any event. Instead, the suggestion is that by having a majority rule approach to collective decision-making we can at least reduce the likelihood that disagreements that cannot be resolved to everyone's satisfaction will lead to prolonged strife. As domestic tranquillity is thought to be in everybody's overriding interest, it is concluded that all have good reason to want to see decisions reached on a majority rule basis (even if they may also have reason to resist particular decisions actually reached on such a basis).[6]

Perhaps the first thing to note is that if *this* is the rationale for majority rule, then it is the second of the three conceptions of "majority winner" articulated by Professor Kramer in his discussion, which is the most appropriate. (In other words, alternatives ought to be presented separately with voters voting for as many as they consider acceptable. If none is favored by a majority, the status quo is preserved. Otherwise, the alternative which receives the largest number of votes is adopted). For it is on this approach that the majority winner (possibly the status quo) can most plausibly be represented as the alternative that the greatest number of electors could live with, or that the smallest number would consider intolerable. Both plurality rule and the pairwise comparisons approach can lead to decisions that are disheartening to many more of the participants in the procedure.

A significant difficulty with this approach, however, is its obvious vulnerability to "devious" or "insincere" voting strategy. The results may not reflect what the greatest number of voters could live with as voters have a definite incentive not to reveal through their voting behavior the *full range* of alternatives minimally acceptable to them. They are more likely to vote only for one or two options which they most prefer (and in some cases only for their very first choice).

Even if it were possible to fashion a version of majority rule which did single out the alternative to which the least number of individuals object, it is far from certain that the threat of social disruption would thereby be minimized. Extremely alienated minority groups—thinking that matters could not be any worse, that they really have nothing to lose—are perhaps the most likely practitioners of terrorism. In their desperation, they can pose as much—or more—of a threat to the public peace than more sizable but far less cohesive dissenting groups.

A third "practical" argument for majority rule might run like this. Some decision procedures typically result in decisions which, though they lead to nothing so dramatic as civil strife or organizational demise, simply do not have sufficient support to be effectively carried out. We might call procedures deficient in this respect "ineffectual." Ineffectuality is not to be confused with indecisiveness. The issue is not "Will following the procedure lead to a decision for any profile of individual preference-orderings?" but rather "Are decisions reached in accordance with the procedure likely to have enough support to be effectively carried out?" Decisiveness is a very attractive property in a collective decision-making procedure, but it is small comfort when decisions thus arrived at are rarely executed satisfactorily. Here it might be urged that decisions reached on a majority rule basis typically do have sufficient support to be translated into effective policy.

It is not difficult to think of at least one objection which—if not fatal—at least narrows the range of cases within which this argument could be said to support majority rule. How much positive support policy decisions must have if they are to be effectively carried out varies considerably according to context. Some policies will require the active support of nearly everyone if they are to succeed. But other policies could be carried out quite well with the *active* support of only a few (and a lack of active opposition on the part of many). Thus, in some cases, it would be wise to insist on a more stringent requirement than simple majority rule; while in other cases a mere concern with whether or not the decision reached can be executed hardly warrants insisting on the positive support of even a bare majority.

More important, to say that a procedure leads to decisions which are more likely to be carried out is not sufficient to justify it. One wants to know if decisions arrived at in this way (however likely they are to be carried out) are worthy of being carried out. The problem is to find—among the procedures that are likely to lead to decisions worthy of being carried out—the procedure that is also likely to generate effective support for those decisions. Such a procedure is surely to be preferred to any procedure that generates effective support for *more* decisions but for *fewer* decisions that actually should be carried out.

III. A UTILITARIAN ARGUMENT

Though the preceding arguments (to whatever extent they go through) would not be entirely without interest to utilitarians, another line of argument attempts to establish a more direct and comprehensive connection between decision making on a majority rule basis and the maximization of social utility.

If each individual who stands to be affected by how an issue is resolved orders the options according to personal preference and votes accordingly, then the option that defeats all the others in a series of pairwise comparisons governed by majority rule could be regarded as the option (among those actually presented to the voters) with the greatest net expected utility (for the group which is voting).[7]

From this perspective, it would seem that the question "Who is to vote?" is to be answered in roughly this way: all who stand to be affected by the decision (to an extent worth the trouble of taking into account) and who are capable of making a judgment about how they will be personally affected by different policies.

There is no need to assume that voters are particularly good at estimating what is socially utilitarian. It is left to the procedure itself to "do" that. It is not even necessary to contend that each is always the best judge of what is conducive to his or her own happiness. Instead, all that need be claimed is that any utility-estimating procedure—other than polling the individuals themselves—is either too costly to operate or too fraught with the opportunity for abuse of power to be worth pursuing.

In any event, the result of following majority rule procedure (conceived in this way) can be no better than the best of the proposals which are put to a vote. Obviously it is important that proposals be well conceived and clearly presented to the voting public. In this connection, one could explore the merits of various procedures for determining the agenda and for arriving at final proposals, but I shall not attempt to do so here.

Objections

Perhaps the foremost objection to representing majority rule in this way is that standard voting procedures only reflect the order of people's preferences, *not* their strength or intensity. A proposal which a majority of individuals mildly prefer can pass although, given the intense dissatisfaction of the minority, it is considerably less utilitarian than some other. (Of course, even if a cardinal and not merely an ordinal measure of utility could be constructed for each individual, there is still the notorious problem of interpersonal utility comparison. No doubt this is a difficulty with utilitarian thought in general, and not just with this particular utilitarian defense of majority rule.)

There are, however, two mitigating factors: (1) That it is tedious or boring to participate in a voting procedure may actually help to correct this deficiency to some extent! Persons who do not have strong preferences are not very likely to take the trouble to vote. Those who do feel intensely are more likely to do so.[8] Here is an argument *against* the practice adopted in some countries of actually *requiring* citizens to vote and imposing a fine on those who do not. Instead of representing the prerogative to cast a vote as a sacred responsibility not to be shirked however little one cares about what is at issue, on this view of the matter we should encourage people to exercise that prerogative when and only when they do have rather strong feelings. If people do not vote even then, the system will not work.

(2) The oft-criticized practice of vote trading or "logrolling" can also help to make the results of majority rule voting procedures

reflect preference-strengths and not merely preference-order. As Luce and Raiffa explain, "A senator who feels strongly about bill *q* and indifferent about bills *r* and *s* will trade his votes *r* and *s* for the desired votes of senators indifferent about *q*. Thus, his strong preference for bill *q* is recorded." [9]

Unfortunately, this last defense seems to depend in turn on two rather important but sometimes questionable assumptions: (1) preferences are so distributed, that in order to have their way on at least some issues which matter a good deal to them, enough voters do have to yield on issues that others feel more strongly about than they do; (2) each voter is able to communicate with sufficiently many other voters in regard to a sufficiently wide range of issues that will come up for a vote to make vote-trading efforts worthwhile.

If, however, voters are permitted to refrain from voting when it suits them, and if they do have the opportunity to effect significant vote-trades, then it might be argued that one measure that we do have (if we have any at all) of how strongly the members of a group feel about various proposals is the way they behave *as voters* (e.g., whether they vote or not, how firmly they hold out for compromises, etc.). In this way, we might think of the results of a majority-rule voting procedure as providing at least a rough index of the social utility, *for* the group which is voting, of the various proposals which are presented to them.

A second difficulty with conceiving of majority rule in this way arises from the fact that when a number of individuals independently act so as to maximize self-interest, the net result is sometimes worse for each (and a fortiori for their society) than if each had been moved by concern for the public interest instead.[10] So long as voters are encouraged to vote and do vote purely in expression of self-interest, majority-rule voting procedure must fail to generate a socially utilitarian decision in contexts such as these.

A third difficulty has to do with the phenomenon of sympathetic identification. Many voters will simply not be able to decide how happy or unhappy the enactment of a certain proposal will make them without taking into account how others will fare under that policy. In these people, the knowledge that others will be either very favorably or very adversely affected could significantly affect their own net satisfaction. Of course, not everyone (not even every utilitarian) is going to be personally moved in this way, but there are likely to be enough such persons around that failure to take their feelings into account could skew the result.

In order to deal with this complication, it might be suggested that the decision procedure be divided into two stages. In the first, voters would assess the options on a narrowly self-interested basis and publicly express whatever preferences they had formed accordingly. In the second stage, a vote would be taken and each would express through that vote how he or she expects to be affected—taking into account, this time, the extent to which personal satisfactions and dissatisfactions will be altered by sympathetic reaction to the condition of others. Some may see a danger here of infinite regress: would yet a third vote have to be taken so that each voter could then take into account the other voters' revised feelings? It *is* at least possible for the "sensitive" members of the community to achieve a certain equilibrium in their mutually responsive feelings, so that this difficulty, at any rate, may be more imaginary than real.

Minority Reconciliation to Majority Rule

Why, on this approach, would voters who do find themselves in the minority have reason to be "reconciled" to the majority rule result? The answer is rather ingenious. Though it is right that the proposal that received a majority of the votes be carried out, it is not to be inferred that the voters who happen to be in the majority were any more "in the right" to have voted as they did than the voters who find themselves in the minority were to have voted as they did. Insofar as all voted—not for what they might have thought was right but for what they thought would be personally most advantageous—*all* voted rightly. For to vote as one *ought* to vote is *not* to vote for what one might think, *prior* to the vote, *ought* to be done (not under that description, at any rate). It is for the procedure itself, not the individual voter, to "decide" what ought to be done (i.e., which option is most *socially* utilitarian). Voters who understand all this and who find that they are in the minority are not really in the position of *having* to revise the judgment expressed through their vote (which was not about what ought to be done) or to reconcile it with the judgment that the majority will ought to prevail.

IV. AN ARGUMENT FROM PROBABILITY THEORY

When certain assumptions can reasonably be made, a strong argument on behalf of majority rule grounded in probability theory can be marshaled.[11] The argument—drawing on a formula of Bernoulli—was first presented by Condorcet. If a randomly selected voter is more likely to be right than wrong in his judgment about a matter which is up for a vote, then the probability that a judgment which is independently arrived at by a majority of such voters is the correct judgment is greater than the probability that the judgment of a randomly selected voter is correct.[12] Thus voters who find themselves in the minority in such circumstances have, in virtue of that, some reason to regard their own opinion as less probably correct than the majority opinion.

More formally, the probability that a judgment independently arrived at by h members of the group will be the correct judgment is

$$\frac{(h + k)!}{h! \, k!} \, v^h e^k$$

where $h + k = N$ (the total number of members of the group), v is the probability that a randomly selected voter will judge correctly, and $v + e = 1$. Through certain algebraic manipulations, it can be shown that this expression is equivalent to

$$\frac{v^{h-k}}{v^{h-k} + e^{h-k}}$$

By taking the appropriate partial derivatives, it can be demonstrated that if h is greater than k—i.e., if h is a majority of those voting—then as v increases, the probability of the correctness of the majority opinion increases continuously from 0 to 1. (The likelihood that the majority is correct approaches 1 as the reliability of the average voter approaches 1.) Similarly, it can be shown that as h increases, the probability of the correctness of the majority opinion also increases continuously from 0 to 1. This means that the reliability of decisions which result from majority-rule voting procedure (assuming that voters are themselves more reliable than not) increases either as the proportion of votes required to carry a proposal is increased or (for a given proportion) as the size of the electorate increases.[13]

To illustrate: if we can assume that the average voter is only slightly more likely to be correct than not, say, 51 percent likely, and if we require only 51 percent of the vote to carry a proposal, then the probability that a 51 percent majority is correct in its judgment when 100 are voting is 51.99 percent. For an electorate of 500, the probability that a 51 percent majority opinion is correct is 59.86 percent. When 1,000 are voting the probability is 69 percent; and when 10,000 are voting, it is 99.97 percent.

If we increase the proportion of votes required to carry to 60 percent, then in a population of 100 voters each of whom is right a mere 51 percent of the time, the probability that the judgment of a 60 percent majority is correct is 69 percent. In a voting population of 1,000, the probability is 99.97 percent.

With more reliable decision-makers, majority rule can yield highly reliable results even when relatively few individuals are polled. For example, if individual voters are correct in their judgments about 60 percent of the time, the likelihood of a correct judgment arrived at by 51 of 100 such individuals is 69.23 percent. If the average voter is correct about 75 percent of the time, the likelihood of the correctness of a judgment reached by 51 out of 100 is 90 percent.

Objections

Condorcet's reasoning provides a powerful defense of majority rule. Though the argument is valid, one may well entertain serious doubts about the appropriateness of the underlying assumptions. For the argument to be sound it must be correct to assume either that the questions that are put to the voters do have objectively correct answers or—at the very least—that there is a certain point of view which it is appropriate for all who are voting to take up and from which everyone who reasons correctly (and is adequately informed) will reach the very same conclusion. It must also be plausible to suppose that individual voters are right more often than wrong. Though they are not infallible (if they were, there would be no disagreement—hence no need for a collective decision-making procedure), they must be moderately reliable. If there were even one infallible decision-maker among them and if it were possible for fallible beings to identify with certainty such a person, it would hardly be necessary to ask anyone else to "vote." On the other hand, if the judgments of the average voter were wrong more often than right, then the mathematics of Condorcet's argument would give us reason to regard an opinion held by a majority of voters as even *more* dubious than that of any randomly selected voter!

Finally, if we think of each voter's reaching a judgment about the matter under consideration as an "event," then the reasoning which leads to Bernoulli's formula is not appropriate unless these events can be regarded as probabilistically independent.[14]

Applications

Now there do seem to be contexts in which there is an inclination to offer in support of majority rule at least an informal analogue to this argument. Thus when we think it is appropriate to consult a number of "experts" on some matter (as Judge Sirica did *twice* during the course of the Watergate affair) and to act on the basis of what a majority of them have to say, or when we think it is appropriate for the Supreme Court to arrive at its decisions on the basis of what a majority of its members judge to be constitutionally correct, it can hardly be because we believe that if such persons were to "slug it out" the majority would "win" in the end, anyway; or because we want to make sure that whatever decision is reached is supported by sufficiently many of the individuals in question that *they* can effectively carry it out themselves; nor could it be because we are trying to maximize the net happiness of the decision-making group. A more natural explanation is that in the absence of any special reasons to the contrary, we presume that the opinion of a majority of such experts is more likely to be correct than the opinion of just one expert. This also seems to be what accounts for the fact that we are more impressed by more nearly unanimous verdicts; though they may be accepted for the time being, very close decisions tend to inspire less confidence and are regarded as less "definitive" than judgments rendered by more clearcut majorities.

Incidentally, whatever doubts one might entertain about the propriety of invoking Condorcet's argument in the collective decision-making contexts which are most familiar to us, it is interesting to note that reasoning of essentially the same sort has found an important application in the design of modern digital computers.[15]

Contrasting Two Arguments for Majority Rule

As it is formulated in highly general terms the argument presented in this section might come to mind whenever it is thought that the making of certain decisions ought to be governed by specific considerations which can be more or less correctly applied. Thus a second utilitarian argument for majority rule could be readily constructed along these lines: if it is possible to identify individuals whose independent judgment about the social utility of competing proposals has, in the past, proven to be correct significantly more often than not, then there is some reason to arrive at policy decisions, according to what, upon due consideration, a majority of them judge ought to be done.

By adapting the Condorcet model of majority rule to the special case of utilitarian decision-making, we can bring into sharper focus a striking contrast between it and the utilitarian conception of majority rule presented earlier. At least three important issues—who is qualified to vote, how voters should decide their votes, and why voters who find themselves in the minority ought to be reconciled to the majority rule result—get settled quite differently.

From the perspective of the earlier argument, we need not insist that voters be at all reliable at estimating social utilities and disutilities. It is only assumed that they can form a fair idea of how they will be personally affected. On the present view, however, individuals who are asked to vote *must be* correct more often than not in their judgments about what is socially utilitarian if the result of following a majority rule voting procedure is not to be *less* rather than more advisable than doing what a randomly selected voter suggests. (The smaller the number of individuals who are relied upon for a decision, the more plausible it must be to represent them as *experts* at estimating what is socially utilitarian.)

On the view presented earlier, it is thought to be more utilitarian to have voters vote in expression of their private interests while leaving it to the procedure itself to decide where the public interest lies. From the point of view expressed here, majority rule voting procedure makes sense only if voters do try to arrive at the objectively correct, i.e., the most socially utilitarian, decision. Each must vote, not in expression of purely private interests, but from the point of view of what is in the public interest.

Finally, on the earlier utilitarian view, voters who find themselves in the minority can regard decisions which emerge from majority rule voting procedures as reasonably utilitarian, *without* having to think of themselves as having expressed through their votes a contrary judgment. In voting as they did they did not really express any judgment at all about the social utility of the alternatives which were before them. On the present approach, however, each vote ought to represent someone's most considered judgment—at the time of the vote—in regard to the social utility of the respective options. Thus the problem of minority reconciliation to majority rule seems to be more pronounced. The solution, of course, is this: voters who find themselves in the minority are said to have—in virtue of so finding themselves—good reason to regard the view for which a majority has expressed support as more likely to be correct than the view which they themselves held just prior to the result of the balloting.

V. MAJORITY RULE AND FAIRNESS

Finally, it might be suggested that recourse to majority rule is, at least in certain contexts, recommended by considerations of justice and fairness. Remarks near the very end of Professor Kramer's paper suggest that he had in mind such a justification himself when he afforded the majority principle so prominent a place in his discussion:

> The rules of elections ostensibly satisfy the majority principle since they require absolute majorities to elect; upon analysis, however, it turns out they do not satisfy it functionally, and can lead to results inconsistent with it. This suggests the question of whether some ostensibly fair procedural safeguard is functionally fair, i.e., does improve justice.[16]

In *A Theory of Justice,* John Rawls also seems to associate majority rule with fairness in the matter of political participation (though not with the justice of the social system as a whole):

> Whenever the Constitution limits the scope and authority of majorities . . . equal political liberty is less extensive.[17]
> . . . if minority rule is allowed, there is no obvious criterion to select which one is to decide and equality is violated.[18]

But just what *is* the connection between fairness and majority rule? There is at least some temptation to maintain that whenever a number of individuals are entitled (for whatever reason) [19] to an "equal voice" in the making of a certain decision, the fair way to resolve into a single policy decision their many (potentially conflicting) views about what ought to be done is to assign to each person one vote and to have votes translate into results on a simple majority rule basis. In this way, the connection between fairness and majority rule is mediated by the requirement that there be "one person, one vote." In some cases, it is thought to be only fair that persons have an "equal voice"; this ideal is served by letting each person have one vote and no person more than one vote. Finally, "one person, one vote" is seen as somehow entailing that the majority shall rule!

At this point, however, several questions still remain:

(1) What is the connection between the ideal of "equal say" and the procedural requirement of "one person, one vote"? If the point is to give people an equal voice, why take a vote at all? Why not, instead, have them take turns dictating decisions to one another?

(2) What connection is there between "one person, one vote" and majority rule? Would some version of minority rule (e.g. "whichever alternative receives the least number of votes shall win") not meet this requirement just as well?

(3) Is rule by *bare* majority any more or less closely connected either with the requirement that there be "one person, one vote" or with the underlying ideal of "equal voice" than rule by more inclusive majority or rule by mere plurality?

Taking Turns Dictating Decisions; Assigning
Authority to Decide by Lot

If the point is to give to each person an "equal voice," why take a vote at all? Why not, rather, have those who are entitled to an equal voice take turns dictating decisions to one another? One problem is that in reasonably large associations, at any rate, a rotation scheme would not really be fair in practice; too many members might die before their turn ever came up! To get around this, it might be suggested that authority to decide be assigned by lot: in this way, persons would at least stand an equal *chance* of having their way. Thus it could be argued that, if in small associations members take turns dictating decisions to one another while in large associations the authority to decide each matter is assigned by lot, the ideal of "equal voice" will still be served although no votes are taken and, a fortiori, the precept "one person, one vote" is not satisfied.

Either approach, however, is subject to an important objection. When people know that they can get a proposal to prevail as policy only if a *majority* of voters can be persuaded to see the matter in the same way, they are more likely to take the trouble of presenting their views *to one another* and *to pay more attention* to what others have to say (if only to get a better idea of how they might dissuade them) than when everyone knows that in the end one particular individual has full authority to decide. As persons are less likely to take one another's views into serious consideration when they merely have the opportunity to express an opinion and not also the prerogative of casting a vote, voting procedure might be regarded as effectively fairer than rotation schemes and lotteries.

A further point which may militate in favor of voting procedure is that better decisions are more likely to result when people are induced to exchange information and see matters from one another's perspective. Though to some extent this can happen even when people take turns dictating decisions or assign the prerogative to decide by lot, it seems more likely that it will happen when they have the task of persuading a majority of their group rather than just one individual.

Finally, with either a rotation scheme or a lottery, each day a decision is rendered, the preceding day's decision may be completely undone or reversed. Of course, it is not desirable that policies be irreversible. Past decisions may come to be seen as mistaken, or if not wrong when rendered, then unsuited to changing circumstances. But while policies should be subject to change if possible, it is also true of many policies that if they are to succeed at all, they must be in operation for awhile. Obviously, some balance must be struck between the need for reasonably sustained effort and a certain continuity on the one hand and the need for mechanisms of change on the other. Of course, even with a voting procedure, shifts in policy may be more sudden than is ideally to be desired. With rotation schemes and lotteries, however, the problem of discontinuity and interruption would seem to be more pronounced.

Of course, none of this is to deny that when decisions to be reached are relatively "low-level" and operational, the ideal of "equal voice" might be served well enough by one of the other "fair" schemes for delegating authority, for it does take extra time and effort to run an electoral procedure and some matters are not important enough to warrant the added cost.

Minority Rule and "One Person, One Vote";
Simple Versus Qualified Majority Rule

Is it not possible for some version of minority rule to satisfy the precept "one person, one vote" no less than do various versions of majority rule? Is there any reason to regard simple majority rule as fairer than other versions of majority rule? Though for the sake of brevity I shall not explore these questions here, I believe that with some difficulty the following points can be established:

(1) A commitment to "one person, one vote" carries along with it a commitment to majority rule in some form or other. (2) Each voter's chances of getting new action taken are greater under rule by bare majority than under rule by more inclusive majority. And this is so whatever probabilities can be associated with various possible distributions of voter preference and/or patterns of voter turnout. (3) In the event there is no institutional status quo to which matters can revert, rule by bare majority is more decisive than rule by more inclusive majorities; i.e., it is decisive for more possible distributions of voter preference and/or patterns of voter turnout. (4) When, however, there is a status quo to which matters can in fact revert, rule by more inclusive majority tends to favor those who support the

status quo in any given matter, inasmuch as they can have their way with fewer votes on their side, than the proponents of change must have on theirs. Simple majority rule, on the other hand, sets the same task for both. (5) Whether, in virtue of this, simple majority rule is fairer or more just than more stringent requirements will depend on further factors which vary from context to context, e.g., how "reformist" and "conservative" tendencies are distributed among the voters; how just the status quo is; how responsive voters are to the legitimate claims of others. (6) In the absence of special background information of this sort, instituting simple majority rule could be construed as a reasonable attempt to give voters as much power to take action as to block action.

"One Person, One Vote" and "Equal Voice"

Now even if it *can* be established that majority rule in some form or other is intimately—perhaps inevitably—connected with the requirement that there be "one person, one vote," it is still appropriate to ask how satisfactorily does any essentially "one person, one vote" procedure express the ideal of "equal say." Though in one sense such procedures rather obviously answer to the demand for equal say, it may yet be the case that over time the burden of getting one's way in respect to matters of common concern will fall rather more heavily on some voters than on others. It is not merely that individuals differ considerably in respect to their oratorical abilities or with respect to the time and effort that they can afford to expend debating policy. More disturbing in this connection is the possibility that one group of voters will be so similar in outlook and so numerous that they have their way significantly more often than the rest of the electorate. This, of course, is the problem of the permanent majority. The point is that "one person, one vote" does *not* insure that voters have an *effectively equal* say because it is by no means certain that voters will actually get their way more or less equally often over time.

Clearly certain further conditions would have to obtain if we were to be able to conclude that "one person, one vote" tends toward equality in the sense of equal effective influence. It would be most interesting to know just what the relevant background assumptions are. Certainly we would have to be able to rule out the aforementioned possibility of a permanent majority. But this is not sufficient. The formation of a permanent majority *coalition* would also relegate a number of voters to permanent minority status. Somehow preferences must be so distributed that each voter finds himself aligned with a majority of voters on a fair number of issues. Instead of rule by fixed majority or majority coalition, circumstances must conspire to produce rule by constantly shifting coalitions of minority groups. In trying to determine just what those circumstances are, a good deal of attention would probably have to be paid to the dynamics of the "vote-trading" phenomena (in those contexts which allow for it and in which the need to forge a majority coalition is sufficiently great to stimulate it).[20]

Actually, there are two important questions worth raising here: When does "one person, one vote" lead to a roughly equal distribution of effective influence? When *should* such a distribution be demanded as a corollary to the demand that there be "equal voice"?

An argument for supposing that the fairness of a voting procedure *does* hinge on whether or not voters have *effectively* equal influence over time might run like this: There are important benefits associated with the existence of an established procedure for peacefully resolving disputes about group policy matters. Moreover, each person who stands to benefit is prima facie bound to bear a *fair* share of the burdens of making such a procedure work. If the procedure benefits all alike, then people should bear an equal share of the burden. But when do all benefit equally? Just what are the burdens of making such a procedure work? What is a fair share of the burdens? Talk about the bother of engaging in public debate or the trouble of having to go cast a vote in a prescribed place at a prescribed time does *not* exhaust the subject of burden bearing. The *major* burden which the participants in a collective decision-making procedure must shoulder if the procedure is really to "work" (if anyone is to benefit from it) is the burden of having to acquiesce in decisions which one would not *otherwise* find agreeable.

Thus it cannot be argued with plausibility that the burdens of making such a procedure work are borne equally over time, or that on balance all derive equal benefit from the operations of the procedure (and hence that all should bear an equal share) unless the burden of having to acquiesce in disagreeable decisions is distributed more or less equally over time. This is why—if one wishes to argue that a collective decision-making procedure is fair and that there is consequently a duty of fair play to acquiesce in the results of the procedure if one has participated in it—it does not suffice to point out that each person participating in the procedure has one vote and that no person has more than one vote.

With a somewhat richer set of assumptions, however, perhaps it *can* be argued that fairness does *not* require a roughly equal distribution of the burden of not getting one's way (but demands only a roughly equal *opportunity* to win). If we can assume, for example, that (a) voters have an effectively equal opportunity to express their views to one another; (b) that they earnestly try to vote in expression of what they believe to be in the public interest rather than in expression of purely private interest; (c) that while each has views about what is in the public interest that he or she does wish to present to the others, most voters *are* genuinely open to reasoned argument in respect to what is and is not in the public interest—if we can say all this and perhaps more, then perhaps we can conclude that each voter has a "fair crack" at getting his or her views to prevail and that this does suffice to make the collective decision-making procedure fair. Should someone find that his opinions seldom prevail, there are several ways to respond. Initially, he might take this merely as evidence that his views have not been presented in the best possible way; eventually, however, he might either come to doubt the wisdom of his point of view or to question the seriousness and sincerity of his fellow voters. (In taking the latter course, he might then cease to think of himself as having any obligation of fair play toward his fellow voters to work in and through the procedure or to acquiesce in its results.)

(Incidentally, in very limited-purpose, highly voluntary associations, that some individuals get their way significantly less often than others may not be cause for much consternation. The remedy may be simply for those individuals either to join or to form an association of more like-minded individuals. The charge of injustice would be more appropriate, however, (a) if there were actually a conspiracy to shut these individuals out from the mechanisms of group policy-making; or (b) if the association were nominally voluntary but the option to secede were not a live option (e.g., the cost of withdrawing would be excessive, or the purposes served by

belonging to the association could not be served very well by joining
any other association).

Fair Procedure, Unjust Results and the
Need for Background Constraints

Now, even if it can be argued that individuals either do get their
way equally often or have at least an equal opportunity to get their
way in matters calling for a collective decision, it is still possible that
a gravely unjust policy will be approved by a majority of voters on
any particular decision-making occasion. The preceding discussion—preoccupied as it was with whether the burden of not getting
one's way is equally distributed over time—might be regarded as
entirely *misguided*. For what if some voters want what they have *no
right* to get? It is even possible that when voters get their way
equally often, the result will be mutual exploitation rather than
equal justice.

Instead of asking how people fare from the point of view of their
own interests, we might look at the matter from the perspective of a
particular conception of justice. It could then be argued that merely
counting occasions on which each person gets his or her way—
without paying attention to the moral legitimacy of their respective
claims—is hardly an adequate way to appraise the workings of a
decision-making procedure. (This seems to be the analogue, from
the standpoint of justice, to the "intensity of desire" problem which
arises in utilitarian theorizing about majority rule.)

Thus at least two sorts of injustice may be associated with the
workings of majority rule or any other decision-making procedure:
(1) over time, the burden of being a loser (of not getting one's way
in respect to public policy) may fall rather more heavily on some
individuals than on others; (2) on any particular decision-making
occasion, a decision may be reached which seriously and adversely
affects the rights of certain members of the community. (Obviously
injustice of the latter sort can be said to arise only when it does
make sense to think of substantively unjust policy decisions.)

The preceding remarks reflect the obvious need to limit what can
be decided on a majority rule basis. Some time ago Herbert
McClosky tried to argue on "logical grounds" that majority power
is not absolute.[21] Claiming "it is the very nature of a principle that
it prohibits its own negation," [22] McClosky inferred that it would be

inconsistent with the majority principle itself for a majority either to repeal majority rule or to enact measures which would undermine those rights (primarily political) whose recognition is essential to the effective operation of a majority rule system. "On logical grounds alone, then, it becomes apparent that a majority, deriving its sanction from the principle of majority rule, is limited by that principle to the extent, at least, that it cannot abrogate the rules that authorize the power it can properly exercise." [23]

Now there are two problems with McClosky's approach. First, in attempting to construct an argument for limited majority rule on "purely logical grounds," we are likely to articulate—as McClosky himself did—an excessively modest conception of the limits appropriate to the exercise of majority authority.[24] Second, there is no point in trying to distinguish what the "majority principle" itself forbids a majority to do from what is on more general moral grounds forbidden. For it is difficult to believe that the "majority principle" is a first-order consideration rather than a principle grounded in other more fundamental considerations. Once we recognize this, we can determine the appropriate limits to majority authority by appealing to these and *other* more fundamental considerations. It is my claim that we can then appreciate more clearly (a) why majority power ought not to be regarded as absolute; and (b) why constraints on majority rule authority ought to be more extensive than the majority-rule-preserving constraints for which McClosky argued.

McClosky's "logical" approach to the problem will not do; for a principle can—without absurdity—warrant its own "suspension" in favor of other principles. For example, many utilitarian theorists have argued, *on utilitarian grounds,* that we had better not live *directly* by the principle of utility itself but by more concrete and specific rules instead. More generally, it can be said—and with good reason—that a person who is committed to living in accordance with the dictates of reason need not be constantly reasoning about what to do. So, too, if we read the majority principle as "decisions rendered ought to be in accordance with the will of a majority," it is perfectly conceivable that the will of the majority of people in a particular place is better served over time if there is autocratic rule or unanimous rule or martial rule, etc., rather than direct majority rule.

On the other hand, if we regard the majority principle as an *operational principle;* i.e., as the principle that as a matter of standard operating procedure each decision ought to be reached by directly determining what is favored by a majority of persons, then we ought to be able to ask *why* this should be so. If there are *reasons* for a procedure (or reasons for acknowledgement of whatever principle bids us to follow such a procedure), then, for all we know, with appropriate changes in circumstances, these same reasons may warrant revising the procedure or replacing it altogether. Hence from a *purely* logical point of view it cannot be established that a majority's action to revoke the majority rule system is inconsistent with whatever considerations might have warranted its having the power to act in the first place.

To rescue McClosky's point about the limits of legitimate majority rule, we must look at the *particular* moral reasons for regarding majority rule as wise in the first place, rather than appeal to more general and allegedly logical considerations (e.g., that principles *prohibit* their own "negation").

Let us suppose that majority rule *is* to be argued for on grounds of fairness. Then certainly there are measures whose majority enactment would not be consistent with the grounds for regarding majority authority as legitimate in the first place; for example, measures which undermine the *fairness of* the majority rule decision-making procedure itself, by violating the equal freedom of citizens to express their opinions, to assemble peacefully, to vote, etc. But the *moral* "logic" of the situation should carry us further; i.e., beyond these procedure-preserving constraints to more substantive constraints. Thus, if the persons who find themselves in the minority could legitimately be expected to acquiesce in the rule of the majority, there would also have to be restrictions on the exercise of majority power in various other ways which subvert the *equal* status of citizens as free persons more generally.

I believe that essentially the same point may be found in the following passage from Roland Pennock's *Liberal Democracy:*

> But no absolute right of majority rule has been established, nor in the writer's opinion can it be established. From our argument that there is an equal right of self-government it would follow that votes should count equally. But this right of self-government itself was derived from the basic rights of

liberty and equality. Because it was the most apt instrument for the realization of these values it became entitled to the status of a right. The liberties that liberal democracy includes are fully as basic to the ultimate goal as is the power of self-government. In fact, in no small measure the latter is justified by its tendency to protect the former. Surely, then, the right of the majority cannot be advanced against one of the rights it is designed to protect.[25]

Three Levels on Which Questions of Justice May Arise

Any discussion of majority rule from the standpoint of justice and fairness seems to be complicated by the fact that the goods in respect to which questions of distributive justice can and do arise are of three different sorts:

(1) The good of having access to and of participating in the mechanisms for effecting policy change (and/or for selecting officers);

(2) The good of having influence and of exercising it effectively (i.e., of actually getting one's way in regard to group policy matters);

(3) The goods of life, liberty, health, education, income, etc.

There is clearly some temptation to argue that a nearly equal distribution of the good of political participation produces a nearly equal distribution of political power, and that a nearly equal distribution of political power tends to produce a just or equitable distribution of other important goods. (Consider in recent years the emphasis placed on "black power," "gay power," etc.) Much of the appeal of "democratic processes" can probably be understood in these terms. No doubt, there *are* important connections here but what they are and how firm they are would seem to depend on circumstances that can and do vary. At the very least, perhaps, it can be said that without equal political participation it is most unlikely that people will enjoy equal political influence and that without equal political influence it is most unlikely they will enjoy an equal share of the other goods in life. It might also be noted that while political participation and the effective exercise of power are in some degree instrumental to the realization of other ends, individuals may value these for their own sake as well.

Minority Reconciliation to Majority Rule from the Standpoint of Justice and Fairness

Why, from the standpoint of justice and fairness, should persons who find themselves in the minority be reconciled to the results of majority rule? Cases arise in which, though there is room for conscientious disagreement, a collective response to the situation is advisable. Fair-minded persons realize this and are prepared to "accept the risks of suffering the defects of one another's knowledge and sense of justice in order to gain the advantages of an effective legislative procedure." [26] They are prepared to do so provided that the risks are equitably shared and that injustice does not exceed certain limits in any event. The explanation for this willingness on their part would appear to be that arriving at a policy decision through a peaceful, reason-governed procedure that affords persons an equal status in the actual process of decision making is, in many cases, as important as resolving the matter under consideration in one way rather than in another.

If background circumstances are favorable to its fair operation and if the range of cases with respect to which the majority is permitted to rule is sufficiently restricted, persons with a sense of justice may regard themselves as having a weighty though prima facie duty to work in and through majority-rule decision procedure rather than around it. In addition, they will think of themselves as incurring a prima facie obligation of "fair play" to go along with what results from a fair procedure in which they have actually participated.

In contrast with the approach in each of the two preceding sections, fair-minded persons can think that there is *some* reason to go along with what is decided through a fair majority rule procedure in virtue of its having been so decided (and in virtue of their own participation in the procedure), *without thinking* that the decision is itself a better or more reasonable decision on that account. The decision procedure does not literally define what is just; it is rather that in order to assess the rightness of going along with the result of the procedure, one must look at the whole picture—including the fact that proceeding in a certain way has moral significance in its own right.

As it *is* important that people do continue to relate to one another through fair and peaceful procedures, it is to be hoped that unjust decisions are neither serious enough nor frequent enough to warrant extraprocedural steps. But even when fair-minded persons "submit their conduct" to the rule of the majority, "they do not submit their judgment." [27] As they do not generally regard the majority decision as more likely to accord with what justice demands than their own view, it is possible for voters who find themselves in the minority to reach the judgment that—all things considered—the injustice of a particular decision or of a series of decisions *is* grave enough to warrant either going outside the established framework or—at the least—not fully acquiescing in what has been decided within it.

A Classification of Cases

Perhaps we can put in order some of the reflections of this section by classifying cases according to whether substantive considerations of justice do or do not relate to the matter under consideration by the electorate, and, if they do, how. It is possible, for example, that considerations of justice do not engage the *substance* of a particular issue at all. It is a question of purely subjective preference (a "chocolate or vanilla?" case, so to speak). Morally speaking, what is decided in any one of these cases—considered in isolation from the others, is immaterial. But it is *not* immaterial (1) how decisions are reached; i.e., what role each person plays or what status each person enjoys in the decision-making process; or (2) how the burden of not getting one's way in such matters is distributed over time. Another way to characterize these cases is to say that questions of justice do arise but not so much in respect to the substance of the issues as to the goods of participation and power and how these are distributed.

It may also be that while considerations of justice do relate directly to the matter under consideration, justice is *equally* well served by each of the proposals which happen to be before the electorate. Whereas in cases of the preceding sort it is equally irrelevant from the standpoint of justice what is decided, in cases of this sort it is equally fortunate. Still it remains a matter of some concern how people relate to one another in the decision-making process itself.

More interestingly, there are cases in which what is decided matters a great deal from the standpoint of justice. Considerations of justice engage the issue that is before the voters clearly and directly. Justice in such cases is not primarily a matter of people getting their way equally often, for some individuals may want what they have no right to get. If people who are not constrained by a sense of what is just, who are not responsive to the legitimate claims of others, get their way as often as one another (simply counting up occasions), the end result *may be* injustice all around rather than equal justice. Though to some extent a just constitution can circumscribe the sphere of majority rule operations, it is surely not possible to spell out in advance and in full specifics a just solution to every significant problem which might arise. Much also depends on the good will of those who participate in the decision-making process.

Finally, there are cases in which, though it clearly does matter from the standpoint of justice what is decided, it is far from clear what should be done. While basic considerations of justice are relevant and should be controlling, there *is* room for *reasonable* disagreement about the precise implications of these considerations in the more complicated real-life situations. Were circumstances such as these never to arise, there might be little need for collective decision-making procedures in the first place; when they do, though, it is not very clear how we should expect a collective decision-making procedure to work. One suggestion, at any rate, is that we look for a roughly equal distribution over time of the burden of not getting conscientious convictions translated into group policy. There is also some temptation to hope for a *growing* consensus as discussion and debate continue and as more relevant information comes to light.

A Summary of Possible Positions

From the standpoint of justice and fairness, there are a number of different ways of favorably representing majority-rule decision making or, indeed, any collective decision-making procedure.

Among these are the following:

(1) It might be argued that decisions reached on a majority rule basis are just solely in virtue of having been thus decided. There is no other criterion for assessing their correctness. (On this view of the matter, majority-rule decision making would be understood as a case of what Rawls has called pure procedural justice, that is, it does not matter what is decided so long as decisions are reached in accordance with a correct or fair procedure.) [28]

(2) Though the just result cannot be literally defined as whatever decision (or pattern of decisions) has resulted from following a certain procedure, it might be said of a particular decision-making procedure that it always leads to just results. (On this view of the matter, the procedure would be a case of what Rawls has called perfect procedural justice.) [29]

(3) Though of course no feasible procedure is sure to lead to a just decision in every case, some procedures are more likely to do so than others. On this line there is no need to argue that majority rule (or whatever procedure one is recommending) is *very* likely to lead to decisions which are just, but only that no other procedure is *as likely* to do so. (Recall Winston Churchill's remark to the effect that democracy is the worst form of government with the exception of all the others.)

(4) Although it can be an instrument of injustice, the procedure in question is not less likely than any other procedure to lead to just results and has, in addition, certain other merits;[30] most notably, in virtue of how the participants are situated with respect to one another and must relate to one another in the course of following the procedure, it is fairer. Thus the balance of right-making considerations is in its favor.

(5) Though some other procedure may even be somewhat more likely to lead to just results, the procedure in question is not so much less likely to do so that the superiority it can be said to have in virtue of its "intrinsic" fairness is offset.

(6) Whatever its merits may be, whether it is to be appreciated for reasons of justice and fairness or even chiefly for other reasons, majority-rule decision procedure can at least be made reasonably compatible with what justice demands if the sphere of its operations is appropriately circumscribed.

Which of these representations (or which conjunction) is most accurate? Although there are times when what is decided is far less important than how things are decided, we would not be wise to extrapolate from one rather limited class of cases a purely procedural conception of justice in matters of collective decision-making. Nor is it plausible to maintain that majority rule or any other procedure always results in just decisions.

More interesting is the contrast between the third position and either the fourth or the fifth ways of appreciating majority rule suggested here. On each of these views, we are in a position to say that majority rule is a *fair* procedure which may nevertheless yield *unjust* results. Evidently, however, there are at least two different ways of making sense of this claim. On the one hand, we might say that a procedure is fair just in case no other procedure that anybody can think of is any more likely to lead to just results. On this way of thinking a fair procedure is a procedure reasonably designed to yield just results. The thought is that it can hardly be unfair to proceed as we do, even though injustice may result, if we can really do no better in this regard. On the other hand, we might say that the fairness of a procedure has also to do with *how* the parties are situated with respect to one another and must *relate* to one another *in the process* of arriving at a decision. On this way of thinking, if the parties are *entitled* to an equal voice, then the more nearly equal their prerogatives as participants, the fairer the procedure is. We might call what is at issue here "intrinsic" fairness.

As it matters *what* decisions are reached, so also does it matter *how* they are reached. But the "how" of decision making can be important in its own right and not only in relation to possible end results. In dismissing the view that decisions are correct *solely* in virtue of having been generated by a certain kind of parliamentary process, we need not go to the other extreme of supposing that all that matters about a decision procedure is how likely it is to issue in decisions of a certain sort. We can, and I believe we should, give (independent) weight to both process and result.

In (4) and (5), we have two ways in which one might arrive at a view favorable to majority rule after having taken into consideration both process and result.[31] To assess these positions one must be able to evaluate the claim that proceeding on a majority rule basis is "intrinsically fairer" (assuming, that is, that the persons who are to vote ought to have an equal voice). Clearly the force of this claim depends—at least in part—on how intimate is the connection between majority rule and "one person, one vote" and on how comparatively well "one person, one vote" procedures satisfy the ideal of equal voice. But one must also be able to evaluate various claims about the relative likelihood of majority rule's success in helping to produce just decisions (or a just pattern of decisions). A number of points in the preceding discussion bear on this issue.[32] Obviously, much depends on background circumstances and, in particular, on the motivation of the individuals who participate in the procedure. By employing several different arguments sketched earlier, a defender of majority rule might try to show that just results are as or more likely with majority rule than without it, under any one of a variety of motivational assumptions.[33]

Finally, it might be said that at least one "virtue" of a majority rule procedure is that not all questions of justice need be settled by it. This position (corresponding to (6)) is perfectly consistent with the other more positively favorable views insofar as the claims they make may be understood to apply within a restricted domain. For, even if one procedure is more likely to yield just results than another, we do well to regard any collective decision-making procedure as operating (explicitly or implicitly) under certain constraints.

VI. CONCLUSION

Several lines of argument for majority rule have been sketched and various objections entertained. What is evident is that each case for proceeding on a majority rule basis carries its own set of answers to important questions about the nature of the procedure (e.g., who is to vote, how voters are to decide their votes, which issues are to be put to a vote). Special attention was paid at each turn to the question of why persons who find themselves in the minority ought to be "reconciled" to the rule of the majority. For without a satisfactory theory of minority reconciliation, it is particularly difficult to see how majority rule can be plausibly recommended as a matter of parliamentary "due process," as a procedural condition whose violation can be said to constitute a violation of anyone's rights.

As each case for majority rule requires us to make certain

background assumptions which limit the scope of its defense, it is likely that no single line of argument is adequate to support the "majority principle" in all the circumstances in which majority rule does seem to make some sense. It is also likely, in view of the objections to which each defense of majority rule is subject, that majority rule cannot be defended in every circumstance in which it is practiced. Finally, as there are so many different views of majority rule—views about what it is and about why we ought to have it—and as each view may be appropriate in at least certain contexts—perhaps we do better not to speak of *the* majority principle at all.[34]

NOTES

1. This paper grew out of remarks which I made as commentator on Professor Kramer's presentation at the 1973 meetings of the American Society for Political and Legal Philosophy in New Orleans. In the opening paragraphs, therefore, I try to relate my efforts here to certain passages in the original draft of his paper. If any of my references to Professor Kramer's remarks are no longer appropriate, I think they can either be omitted without losing the sense of my discussion or else be read as representing at least one possible point of view—even if it is no longer Professor Kramer's.

2. For Kramer's revised discussion of the majority principle, see pp. 265-78 (Eds).

3. Though in his study of the extent to which various procedures meet these requirements, Professor Kramer says he is concerned with the rules for what he calls "voluntary, nongovernmental assemblies" rather than for "official parliamentary or legislative assemblies," I shall not try to limit this discussion of the majority principle in the same way. I think there are two good reasons for not observing such a limitation: (1) the majority principle is widely thought to apply to the operations of official, governmental bodies; in some form or other, majority rule is a prominent feature of political life. (2) If, as might well be surmised, the majority principle should *not* be afforded precisely the same status in the context of official governmental deliberation as in the deliberations of unofficial and voluntary associations, it would be interesting to know *why* this is so.

4. Pp. 271-74.

5. The question of how voters ought to decide their votes becomes immensely more complicated when voters are supposed to "represent" other individuals or groups of individuals. Unfortunately, I

must leave aside such complexities here. But for extensive treatment of this subject, see J. Roland Pennock and John W. Chapman (eds.), *Nomos X: Representation* (New York: Atherton Press, 1968).

6. In turning to the philosophical tradition, one might expect to find such an argument in the writings of Thomas Hobbes, were it not for the fact that Hobbes himself had deep doubts about *group* decision-making of any sort. Thus I originally conceived the argument as "Hobbesian" (in spirit, if not in letter). Actually, a rather clear and forceful statement of it can be found in the writings of Henry Sidgwick:

> But further, democratic government, in the sense of government resting on the active consent of the citizens, may—as we have seen—reasonably be preferred, not because it is likely to be better conducted, but because it is likely to be better obeyed,—because it reduces the danger of revolution. If the majority of a nation are able to modify, in an orderly and regular way, their laws and the action of their government, a minority desirous of change will, ordinarily, be only tempted to resort to physical force when it is hopeless of becoming a majority; and as such a minority must expect to have opposed not only the majority of persons averse to the change, but also all other citizens who consider the advantage of the change, if any, to be outweighed by the evils of revolution, it will only be under exceptional circumstances that the temptation to revolution will be strong.

Henry Sidgwick, *Elements of Politics* (London: Macmillan & Co., 1929), pp. 615-16. I am indebted to Alan Kussack for bringing this passage to my attention.

7. It is beyond the scope of this paper to explore various ways of dealing with the problem of cyclical majorities, but I would suggest that the problem can—and probably ought to—be looked at from a number of different perspectives on why we ought to have majority rule in the first place. It would be interesting to consider, in this connection, which if any of the suggested approaches to the problem are especially to be recommended on utilitarian grounds.

8. Of course, a background assumption here is that the "tedium" of participation is about the same for everyone; if, however, it could be said that some people like participating in the procedure for its own sake a good deal more than others do, this argument would not hold

up. If we are ever to make meaningful interpersonal utility comparisons, somewhere along the way we must find a "yardstick" which we can plausibly claim marks off equal amounts of happiness and/or unhappiness in different persons.

9. Luce and Raiffa, *Games and Decisions* (New York: John Wiley & Sons, 1967), p. 36.

10. These situations might be called "prisoner's dilemma cases" in view of the celebrated anecdote attributed to A. W. Tucker. See Luce and Raiffa, *Games and Decisions,* pp. 94-97.

11. See Duncan Black, *The Theory of Committees and Elections* (Cambridge University Press, 1958, 1971), pp. 164-65.

12. Obviously at work here is a conception of how voters ought to decide their votes which is quite different from that of the preceding argument. See pp. 308-09 for a fuller elaboration of the contrast.

13. With rule by bare majority, more reliable results are not *necessarily* to be had as the size of the electorate increases; if majority support exceeds minority opposition by precisely one vote the judgment of the majority is *as* likely to be correct as the judgment of any randomly selected voter, but not more likely. On the other hand, rule by some fixed (majority) proportion—however close to one-half that may be— *does* yield more reliable results with larger electorates.

14. Cf. John Rawls, *A Theory of Justice* (Cambridge, Mass.: Belknap, 1971), p. 358.

15. In order to increase the reliability of "circuit package" performance, computer engineers have resorted to an approach which is known as "majority redundancy." A circuit package consists of a number of subcomponents, each of which receives one or more inputs and yields a determinate output according to a certain logic which it has been designed to observe. On the approach in question, each subcomponent is replaced by an odd number of subcomponents which are identical to it and by a so-called "voter circuit." The output of each replica of the original subcomponent is then fed into the voter circuit which, appropriately enough, "decides" the final output on a majority rule basis. The current either passes through or does not pass through the voter circuit, according to whether it has or has not passed through a majority of the identical subcomponents that feed into it. To increase the reliability of the "vote-counting" operation— i.e., to reduce the likelihood that voter circuit malfunctioning will in turn contribute to the unreliability of the overall computer operation—the original complex of voter circuit and subcomponents that feed into it can be replicated an odd number of times and their respective outputs fed into a higher-order voter circuit.

If the average reliability of the replicated subcomponents and of the voter circuits is greater than 50 percent (if they work as they are supposed to, better than half the time), then an *arbitrarily high degree of reliability* can be achieved for the whole system merely by increasing the replication factor in respect to subcomponents, voter circuits, higher-order voter circuits, etc. Thus, without having to manufacture circuit components which are any more reliable than those which can be manufactured presently (assuming that these are more reliable than not), we can build computers which are as reliable as we like. We have only to manufacture many more such components and to structure their functioning in the manner suggested above.

In view of its application to computer design, we might think of the Condorcet argument from probability theory as the "voter circuit" model of majority rule. To see it in this light is to see more clearly how—from the point of view in question—majority rule is essentially a strategy for achieving greater decision-making reliability through *redundancy*. The thought is that by proceeding on the basis of what a majority of "experts" who independently make the appropriate investigations and engage in the relevant thought processes have to say, we will get the most reliable results we can get, given the level of expertise available to us and the possibility of error in judgment.

I am indebted to Stephen J. Gruen, IBM Corporation, for calling this application to my attention and explaining it to me.

16. These sentences are omitted from Kramer's revised paper (Eds.). The question of how majority rule is to be viewed from the standpoint of justice and fairness is extremely complex (even leaving aside all the more general difficulties which would plague any attempt to work out a complete theory of justice). It would be difficult to treat this matter adequately in sufficient detail on less than book-length scale. I shall try, therefore, merely to set out what I take to be a few of the more important issues and arguments which arise in this connection.

17. Rawls, *A Theory of Justice* p. 224. Rawls is *not* opposed to restrictions on the scope of majority rule; in fact, he clearly believes that justice requires such restrictions (cf. pp. 228-31, 356). In the remarks cited here, he is connecting majority rule with greatest equal *political* liberty.

But political liberty is just one of a number of basic liberties which must be taken into consideration when the "greatest equal liberty" principle—which for Rawls is the first principle of justice—is applied. "The best arrangement is found by noting the consequences for the complete system of liberty." Thus, to justify restrictions on majority rule, "one must maintain that . . . the less extensive freedom of participation is sufficiently outweighed by the greater security and extent of the other liberties." (p. 229).

18. Ibid., p. 356.

19. Unfortunately, I must leave aside here many important questions about when and why persons could be said to have such a right.

20. If there is no way of knowing what issues will come before the group in the future, or if it is not possible to communicate with all but a few of those who will vote, it will either not be possible or not worth the effort to effect a "trade." Vote trading is more characteristic of relatively small deliberative bodies (e.g., representative assemblies) than of large associations which resort mainly to the referendum.

21. Herbert McClosky, "The Fallacy of Absolute Majority Rule," *The Journal of Politics,* 11 (1949), 637-54.

22. Ibid., p. 643.

23. Ibid.

24. Thus he writes: "It may be ... that such matters as freedom of worship can be secured against governmental control by some principle other than the majority principle. It needs, however, to be made clear that while the majority principle imposes restraints on majority power, it does not sanction freedom from any sort of control. On the contrary, it *authorizes* the exercise of power, except over those matters upon which the authorization itself depends." (Ibid., pp. 646-47).

25. J. Roland Pennock, *Liberal Democracy* (New York: Rinehart and Company, Inc., 1950), pp. 118-19. Published shortly after McClosky's article, this argument contrasts nicely with McClosky's more formal and, I believe, less successful argument.

26. Rawls, *A Theory of Justice,* p. 355.

27. Ibid., pp. 357, 360.

28. Ibid., p. 86.

29. Ibid., p. 85.

30. Here I have in mind *whatever* good features a decision-procedure has *apart from* its tendency to eventuate in *decisions* of a certain sort. To be instrumental to the making of wise or just decisions is no small merit but following a decision-procedure may also be instrumental to the realization of other goods (e.g., increased self-esteem on the part of the participants or a greater sense of community among them). Following a procedure can be *intrinsically* significant as well. Suppose, for example, that a certain procedure requires people to relate to one another in certain ways (e.g., peacefully, through reason and argument, with more or less the same participatory status). If to follow the procedure *is* to relate in these ways and if people relating to one

another in these ways has *intrinsic* moral significance, then we can say that the procedure itself has intrinsic moral significance.

31. Of course, there are other possible positions. For example, one might judge that while a procedure is less attractive when viewed simply as a process, it is so much more attractive as an instrument for generating just decisions that on balance it is to be preferred. Or one might judge that it is to be preferred because it is superior in both respects. Moreover, for each way of representing a procedure favorably, there is a correspondingly *unfavorable* representation.

32. See pp. 305-06, 311, 313-15.

33. Here, for example, is a three-pronged argument: (1) If we can assume that people are motivated by considerations of justice, then their having to persuade a majority of one another of any particular opinion about what ought to be done is likely to induce an exchange of information and ideas which in turn will lead to better—i.e., more just—decisions than would result otherwise. (2) If, however, we assume that the people who are to participate in whatever procedure we contrive are motivated primarily by self-interest, it can be argued that the necessity of having to put together a majority of votes makes even self-interested voters at least somewhat more responsive to the interests of a wider range of individuals than they would otherwise be. An obvious objection is that these good effects depend on there not being a permanent and ill-willed majority. In response, one could argue that if a majority of persons are bent on perpetrating injustice (because, for example, self-interest moves them to do so), justice is not very likely in any event, that conditions not favorable to the just operation of a majority rule system are not any more favorable to the just operation of other systems. A thought like this seems to have motivated Henry Steele Commager's attack on nonmajoritarian devices (such as judicial review) for securing minority rights against the tyranny of the majority. (See his *Majority Rule and Minority Rights* (London: Oxford University Press, 1943). (3) Finally, we might suppose that people are a mixed lot. Some are willing and able to look at matters in a just-minded way, and some are not. If so—and if there is a plausible way to institutionalize the selection of those who have the requisite character and intelligence—then it can be argued, either as in (1) above or in the manner of Condorcet (assuming, however, that the voters are to reach their judgments through independent deliberation), that at least we ought to proceed on the basis of what a majority of *them* have to say.

Obviously the idea of all this is to show how, given *comparable* motivational assumptions, just results are as or more (though not always very) likely when there is rule by majority (conceived in one way or another) rather than not. The argument is presented here only to illustrate this more general strategy.

34. I am grateful to Beatrice Rouse and Richard Grandy for helpful discussion in the course of this paper's evolution. I would also like to thank Claire Miller and Pat Blunden for extensive secretarial assistance.

12

VOTING THEORY, UNION ELECTIONS, AND THE CONSTITUTION

RICHARD A. EPSTEIN [1]

In his paper, "Some Procedural Aspects of Majority Rule," Professor Kramer has discussed the ways in which the general notion of due process may be applied to the rules of order used by parliamentary bodies. In the course of that paper, he has elaborated a notion of majority will that he claims has general acceptance in political theory. In this paper, which began as a comment upon his, I shall use his account of the majority will to discuss in the particular context of labor law two distinct but closely related issues. The first of these concerns the degree to which procedures adopted in certification elections—those which determine which union, if any, in a given bargaining unit should represent the workers in that unit—should conform to his account of the majority will. The second of these questions is, whether as a constitutional matter there is any violation of the due process clause when the federal government sanctions union elections that do not adopt the account of majority will that he proposes.[2] In order to set the stage for an examination of these two issues, it is first necessary to set out in brief form the account of the majority will adopted by Kramer and the reasons why it should be preferred to other accounts that might be substituted in its place.

I. THE CONCEPT OF MAJORITY WILL

The concept of majority will appears to be straightforward enough. In the usual case in which there are but two choices, that outcome chosen by more than half the voters represents the majority will. The only problem in either theory or practice concerns the selection of a mechanism of decision in the event of a tie, and that can be solved in the usual case by simple convention— as, for example, by allowing the chair to vote in deadlocked cases. Difficulties with the conception of the majority will are, however, much more acute in cases that present three or more possible outcomes for decision.

One possible response to this situation is to leave the definition unchanged, and to require one outcome to be the first-place choice of more than half the voters. As such, this response assumes that the concept of majority retains a fixed content no matter how many possible outcomes are under consideration. That result might be sound as a linguistic matter, but is clearly unacceptable as a practical one, because it renders group decisions impossible in all too many cases. To meet this practical objection, it is necessary to give a weaker account of the majority will that is less literal but more functional—an account, perhaps, of the "group choice" and not the majority will.

Regardless of terminology, there are at least three possible accounts of the majority will which produce divergent results in many cases. The first—rightly rejected by Kramer—states that the choice that receives the most first-place votes represents the will of the majority, even if it does not command the support of one-half the voters. The difficulty with this account is that it does not honor (except in cases of ties) the preferences of a given voter beyond his first. Take an extreme case with four possible outcomes, and suppose that one of those is ranked first by 30 percent of the voters, but last by 70 percent of them. Given this proposed definition of the majority will, that outcome will be treated as the choice of the group if each of three other choices commands less than 30 percent of the first-place votes. The second and third preferences of each voter are systematically ignored.

A second account of majority will might turn on a system of runoffs in order to avoid the problems of plurality voting. With a runoff election, the full array of outcomes is first presented to the voters, each of whom is required to select his choice. Where no single choice has the support of more than 50 percent of the voters, a runoff election is held between the top choices—often two, but perhaps three or more—until a single choice has the support of more than 50 percent of the voters. Where the first runoff election is among three or more choices, subsequent runoff elections could be held, if necessary, until one outcome obtains the necessary support.

The problem with the runoff scheme is that it, too, does not take full account of individual rankings outside of the first. Thus, to take the simplest of cases of preferences, one of many that can be constructed:

	I (2 voters)	II (2 voters)	III (1 voter)
First choice	a	c	b
Second choice	b	b	a
Third choice	c	a	c

Figure 1

Here in the first election with all three choices, *a* and *c* make it into the runoff, as each has two first-place votes while *b* has but one. In that runoff election, *a* then prevails over *c* by a vote of 3 to 2, and thus becomes the choice of the group. That result is intuitively unsatisfactory because it ignored the fact that no voter made *b* his last choice while two voters made *a* their last choice. The intuitive uneasiness with this choice is reinforced, moreover, because in the direct comparison between *a* and *b*, *b* prevails by a vote of 3 to 2.

In order to capture the importance of pairwise comparisons, and to escape the unpleasant consequences of both pluralities and runoffs, Kramer adopts the account of the majority will generally accepted by voting theorists:[3]

Definition. A *majority will* exists if and only if there exists a subset M of the outcomes, with the following three properties:
(1) M contains at least one outcome.
(2) At least one outcome is not contained in M.
(3) Any outcome in M defeats any outcome not contained in M (in a direct pairwise vote).

Under this account, outcome *b* is indeed chosen as the *majority will* because it satisfies each of the three requirements of the definition. It is an outcome in set M; there are two other outcomes, *a* and *c,* that are not contained in the set M; and it defeats both *a* and *c* in a direct pairwise comparison by the identical votes of 3 to 2. This definition alone has strong intuitive attraction because it allows all members to have some say on the selection of the group, not only with their first choice but with their subsequent ranking of all the outcomes available for decision. All voters are thus involved in the collective decision, even those whose first choice has no chance of adoption. This account raises, however, distinctive problems of its own in that it is possible to find cases for which there is no obvious majority will. Take the most famous case in the literature, where there are three voters—I, II, and III, who express their individual preferences amongst three choices (a, b, c) as follows:

Voters Choice	I	II	III
First	a	c	b
Second	b	a	c
Third	c	b	a

Figure 2

In the direct pairwise comparisons, *a* is preferred to *b*, *b* to *c,* and *c* to *a,* all by two-to-one votes. While the individual preferences are perfectly transitive, the collective preferences are not. The rule of pairwise comparisons does not permit the determination of the majority will, given the circularity of the collective preferences.[4]

It is, however, possible to put cases that yield cyclical majorities, which intuitively do not look like ties. Thus suppose we had 100 voters whose preferences were as follows:

	40 voters	30 voters	30 voters
First choice	a	c	b
Second choice	b	a	c
Third choice	c	b	a

Figure 3

In this case we have a cycle: *a* is preferred to *b* by a 70 to 30 vote; *b* is preferred to *c* by the same vote; and *c* is preferred to *a* by a 60 to 40 vote. Yet the case should not be treated as a tie given the greater measure of support for the *a, b, c* ordering. The question is whether or not there is any possible way to break the tie in order to make *a* the winner, with *b* in second place, and *c* in third. One possibility is to hold that once the cycle is established, the relative majority criterion should be applied, which in this case will yield the correct result.

There is, in addition, at least one other way to break the cycle. In the simple example just given in Figure 3, the majority that *c* enjoys over *a* is only 60 percent, while the majority in the other two cases is 70 percent. It might not be at all unreasonable to take advantage of that fact to break the cycle between *c* and *a* by putting first the outcome defeated by the smallest majority, thus leaving *a* the clear first choice. Any such technique might need a great deal of refinement, particularly in those cases in which the cycle involved more than three choices.[5] Nonetheless, it might in the end allow a sensible ordering within the elements of the cycle. That task should not detain us here, however. The particular procedures under the labor acts which we will study do not call in question any of these refinements of the basic definition of the majority will. The evaluation of the legal problems can be made with only that basic definition in mind, and it is to that task we now turn.

II. MAJORITY WILL IN THE CONTEXT OF COLLECTIVE BARGAINING

With the concept of majority will thus explicated, we can now ask how it might prove of use in cases that require concrete legal decisions. There are numerous contexts to which voting theory should, in principle, be applicable. In the domain of public law, it might help select the appropriate procedures for choosing representatives to national, state, or local bodies. In the domain of private law, the theory could have obvious application to the study of elections within the corporate context. In this paper, however, I wish to concentrate my attention in one substantive area—that of labor law, which is a peculiar amalgam of public and private law.

Under current labor law, a union has both its private and public aspects. It is private in that only those workers who want to join it need do so; the union cannot avail itself of the force of the state to conscript a worker into its ranks. But the consequences that attach to a worker's decision not to join a union nonetheless do give it a weak form of sovereignty and thus the form of a public organization. Those who choose not to join the typical voluntary organization are not entitled to the benefits of membership in that organization. They may be worse off because of their decision not to join; but regardless, they do remain free to conduct their individual affairs just as they did before, and need not yield any of their rights to the organization of which they do not approve.

The situation in labor law is quite different. Here is not the place to dwell at length upon the complex relationship between an employee who does not want union representation and the union which has received a federal mandate to represent him. Suffice it to say that the individual worker who does not (or cannot) join the union will be required to accept union representation if he wishes to keep his current employment. Under no circumstances can he negotiate with his employer over the terms and conditions of employment as if no union had been selected to represent the workers within the unit. The institution of collective bargaining requires *all* the workers within a given bargaining unit to accept union representation if a *majority* of the workers within that unit so desire it. Individual negotiation by individual workers is no part of the scheme.

Under this legal regime, it is crucial to answer two distinct but related questions. First, how do we determine the boundaries of the bargaining unit in which the principle of collective bargaining is to operate? Second, what are the appropriate procedures to insure the dominance of the majority will within the unit after its boundaries are determined?

a. The Scope of the Bargaining Unit

To turn to the first of these questions, the question of eligibility—the question of who votes—cannot be solved in the straightforward way appropriate to voluntary organizations. In voluntary organizations, all who choose to join will be entitled to vote in the elections of that association, subject only to whatever restrictions they agree to accept as a condition of membership. But these simple consensual techniques are not available in certification elections (those to decide whether a given union will represent the workers in a given unit) because voting cannot determine who is allowed to vote. The boundaries of the bargaining unit cannot be determined by the members of that unit precisely because there is no elective mechanism that allows us to say which individuals are members and which are not.

There is, moreover, no recourse to the easy political tests of residence and age that are applicable in political elections.[6] In a typical case, one union might urge that all the workers at a particular plant should constitute an appropriate bargaining unit.[7] The employer—or perhaps another union—might contend that one particular craft is entitled to separate representation of its own because of its distinct economic interests. Do craft employees alone—or all plant employees—vote on the question of representation? As the question of "which employees" cannot be determined by majority rule, it must be resolved by some objective tests that do not seek to aggregate a set of individual preferences.

Labor law has for years struggled with but mixed success to develop a set of principles which will decide who should vote in any given election. The Labor Board and the courts have thus paid attention to such matters as the degree to which the separate craft traditionally has enjoyed the benefits of separate representation, the extent to which the work of the members of the craft is separated from that of the other workers in the plant, the adequacy of the representation that a plant union could be expected to give to the craft workers, and the effects that a separate unit for craft employees will have upon the stability of labor-management relations. These "tests" are plausible for all their imprecision, given the collective bias of the National Labor Relations Act. Even if we assume the highest levels of the judicial art, it is easy to put cases that could be decided as well one way as the other. One could dwell on the problems created by the use of many-factored tests, but it is doubtful that much could be done to improve them within the framework of the labor law. Indeed, their best justification is the difficulty in improving upon them. Criticism is one thing, but constructive alternatives are quite another.

b. Voting Procedures in Certification Elections

The second task—that of using the appropriate internal procedures to determine representation with a bargaining unit—can in principle be discharged with greater precision than the first, as it should be, given the implicit coercion in the decision to impose collective union rule in labor-management relations. Yet here little attention has been paid to the formal procedures of voting discussed by Kramer and other voting theorists. The most striking example I have found is in standard practices adopted by the National Mediation Board (N.M.B.) in certification elections by employees of the common carriers. Under the procedures prescribed by the N.M.B., when two unions compete for representation, only two choices are set out on the ballot; one for each union. The workers are entitled as a matter of substantive law to reject all union representation, but to express that preference under N.M.B. procedures, they must not vote at all. If over 50 percent of the workers choose one union or the other, then the union with more votes is certified as the representative of the unit. The procedure has the obvious difficulty that all "no" votes are ambiguous—for they could mean simple disinterest, inability to vote, or a clear preference for no union. But even if we put that problem aside, there are still grave defects with this procedure.

Suppose a group of workers has the following preference scheme: (i) no union, (ii) union A, (iii) union B. If they (or some of them) decided not to vote, in order to "express" their first preference, they might find themselves in the position where over half the workers have voted for one of the unions, and a majority of those for union B. By not voting in order to express their first choice, it is possible that union B will be chosen even though in the direct pairwise comparison between the two unions, more workers prefer union A to union B.

On the other hand, these workers could vote for union A and thereby abandon their first choice in the hope of getting their second. While that strategy could succeed, it is open to two major risks. The votes of these workers could indeed give union A its necessary votes, while if they did not vote, their first choice of no representation might have prevailed. Worse still, their votes for union A could bring to over 50 percent the number of workers who voted for some union, while still leaving union A with fewer supporters than union B. In a set of direct pairwise comparisons, union B might well be the last choice of the group, yet it is possible that it could be nonetheless regarded as representative of the majority will.

There are problems as well for those employees whose order of preference is (i) union A, (ii) no union, (iii) union B. Here again, strategic guesses must be made before the workers cast their ballots. If they vote their honest preference for union A, it is only at the risk of helping to select union B. Fewer votes may still be cast for union A than for union B. Yet these very votes themselves might place the total votes for some union representation over 50 percent, such that union B is selected, even though union A is preferred to union B in the direct pairwise comparison. On the other hand, the decision by these employees not to vote at all (in order to express their second preference) could also help bring about the selection of their third, union B. Thus if more than 50 percent of the workers choose to vote for some union, the decision of these workers not to vote could allow union B to prevail over union A, even though union A would be selected in a direct pairwise comparison.

There are, of course, some workers who will not be put to any strategic choices by the N.M.B.'s voting system. Thus those whose preferences are:

(1) (i) union A, (ii) union B, (iii) no union; or
(2) (i) union B, (ii) union A, (iii) no union; or finally,
(3) (i) no union, (ii) either union A or union B;

will all be able to vote their first preferences without creating the risk that they will thereby advance their second or third at the expense of their first. Thus with case (1), the workers will always vote for union A, even if that union might not win. Their votes cannot help union B as against union A, and they will help ensure that at least 50 percent of the workers will support some union, and thereby tend to work for their second choice as against their third. These arguments apply with equal force to case (2). In case (3), the workers will abstain because once one union is selected, they do not care which. Nonetheless, these easy cases do not constitute any sort of justification of the procedure, for it is clear beyond question that some workers will rank the choices (i) no union, (ii) union A, (iii) union B; or (i) union A, (ii) no union, (iii) union B. This last choice, moreover, would be especially appropriate for workers who worked for union A against union B in the certification election. The system of pairwise comparisons allows those workers to express their preferences in unambiguous fashion and does not deny that right to anyone else. There is no reason why they should not be adopted as a general administrative matter.

III. DUE PROCESS AND VOTING PROCEDURES

What is to be done where the government agency wishes to retain this procedure, and some individual employee (or perhaps the employer) wishes to challenge it? One response was given by the Supreme Court when it considered the problem in Brotherhood of Railway & Steamship Clerks, etc. v. Association for the Benefit of Non-Contract Employees.[8] In *Railway Clerks,* the Court did not address itself to the merits of the procedure, even though the brief for United Airlines pointed them out in graphic detail.[9] Instead, it contented itself with the view that it was within the discretion of the N.M.B. as Congress's chosen administrative agency to determine the appropriate procedure for these certification elections, and brushed aside without any real argument the simple contention that a procedure so ill-suited for its stated end could not be regarded as appropriate for its appointed task.[10]

The statutory point, however, is not what should concern us here. The topic of this volume of NOMOS is due process, and the truly interesting point—one not even considered in the case—whether the procedures sanctioned by the N.M.B. are subject to constitutional attack under the due process clause. The due process clause of the Fifth Amendment provides that no person shall "be deprived of life, liberty, or property without due process of law." The clause has been construed to apply only to deprivations that are a result of actions by the federal government. While there is serious question whether the reach of the amendment extends to the actions of the union itself, there can be no question but that it covers the actions of the N.M.B. when it controls certification elections pursuant to its statutory grant.[11]

The next question concerns the employee's ability to show that there has been a deprivation of his "liberty or property," as those terms are used in the due process clause. One possible construction of these terms is a narrow one that limits "liberty and property" to the class of "vested rights" already entitled to protection under ordinary common-law principles. The paradigm case of rights protected under this view are, with respect to property, ownership rights over land, chattels, or intangibles; and with respect to liberty, to the physical ability to move about without physical obstruction or hindrance. On this view, the acts of the state subject to judicial scrutiny are, for their respective cases, confiscation or imprisonment. Nonetheless, that view of the subject does not by any stretch of the imagination represent the current view of the law, as embodied a uniform line of recent Supreme Court decisions, all of which envisage a much broader place for the due process clause. Instead, the current conception is much more inclusive and focuses upon the "legitimate" interests of the plaintiff, the loss of which will condemn him, in the standard phrase, "to suffer grievous harm" [12] of a personal or financial kind.

The consequences of this view, in connection with the term "property," are illustrated, in one case among many, by Goldberg v. Kelly.[13] There it was taken as settled law that welfare benefits count as "property" which the state could terminate in the individual case only after the recipient in question is afforded the procedural protections required by the due process clause—in this case, some form of hearing. Yet no one would argue that the state could not decide to abandon its welfare program if it chose. True, those who are now recipients would be worse off because of the change, but that fact alone does not mean that they have proprietary interest which could be condemned by the state only upon payment of compensation. But whatever the differences between welfare benefits and private property, it is quite sufficient for purposes of due process that some grievous loss could follow from their termination. The "better off"-"worse off" test seems to control in constitutional litigation where there is any nexus (such as welfare benefits) between the individual and the state.

Even more to the point here, the same broad construction has been given to the term "liberty." In but one recent case, Morrisey v. Brewer,[14] the Supreme Court held that the prisoner had a constitutional right to some form of hearing before his parole was revoked. To reach that conclusion, the Court had to find that the revocation of parole amounted to a loss of "liberty," as that term was used in the due process clause. It is settled law that no prisoner can insist upon parole as a matter of right, and settled as well that the state may attach terms and conditions when it grants parole that it could not apply to ordinary citizens. But the Court held it was quite immaterial that parole was in the first instance at the discretion of the state. Once it could be shown that the individual is condemned to suffer "grievous loss," there is a deprivation of "liberty" under the due process clause.

There is one sense, however, in which cases like *Goldberg* and *Morrisey* do not apply to this discussion. In both cases, the terms "liberty" or "property" were given an expansive construction in order to determine if the individual is entitled to procedural protection—usually of notice and hearing—from the state. Now if the Due Process Clause were construed—as its language suggests—solely as a procedural safeguard, it would be a difficult question whether it would be of any assistance to a worker who wished to challenge the voting methods of the N.M.B.—or, for that matter, those of the N.L.R.B. (runoffs), could fashion a constitutional claim. The essence of voting is process, but it does not appear to be the kind of process associated with the traditional conceptions of procedural due process. In the two cases just mentioned, as in the others of this group, the question of procedural due process arose in connection with the adjudication of individual claims before the state. Notice, hearing, right to counsel, and rules of evidence are the stuff of which procedural due process claims are made. And whatever the importance of these voting procedures, they simply do not deal with the modes of adjudication before courts or administrative bodies.

There is today, however, less need to try to press the due process claim into the classic procedural mold, for some of the recent decisions of the Supreme Court have utilized the once-discredited doctrine of "substantive due process." Under this doctrine there is no procedural threshold that must be crossed before the Court may pass on the constitutionality of laws that determine the rights and duties of the individual against the state. The most famous recent case of this sort is Roe v. Wade,[15] in which the Supreme Court struck down all state criminal abortion statutes on the grounds that they placed an unjustified limitation upon a woman's right of privacy. There have been other decisions, less dramatic, that are in the end substantive due process cases as well. Thus, for example, in the recent case, Cleveland Board of Education v. LaFleur,[16] the Supreme Court held that the state could not require all woman teachers to take an unpaid pregnancy leave five months before the expected delivery date. Here the state rule, denounced in the opinion as a "conclusive presumption," could not be attacked on procedural grounds. The vice of the statute was not its failure to provide a hearing for all teachers in which the only issue would be the number of months that the teacher was pregnant; instead it was whether the state could by contract require the teachers to take an unpaid pregnancy leave. That is a substantive rule—one that determines the primary rights and duties of citizens. It could be called "procedural" only if all public regulations were so classified.

The concern is not with the soundness of either of these decisions, but with the method of analysis they employed. In each case, the Court identified the "liberty" of the individual. In both it was the "freedom of personal choice in matters of marriage and family life." Once identified, the next question asked was whether the state could find any sufficient justification which permitted it to restrict the liberty in question in order to achieve some higher goal. How, then, does this general form of argument apply to the voting cases? In the first place, one must first identify the individual interest in "liberty and property." In my view, that interest is found in the "freedom of contract." It is arguable that freedom of contract is an essential liberty even if we adopt the narrow conception of liberty, and difficult to deny that it falls within the broader conception of liberty that the Courts have fashioned in connection with both procedural and substantive due process.

In *LaFleur*, the conclusion is inescapable that the Court allowed the plaintiff in the name of liberty to impose a term upon her employer, the state, which it did not wish to accept. A fortiori, then, it appears that individual liberty must be abridged if the state prevents two parties—here the individual worker and his employer— from establishing contractual arrangements for their mutual bene- fit. Indeed, even though freedom of contract (but note: not freedom of speech) is often viewed as one of the great relics of the nineteenth century, it nonetheless holds a central place in the classic accounts of liberty invoked by the Supreme Court to this very day. Thus the Court said in Meyer v. Nebraska:

> While this Court has not attempted to define with exactness the liberty thus guaranteed, the term has received much consideration and some of the included things have been definitely stated. Without doubt, it denotes not merely freedom from bodily restraint but also the right of the individual to contract, to engage in any of the common occupations of life, to acquire useful knowledge, to marry, establish a home and bring up children, to worship God according to the dictates of his own conscience, and generally to enjoy those privileges long recognized at common law as essential to the orderly pursuit of happiness by free men.[17]

Again, in another early case, Truax v. Reich, the Supreme Court said:

> It requires no argument to show that the right to work for a living in the common occupation of the community is of the very essence of the personal freedom and opportunity that it was the purpose of the Amendment to secure.[18]

There is thus an initial individual interest. This interest is one, moreover, that is limited by the application of the national labor acts, for they make it impossible for an employee to negotiate directly with his employer once a union has been certified as the exclusive statutory agent of the bargaining unit. The crucial question is can we find any state justification for the restriction in question? Here it is clear that no court today would deny that the state interest is sufficient if the entire substantive scheme of either the Railway Labor Act or National Labor Relations Act were challenged on constitutional grounds. The general view is that the interest of the individual employee must yield to the greater interest of the group in order that they might deal with their employer with sufficient economic power effectively to protect their interests during negotiations.

That line of argument does not, however, provide automatic

protection for the procedures that are adopted by the N.M.B.—or, for that matter, by the N.L.R.B. Here the individual worker could well claim that his individual freedom to contract may be overridden on these general balancing tests by the will of the majority. But there is no reason at all to allow it to be overridden by the will of a minority. There is no question but that the principle of majority rule is regarded by the Supreme Court as central to the scheme of collective bargaining.[19] To take but one example, it will not enforce contracts negotiated before employer and union where the union does not represent the majority of workers, even if both parties to the contract believe in good faith that it does.[20]

On this view of the appropriate balance of interest, it seems both necessary and appropriate to use that formal system of voting which best allows the realization of that majority will. Let there be at least three votes and three choices, and the definition of the majority will, with its attention to pairwise comparisons, given earlier in the paper, is better than all its alternatives. It is a definition, moreover, capable of easy implementation, in that a single ballot that ranks all of the choices will provide all of the information to decide, first, whether there should be representation and, if so, by which union.[21] The ballot in this form will not have any built-in bias in favor of unionization, but, given that the labor law allows employees to refrain from collective bargaining if they so choose, this feature conforms to the statutory scheme and counts therefore as a strength and not a weakness of the system. The fit between means and ends is perfect, and, more importantly for our purposes, it suggests how it is possible to attack voting schemes such as those developed by the N.M.B. in a manner that is consistent with the current modes of constitutional interpretation.

The argument, however, has still not wound its way to a final resting point. The resurgence of "substantive due process" has not been complete, and scars of earlier days remain visible today, so great is the fear that the Supreme Court will act as a "superlegislature," entitled to strike down whatever economic and social legislation that is inconsistent with its own political beliefs. To avoid that institutional peril, one essential task of a sound constitutional theory—and one that has never adequately been discharged—is to fashion a set of rules that allows the Court to distinguish between legislation that is unconstitutional and that which is only unwise.

348 RICHARD A. EPSTEIN

The task is difficult enough even with specific prohibitions, as, for example, those of the First Amendment on freedom of speech. It is much more difficult when there is only a reference to a formal principle like "due process." But unless that task is discharged, it will be difficult to find any grounds on which the powers of a court differ from those of a legislature. Yet once that distinction is borne in mind, it becomes difficult to require as a constitutional matter the use of those voting procedures dictated by adoption of proper definition of the majority will. Is it unconstitutional—or just unwise—to have plurality elections when there are three or more possible outcomes? Unconstitutional—or just unwise—to have runoff elections between the first two or three candidates, when no single candidate is able to command a majority of votes?

Concern with substantive due process in itself, however, is not decisive. Simple pluralities and runoff elections might well be sustained as the kind of error made respectable by inveterate use. The switch from imperfect logic to inveterate practice might well save the runoffs used by the N.L.R.B. But it does not, however, offer any justification for having the N.M.B. run certification elections in the manner sketched above. To put the point somewhat differently, the sense of skepticism about substantive due process is responsive to Holmes's famous remark that "a constitution is not intended to embody a particular economic theory, whether of paternalism and the organic relation of the citizen to the state or of laissez-faire." [22] But here we are not faced with that sort of a choice, for Congress displaced the principles of laissez-faire when it introduced collective bargaining into labor relations. The only question left is whether it has implemented that intervention in a manner that is consistent with its major premise, and it is hard to see what system of voting is less likely to reach the majority decision than that adopted by the N.M.B. As a matter of policy, nothing can be said in favor of that system. Perhaps, then, this is the case to upset the administrative procedure even in the face of the presumption of constitutionality.

The constitutional question thus remains in balance. All the convolutions and twists in the argument are themselves unable to clarify the legal question of constitutionality. They show that the N.M.B. procedures are wrong, and that is like showing that 2 + 2 does not equal 5. But the constitutional question of due process— when all is said and done—asks not whether 2 + 2 equals 5, but whether it is reasonable (even if erroneous) for the legislature to act as though they do. Here the problem is somewhat different from that encountered in the usual run of cases, because the error in question can be demonstrated by formal procedures alone without the delicate adjustment of incommensurable interests demanded in the typical constitutional case. And so the legal question remains worthy of theologians as it remains unanswered and perhaps unanswerable by conventional techniques: is a procedure for determining majority will that in fact does not determine it nonetheless reasonable? It is a question on which voting theory—and perhaps all theory—has nothing to say.

NOTES

1. I should like to thank my colleagues Bernard D. Meltzer and Geoffrey R. Stone for their helpful comments on an earlier draft of this paper.
2. There are two distinct due process clauses in the Constitution. The Fifth Amendment provides that "no person shall be . . . deprived of life, liberty or property, without due process of law." The Fourteenth Amendment provides: "nor shall any state deprive any person of life, liberty, or property, without due process of law." The Fifth Amendment has been construed to cover cases in which the United States government was responsible for the deprivation in question, and strictly speaking is the clause involved here, even though most of the case law presented concerns deprivations by the state under the parallel provisions of the Fourteenth Amendment.
3. See, Kramer, p. 000 for his discussion of the definitions.
4. In practice, however, it has been argued that the problem is not likely to be acute. In an election with two outcomes, the probability of a tie decreases as the number of voters increases, and the same is true—only more so—in elections with three or more possible outcomes, or so it has been contended. See Duncan Black, "On Arrow's Impossibility Theorem," 15 Journal of Law and Economics (October 1969) 227, 238. But see Kramer, p. 000.
5. It should not create much difficulty where the three blocs of voters are of different sizes, however. Thus, if the ordering *a, b, c* had 40 votes, while *c, a, b* had 33, and *b, c, a* had 27, the cycle would still be broken between *c* and *a*, as *c*'s 60 percent majority remains the smallest.
6. Even here there are occasional questions of eligibility in the political context. See, e.g., Carrington v. Rush, 380 U.S. 89 (1965) in which the

Supreme Court held that members of the military cannot be prohibited by state law from casting their ballot in the county in which they reside.

7. See, e.g., Mallinckrodt Chemical Works, 162 National Labor Relations Board 387 (1966).

8. 380 U.S. 650 (1964).

9. For relevant excerpts, see Bernard D. Meltzer, *Labor Law, Cases, Materials and Problems* (Boston, Little, Brown, 1970), p. 328, n. 8.

10. 380 U.S. at 668-71.

11. See Harry H. Wellington, "The Constitution, The Labor Union, and 'Governmental Action,' " 70 Yale Law Journal 345 (January 1961). Comment, "Individual Rights in Industrial Self-Government—A 'State Action' Analysis," 63 Northwestern Law Review 4 (March-April 1968).

12. The use of the phrase in the context of the Due Process Clause dated from Joint Anti-Fascist Refugee Committee v. McGrath, 341 U.S. 123, 168 (1951).

13. 397 U.S. 254 (1969).

14. 408 U.S. 471 (1972).

15. 410 U.S. 113 (1973).

16. 415 U.S. 130 (1974).

17. 262 U.S. 390, 399 (1923). The case itself concerned the constitutionality of a Nebraska statute that made it a misdemeanor to teach the German language to students in elementary school. *Meyer* could be viewed as being not concerned with the freedom of contract, but with the rights of education; and this sort of interpretation will be pressed by those who like the result in the case even as they distrust the doctrines of freedom of contract. Nonetheless, the case does not concern the contract of employment between teacher and parent, and was—at least at some points—so considered by the Supreme Court, 262 U.S. 390, 400. Once the case is so viewed, the freedom of contract rationale is compelling in the defense of its results.

18. 239 U.S. 33, 41 (1915).

19. J.I. Case Co. v. National Labor Relations Board, 321 U.S. 332, 339 (1944).

20. International Ladies' Garment Workers Union v. National Labor Relations Board, 366 U.S. 731 (1961).

21. Indeed, at this point it is worth noting that most of the problems that Kramer discusses in connection with the rules of order arise because the three (or more) proposals are considered on two (or more) distinct ballots. Indeed, these procedures, even if "admissible," see Kramer,

pp 278-85. [Sec III]) ., will yield unique results in the situation found in Figure 2, even though there is a tie which no one should be able to break. See Robin Farquharson, *A Theory of Voting* (Oxford, 1969) Appendix I for a table of outcomes under both honest and sophisticated voting.

22. Lochner v. New York, 198 U.S. 45, 75 (1905).

INDEX

353